Preface

This pocket guide to California is one of the new generation of Baedeker guides.

Baedeker pocket guides, illustrated throughout in colour, are designed to meet the needs of the modern traveller. They are quick and easy to consult, with the principal places of interest described in alphabetical order, and the information is presented in a format that is both attractive and easy to follow.

The present guide is concerned with the entire state of California, in particular with the Federal US State, but also included are the two parts of the Mexican State of Baja (lower) California – B.C.Norte and B.C.Sur.

The guide is in three parts. The first part gives a general account of California, its climate, flora and fauna, population and religion, economy, notable personalities, history, art and architecture. and suggested itineraries. In the second part towns, villages, scenery, national parks, etc. which are of interest to the tourist are described in some detail. The third part consists of practical information arranged in alphabetical order.

The neo-classical Capitol in the Californian capital of Sacramento, or the bizarre limestone turrets in the Mono Lake – California has both natural and man-made constructions to offer

The new guides are abundantly illustrated and contain many newly drawn plans and numerous colour photographs. Each entry in the A to Z section gives the co-ordinates of the square on the map in which the particular feature can be located. Users of this guide, therefore, will have no difficulty in finding what they want to see.

Contents

Baedeker Specials

5

Go West to

This call to the "Promised Land" was followed by thousands upon thousand of people from all nations once gold was discovered in the American River i 1848. "Heureka" – "I have found it" is the official motto of California. To begi with it was gold, the hope of getting rich quick that attracted adventurers an soldiers of fortune. After them came the wagon trains, bringing those wh dared to undertake the arduous journey from the east coast of the USA throug prairie, desert and high mountains, to make a new life for themselves in the fe tile tract of land along the Pacific. More recently it has been the Hollywoo dream factory that has attracted artists, or the computer industry of silico valley that has attracted "yuppies" here from far and wide. Today visitors from all over the world flock to this fascinating land of dreams which from the outset has lent wings to the imagination.

California's attraction for visitors lies above all in the variety of its landscapes: a drive along Highway 1, "the world's dream highway" takes in a rugged coastline, lashed by the waves of the Pacific. The tallest and oldest trees in the world, red-woods and giant sequoias, grow on the north coast and in the Sierra Nevada – living monuments from prehistoric times. Breathtaking rock formations in the Yosemite National Park provide scenery as impressive as any that might have been cre-ated by Hollywood. Then the seemingly endless deserts, Death Valley, Joshua Tree or Mojave, make up just under a quarter of the state's land area. In the middle of the

San Francisco

Symbol of the financial district – the Transamerica Pyramid

Yosemite Falls

Impressive display of nature in the Yosemite National Park. After the snow melts in the spring waterfalls cascade down the rocks

San Diego

View of Downtown San Diego with the harbour in the foreground

Baedeker's

CALIFORNIA

How to use this book

Following the tradition established by Karl Baedeker in 1846, sights of particular interest and hotels and restaurants of particular quality are distinguished by either one★ or two★★ stars.

To make it easier to locate the various sights listed in the "A to Z" section of the Guide, their coordinates on the large map are shown in red at the head of each entry, e.g. ★Sacramento G/H 2/3.

Only a selection of hotels and restaurants can be given; no reflection is implied, therefore, on establishments not included.

The symbol ⓘ on a town plan indicates the local tourist office from which further information can be obtained. The post-horn symbol indicates a post office.

In a time of rapid change it is difficult to ensure that all the information given is entirely accurate and up to date, and the possibility of error can never be completely eliminated. Although the publishers can accept no responsibility for inaccuracies and omissions, they are always grateful for corrections and suggestions for improvement.

California

nd dunes, where only cacti can survive in the unrelenting heat, artificial
ses such as Palm Springs have sprung up, with luxuriant green golf courses.
lifornia also offers another almost deserted wilderness in the north east,
aginificent skiing areas around Lake Tahoe, and lovely wine valleys such as
apa or Sonoma, reminiscent of the Mediterranean region.
No less delightful are the individualistic cities of California: the unforgettable
yline of San Francisco with the Golden Gate Bridge swathed in mist, or a trip
the historic cable car over the many hills of this, probably the most European
y of the USA. By visiting Old Sacramento you can go back in time to the days
of the Wild West, when the Californian capital was still a notorious settlement of the first golddiggers. In San Diego, where Spanish missionaries began the colonisation of Alta California, you can enjoy visiting the Aquarium Sea World or Balboa Park. And last but not least, Los Angeles, now growing into a boundless metropolis which owes it worldwide reputation to its countless film studios, is well worth a trip. Memories from the film and television industry come to life in the ever-popular Disneyland theme park and Universal Studios. Many smaller towns also have their own particular charm, such as Santa Barbara with its Spanish influence, the Danish town of Solvang, idyllic Carmel, the dreamy houseboat settlement of Sausalito, the university town of Berkeley, and the lively bathing resorts of Santa Monica and Venice.

Hollywood

*Walk of Fame:
permanent reminder
of the stars and
starlets on the way to
fame*

Getty Museum

*in Malibu was built in the
style of a Roman villa*

Sacramento

*The old town of the
Californian capital
has reminders of the
days of the Wild
West*

Nature, Culture History

Facts and Figures

California lies on the Pacific coast of North America and consists basically of the US Federal State of California (originally Alta California), but also includes the adjoining narrow peninsula of Lower California to the south; this consists of the two Mexican states of Baja California Sur and Baja California Norte.

General

California, after Alaska and Texas, is the third largest of the 50 American federal states, and covers an area of 411,012 sq. km (158,693 sq. mi.) – almost twice as large as Great Britain. It lies between latitudes 328 and 428 north and longitudes 114° and 124° west. In the north it is bounded by the state of Oregon, in the east by Nevada and Arizona, and in the south by the Mexican province of Baja California. The Pacific Ocean forms the western boundary. Its length from north to south as the crow flies is 1248 km (780 mi.), and the coast has a length of 2024 km (1224 mi.). The width from east to west is 240–560 km (150–350 mi.).

Geological faults

It has been said that the physical picture of California is as restless as the inhabitants of its towns. The reason for this is primarily the 900 km (560 mi.) long San Andreas fault (see Baedeker Special p. 12) which extends from Mexico to Point Reyes north of San Francisco. Since the western side of the fault moves every year about 3 cm to the north, California is in great danger from earthquakes. This danger is increased by numerous other faults.

The Sierra Nevada fault caused the most extensive earthquake in California in 1872, particularly in Owen's Valley. The so-called white wolf fault was the cause of the earthquake at Bakersfield in 1952. The Santa Inez fault was responsible for the earthquake which devastated Santa Barbara in 1925. Movement of the Newport Inglewood fault destroyed Long Beach in 1933. In addition the San Jacinto fault, a southern extension of the San Andreas depression mentioned above, and the Garlook fault were responsible for minor earthquakes.

Surface

Three mountain ranges and two great valleys characterise the central geography of California. Parallel to the coast runs the Coastal Range which reaches a height of 2700 m (8861 ft). To the east, in the north of the state, rises the Cascade Range up to a height of 4390 m (14,408 ft), and along the frontier of Nevada extends the Sierra Nevada which can only be crossed by passes and which has a maximum height of 4418 m (13,500 ft). Between the two mountain ranges stretches the great valley of California, called the Great Californian Long Valley, with a length of almost 700 km (435 mi.) and a width of 60 km (37 mi.). It is formed by the Sacramento Valley in the north and the San Joaquin Valley in the south. The other great valley, Imperial Valley, is one of the most important territories of the state and extends from the Salton Sea as far as Mexico.

Lakes

The lakes in the north of California were formed more than 20,000 years ago by glacial water rushing down into the valleys of the Sierra Nevada. These include Lake Almanor, Honey Lake and Eagle Lake. One of the

◀ *Highway 1, the "Dream Highway of the World", runs along the Pacific Coast. Here is the stretch south of Monterey*

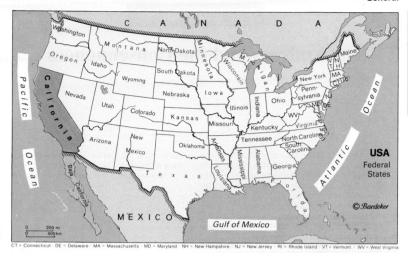

CT = Connecticut · DE = Delaware · MA = Massachusetts · MD = Maryland · NH = New Hampshire · NJ = New Jersey · RI = Rhode Island · VT = Vermont · WV = West Virginia

largest is Lake Tahoe which is shared by California and Nevada. The most southerly of these lakes is Mono Lake, not far from the Yosemite National Park. The inland lakes cover an area of more than 5600 sq. km (2162 sq. mi.)

In addition to the natural lakes there are others which have been formed by the construction of dams and these include Lake Oroville, Lake Beryessa, Lake Shasta and Lake Clair Eagle.

A particular feature of California are the four great wilderness areas which are not covered with sand but in places have rich animal life and vegetation, and which cover more than a quarter of the entire surface of the state.

Wilderness areas

The Colorado Desert in the south-east of the state is partially used for agriculture (Imperial Valley, Coachella Valley) and provides space for recreational centres (especially in Palm Springs).

The Mojave Desert, which borders the Colorado Desert at the Joshua Tree National Monument, occupies one sixth of the area of California. Thanks to irrigation there are also extremely fertile areas here.

Contrasting areas such as Owen's Valley or Death Valley are part of the Trans-Sierra Desert.

Regions

Because of its extent and soil conditions California has extremely vary-ing climatic zones and the expression "twelve Californias" is often used:

The north coast with its rock formations, giant redwood trees and vineyards.

North coast

To the east lies the Shasta Cascade territory where the mountain tops are always covered with snow, where there are forests, caves and innu-merable mountain lakes.

Shasta Cascade

The territory of the high Sierra Nevada adjoins to the south-east with the Yosemite National Park, the Kings Canyon and Sequoia National Park and probably the most popular skiing areas of the state especially around Lake Tahoe and the Mammoth Lakes.

High Sierra

San Andreas and the Consequences ...

At 4.31am on January 17th 1994 the inhabitants of Los Angeles had a rude awakening. A moderately severe earthquake (measuring 6.6 on the Richter Scale) resulted in billions of dollars' worth of damage to property. The disaster claimed more than 40 victims, many of them killed when houses and bridge structures collapsed. Five years earlier in 1989 San Francisco Bay was hit by one of the strongest earthquakes ever recorded in California, and 59 people lost their lives. The reason for these serious movements in the earth's crust is to be found in the continental shift. Of all the states in the USA, California is the one most under threat of earthquakes.

Famous, because it is also evident in the spectacular landscape, is the San Andreas Fault, which extends from the northern end of the Gulf of California, passing in a north-westerly direction through Imperial Valley, and on through the Mojave Desert to the San Bernardino mountains. At this massif the fault line initially veers off towards the west, only to turn back towards the

north-west at Santa Barbara. It then runs along the Coastal Range, or Great Californian Long Valley to Point Arena,

which juts out into the Pacific some 180 km (112 mi.) north-west of San Francisco. From there it continues along the seabed. Along the San Andreas Fault the Pacific plate, which is drifting to the north-west, collides with the North-American plate, which is pushing to the south-east. During the past 150 million years, the two con-

Goldland	In the west is "Goldland" where there are still remains of the gold digging centres of the nineteenth century, and where you can see the spot on the American River where in 1848 the first gold was found.
Central Valley	South of "Goldland" lies Central Valley, one of the most fertile regions in the United States, with the towns of Sacramento, Fresno and Bakersfield. The last named being the centre of the traditional American rodeo.
San Francisco	The sixth region is San Francisco with the entire great bay territory. In addition to this, perhaps the most attractive town in the state, there are other places which are worth visiting, such as San Jose or the university town of Santa Clara.
Central coast	South of San Francisco lies the central coastal area with the picturesque peninsula of Monterey, Carmel, Point Lobos and the massive castle

tinental plates have scraped approx. 560 km (350 mi.) past each other, creating large tensions in the earth's crust just where the present-day State of California lies. Time and again these tensions have produced major earthquakes.

The city zone of San Francisco, which stretches out precisely along the line of the San Andreas Fault, has already been repeatedly struck by severe earthquakes, in 1857, 1865 and 1868, especially in 1905, 1940 , 1986, and most recently in 1989. Further earth-

San Andreas fault: the cause of frequent earthquakes

quakes must be expected – probably in the very near future. But in spite of all the warnings, people have gone on building dams, canals and housing estates on unstable ground.

Although, as a tourist, the statistical

probability of your being affected by an earthquake is very slight, in the event of this happening you should observe the following procedure:

Get away from furniture that might fall over, crawl under a firm table or stand in a doorway. If you are outside, get as far away as possible from houses. If you are in a car, under no circumstances stop under bridges or in tunnels.

Serious earthquakes in California since the 19th c. (reading on the Richter scale given in brackets):

1812 – South California (7.2)
1838 – San Francisco (7.0)
1857 – South California (8.3)
1868 – Hayward (6.8)
1872 – Owens Valley (8.0)
1906 – San Francisco (8.3)
1925 – Santa Barbara (6.3)
1927 – Lompoc (7.5)
1933 – Long Beach (6.3)
1940 – Imperial Valley (7.1)
1952 – Kern County (7.7)
1954 – Eureka (6.6)
1968 – Borrego Mountain (6.4)
1971 – San Fernando (6.6)
1980 – Eureka (7.2)
1983 – Coalinga (6.7)
1987 – Whittier Narrows (5.9)
1989 – Santa Cruz, San Francisco, Oakland (6.9)
1992 – Los Angeles (7.5), Mojave Desert (6.5)
1994 – Los Angeles (6.6)

which the newspaper proprietor Hurst had built in San Simeon. The area extends as far as Santa Barbara with its Spanish-Mexican atmosphere and the finest of all the mission churches.

From here it is only a short drive to the area of Los Angeles with Hollywood and Beverly Hills, museums and theatres and an almost one-hundred-mile-long unbroken sandy beach.

Los Angeles

Although Los Angeles is located in the desert, the actual great desert area begins to the east of the town. Here are the Joshua Tree National Monument, Death Valley and Palm Springs, the haunt in the season from December to May of many rich Americans.

Wildernesses

Typical of the contrasts in California is the fact that nearby can be found the Inland Empire where the first orange trees were planted and which is today the major region for the growing of citrus fruit. Here there are

Inland Empire

Parched landscape in the "Valley of Death"

lakes and alpine resorts: theoretically it should be possible to indulge in water-skiing and land-skiing on one and the same day!

Orange County

West of the Inland Empire extends Orange County with its many exclusive residential places and the playground of the nation: the amusement parks of Knott's Berry Farm and Disneyland, a motor museum, one of the largest waxworks in the world and probably the most fashionable bathing resort in the state, Newport Beach.

San Diego

The most southern of the "Twelve Californias" is the region around San Diego, which was discovered by the Spaniards 50 years before the east coast of the United States was discovered by the English. Balboa Park, San Diego zoo with its enclosure for game, sailing regattas, one of the finest aquaria and the most elegant suburb La Jolla are the attractions of this region. You can go from here to Tijuana by tram and enjoy in the largest town of Baja California the atmosphere of Mexican life.

Administration

Counties

Like all the federal states California, which in 1850 became the 31st state of the USA, is divided into counties (numbering 58). San Bernadino County with one eighth of the total area is the largest. With an area of 52,400 sq. km (20,226 sq. mi.) it is not only one third as large again as Switzerland but is the largest county in the United States. Its total population is around one million, and the county town of the same name has 165,000 inhabitants. The smallest county is San Francisco, with 113 sq. km (44 sq. mi.) and barely 724,000 inhabitants: it consists only of the city of San Francisco and is the only county which coincides in area with a single town. The county with the largest population (9.1 million) is Los

Angeles; it covers an area of some 16,180 sq. km (6,245 sq. mi.). Alpine
County which borders Nevada has the smallest population; with an area
of 1760 sq. km (679 sq. mi.), it has less than 1200 inhabitants.

At the head of the state is a Governor who with his deputy and the
Minister of Justice is elected every four years by popular vote. He names
the other members of the cabinet who need approval by the Senate.
This consists of 40 members of which half are elected every two years,
so that a continuous process of law-making can be effected. The second
chamber, called the "Assembly", consists of 80 members who are elected every two years. Laws which have been accepted by both chambers
can be vetoed by the Governor, but his veto can be overturned by a
majority of two thirds in both chambers.

Government

   In the Congress in Washington California is represented by 47 members of Congress and two Senators. A total of one tenth of the total
population of America lives in California which has approximately the
same proportion of the total number of Congressmen (435); however, in
the Senate, like all other states, California has only two representatives.
Numerous legislative proposals, especially for alterations to the
Constitution, are decided by referendum, as they are in Switzerland.
These referenda take place annually on American election day, the
Tuesday after the first Monday in November.

The famous Californian poppy, which grows principally on the eastern
slopes of the Central Valley, has been adopted as the state flower.
"Golden Poppy Day" is held in April, although the flower blooms almost
throughout the year.

Symbols

   The chosen state fish is not from the Pacific Ocean; it is the Californian
golden trout which is only found in this part of America, especially in the
High Sierra and the Shasta Cascade area.

State flag of California

Counties

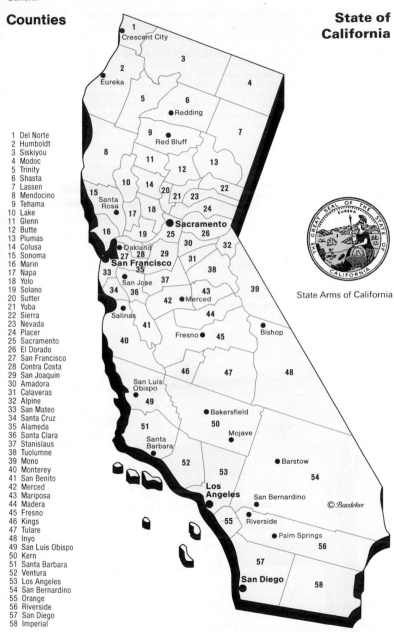

1 Del Norte
2 Humboldt
3 Siskiyou
4 Modoc
5 Trinity
6 Shasta
7 Lassen
8 Mendocino
9 Tehama
10 Lake
11 Glenn
12 Butte
13 Plumas
14 Colusa
15 Sonoma
16 Marin
17 Napa
18 Yolo
19 Solano
20 Sutter
21 Yuba
22 Sierra
23 Nevada
24 Placer
25 Sacramento
26 El Dorado
27 San Francisco
28 Contra Costa
29 San Joaquin
30 Amadora
31 Calaveras
32 Alpine
33 San Mateo
34 Santa Cruz
35 Alameda
36 Santa Clara
37 Stanislaus
38 Tuolumne
39 Mono
40 Monterey
41 San Benito
42 Merced
43 Mariposa
44 Madera
45 Fresno
46 Kings
47 Tulare
48 Inyo
49 San Luis Obispo
50 Kern
51 Santa Barbara
52 Ventura
53 Los Angeles
54 San Bernardino
55 Orange
56 Riverside
57 San Diego
58 Imperial

State Arms of California

The official state bird is the Californian tree-quail which is found all over the state.

The grey bear appears on the state seal and on the Californian flag, but the animal has been extinct for a very long time.

The state flag dates from the foundation of the short-lived independent Republic of California and was raised for the first time on June 18th 1846 at Sonoma. The present state flag was approved by parliament in 1911. On a white background is a red star in the upper left-hand segment; in the middle is a brown bear on a green strip, moving towards a star; below in black are the words "California Republic" with a red strip along the bottom of the flag.

Climate

Central California around San Francisco enjoys a pleasant climate with dry summers and rain in winter, corresponding to the Mediterranean climate in Europe. Northern and Southern California, the interior and the mountains each have their own distinct climatic zones:

Coast Range (including the adjoining Klamath Range)   Climatic zones
Central Valley
Sierra Nevada
Southern California
Mojave Desert

Together with Florida, California is the part of the USA with the least climatic stress, i.e. its summers are neither too hot or oppressive nor its winters too cold. For this reason it is favoured by winter holidaymakers and as a retirement home for older citizens, except for the most northern and eastern regions.

The climates of the individual zones of California can be more precisely   Climatic graphs
described by means of climatic graphs for typical locations. The temperature and precipitation levels throughout the year can be read from left to right (J = January to D = December). The blue rainfall columns show the monthly precipitation (in mm) according to the blue scale at the side. Temperatures are indicated by the orange-red band. The upper line represents the average highest day temperature, the lower line the average lowest night temperature. Temperature figures are given on the red scale at the side. The peculiarities of California's individual climatic zones are apparent when compared to the climatic conditions of Central Europe. There are even differences within the regions.

Coast Range

The climate is warm temperate with rain in winter and dry in summer,   Climatic stations
similar to the Mediterranean climate. In contrast, however, the maxi-   San Francisco
mum average summer temperatures seldom rise above 22°C; the high-   and Eureka
est summer temperatures are in September and, in Point Reyes, even in November. The graph shows that temperatures during the preceding months are not much lower. The diurnal and annual range of temperatures is quite small. In August the temperature in San Francisco is 12° at night and 18° at noon.

This is due to the California Current which flows south. It brings cold water from sub-Arctic latitudes and at the same time stirs up the cold deep water off the coast. The centre of this cold water zone lies north of San Francisco. In August temperatures of 11° are recorded, almost 7° lower than in the open sea far off the coast. To the north as far as the Oregon coast the temperatures reach 17° and 18°C at the Mexican border. In winter the water temperature graduates from 16° at the

Climate

Explanation in text

Seven climatic stations in California typical of their regions

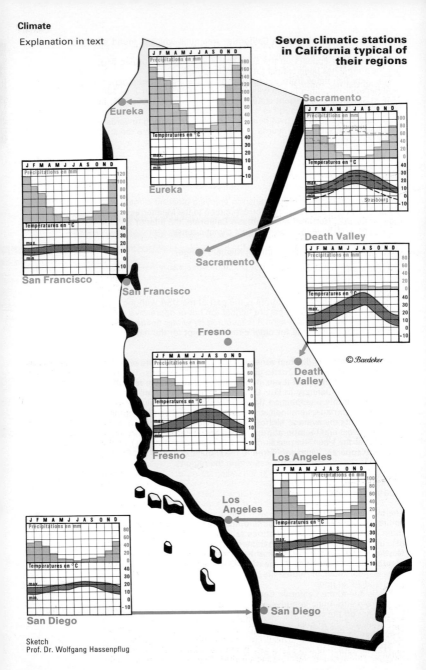

© Baedeker

Sketch
Prof. Dr. Wolfgang Hassenpflug

18

Mexican border to 10° at the border with Oregon. The prevailing west winds (sea winds) in summer cool the damp sea air above the cold water. Fog regularly forms as far as the southern outskirts of San Francisco, drifting inland and hardly rising above 500 m.

During the dry summer trees on the coast range absorb this dampness, so that the grass below them which would otherwise dry up stays green. The sea mist penetrates up to 30 km (15 mi.) inland to the north of San Francisco where the redwoods (Sequoia sempervirens) grow.

In autumn the sea breezes diminish and mainland temperatures are lower causing the mists to be less frequent.

Above the mist the air is normally warmer and drier. Point Reyes on the coast has an average July temperature of 12°C, compared with nearby Mount Tamalpais (724 m (2376 ft)). 19.6°C Relative humidity in Point Reyes in July is 90 per cent, in Tamalpais 39 per cent. From June to September it is on average 4°C warmer on Mount Tamalpais than in San Francisco. If the temperature difference between the two stations is more than 4° by morning then mist will probably form on the coast in the afternoon.

Storms are extremely rare; it is said that an earthquake is more probable than a storm.

A comparison of the San Francisco and Eureka stations illustrates the regular variations from north to south. Towards the south amounts of precipitation and the number of days of rainfall decrease (975 mm on 118 days in Eureka; 529 mm on 67 days in San Francisco). Temperature and hours of sunshine increase (average annual temperature in Eureka 11.3°C, in San Francisco 13.8°C; hours of sunshine 2198 and 2959 respectively). North of Eureka the winter precipitation levels increase further, the climate is maritime with very mild winters and summers which are only moderately warm and dry.

Central Valley

The Central Valley of California – with the exception of the east hinterland of San Francisco – is influenced by the Pacific Ocean through its situation behind the coastal mountains, and escapes extreme weather. Accordingly, the daily and annual temperature differences are larger and the precipitation lower than on the coast. In the climate graphs this is shown in the broad spread across the temperature bands. The summer temperature here climbs to a value comparable with the Mediterranean climate in Europe. The drop in values is not to the north but to the west. The lowest night temperature in July is in Fresno and is as high as the daily maximum temperature in San Francisco.

The reverse happens in winter in the valley bottoms where again and again there are severe night frosts. Delicate crops such as lemons and apricots are therefore grown at an altitude of between 60 and 350 m (197 and 1148 ft) on the sides of the hills above the nightly cold front where frequently mist can form.

Within the valley there is, as on the coast, a clear north–south variation. The small northern part of the Sacramento Valley is damper (411 mm annual precipitation on 60 days in Sacramento), the larger, southern San Joaquin Valley has a steppe-like dry climate (285 mm annual precipitation on 46 days and 3632 hours of sunshine in Fresno).

Sierra Nevada

The mountain climate of the Sierra Nevada in common with the low lying areas is marked by maximum precipitation in winter, but because of the altitude (over 4000 m) it falls mostly as snow (hence its name!). At Tamarack station (2438 m (8000 ft)) for five months the average temperature is below freezing and 88 per cent of the precipitation of 1314 mm falls as snow. This area gets the most snow in the USA (over 6 m), providing the

Climatic stations
Sacramento and
Fresno

No climatic
station

basis for extensive winter sports, e.g. Squaw Valley (Olympic Games 1960). Despite the high snowfall there is a lot of fine weather, mostly of over a week's duration, 40 per cent of winter days and 47 per cent of spring days.

In summer the snow virtually disappears. The snowfalls of the Sierra Nevada are more important than the precipitation of the Coastal Range in providing the source of California's water supply, especially that of Southern California. In nearly all the valleys on its western slopes dams have been constructed. The Sequoia gigantea grows at an altitude of 2200 m; at 3000 m the forest gives way to sub-alpine meadows.

Southern California

Southern California is considerably warmer and drier than Central California. In Los Angeles the annual precipitation is lower and less frequent than in San Francisco (373 mm on 37 days). Lowest night temperatures are somewhat higher than in San Francisco and the highest daytime temperatures are much higher; at 3284 hours annually the amount of sunshine is 300 hours greater than in San Francisco.

Climatic stations Los Angeles and San Diego

Towards the south it gets progressively drier. Los Angeles has a Mediterranean type climate, whereas San Diego has a prairie climate. The overall higher temperatures mean that in the Salton depression at the southern state boundary even the winters are mild.

The dry climate and clear air made Los Angeles the ideal location at the beginning of the century for the Hollywood film studios, as filming could nearly always take place outdoors. Since then, however, the quality of the air has very much deteriorated. Smog forms when warm air from the Mojave Desert meets the cool sea air. As soon as the lowest level of warm air drops to 500 m in the Los Angeles basin it prevents the movement of air. Even when the light wind off the land blows the polluted air partly out to sea at night, it usually returns again in the morning with the sea breeze.

Usually, and ideally, the wind in Los Angeles blows from the west; a light sea breeze brings cooling air into the city. Occasionally, however, the wind changes direction. Winds from the south-east not only bring the danger of fog but also of heatwaves. Coming from the hot desert across the Santa Ana mountains they introduce oppressively hot air into the city. Then the temperatures can exceed 40°C (as recently as April 1989) and are higher than in Death Valley.

Mojave Desert

In the interior or Southern California a veritable hot desert climate prevails owing to its southerly location. Extreme temperatures are reached in the lee of the Sierra Nevada and in the lowest locations in Death Valley (up to 86 m below sea level). The distance from the Pacific and the drop in relative humidity associated with falling air lead to only relatively low and very irregular precipitation levels (average 41 mm annually on 9 days and 334 cloudless days). Heavy rain of more than 10 mm can fall suddenly in any month and leave furrows on the land which remain for years or even decades. The aridity gives rise to great discrepancies in daily and annual temperatures. The highest air temperature on earth was recorded here on July 10th 1913 – 56.7°C (a disputed rival measurement of 58° was taken in Libya in 1922).

Climatic stations Greenland Ranch and Death Valley

The average maximum summer temperatures exceed 45°C. In contrast in winter there are frequent temporary but heavy night frosts, while the average night temperatures do not fall below 3°C.

The extreme conditions of this desert climate make it absolutely essential that adequate clothing is worn (protection against the sun and the cold) and that water supplies are carried. Even without feeling thirsty

◀ *Few plants grow in the hot dry conditions of the Mojave Desert* the human body requires so much water in dry air and high temperatures that a lack of it can quickly lead to collapse.

Flora and Fauna

Thanks to its many natural resources California has a rich panoply of animal and plant life which is spread throughout the various climatic zones and which varies according to the amounts of rainfall.

Flora

Habitat

Despite large areas having been cleared in earlier times, two thirds of California remains forested. There are still considerable tracts of virgin wilderness which are officially protected. The Great Californian Valley between the two mountain ranges belongs to the vegetation zone designated as prairie. However, these fertile valleys were extensively converted for cultivation and are now among the most productive areas of fruit, vegetable and wine producing areas in the USA.

The arid deserts of Southern California have primarily a flora with machia-like scleophyllous scrub (chaparral) as a typical example.

Trees

Some of its native species of trees, especially the giants (see "Redwood Highway"), have made California world-famous. The fan-palm or Washington filifera, growing exclusively in the south of the state, is one of the 1200 species of palm in the world. In the numerous coniferous forests there are several common indigenous varieties of fir and pine, as well as the famous Monterey pine in and around Monterey, the Torrey pine, found only in San Diego County especially in La Jola, and the ancient gnarled bristlecones in upland areas. Apart from the Joshua

Séquoia gigantea

Fan palm

"Teddy-bear" Cholla   Joshua tree

Tree National Monument in the Mojave Desert, this indigenous tree is also found in parts of Arizona, Nevada and Utah.

In addition, most other trees that exist in the world thrive here, especially in the northern mountain area. Significant stands of eucalyptus which originated in Australia are to be found, and the oak in at least a dozen of its various varieties is so widespread that its Spanish name "poble" has persisted in over 130 place names.

Other commonly found arboreal species include cedar, cypress, juniper, poplar and willow.

Approximately one quarter of California is covered by the Southern Desert. In the barren, sometimes wildly romantic strips of land such as Death Valley National Monument, only creosote bushes thrive in patches, their poisonous roots killing all surrounding vegetation which might compete for the minute quantities of life-giving water.

Cacti are indigenous and numerous in the desert, conserving water in their stems and leaves. Most cacti belong to the opuntia family. There are nine distinct types of cholla, one of which, the snake cholla, is found only between San Diego and the Mexican border. One species of opuntia is the platyopuntia, to which belong the nine varieties of prickly pear; these have blossom in many colours following a wet winter, and their fruit is highly prized.

Desert vegetation

Fauna

The grey or grizzly bear, the emblem on the state flag, has been extinct in California since the beginning of the twenties. Much of the land has been enclosed by man, leaving little space for the vast territory which is a precondition for the grizzly's existence. However, his smaller relative, the chiefly plant-eating black bear, is to be found in the Sierra Nevada between Siskiyou and Kern County.

Mammals

23

Flora and Fauna

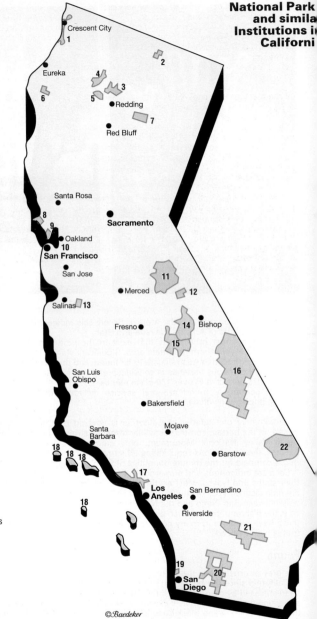

1 Redwood
National
Park
2 Lava Beds
National
Monument
3 Shasta National
Recreation
Area
4 Trinity National
Recreation
Area
5 Whiskeytown
National
Recreation Area
6 Humboldt Red-
woods State
Park
7 Lassen Volca-
nic National
Park
8 Point Reyes
National Sea-
shore Park
9 Muir Woods
National
Monument
10 Golden Gate
National
Recreation
Area
11 Yosemite
National
Park
12 Devils Postpile
National
Monument
13 Pinnacles
National
Monument
14 Kings Canyon
National Park
15 Sequoia
National Park
16 Death Valley
National Park
17 Santa Monica
Mountains
National
Recreation
Area
18 Channel Islands
National Park
19 Cabrillo
National
Monument
20 Anza-Borrego
Desert State
Park
21 Joshua Tree
National Park
22 Mojave
National
Preserve

©Baedeker

24

The coyote, another mammal which played an important role in Indian mythology, is widespread all over the state and can be hunted throughout the year. The pronghorned antelope, living in the mountains of the north, was almost extinct ten years ago but now numbers about 5000 thanks to a hunting ban. Elk, another species threatened with extinction but now protected, can also be found here. Raccoons, badgers, hares, foxes, otters, oppossum and numerous species of squirrel are common. The wolf appears to have become extinct in California.

Of the many golden eagles which must have existed here in past times, as many place names and geographical references suggest, only a few remain today; the condor can only be seen in the zoos of San Diego and Los Angeles. Nevertheless wild ducks, jays, ptarmigans, owls, quails, herons and many other birds are everywhere.

Birds

There are large numbers of sea birds and waders on the Californian beaches and in the bays, lagoons and estuaries. Several types of seagulls, pelicans, cormorants (especially on Point Lobos), black-tailed godwits, avocets, terns, redshanks, pondskaters and oystercatchers are the most notable.

The varieties of fish in Californian waters include sole, perch, salmon, halibut, cod, mackerel, tuna, shark, sea and river trout, pike and marlin.

Fish

The sea holds other delicacies, such as the clawless Californian lobster and the oysters in the beds of Moro Bay, Point Reyes and Humboldt Bay. In San Francisco Bay oyster fishing had to be abandoned some 50 years ago because of the polluted water. Abalone mussels, with their mother-of-pearl shells, are found in southern waters. These large molluscs are an expensive gastronomic delicacy.

National Parks

The extensive exploitation of the past soon had negative consequences. In the USA the necessity to conserve at least parts of the natural environment from further destruction was realised earlier than in other countries. In the face of great resistance this idea led to the establishment of extensive areas of protected countryside, the so-called National Parks, where typical regions of outstanding beauty are preserved in their original form.

The National Park Service is responsible to the State Department of External Affairs and adminsters all protected areas, nature monuments, places of historical interest and long-distance footpaths.

National Park Service

In California there are six parks under the auspices of this department. In order of their establishment these are: Yosemite (1890), Sequoia (1890), Lassen Volcanic (1916), Kings Canyon (1940), Redwood (1968) and Channel Island (1980).

The same department also controls eight so-called National Monuments: Muir Woods (1908), Devil's Postpile (1911), Cabrillo (1913), Lava Beds (1925), Death Valley (1933), Joshua Tree (1936). In addition there are: Port Reyes National Seashore (1962), three national recreation areas – Golden Gate, Santa Monica Mountains and Whiskey-town Trinity Shasta – and six national wild and scenic rivers – American River, Eel River, Feather River, Klamath River, Smith River and Trinity River.

There are also 20 national wildlife refuges in California controlled by the Federal Government, covering a million ha (2471 million acres), 18 national forests with a total area of nine million ha (22,240 million acres) and two so-called national resource lands – Kings Range in the north-west and Owens Valley in the south-east.

The various Indian reserves have been taken out of the control of the State of California and are now the responsibility of the Indian Affairs Bureau of the State Department. The largest, with an area of approximately 35,000 ha (86,485 acres) is that of the Hoopa Indians in Humboldt County in the north-east of the state.

Indian Affairs Bureau

GENERAL SHERMAN

Population

California, American's most densely populated state, is a "melting pot" of different races and nationalities. During the 1840s, when California became one of the American states, it was inhabited by approximately 100,000 Indians and about 14,000 others. The gold rush which was soon to follow brought an influx of people from many different countries; towns such as Sacramento and San Francisco experienced a real population explosion, while the gold towns were soon abandoned after the gold seams were exhausted and became genuine ghost towns. In the following years the European settlers were joined by Afro-Americans, Mexicans, Chinese, Japanese, Koreans and more recently other Asians such as Vietnamese and Cambodeans. Latterly the percentage of Whites in the population has fallen from 66 per cent to just over 50 per cent; Hispano-Americans (over 25 per cent) and Asians (about 10 per cent) form the next largest groups, followed by Afro-Americans (under 8 per cent).

Indians are supposed to have lived on California soil over 7000 years ago. The first mission stations were founded to convert the pagan inhabitants, consisting of about 300,000 Indians of whom around one sixth went over to Christianity. Maltreatment and torture by the whites together with imported disease reduced their numbers to almost 58,000. By 1913 the decimation of the Indian population had reached its peak. There were still about 13,000 distributed among a multiplicity of tribes. With the establishment of Indian reserves and increasing state protection their numbers increased gradually; in 1928 there were 23,000, in 1970 91,000 and 236,000 by 1990 when the last census took place. This is still less than 1 per cent of the total population and only about one fifth live in reserves. Numerous places and rivers in California have Indian names.

Indians

The first Chinese arrived in California around 1850. They were engaged in gold-mining and treated almost like slaves by their employers. In former gold-mining towns such as Dutch Flat or Weaverville, which are relatively unknown today, as many as 2000 Chinese were employed. Later thousands worked on building the trans-continental railway line (for a dollar a day). By 1875 50,000 Chinese were living in the Chinese quarter of San Francisco.

Chinese

The Japanese first came to America in 1868, as emigration was not allowed before then. In 1942 they were interned, including those born in the USA, the so-called Nisei, and those with Japanese citizenship. Not until 1988 were they awarded damages from the US government for the injustice they suffered.

Japanese

Since the end of the Vietnam War in 1975, some 280,000 Vietnamese and Cambodians have settled in California, mostly in or around Los Angeles. Koreans, some of whom came to California at the beginning of the 20th century, arrived in greater numbers following the Korean War and then again after 1976; their total number is estimated at 260,000, of whom the majority live in Los Angeles.

Other Asians

Before 1850 there were at the most 1000 Afro-Americans in California, and even at the beginning of the 20th century there were only about 11,000. In 1920 their numbers rose to 38,000, 20 years later to 124,000 and by 1950 to 462,000. Another 20 years later 1,400,000 were counted, and in the last population census in 1990 there were about 2,209,000.

Afro-Americans

The largest proportion of the non Anglo-Saxon population consists of the Mexicans with about 20 per cent; in 1990 there were around

Mexicans

◀ *General Sherman Tree – one of the giants in the Sequoia National Park*

6,119,000, of whom about one quarter were born outside the USA. Already today there are more Mexicans in Los Angeles than in any town in Mexico apart from Mexico City. San Jose and to lesser extent San Diego and San Francisco also have large Mexican populations.

Growth

Less than half California's 32 million inhabitants were born in the state; the continued annual increase of more than 400,000 people (1.6 per cent) shows that the attraction of California for Americans from the other 49 states and from abroad remains undiminished.

California has been the most populated state since 1963 when it overtook New York. While it had only 5 million inhabitants in 1930, that is about two thirds of the population of New York City, it reached 9 million after the Second World War and has since risen to over 25 million. The growth is primarily due to immigrants from other parts of the USA who were attracted by the prosperous economy and the "eternal spring" of the coastal area. Los Angeles and San Diego – the two cities with a population of over one million – and their suburbs were the most popular areas and experienced tremendous growth. By 1982 Los Angeles has become the second largest city in the United States, overtaking Chicago which had been second since 1890.

Religion

Denominations

Christianity – or more precisely Catholicism – was introduced into California by the Spanish missionaries and spread widely following the first wave of immigrants with the 1848 Gold Rush. The fortune hunters were accompanied into the promised land by Protestant priests – Baptists, Congregationalists, Methodists and Presbyterians. By 1900 almost half the population were adherents of the Christian faith.

Despite the rise of various sects at the beginning of the 20th c. the traditional churches remained the dominant force. In 1980 they had more than eight million members: 3,322,117 Protestants, the Mormons (Church of Jesus Christ of Latter Day Saints) having the largest number, followed by the Baptists, Methodists and Presbyterians. In 1984 almost 5½ million belonged to the Roman Catholic Church.

The Jewish population of 792,515, of whom some two-thirds live in the metropolis of Los Angeles, is the second largest in the USA, and this is also true of the Catholics.

Cults

As well as the expansion of the established Churches, the last one and a half centuries has seen the growth of every possible type of cult in California – perhaps for the same reasons which make the state so attractive to other Americans and foreigners: the hope of an easier and more fulfilled life. When demagogues promise the new arrivals heaven on earth under the guise of alternative religions, they are more likely to be believed here than in other parts of the country. The fact that most of these movements are only short-lived has not deterred the introduction of new cults.

Theosophists, Angelus and People's Temple

Most of these cults were only of interest to the sociologist. The most notable were the Theosophists, led by Anny Besant and Katherine Tingley, who founded a secret society in Point Lorna, the Canadian Aimee Semple McPherson, whose Angelus Temple in Los Angeles had many adherents, and more recently Jim Jones, whose People's Temple, first in Ukiah and subsequently in San Francisco, abused the blind faith of thousands of followers, driving about 900 of them to commit mass suicide in Guayana in 1978.

Utopian and Communist communities

There has been no shortage of Utopian societies in California. One of the first was founded in Anaheim by the Polish author Henryk Sienkiewicz and the actress Helena Modjeska, but it disintegrated in 1878 after only two years. Sienkiewicz returned to Poland while Modjeska began a suc-

The Cult of Bodybuilding

One of the many cults and trends which started in California and gradually spread all over North America, is a new physical awareness which finds its strongest expression in bodybuilding. Physical fitness at any price is what life is all about to Californians ("motion is progress"), and is demanded of anyone who wants to achieve social recognition.

There are no age barriers to training either in the studio or out in the open air in the form of various sports. Along the beaches of California, where the sun almost always shines, watch out for determined joggers and roller skaters showing off their skills; "Beach boys" boldly surf the waves or play beach volleyball. It was on the legendary Venice Beach in the Los Angeles area that the aerobics movement was born. Today, on "Muscle Beach" tanned, steel-muscled bodies tense their biceps and demonstrate to passers-by the ideal of male physical beauty.

This fitness fever goes hand-in-hand with the slimming cult. In contrast to the rest of the USA, there are few overweight people to be seen in California. The "Californian way of life" gave rise to the invention of "California Nouvelle Cuisine", which uses only seasonal vegetables, fresh from the field and, if possible, cooked "al dente". The food is high-fibre, low-fat and cholesterol-free. Thick sauces and animal fats are practically excluded from the menu and it goes without saying that smoking and excessive alcohol consumption are frowned upon.

The body-building cult on "Muscle Beach" in Venice (Los Angeles)

cessful stage career. A mountain close to Anaheim and an island off the coast of Newport are named after her.

Socialist and communist communities also had a following in California but lasted only a short time. Among them were the Kaweah Cooperative Commonwealth (1885–92), near the present-day Sequoia National Park and the Llano-del Rio (plain by a stream) Commune (1914–18), between the Mojave Desert and the San Gabriel Mountains, which in its heyday had 900 members.

Beat and Hippy movement

In 1956 the Beat movement started in San Francisco, followed a few years later by the Hippies. Both movements sought happiness through alcohol and drugs, and rejected the establishment completely. Allan Ginsberg, Jack Kerouac and Lawrence Ferlinghetti were poets of the Beat generation, but the Hippies left behind no such talent. With the grisly murders of the rich and famous by the Manson family (originally with 26 members, 20 of them women) in 1969, the movement degenerated into an anti-social lifestyle without any ideals. The San Francisco suburb of Haight-Ashbury, which was home to the Hippies 20 years ago, has again become a very middle-class area.

Bodybuilding

This decidedly harmless cult which began in California has gradually spread over the whole of the country. Male and female bodybuilders alike, for whom obsessive physical training often degenerates into exhibitionism, are active all over California. In particular these muscle-men and women frequent the beaches of central and southern California, where the sun nearly always shines, and can even be seen demonstrating their prowess in front of the Mission Church at Santa Barbara.

Economy

About half of California's gross national product comes from industry. The most important sectors are aerospace, electronics, metallurgy and chemicals, with food-processing (preserves and deep-frozen food) overlapping both agriculture and industry. The production of television and cinematic films is concentrated on Hollywood. Tourism is of increasing importance; the number of visitors to California each year from other states of the USA and from abroad can be counted in millions. Both the state and individual towns actively promote tourism.

Prosperity

California has the highest GNP of any state in the USA. Were it an independent country it would rank sixth in the world after the USA, the CIS, Japan, West Germany and Great Britain.

Recession

Even the "sunshine State" has felt the effects of the recession in the United States, though relatively late to do so. For the first time since the worldwide economic crisis, California finds itself facing severe financial difficulties, with cuts in expenditure and rising unemployment (9.5 per cent in 1992) due in no small measure to the drastic reduction in US defence expenditure following the end of the Cold War. High taxation, transport problems and the additional burden of costly environmental levies, have contributed to some once thriving industries moving elsewhere.

Aerospace

The origins of the aerospace industry go back to the time before the First World War, when pilots such as Glenn Martin, Allan Lockheed (actually Loughead), Donald Douglas and John K. Northrop founded small firms bearing their own names. With the exception of Martin, who settled in Baltimore, the remaining pioneers remained loyal to California and others joined them. In 1939 no more than 20,000 people were employed in the industry, but this number increased tenfold over the following four years. After the Second World War a slump set in, which, however, was soon overcome owing to the increase in civilian air traffic.

The container port in Oakland is an important exchange point for cargo

Thereafter the Californian aerospace industry inexorably expanded, not least because it received almost 25 per cent of US government armament contracts. With the subsequent drop in orders as a result of the so called "peace dividend" however, more than 86,000 jobs have been lost in the aerospace industry and a further 50,000 among supply industries. The California-based firm of McDonnell Douglas (with headquarters in Burbank, a suburb of Los Angeles), once one of the world's leading aircraft manufacturers, has increasingly failed to keep pace with its major competitors Boeing and Airbus.

Whereas the aircraft industry is concentrated in southern California, the newer electronics industry has developed almost exclusively in Silicon Valley, in the region between Palo Alto and San Jose, to the south of San Francisco. Although the first of the firms had sprung up by 1920, the real boom did not begin until after the Second World War. In addition to major concerns, such as Hewlett-Packard, IBM and Fisher, there are countless smaller firms specialising in the latest electronic developments.

Electronics

The concentration of these firms in a relatively restricted space is due to the proximity of Stanford University in Palo Alto, where Frederick E. Terman, who was responsible for the electronics department, placed engineers trained by him to combine research and its practical application. He supported the creation of Stanford Industrial Park on sites owned by the university, where factories could be built near the university laboratories. Terman died in 1982 but he was able to witness the results of his endeavours.

The oil industry's modest beginnings date back to just after 1860 when the first oil was found in Ojay Valley. It really expanded with the discovery of oil in several parts of the state towards the end of the 19th century. The first oil in Los Angeles was found in 1892, soon followed by oil fields in Santa Barbara, in Ventura, Kings and Kern County. From four million barrels in 1900 the annual quota rose to 105 million barrels in

Oil

31

1920. Oil was also discovered off the coast in the Pacific Ocean, especially around the Channel Islands. But since large quantities of oil were washed up on the coast from an accident in 1969, an influential ecological movement has been formed which has been successful in campaigning against further drilling for oil. As a result of this the planned drillings around the coast of Mendocino and Fort Bragg have been postponed.

Large quantities of natural gas, found in all oil fields and also on its own (a distinction is made between "wet" and "dry" natural gas), are obtained in California but not sufficient for domestic demand, so that additional gas has to be imported from Texas and Canada.

Minerals

Apart from the almost exhausted gold reserves there are other minerals important to industrial processes. These are borax, especially in Death Valley, gypsum, molybdenum, tungsten, antimony, lead, manganese, mercury and potash. Iron and copper are scarce.

Agriculture

Agriculture owes its importance to the fertile soils and favourable climatic conditions widespread throughout the state. Some statistics illustrate this: in 1992 about 78,000 farms earned almost 20 billion dollars. No less than 250 different agricultural products are grown, more than in any other state. Almost 80 per cent of the USA's requirement for fruit and vegetables comes from California, which is also the leading producer of cotton, eggs and greenhouse vegetables.

Fruit and vegetables

With the exception of coffee and bananas every conceivable type of fruit and vegetable is grown here, and wheat production is only surpassed by the Mid-West states.

Fruit in abundance

Apples, apricots, cherries, dates, figs, grapes, melons, nectarines, nuts, peaches, pears, plums and especially citrus fruit are harvested in almost wasteful quantities. Tomatoes are the most important vegetables, followed by asparagus, carrots, lettuce, cauliflower, sprouts, spinach and broccoli.

The warm climate is conducive to horticulture with the result that California is the main area of flower-growing in the country. The chief areas of cultivation are the counties of Monterey and Santa Clara, the valleys north of Santa Barbara and Orange, Ventura and San Diego counties. Until about 60 years ago France was the main supplier of seeds to the USA. Lompoc in Santa Barbara County has now taken over this position.

Flowers

Agriculture is concentrated in Imperial Valley, but from the economic viewpoint equally as important as fruit and vegetable production (especially oranges and lemons) is the cotton-growing industry in San Joaquin Valley. Almost the total US production of sultanas, dates, figs, olives and walnuts comes from the south. Peaches, almonds, cherries and apricots are produced in the north. Timber production is of only limited importance today, whereas the fishing industry remains buoyant.

Cultivated areas

Around 80 per cent of all American wines originate in California. Chief growing areas include the Nappa and Sonoma Valleys north of San Francisco, Santa Clara and Joaquin Valley, the region around Monterey, and Cucamonga south of San Francisco. There are also vineyards further east of Los Angeles and further south in the region of Temecula, halfway between Los Angeles and San Diego. There are some 400 wine-producing concerns in the USA.

Water supply is of concern to agriculture, as rainfall has been unusually low in recent years. Californian agriculture needs 80 per cent of all water which, because of the dry summers, has to be imported from further afield. The cotton planters are accused of using too much water for a product for which there is little demand worldwide. However, California has succeeded in recent years in producing new markets for its products in Japan.

Irrigation

Water supply

The very existence of California with its big cities and agriculture depends upon an adequate water supply. One problem is caused by the northern part of the state with most of the rivers and lakes having a small percentage of the population, whilst the majority of the population is concentrated in the desert areas of the south. In other words 70 per cent of the water supply is in areas which are thinly populated, whereas 80 per cent of the water is required by the south. Redirecting water from the north to the south is no solution owing to the occasional extremely low amounts of rain and snow in the north. This was the case in 1976 and 1977 and again a decade later in 1987 and 1992. It is only a small consolation that in 1978 and 1979 so much rain fell that drought-stricken Los Angeles was threatened with flooding! San Francisco, which introduced water-rationing in May 1988 in anticipation of a hot summer, "helped itself" to water from Hetch-Hetchy Valley at the beginning of the century. Los Angeles built a 250 m long aqueduct to direct water south from the Owens River.

Reserves

With the rapid growth of Los Angeles the water from the Owens River no longer sufficed. A second aqueduct, not quite so long, was built from Colorado, using water belonging to the neighbouring state of Arizona which finally agreed to the building of the Hoover Dam for electricity production, flood control and irrigation. The "All American Canal" irrigated the Imperial and Coachella Valleys. Other rivers which have been tapped for the south's water include the Sacramento, Joaquin, McCloud, Pit, Feather and Stanislaus rivers. Hundreds of dams and reservoirs have been built and new water projects are constantly being considered to appease the insatiable thirst of Southern California.

Hoover Dam

Economy

Projects

Massive amounts of money have been invested in these water projects to provide at any cost all taxpayers of Southern California with cheap water. The major investor is the Federal Government (e.g. the Central Valley Project incorporating the Shasta Dam) though the state is also involved (State Water Project). The state has to strike a balance between the arid but rich and powerful south and the well-watered but under-populated north. Finally it is not only the cities which benefit from this, as 80 per cent of the water required is used in cattle rearing and agriculture which is concentrated in the south.

Transport

Age of the car

Nothing symbolises the life of the Californian better than the automobile, without which the steady economic prosperity of the state would have been inconceivable. On the other hand it has meant that the development of a good public-transport network was neglected in the built-up cities.

Los Angeles

Los Angeles is a typical example of a city which developed during the age of the motor vehicle. Automobile clubs, which were founded at the beginning of the 20th century encouraged the development of roads, with the result that two decades later one in three of the population was a car owner. In 1982 17 million of California's population of 25 million had driving licences, a proportion not even approached by any other state. In 1991 there was a car to almost every one of California's 31 million inhabitants.

Freeways

The dramatic rise in car ownership led to the development of the highways and so-called "freeways", which are toll-free throughout the state. California has over 180,000 miles of metalled roads, of which almost 39,000 miles were built by the government and 15,000 by the state. The first enormous highway was not constructed until 1940; this is the Pasadena freeway from Los Angeles to Pasadena, with fly-overs instead of intersections. Nowadays such dense road networks can be found everywhere, especially on the approaches to large cities, with as many as twelve lanes in each direction, as in Los Angeles.
The most important roads are:

No. 1 along the coast from Eureka to San Juan Capistrano;
No. 5 from the Oregon border via Los Angeles and San Diego to the Mexican frontier;
No. 10 from Santa Monica via Indio and Blythe to the border with Arizona;
No. 15 between San Diego and Las Vegas (Nevada) via San Bernadino and Barstow;
No. 80 from San Francisco via Sacramento to Reno (Nevada) and thence to the east coast of the USA;
No. 101 from the Oregon border via Eureka, San Francisco, San Jose, San Luis Obispo and Santa Barbara to Los Angeles;
No. 395 from San Bernadino via Lone Pine and Bishop past the Yosemite National Park to Carson City (Nevada).

Environment

Before 1973 low fuel prices made the automobile not only the most convenient but also the cheapest form of transport. Since then increased prices have not hindered the unrestrained increase in car ownership. Even in recent years the environmentalists' strong objections that cars are the principal contributors to smog have had little impact. The speed limit on motorways (in some places 100 km (65 mi.) per hour, generally 83 km (55 mi.) per hour)) has helped to restrict pollution. Since the mid-1970s, all petrol in California has been lead-free.
To tackle the threat of pollution, the government of California has

passed the most stringent anti-smog legislation in the USA, which should result in a 70 per cent reduction in pollutants from cars by 2003. This is also the thinking behind the underground railway and tram network planned for Los Angeles.

Only San Francisco and more recently Los Angeles have underground rail systems. The San Francisco network links the five city centre stations with Oakland, Berkeley and other nearby towns. Although an underground was planned for Los Angeles as long ago as the 1920s, it was not until 1990 that the first stretch of the city's metro and urban railway opened with the completion of the Downtown Los Angeles-Long Beach section.

Underground railway

History

1510   The name "California" meaning "land of fantasy" appears for the first time in "Las Sergas de Esplandián", a work by the Spaniard Garcí Ordóñez de Montalvo.

1533   Fortún Jiménez discovers the peninsula of Baja California on behalf of Hernando Cortes.

1540   Hernando de Alarcón discovers the Colorado River and is the first white man to set foot on Alta California, which today is the Federal State of California.

1542   Juan Rodriguez Cabrillo is the first to enter San Diego Bay and discovers the offshore islands.

1579   Sir Francis Drake lands his ship the "Golden Hind" in an unidentified harbour, probably north of present-day San Francisco and claims the country for Queen Elizabeth I as Nova Albion.

1601   Sebastian Vizcaíno sails along the coast and lands where San Diego, San Pedro and Monterey Bay are located today.

1613   Juan Torquemada believes that California is an island.

1697   The Jesuit Juan Maria Salvatierra founds the first mission station in Baja California.

1701   The Jesuit Eusebio Francisco Kino is the first to cross the Colorado and reach Alta California.

1768   The Spanish government replaces the Jesuits with Franciscans.

1769   Junípero Serra, the chief missionary in Alta California, founds the first of Alta California's 21 missions in San Diego.

1770   Founding of the San Carlos Mission in Monterey. Pedro Fages becomes the first "Commandante militar" and "gobernante" of the two Californias.

1775   Monterey is proclaimed the capital of Alta California.

1776   Founding of the mission stations Dolores (in what was later San Francisco) and San Juan Capistrano.
       At the head of a Mexican overland expedition Bautista de Anza reaches the area of San Francisco.

1781   Los Angeles is established by Felipe de Neva as El Pueblo de Nuestro Señora de la Reine de Los Angeles de Porciúncula with 44 settlers.

1784   Serra dies and Francesco Paulo is named as head of the mission stations in Alta California, but only one year later he is succeeded by Fermín Francisco de Lasuén who remains in charge until his death in 1803.

1786   Founding of the Santa Barbara Mission, followed one year later by the mission La Purísima Concepción at Lompoc.

Mission stations are founded at Santa Cruz and Soledad. The English captain George Vancouver arrives on the first of four journeys to California to chart a map of the coast.   1791

Four mission stations – San José, San Juan Bautista, San Miguel Arcangel and San Fernando Rey de España – are founded, followed the next year by the San Luis Rey de Francia Mission.   1797

Estevan Tapis is the new head of the mission stations. An earthquake destroys the San Diego Mission.   1803

California is divided into two provinces: Alta California and Baja California. José Joaquin de Arrillaga is the first governor of Alta California.   1804

The Russian Nikolai Petrovich Rezanow, founder of the Russian-American Company, sails into the bay of San Francisco, becomes engaged for political reasons to the 16-year-old daughter of the second governor, José Dario Arguella, but dies in Siberia on the return journey to St Petersburg.   1806

Russians begin to settle at Bodega Bay.   1809

Four mission stations, Santa Barbara, La Puísima Concepcion, San Buenventura and San Juan Capistrano, are destroyed by an earthquake; the Russians establish the fortified trading post of Fort Ross.   1812

John Gilroy is the first non-Spaniard to settle in California.   1814

A Russian expeditionary fleet under the command of a German, Otto von Kotzebue, spends a month in San Francisco Bay; among those on board is Adalbert von Chamisso, who described his Californian experiences in "Reise um die Welt" (Journey around the World; 1836).   1816

The non-Indian population is estimated to be around 3500, 650 of whom live in Los Angeles.   1820

Mexico gains independence from Spain; Emperor Agustin I proclaims Alta California to be a province of the Mexican Empire.   1822

The last of 21 mission stations, San Francisco Solano, is founded in Sonoma.   1823

Jehedia S. Smith, leading a group of trappers, is the first white man to conquer the peaks of the Sierra Nevada.   1827

Governor José Figueroa proclaims the secularisation of the mission stations.   1833

Rosalia Leese is the first white child to be born in what is to become San Francisco.   1838

Johann August Sutter (later calling himself John Augustus Sutter) arrives in California from Germany, becomes a Mexican citizen and receives from the governor Juan Bautista Alvarado a vast territory at the confluence of the American and Sacramento Rivers, which he names Nueva Helvetia. He establishes a fort here and buys Fort Ross from the Russians, thereby ending the Russian attempt to colonise California.   1839

1841

Thomas Oliver Larkin is named first US consul of Alta California.   1844

Pio Pico, the first native born governor, becomes the last Mexican governor of California.   1845

Covered wagons en route to the West

1846	On May 13th war breaks out between Mexico and the USA; from June 10th to July 9th California is a republic under the flag of the bear. War ends in 1847. Captain George Stock and John Charles Frémont conquer Los Angeles; the US flag is raised over Yerba Buena ("good pasture") and its name is changed to San Francisco, with Washington A. Bartlett as the first American "alcalde" (mayor). California becomes one of the United States of America.
1848	The loss of California is recognised by Mexico in the Treaty of Guadalupe Hildalgo. James W. Marshall, a partner of Sutter, discovers gold during the construction of a sawmill near Coloma on the southern fork of the American River.
1849–1850	The state constitution is ratified in 1849 and on September 9th 1850 California is accepted as the 23rd state of the Union. Its first capital is San José. The population of the new state is estimated at 92,597; in Los Angeles there are 1611 inhabitants, while San Francisco, attracting thousands of golddiggers, has a population of 24,000.
1851	The capital is transferred to Vallejo. The first universities are founded: Santa Clara and the University of the Pacific in San José.
1852	The population of the state reaches 255,000.
1853	Benicia, only founded in 1847, becomes the third capital within a year. Foundation of the Californian Academy of Sciences. Opening of San Quentin Prison.
1854	Sacramento is the fourth and final capital of California.

Gold diggers working by a river

The first overland stagecoaches arrive in San Diego.	1857
Discovery of the Comstock Lode, an area about 3 km (2 mi.) wide and not quite 100 km (62 mi.) in length near Virginia City, abundant in gold and silver deposits.	1859
The population rises to almost 360,000 (52,802 in San Francisco, 4385 in Los Angeles).	1860
Transcontinental telegraph line from New York to San Francisco is finished.	1862
Outbreak of anti-Chinese demonstrations in San Francisco.	1867
University of California is founded. Naturalist John Muir arrives in California.	1868
Central Pacific and Union Pacific railway lines meet at Promontory Point (Utah), thereby establishing transcontinental transport between the east and west coasts.	1869
State population is now 560,000; 150,000 of whom live in San Francisco but only 5700 in Los Angeles.	1870
Serious anti-Chinese disturbances in Los Angeles. California Historical Society and San Francisco Art Institute are founded.	1871
First of the cable-cars comes into service in San Francisco.	1873
The second meeting of the Constitutional Assembly. Foundation of the	1879

University of Southern California in Los Angeles. Tennis is introduced into California.

1880	State population rises to 865,000; 234,000 live in San Francisco and 11,200 in Los Angeles.
1885	The Santa Fe Railroad reaches Los Angeles. Competition between railway companies leads to price cuts, attracting many people to the south and causing real-estate sales to flourish.
1890	The population reaches 1,200,000; San Francisco is the largest city with 300,000 inhabitants, followed by Los Angeles with 50,000. Congress establishes the National Parks of Yosemite and Sequoia.
1891	Oil is discovered in Los Angeles. Opening of Stanford University in Palo Alto. Throop Institute, the forerunner of the California Institute of Technology, is founded in Pasadena.
1892	The Sierra Club is founded.
1893	Stephen M. White is the first federal senator born in California.
1900	Population of California reaches 1,485,053; 343,000 live in San Francisco, and Los Angeles exceeds 100,000 for the first time.
1903	The yellow poppy is declared the state flower; Chamisso gave it its scientific name "Eschscholtzia California" in honour of Johann Freidrich Eschscholtz, the doctor on the Kotzebue expedition (see 1816).
1906	Earthquake followed by fire destroys large areas of the city of San Francisco. Founding of the the Los Angeles suburb of Beverly Hills. First film studio comes into operation in Los Angeles.
1910	Population now numbers 2,377,549; almost a third live in San Francisco (416,912) and Los Angeles (319,198). First film studio in Hollywood comes into operation.
1915	Panama-Pacific International Exposition takes place in San Francisco. First trans-continental telephone conversation between San Francisco and New York.
1919	Founding of Hoover Institution in Palo Alto. Hearst begins to build his castle in San Simeon.
1920	For the first time the population of Los Angeles (576,673) exceeds that of San Francisco (506,676); total population is 3,426,861.
1921	Huge oil reserves are discovered at Signal Hill, Long Beach.
1922	The Hollywood Bowl is opened.
1924	First airmail letters sent from San Francisco to New York.
1925	Serious earthquake in Santa Barbara
1928	A regular air connection is established between San Francisco and Los Angeles.
1929	First Academy Award (to Emil Jannings and Janet Gaynor, and to the film "Wings").

Population reaches 5,677,251, of whom 1.2 million live in Los Angeles and 634,000 in San Francisco. — 1930

Olympic Games in Los Angeles. — 1932

Earthquake hits Long Beach. — 1933

The Golden Gate Bridge in San Francisco is acclaimed at its opening as a new wonder of the world. — 1937

Within a decade the population has increased by a million to 6,907,000; Los Angeles has 1,504,277 inhabitants and San Francisco 634,536.
    The Pasadena freeway, the first motorway in Los Angeles, is completed. — 1940

Japanese submarines attack an oil field near Goleta.
    A detention camp is set up for Japanese nationals. — 1942

The All American Canal providing irrigation for Imperial Valley is completed, and is extended to Coachella Valley in 1948. — 1943

United Nations Organisation (UNO) founded in San Francisco. — 1945

Population has risen to 10,586,223; Los Angeles 1,970,000 and San Francisco 775,000. — 1950

"I love you California", a song by F. B. Silverwood (words) and A. F. Frankenstein (music) published in 1913, becomes the official state anthem. — 1951

The redwood tree and the grey bear become new state emblems. — 1953

Disneyland is opened at Anaheim. — 1955

Approval is given for a water supply system to ensure provision of water throughout the state, and for the building of the Oroville Dam to begin. — 1957

The move from New York by the Giants and the Dodgers means that California has the two leading baseball teams playing in one of the two main leagues. — 1958

In ten years the population has increased by 50 per cent to 15,717,000, with 2,480,000 living in Los Angeles and 740,000 in San Francisco. — 1960

California overtakes New York state as the most populated state in the USA, with 17.3 million inhabitants.
    John Steinbeck is the first native Californian to receive the Nobel Prize for Literature. — 1963

Serious disturbances in Watts, a suburb of Los Angeles predominantly inhabited by blacks. — 1965

In Oakland Bobby Seale and Huey Newton found the militant Black Panther organisation; Eldridge Cleaver joins soon after its foundation and becomes its spokesman. — 1966

Ronald Reagan is elected 33rd governor of the state and re-elected four years later. — 1967

International attention is aroused by a series of murders committed by the Manson family who, on two consecutive days in Los Angeles, kill seven strangers. — 1969

1970	The ever increasing population reaches almost 20 million, with 2,809,000 inhabitants in Los Angeles and 715,000 in San Francisco. Indians occupy Alcatraz Island off San Francisco.
1971	San Fernando Valley is affected by a serious earthquake.
1972	In San Francisco the BART rapid transport system for local traffic is opened.
1974	The Symbionese Liberation Army, an underground terrorist group, kidnaps Patty Hearst a student at the University of California in Berkeley. The granddaughter of the newspaper magnate William Randolph Hearst joins her kidnappers, participating in their crimes and, after being in hiding for a year and a half, is sentenced to seven years' imprisonment.
1977	Second year of low rainfall levels leads to a drought and water rationing in several regions of the state. Parliament reintroduces the death penalty.
1978	Floods and landfalls cause severe damage around Los Angeles. Voters decide on an addition to the constitution "Proposition 13" which restricts ground taxes and requires spending cuts in many counties and throughout the state.
1980	Population has risen to 23.6 million, a fivefold increase in 50 years.
1981	The state parliament passes a law to make all houses in the earthquake zone proof against future quakes.
1982	The "Peripheral Canal" is rejected in a referendum.
1984	23rd Olympic summer games in Los Angeles.
1987	According to the latest demographic census the Californian population will reach 33.5 million by the year 2000.
1988	Contrary to the Indians' wishes the Franciscan father Junípero Serra, who founded the first mission stations in the 18th c., is canonised; the Indians regard him as an oppressor of their forefathers. Many communities oppose further growth; the electors support about half the initiatives which are necessary for a referendum.
1989	On October 17th the Bay of San Francisco is hit by the most severe earthquake (6.9 on the Richter scale) since 1906 (8.3 on the Richter scale) at 5.04pm during the rush hour. It causes serious damage in San Francisco, Oakland, Santa Cruz and in Silicon Valley. The epicentre of the quake lies about 80 km (22 mi.) south of San Francisco in the mountains between Santa Cruz and San José. Tremors are felt as far away as Nevada in the north and Los Angeles in the south. After being in the forefront of economic development for six years (1982–88) California faces a recession and economic growth is expected to slow down over the coming years.
1992	Racial unrest follows the acquittal of four white Los Angeles policemen who had come close to beating a black driver to death for exceeding the speed limit. There is considerable damage to property in the city. Late in the year heavy rain and snow bring an end to the almost six year-long drought in California, by which time the water shortage had become critical. The worst economic and financial crisis since the Great Depression results in rising unemployment and reduced social expenditure.
1993	A proposal is put to the Senate that California be divided into three sep-

arate states, to be known as South, Central and North California, on the grounds that the expanding population and falling revenues have rendered the unitary state "ungovernable".

In the autumn nineteen bushfires (possibly started deliberately) cause extensive damage to property in the Los Angeles area and south as far as the Mexican border. As well as tracts of woodland, the towns of Laguna Beach and Malibu are badly affected.

It is decided to set up the Death Valley and Joshua Tree National Parks, and the Mojave National Preserve. Off-road vehicles are banned from driving in dunes and dried-out salt lakes. 1994

Heavy rainfall – especially in the Monterey area – causes damage probably amounting to more that 300 million dollars. 1995

In the west, high summer temperatures of up to 104°F (40°C) and excessive demands on the electricity supply from air-conditioning and cooling systems lead to the most serious power failures (up to 8 hours) in the history of the USA. 1996

Famous People

The following alphabetical list of names consists predominantly of people connected with California through birth, residence, influence or death, who have achieved national, even international importance.

Anselm Adams
Photographer
(1902–84)

Born in California, Adams became famous chiefly for his clear and sympathetic photographs of the Yosemite National Park and other protected areas, nearly all of which are in the west of the United States. Together with several books about the Sierra Nevada, the Californian desert and the National Parks, he also published photographic text-books and a book about the Nisei (the Japanese born in California). His photographs can be seen in nearly every museum in the US which has a photographic collection. Prints made by him fetch high prices at auction. He died in Monterey, not far from his last home in Carmel.

David Belasco
Theatre director
(1859–1931)

It is impossible to discuss the early theatre in America without mentioning Belasco – actor, producer, director, theatre owner and playwright. Born in San Francisco, he went as a child with his parents to Canada and then at 20 to New York to try his luck on Broadway. After a few difficult years he found success and played an active role in the American theatre for almost the next half-century. His distinctive style of direction was apparent even in his plays, two of which – "Madame Butterfly" and "The Girl of the Golden West" – formed the basis for the libretti of two of Puccini's operas. There is a theatre named after him in a side-street off Times Square in New York.

Luther Burbank
Botanist
(1849–1926)

Burbank was 26 when he came from Masssachusetts to California, where three of his brothers were already living. Influenced by the ideas of Darwin, he tried to grow new plants by cross-fertilisation. His experiments were so successful that he almost achieved mythical status in Santa Rosa, where he lived until his death. He succeeded in growing no less than 40 new varieties of plums and damsons, ten new berries, and new strains of tomatoes, peas, maize, roses, lilies and poppies. As well as his memoirs he wrote several books recording his successful work.

John Cage
Composer
(1912–92)

Whereas many famous Californians came from the north-east or the mid-west of the US to the "Golden State", the composer John Cage arrived from the other direction. He was a student at Pomona College (the town of the same name is located in the outskirts of Los Angeles) and studied musical theory under Arnold Schinberg and Henry Cowell. Cage taught for a period at Mills College in Oakland. For decades he has been known as the "enfant terrible" of the contemporary music scene, which he continues to surprise with new and difficult compositions. His own piano concertos often give the impression of being "happenings". He has published numerous books on ballet and the theatre.

James J. Corbett
World champion
boxer
(1866–1933)

James J. Corbett, the first world heavyweight boxing champion (known as "Gentleman Jim"), began his career as a bank employee in San Francisco. He won his world title there in 1892; after his victory over John L. Sullivan he lost the title five years later to Bob Fitzsimmons. It is said that he never fought unfairly.

Henry Cowell
Composer
(1897–1965)

Cowell's career soon took him from his birthplace of Mento Park near Palo Alto to the east, where he lived until his death in New York. His study of comparative musical theory at the University of Berlin from 1931 to 1932

Cecil B. DeMille   *Walt Disney*   *Isadora Duncan*

gave him new inspiration for his individual compositions. He taught at several of the universities of California, including Stanford, Mills College and the University of California. He left behind a comprehensive collection of works which contributed to his reputation of being distinctly avant-garde; they are difficult to perform and not much of his output has been published.

Born in Pala Alto, Alan Cranston is one of the two men who have represented California in the Senate in Washington since 1949. He attended Stanford University, became involved in the real estate business shortly afterwards, and was active in the Democratic Party. He was financial controller of the state from 1959 until 1967.

Alan Cranston
Politician
(b. 1924)

Born in Ashfield (Massachusetts), DeMille is one of the legendary film pioneers who made Hollywood famous. Following in his parents' footsteps, he joined the theatre as an author, producer, actor and manager. Soon after starting a production company in 1912 and making his first film "The Squaw Man", his fame spread. Owing to vehement criticism of the alleged immoraltity of his earlier social comedies, such as "Male and Female", he turned his attention to higher budget films with patriotic and religious themes, their exciting and sometimes superficial storyline having a wider public appeal.

Cecil B. DeMille
Producer and film director
(1881–1959)

Novels, essays and film scripts – the latter co-written with her husband John Gregory Dunne – have contributed to the fame of this writer from Sacramento, the capital of California. She attempts to capture the atmosphere of the 60s and 70s in the form of a social critique. Her meticulous stylistic detail is especially evident in "Run River", one of her most important novels, which shows the changes which have affected her home town where the 1849 Gold Rush began. In contrast, her novel "Play it as it Lays" is set in southern California.

Joan Didion
Writer
(b. 1934)

Hardly known outside America, the 81-year-old former baseball player DiMaggio, Marilyn Monroe's second husband, is still an idol. He comes from the small town of Martinez to the east of San Francisco; he began his career in 1932 as a national player in that town but was soon to become a member of the Yankee team in New York. He holds the unbroken record of having scored in 56 consecutive games.

Joe DiMaggio
Baseball player
(b. 1914)

Born in Chicago, Walt Disney began his career as an advertising artist, and after his first attempts at film cartoons he drew the popular "Mickey Mouse" series in 1928. He developed colour cartoon films ("snow White" 1937; "Bambi" 1942) and produced adventure films ("Treasure

Walt Disney
Cartoonist and film producer
(1901–66)

Jack London

Marilyn Monroe

George S. Patton

Island") and award-winning nature films ("The Living Desert" 1953; "The Wonders of the Prairie" 1954) as well as films for television ("Mickey Mouse Club", "Davy Crockett", "Walt Disney's Wonderful World of Colour"). In 1955 he set up the ever-popular recreational fairy-tale park "Disneyland" at Anaheim near Los Angeles and planned the larger than life amusement centre "Walt Disney World" at Orlando, Florida (opened 1971).

Isadora Duncan
Dancer
(1878–1927)

Born in San Francisco, Isadora Duncan had her first real breakthrough in Europe, because the reactionary Americans disapproved of her carefree lifestyle and were opposed to her sympathy for the Russians. Living most of the time in Paris, she opened her first school in Berlin in 1904 and another school in Moscow in 1921 which lasted only a short time. She distanced herself from traditional classical ballet and sought inspiration in the free movements of ancient Greek dances. The importance of her pioneering work was only recognised after her premature death, as a result of a car accident in Nice.

Lawrence
Ferlinghetti
Poet and
publisher
(b. 1919)

Ferlinghetti, born in New York, had a lasting influence on the cultural life of San Francisco and California. A member of the "Beat generation", he helped its poets to gain recognition by publishing their works and selling them in his City Limits Bookshop in San Francisco. He was, for example, the first to publish Allen Ginsberg. His own work is notable for having peculiar speech rhythms and unusual typography.

Sam Francis
Artist
(b. 1923)

Francis, from San Mateo, is considered one of the most important of present-day artists. His works can be seen in every museum of contemporary art. he was educated at the University of California in Berkeley and at the Californian School of Fine Arts (now San Francisco Art Institute). His mostly large abstract paintings stand out for their richness of colour and for their distinct feeling of space.

William Randolph
Hearst
Newspaper
magnate
(1863–1951)

Hearst's father came to California on foot from the mid-west in 1850, and within a decade he was one of the nouveau riche of San Francisco, thanks to acquiring silver mines in Nevada as well as other mines. His only son, William Randolph, born with the proverbial silver spoon in his mouth, was made publisher at the age of 24 of the daily newspaper "san Francisco Examiner" by his father, but built up his newspaper and magazine empire from New York. Hearst's publications were characterised by sensationalism and patriotism; it was also he who introduced comics into the daily press. Later he bought up radio stations and film companies, as well as real estate, yet he did not neglect his father's mines. He lived in grand style, had a castle built at San Simeon, where his lover Marion Davies was mistress. Orsen Wells paid a not exactly flattering tribute to Hearst in the film "Citizen Kane".

His granddaughter Patricia (Patty) Hearst, born in 1954, was kidnapped by terrorists in 1974. She was seized by the FBI in 1975 and sentenced to several years' imprisonment in 1976 for involvement in her kidnappers' crimes. She was reprieved in 1979.

Hoover was the first of three presidents of the USA who lived in California. He came as a young man from Iowa in the mid-west and studied engineering science at Stanford University. He had a successful career as a mining engineer and expert on international mining problems behind him when he enlisted for official duties in the First World War. At first he organised aid for Belgian and French civilians; on America's entry into the war he became responsible for food supplies to his own country, and after the war he despatched food to young people in countries in need. He was Minister of Trade from 1921 to 1928 and in the latter year, as the Republican candidate, was elected President. The Stock Exchange crash of 1929 occurred during his presidency and the ensuing economic depression ruined his political reputation, with the result that Franklin D. Roosevelt won the 1932 election.

Herbert C. Hoover
US President
(1874–1964)

At the age of sixteen Jeffers came to Pasadena with his family from Pittsburgh where he was born. He attended the Occidental College in Los Angeles where he studied medicine and forestry science. From 1916 to the end of his days he lived in Carmel and helped to give the town its reputation as a favoured residence for writers, up-and-coming artists and leading retired academics. Much of his philosophical and complex work reflects the ambience of Carmel and its surroundings, where "for the first time he saw people living in the midst of magnificent unspoiled countryside, as in the idylls and legends of Homer's Ithaca". He wrote more than a dozen volumes of poetry and a few adaptations of Euripides' tragedies. The interpretation of the poems, most of which do not rhyme, is made more difficult by ambiguous poetic images and symbols. His works, published during the Second World War, are filled with hatred of civilisation and social criticism.

Robinson Jeffers
Poet
(1887–1962)

Of the numerous early film producers Lasky is the only native Californian (he came from San Francisco). With his brother-in-law Samuel Goldwyn he founded his first film company which became Paramount Pictures. After losing control of the biggest film concern of its time, he remained active as a producer for other companies, such as Fox, Warner and RKO. His most successful films include "Sergeant York", "The Adventures of Mark Twain", "Rhapsody in Blue" and "The Great Caruso". Shortly before his death at Beverly Hills he published his memoirs.

Jesse Lasky
Film producer
(1880–1958)

The illegitimate son of an itinerant astrologer and of a mother who was not over-concerned for him, London was born in San Francisco. At fourteen he left school and made his way as a fisherman, harbour policeman (in Oakland) and sailor. He was first arrested for vagrancy and again for making an inflammatory Socialist speech. He was also among those who searched for gold on the Canadian River Klondike. He began his work as an author by writing short stories reflecting his varied experiences; these were first published separately in magazines and in 1900 in a book edition entitled "The Son of the Wolf". Over the course of the next fifteen years he wrote 40 novels. "The Call of the Wild" became his most famous work worldwide. Jack London had a house built in Glen Ellen which, however, burnt down as soon as it was completed in 1913. During the last years of his life he became a depressive and at 40 he committed suicide.

Jack London
Writer
(1876–1916)

Famous People

Marilyn Monroe
Film actress
(1926–57)

Born Norma Jean Baker or Mortenson in Los Angeles, Marilyn Monroe began her heady career as a photographic model, was then discovered as a "sex-bomb" in Hollywood and marketed in almost 30 films. After playing mainly minor roles from 1948 to 1952, she became famous overnight by her part in the film "Niagara". "Gentlemen Prefer Blondes", "The Prince and the Showgirl" and above all "some Like It Hot" were among her best-known films. This undoubtedly talented actress became a tragic, frustrated victim of Hollywood's idol factory. Several biographies of her have appeared. Her third and final marriage was to the author Arthur Miller.

Julia Morgan
Architect
(1872–1957)

Julia Morgan, born in San Francisco, was the first Californian woman to qualify in engineering, and to graduate as an architect at the Ecole des Beaux Arts in Paris. In 1905 she opened her own architect's office in San Francisco and in the course of her long career designed about 600 blocks of flats. Her most important achievement was the planning and completion of the castle built for William Randolf Hearst in San Simeon. She worked on this project from 1919 until 1947.

John Muir
Naturalist
(1838–1914)

John Muir came with his family to the United States as an eleven-year-old from Scotland. He grew up in Winsconsin and first visited California in 1868, where he found his life's work, and where he stayed until his death. (He died in Martinez.) Muir had studied chemistry, geology and botany, and first ran a fruit farm for ten years near Martinez, east of San Francisco. Then he devoted his attention to the preservation of forests, and played a decisive role in the creation of the Yosemite National Park (1890). It was due to his initiative that dozens of forest reserves were created in California. Many places of interest are named after him: the Muir Woods near San Francisco, the John Muir Trail through the High Sierra, the Muir Ravine in the Yosemite National Park, the Muir Grove in Sequoia National Park and the Muir Pass in Kings Canyon National Park.

Richard M. Nixon
US President
(1913–94)

Of the three Presidents of the USA who lived in California, Nixon is the only one who was born in the state. His birthplace was Yorba Linda, east of Anaheim, now a town with 36,000 inhabitants. His family was quite poor, but he had the opportunity to attend a college and then to study law at Duke University in North Carolina. He settled down as a lawyer in Whittier, served in the navy in the Second World War and was elected to the House of Representatives in 1946. Four years later he was elected senator, and in 1952 became Vice-President under Eisenhower. In 1960 he lost the presidential election to John F. Kennedy and in 1962 he was also defeated in the election for State Governor in California. Not until 1968 did he fulfil his life's ambition to become President, and four years later he was re-elected. Nixon advocated detente between the great powers, recognition of the People's Republic of China and the introduction of a ceasefire in the Vietnam War. His increasingly authoritarian style of government and finally his involvement in the Watergate affair forced him to resign, the only one of 40 US Presidents to do so.

Isamo Noguchi
Architect and
sculptor
(1904–88)

Born in Los Angeles the son of a Japanese lyric poet and an American authoress, Noguchi went to school in Japan and returned to the USA in 1918, where he received his artistic education. He worked for six months in Paris as a Guggenheim scholar and assistant to Brâncusis. In his buildings (for example the UNESCO Building in Paris and the Billy Rose Sculpture Gardens in Jerusalem) he combines oriental and surrealist elements with his teacher's initiatives, and he achieves elegant abstractions and an integration of architecture and sculpture. Active until the end of his life, he lived in the USA, Japan and Italy. In 1985 he created the Isamo Noguchi Garden Museum in New York City, the place where his productive life ended.

Patton was a controversial figure but this never worried him. Born in San Gabriel, he grew up on his maternal grandfather's ranch, attended the military academy of West Point and commanded a tank brigade in the First World War. During the Second World War he was commander of the US Third Army which advanced from France as far as Czechoslovakia. His attacks which were often improvised have become almost legendary. Patton was killed in a road accident in Heidelberg shortly after the end of the war.

George S. Patton
Military
commander
(1885–1945)

Peck is one of the few film stars who were born in California. He comes from La Jolla, a suburb of San Diego, studied at the University of California in Berkeley, was a successful actor on Broadway, yet in 1944 decided to concentrate on the cinema. He became known for his reserved and cool acting, as in his most famous films "Duel in the Sun" and "To Kill a Mockingbird". From 1967 to 1970 he was president of the Academy of Motion Picture Arts and Sciences.

Gregory Peck
Actor
(b. 1916)

The 33rd Governor of California (1967–75) and the 40th President of the United States was born in the state of Illinois. He was for five years a sports announcer with a radio station in Iowa before coming to Hollywood in 1937 where he had a rapid career in B films. After the war, during which he served in the air force, was president of the Film Actors' Union for twelve years, became a Republican in 1962, and was elected governor four years later without ever having held office previously. In 1976 he was defeated in the Republican primaries for the presidency, but was elected four years later and re-elected in 1984. He now lives in Bel Air, probably the most prestigious suburb of Los Angeles.

Ronald Reagan
Governor,
US President
(b. 1911)

Born to Armenian parents in Fresno, William Saroyan spent part of his childhood in an orphanage as his widowed mother was too poor to keep him. He left school at the age of twelve; his first job was as a telegraph messenger, and he only had casual work over the next 20 years, although he wrote short stories on the side, which he completed in the edition "The Man of the Flying Trapeze" in 1934. His works are renowned for their often excessively optimistic style which is not always without sentimentality, and they frequently contain autobiographical material. He has also written half a dozen novels as well as several plays. He was awarded the Pulitzer Prize in 1939 for the play "The Time of Your Life", but he did not accept it. Saroyan's uncritical belief in the "American Dream" and the naïve viewpoint of his characters have received a mixed critical response. He died in Fresno.

William Saroyan
Writer
(1908–81)

After a successful career in the east of the country, this Baltimore-born writer first came to California in 1909 and settled in Pasadena in 1917. Among his earlier successes was "The Jungle" (1906), a novel which portrayed the atrocities of the slaughterhouse of Chicago. After settling in the west he wrote almost 100 works in which he criticised the inadequacies of American society. He still found time, however, for political activity, applying as a socialist in 1920, 1922 and 1926 for several positions without success. In 1934 he stood as a Democratic candidate for governor but was defeated by his Republican opponent. He described himself as a religious socialist.

Upton Sinclair
Writer
(1878–1968)

He was born in San Francisco, and grew up in Sacramento in a gabled Victorian house which later became the residence of the governor. Steffens gained an international outlook through studying in several European countries, which stood him in good stead as a journalist. His struggle was primarily against corruption in the big American cities, San Francisco being no exception at the turn of the century. His book "The Shame of the Cities" not only created a sensation, but also had practical consequences for some of the cities that were the subject of his

Lincoln Steffens
Writer
(1866–1936)

William Saroyan   *Upton Sinclair*   *John Steinbeck*

criticism. His most widely read book is his autobiography which appeared in 1931, in which he openly expresses his scepticism about the structure of American society, and which has much to say about the introduction of a different economic and political system. Steffens died in Carmel.

John Steinbeck
Writer
(1902–68)

Like so many American writers Steinbeck cannot get away from his roots. Those who know his birthplace Salinas and the surrounding Monterey Peninsula will keep finding references to his home among the best pages of his books. He studied at Stanford University without taking his finals, and had several short-term jobs before publishing the novel "Cup of Gold" in 1929. He wrote his most important works during the thirties: "Of Mice and Men" (later adapted for the stage) and "The Grapes of Wrath" which represented the tragedy of people driven from their land by economic depression and drought. He was awarded the Nobel Prize for Literature in 1962 for his collected works.

Irving Stone
Writer
(b. 1903)

Irving Stone, another writer born in San Francisco, is famous for biographical novels of famous people. Works connected with California include "sailor on Horseback" (about Jack London), "Immortal Wife" (about Jessie FrÉmont, whose husband was a soldier of fortune, a Californian senator and a major-general in the Civil War) as well as the novel "Men to Match My Mountain" about Californian pioneers.

Levi Strauss
Textile merchant
(1829–1902)

Levi Strauss, whose jeans produced in San Francisco since 1850 have achieved world fame, came to America from Bavaria when he was fourteen. Before setting off on a three-month sea journey around Cape Horn he laid in, from his brother's textile business in New York, a store of various types of material and some rolls of canvas for stage-coaches. Even before he arrived in San Francisco he had sold all his wares except the canvas. One day a gold miner complained that his trousers tore so easily because of his strenuous work, and Strauss hit upon the idea of making trousers from the canvas; these were an immediate success. In 1853 he founded with his brother the firm which is still in existence today. The idea of reinforcing the pockets with copper studs was that of a local tailor (patented in 1878). Later, instead of canvas, resistant cotton drill was used and was named after its French town of origin, "serge de Nímes" which became known as "denim".

Johann August
Sutter Landowner
(1803–80)

An unhappy marriage and the failure of his haberdashery business led Sutter to emigrate to America, the paradise at that time for "black sheep". He was born in Germany and grew up in Switzerland. Johann August

Levi Strauss

Johann A. Sutter

Orson Welles

Sutter arrived in 1839 after adventures which had taken him to Alaska and Hawaii. He became a Mexican citizen and received the largest possible grant of land from the Mexican governor of that time, and farmed it with the help of Indian slaves. Sutter built a fort on the land and called his empire "Nueva Helvetia". He bought the Russian owned Fort Ross and Bodega Bay, and supported the Americans in conquering California. He became a delegate to Congress and from then on called himself John Augustus Sutter. Near Sacramento, the capital of California, which was founded by Sutter, James W. Marshall discovered in 1848 the first Californian gold. Gold was also discovered in 1949 during the construction of a saw mill on Sutter's land and soon his property was overrun with fortune hunters who destroyed everything that was not nailed down. Sutter lost everything, lived sixteen years on a small pension which the Senate allowed him, but his claims for compensation were never recognised by the Federal Government. He died penniless and in obscurity.

The actress from Santa Monica was only three years old when she first faced the camera. By the age of six she was a favourite with audiences both young and old with her winning smile, blond curly hair and indisputable talent. The success of her earlier films ("Little Miss Marker", "The Littlest Rebel" and "Rebecca of Sunnybrook Farm") made between 1934 and 1938 was not to be repeated. At 22, an age when many are just beginning, she gave up her film career, married a rich businessman and joined the diplomatic service, becoming ambassador to Ghana.

Shirley Temple
Actress
(b. 1928)

Earl Warren studied law in Los Angeles where he was born, and took part in the First World War. After returning to civilian life and a short spell as a lawyer, he was elected district attorney, i.e. chief prosecutor, of Alameda County in Oakland. As state Justice Minister (attorney general), the next rung on his ladder to success, he was a successful campaigner against organised crime. Contrary to his otherwise liberal outlook, one of his last official acts was to sanction the internment of the Japanese in the coastal areas. Elected governor of California in 1943 and twice re-elected, his twelve years of service meant he was in office longer than any other governor. President Eisenhower appointed him to the Supreme Federal Court in 1953. During his sixteen years in office he made important judgements in favour of minorities; he declared racial segregation in schools to be unconstitutional.

Earl Warren
Governor
(1891–1974)

Orson Welles, born in Kenosha (Wisconsin), thrilled his theatre audiences from the beginning with his distinctive individual productions. His realistic radio production of H. G. Wells "War of the Worlds" caused

Orson Welles
Actor and director
(1915–85)

mass hysteria and brought him the unique contract for Hollywood of making a completely independent film every year. His first film was "Citizen Kane" which with its editing and lighting techniques, together with the alienating perspective, broke new ground. However, interference and disputes caused him to leave Hollywood in 1947. Often supported by patrons, he experimented as a director in different countries and as an actor – he normally played the leading role in his films – with different kinds of artistic forms. "Macbeth" (1947) and "The Third Man" (1949) are two of his best known films.

Edward Weston
Photographer
(1886–1968)

Edward Weston was born in the state of Illinois and came to California at nineteen where he went about knocking on doors to get portrait commissions. As well as portraits of people he also photographed landscapes, nudes, plants and vegetables. He also used to earn money making prints in his laboratory. During the twenties he spent several years in Mexico but in 1928 he settled in Carmel where he spent the last 30 years of his life, paralysed from 1958 by Parkinson's disease. Like Adams he captured on camera the beauty of the coast of California, especially Point Lobos, rather than the mountains and forests.

Culture

Education

A rudimentary education system became established in California in the middle of the last century. Whereas the Franciscan monks were making efforts even earlier to educate those Indians who were willing to learn, neither the Spanish nor the Mexican colonial governments provided schools for their people. The American settlers who had been coming to California since the early 1840s opened the first school in 1846 at the Santa Clara Mission; another appeared a year later in Monterey. San Francisco got its first school in 1850, about the time when California was accepted into the Union. Chinese, Indian and Black children were excluded from lessons. The legal requirement to establish a school providing three months' teaching in every school district was only gradually complied with, and it was decades later before a higher education system existed throughout the state.

Secondary

The first high schools were private institutions of a religious nature. In 1851 the Jesuits founded Santa Clara College (Santa Clara University from 1885) in the town of the same name, and the Methodists founded the College of the Pacific in neighbouring San José. The latter was transferred to Stockton in 1961 and is now called the University of the Pacific. Both institutions are open to members of other denominations.

State universities

The extensive network of the University of California, now famous throughout the world, had its origins in 1873 in the College of California in Oakland. The State University was founded in 1868 and moved to Berkeley in 1873, where in the same year the first class of twelve men received their diplomas. Three decades later the first branches were founded in Riverside, La Jolla, San Francisco (the Foundation for Medical Research was taken over) and Los Angeles. Later the Universities of Davis, Santa Barbara, San Diego, Santa Cruz and Irvine were added. The network of state universities had now spread throughout the whole state. The Universities of Berkeley and Los Angeles rank among the most pioneering of all the higher education establishments of America. The State also maintains a separate system of state colleges, of which there are currently nineteen with over 320,000 students. A college is the equivalent of an English sixth-form and the foundation year of a university course, and it attendance is a prerequisite for a university place. Not until this stage has been reached does specialisation in individual subjects begin.

Private universities

Some private universities also enjoy an outstanding reputation. These include the University of Southern California in Los Angeles, founded in 1880 by the Methodists and today the largest private university in the State. Others are the world-famous Stanford University in Palo Alto (1891), created by one man, the "railway king" Leland Stanford, the Occidental College in Los Angeles, founded by the Presbyterian religious community, and, last but not least, the Californian Institute of Technology in Pasadena, which owns the Palomar Observatory. This institute is noted for its high staffing ratio – 800 university lecturers to 1800 students.

In the south-east of Los Angeles County at the foot of the San Gabriel Mountains, in the town of Claremont with only 35,000 inhabitants, there is a noteworthy group of six colleges which originated between 1887 and 1946: Pomona College, Claremont Graduate School, Scripps

College, Claremont McKenna College, Harvey Mudd College and Pitzer College.

Arts

The cultural life of California has developed in less than a century. Although folk music and folk dancing were practised in the 1850s and there were even early dramatic performances, these were put on by amateurs and lacked suitable premises. However, as long ago as the 1860s some of the most prominent American actors of the time, including Edwin Booth, Edwin Forrest and Laura Keene, came to California. Even Lola Montez, the mistress of Ludwig I of Bavaria, appeared in San Francisco and some gold-mining towns after her expulsion from Munich.

California's first theatre was built in 1869 in Bath Street and held an audience of between 1478 and 2150. Seven years later there followed the Baldwin Academy of Music, converted from part of an hotel and accommodating 2100, and Wade's Opera House for an audience of 2234.

Theatre

In Los Angeles theatrical life first began in the nineties with the building of the Majestic and Burbank Theatres, which at first only featured guest productions from New York with such famous stars as Joseph Jefferson, James O'Neill (the father of Eugene O'Neill), Sarah Bernhardt, Julia Marlowe and Ellen Terry. Only gradually did Californian actors, such as David Belasco and David Warfield make a name for themselves, but they soon tried their luck on the stages of New York.

The development of theatrical life began to stagnate with the arrival of the cinema. Even in the early days of motion pictures (around 1917) there were more picture houses than theatres in San Francisco. Today the theatrical landscape has radically changed. Not only San Francisco but also Los Angeles have dozens of large and small theatres; San Diego, Sacramento, San José, Santa Barbara, Monterey and numerous other towns can also accommodate permanent theatrical ensembles. The American Conservatory Theatre in San Francisco, the Mark Taper Forum in Los Angeles and the Old Globe Theatre in San Diego now rank among the leading theatres in the country.

The development of musical life was also slow at first, even with the establishment of a philharmonic orchestra in San Francisco as long ago as 1852, which was subsidised mainly by German clubs. Regular operatic performances began in 1877 with mostly Italian opera in the Tivoli Opera House and the Grand Opera House, both of which disappeared in rubble and ashes in the 1906 earthquake. It was 1919 before a new start was made with the San Francisco Opera Company which still exists today.

Music

The first symphony orchestra came into being in San Francisco and from the outset it was able to call on famous conductors. It was followed in 1919 by the Symphony Orchestra of Los Angeles. The construction of the Music Centre for the Performing Arts (completed in 1967) provided a permanent home for the Los Angeles opera which had existed since 1919 in the Dorothy Chandler Pavilion. Summer concerts in the enormous Hollywood Bowl, "symphony under the Stars", can accommodate an audience of 20,000 sitting and a further 10,000 standing. Today other Californian towns have their own orchestras, including Oakland, San José, San Diego, Fresno, Stockton and Sacramento. Music concerts are frequently held in other towns, such as Carmel and Ojay.

The founding of the first conservatory of music (San Francisco Conservatory) in 1917 gave a vital impulse to musical life. The exodus of

◀ *Palo Alto: Stanford University, tower of the Green Library*

San Diego: Old Globe Theatre

renowned composers from Europe in the years following 1933 brought world-famous musicians to Californian universities; a representative selection include the Swiss Ernest Block (University of California in Berkeley), Arnold Schînberg (University of California in Los Angeles where there is also a Schînberg research centre), and Darius Milhaud (Mills College in Oakland).

The importance of popular music in recent times, especially rock music, is worth mentioning. Groups such as "The Grateful Dead", "Jefferson Airplane" and "Beach Boys" have left their mark on the American popular music scene.

Museums   Museums appeared in California even later than theatres and concert halls, indeed not until the present century. The fact that they are among the most important in the world is a reflection of the great hunger for culture of this young state. In this area, too, San Francisco took the lead. In 1916 the M. H. de Young Museum received a purpose-built extension. In 1960 there was added the Asian Art Museum to house the exhibits from the collection of Avery Brundage, the long-serving Chairman of the Olympic Committee. The San Francisco Museum of Modern Art and the California Palace of the Legion of Honour (containing exclusively French works of art) were founded in the twenties.

Until the gigantic Getty Center opened in 1997, the most significant museum in Los Angles was the County Museum of Art, which, built only in 1965, has, over three decades acquired an enviable collection. This was followed by the opening of the Museum of Contemporary Art in 1987. The Southwest Museum ranks as one of the best museums with exhibits illustrating Indian culture. Close to Los Angeles are the Henry E. Huntington Library and Art Gallery (opened 1919) and the Norton Simon Museum of Art in Pasadena (since 1974), the J. Paul Getty in Malibu (1973; the exhibits were moved to the Getty

Center in 1977; reopening with collection of antiques planned for 2001) and the Henry Huntingdon Library and Art Gallery in Pasadena (since 1919).

Other notable museums are the Stanford University Museum in Palo Alto, the E. B. Crocker Art Gallery in Sacramento, the Berkeley University Art Museum, the Oakland Museum, the Santa Barbara Museum of Art, the Museum of Art in Long Beach, the Museum of Contemporary Art in La Jolla, together with the Fine Arts Gallery and the Timken Art Gallery in San Diego. There are also numerous museums of local history and science throughout the state.

During the 19th century a whole range of painters lived in California. They were either European immigrants, such as the German Albert Bierstadt and the British-born Thomas Hill, or artists who had at least studied in Europe. Not until after the Second World War did native painters or those working in the state make a name for themselves; these include Clyfford Still, Mark Rothko, Richard Diebenkorn, Robert Motherwell and Sam Francis.

Painters

Architecture

Californian architecture is as varied as the countryside. It ranges from the adobe houses with flat roofs dating from the colonial period to the skyscrapers which have dominated the outlines of San Francisco, San Diego and Los Angeles for the last decades. Nothing remains of the skittle-shaped huts of the Yurok Indians.

Spanish missionaries came from Mexico to California. They built their mission stations to match the local building style of the pueblo (village). Building materials used were wooden beams and adobe, which consists of a mixture of dried clay and vegetable fibres and was used by the Indians. With this method of building the characteristic adobe architecture developed, and this can be seen throughout California. As well as the special materials used, the main features of this building style, which is still popular today, are a crude, castle-like appearance, façades without windows, and rounded corners.

Adobe style

The mission stations built in the second half of the 18th c. were the first Californian buildings not intended solely for habitation. A right-angled inner courtyard ("patio") was enclosed by the church and the domestic and residential buildings of the monastery. The builders of the mission stations, the Franciscan fathers, basically followed essentially Mexican models, although occasionally Roman architects such as Vitruvius were copied, for example in the construction of the façade of Santa Barbara Mission Station. The work was frequently carried out by the Indians.

With the arrival of the Americans from the east coast of the United States, a mixture of New England style and Spanish-Mexican elements developed which is referred to in architectural history as Monterey Colonial style.

Monterey
Colonial style

The construction of the saw-mills led to an increased number of shingle-built houses and to various kinds of wood being used in construction work. As a result of the fire hazard shops and offices soon came to be built of brick or stone, but wooden houses continued to be constructed for private use until late in the 19th century. Eclectism reigned in Californian architecture; there are examples of Neo- Classicism, Romanesque and Renaissance in the cities, particularly in San Francisco. Whole suburbs were characterised by the large number of Victorian wooden houses from around 1870 until the earthquake of 1906. The

Eclectism

architects did not shy from exaggeration as the "san Francisco Stick" proves. The wooden decorations of these houses could be bought ready-made. The "Eastlake" style can be traced back to England furniture designs, and the Queen Anne style is typified by asymmetrical houses with high gabled roofs and decorated towers. One of the best examples of this style is the Carson House in Eureka.

Los Angeles

Los Angeles, having no more than 10,000 inhabitants in 1880, was untouched by these architectural trends. As the town expanded the number of architects who settled there and who influenced the town's appearance grew. In any case it was some time before a distinctive style emerged. At first the mission style was recreated, then the Beaux Arts style spread, of which there are many examples to be found in Los Angeles. Art Nouveau is more prevalent in Los Angeles than in other Californian towns. The influence of the Austrian architects Richard Neutra and Rudolph Schindler who worked there is still of paramount importance today. Numerous private houses in and around Los Angeles, as well as some public buildings by the American Frank Lloyd Wright, seem to indicate an original style.

Sculpture by J. Lipchitz in Los Angeles

Skyscrapers

By American standards skyscrapers came late to San Francisco and Los Angeles, not least because of the continued threat of earthquakes. In Los Angeles from the end of the twenties blocks of flats were not allowed to be built. Not until the advent of earthquake-resistant buildings could skyscrapers be constructed in California, and even today, particularly in downtown Los Angeles, this trend still continues.

San Francisco with its many hills did not appear to be a favourable site for skyscrapers; gradually they came into being but are not as high as in Manhattan. A referendum prevented the unrestricted construction of high-rise buildings after building restrictions had been over-ruled three times during the seventies.

Quotations

The people (in Hollywood) are unreal, they don't smell. The fruit is unreal, it doesn't taste of anything. The whole place is a glaring, gaudy, nightmarish set, built up in the desert.

Ethel Barrymore
American actress
(1879–1959)

Sometimes when I think of what the polyp of a town (Los Angeles) was like thirty years ago, I get a bit sentimental. Since we have been living in this stifling, evil-smelling khaki-coloured smog, we scarcely know what it was once like; a gentian-blue sky, cold nights with the heavens filled with stars, and the smell of jasmine ... the air so pure that you could not only breathe it, you could even have drunk it.

Vicky Baum
German author
(1888–1960)

The mist which the mighty winds from the sea blow over the coast dissolves in summer over the hot thirsty land, and in autumn the landscape has the appearance of bare space, burned brown by the heat and broken by sparse stunted bushes and dazzling deserts of quicksand. Here and there on the crests of the mountains dark pine forests can be seen.

Adalbert von
Chamisso
German author
(1781–1838)

California, the most spectacular and most diversified American state. California so ripe, golden, yeasty, churning in a flux, is a world of its own ... It contains both the most sophisticated and the most bigoted community in America; it is a bursting cornucopia of peoples as well as of fruit, glaciers, sunshine, desert and petroleum. There are several Californias, and the state is at once demented and very sane, adolescent and mature, depending on the point of view.

John Gunther
American
journalist
(1901–70)

The feeling of the sanctity of science and of a true communal spirit in the service of an ideal was never so clear to me as on the day I spent with the workers on Mount Wilson, the great observatory at Pasadena in California. In Europe art has taken over the functions once fulfilled by religion; in America this position appears to have been assumed by science.

Johan Huizinga
Dutch historico-
cultural writer
(1872–1945)

Remember that the men who stocked California in the 50s were physically and as far as certain tough virtues are concerned, the pick of the earth ... To this nucleus were added all the races of the continent – French, Italian, German, and, of course, the Jews. The result you can see in large-boned, deep-chested, delicate handed women and long, elastic, well-built boys. It needs no little golden badge ... to mark the native son of the Golden West ... Him I love because he is devoid of fear, carries himself like a man, and has a heart as big as his boots.

Rudyard Kipling
British author
(1865–1936)

Broadway in L.A. was no shopping street for the rich; it belonged to the people and never before did I see such folk. Whites of all shades, Blacks both light and dark, Asians both yellow and brown, Filipinos, Mexicans, Latin-Americans, Indians; old races, new races, who worked and walked handsomely, proudly, uninhibited and free.

Wolfgang
Koeppen
German author
(b. 1906)

California is a queer place – in a way it has turned its back on the world, and looks into the void Pacific. It is absolutely selfish, very empty but not false, and at least not full of false effort ... It is sort of crazy-sensible. Just the moment: hardly as far ahead as "carpe diem".

D. H. Lawrence
British author
(1885–1930)

Nature in California is neurotic, its apparent stability a mask for anguish and anxiety; drought and fire are her most frequent aggressions, but earthquake her constant menace.

Carey McWilliams
American
Sociologist
(1905–60)

Quotations

H. L. Mencken
American author
(1880–1956)

Nineteen suburbs in search of a metropolis (description of Los Angeles).

The Californian climate makes the sick well and the well sick, the old young and the young old.

Henry Miller
American author
(1891–1980)

Big Sur is the California that men dreamed of years ago, this is the Pacific that Balboa looked at from the peak of Darien, this is the face of the earth as the Creator intended it to look.

Ashley Montagu
Anthropologist
(b. 1905)

It (California) is the land of perpetual pubescence, where cultural lag is mistaken for Renaissance.

John Muir
American
naturalist
(1838–1914

The Pacific coast in general is the paradise of conifers. Here nearly all of them are giants, and display a beauty and magnificence unknown elsewhere. The climate is mild, the ground never freezes, and moisture and sunshine abound all the year. Nevertheless, it is not easy to account for the colossal size of the sequoias. The largest are about 300 feet high and 30 feet in diameter.

J. B. Priestley
British author
(1894–1984)

California, the advance post of our civilisation, with its huge aircraft factories, TV and film studios, automobile way of life ... its flavourless cosmopolitanism, its charlatan philosophies and religions, its lack of anything old and well-tried, rooted in tradition and character.

George Santayana
Spanish author
(1865–1952)

I am struck in California by the deep and almost religious affection people have for nature ... it is their spontaneous substitute for articulate art and articulate religion.

John Steinbeck
American author
(1902–68)

The spring is beautiful in California. Valleys in which the fruit blossoms are fragrant pink, and white waters in a shallow sea. The first tendrils of the grapes swelling from the old gnarled vines, cascade down to cover the trunks.

Oscar Wilde
Irish author
(1854–1900)

California is an Italy without its art. There are subjects for the artist, but it is universally true that the only scenery which inspires utterance is that which man feels himself the master of. The mountains of California are so gigantic that they are not favourable to art or poetry. There are good poets in England, but none in Switzerland. There the mountains are too high. Art cannot add to nature.

Edmund Wilson
American author
(1895–1972)

California, since we took it from the Mexicans, has always presented itself to Americans as one of the strangest and most exotic of their exploits.

John Phillips
Michelle Gillian

All the leaves are brown and the sky is grey
I've been for a walk on a winter's day
I'd be safe and warm if I was in L.A.
California dreamin' on such a winter's day.

"California Dreamin'"

At the beginning of the 60s the Hippy movement spread from California. The song "California dreamin' ", made popular by the American pop-group "The Mamas & the Papas" is an expression of this philosophy.

Suggested Routes

The following suggested itineraries are intended to help the motorist touring California, without denying him freedom to make his own plans and choice of route. The routes have been chosen so that the principal places of interest in the state are visited. However, not all the places of interest in this guide can be covered without making detours. The proposed routes can be followed on the map at the back of this book.

Departure points, to which the motorist will return at the end of each tour, are principally the towns of San Francisco, Los Angeles and San Diego.

For most journeys several days are needed and the overnight stops must be planned in advance.

Places and areas which are covered in the A to Z section under a main heading are printed in **bold**.

1: San Francisco along the Pacific coast to the north and into the vine-growing area (537 km (342 mi.))

Leaving San Francisco on Highway 101 over the Golden Gate Bridge you first reach the picturesque town of **Sausalito**, and from there go north on the CA 1 to **Muir Woods National Monument** where there is a fine stand of giant redwoods. Continue along the coast road (extremely winding) to Inverness and Point Reyes peninsula with **Point Reyes National Seashore** at its south-west end (February to July flowers; (50 mi. (80km) of footpaths), then via **Bodega Bay** to **Mendocino**, originally a fishing village which has interesting traces of its past.

From there go inland on the CA 20 and CA 29 via Willits to Clear Lake, which is popular with local people, and past the south end of the lake as far as **Calistoga**, continuing via **St Helena**, Rutherford, Oakville and Yountville, where there are numerous wineries, to **Vallejo** and then along the 1–80 to the university town of **Berkeley**.

From Calistoga an alternative route (adds another 64 km (40 mi.)) can be followed back to San Francisco: go north-west on the CA 128 to **Geyserville** and **Healdsburg**, both centres of viniculture, and then on the US 101 to **Santa Rosa**. Continue south on the CA 12 to the Jack London State Historic Park about 2.5 km (1½ mi.) west of **Glen Ellen**. Here can be seen the ruins of burnt-out houses which the author Jack London had built, and also his grave. From here you drive to **Sonoma** once the capital of the short-lived Californian Republic and now the headquarters of numerous wine-producing firms. Continue south along the CA 121 and then take the CA 37 to the west; at San Rafael you turn on to the US 101 and finally arrive back at San Francisco.

2: San Francisco into Goldland, to Lake Tahoe and into the Yosemite National Park (1240 km (775 mi.))

This route starts on the US 80 crossing the San Francisco Oakland Bay Bridge, with a view of the hilly island of Yerba Buena. It then goes via **Oakland** and **Berkeley** from where there are beautiful views over San Francisco Bay and of the silhouette of **San Francisco**. Continue along San Pablo Bay via Richmond to **Vallejo** where the Napa River flows into San Pablo Bay. To the north-west extend the well-known Californian

Routes through California

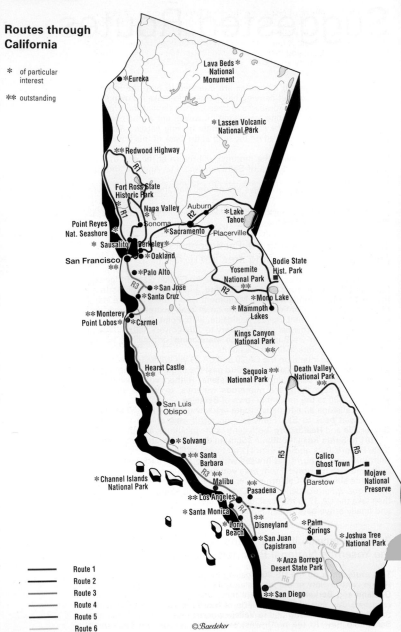

* of particular
  interest

** outstanding

Lava Beds *
National
Monument

*Eureka

*Lassen Volcanic
National Park

**Redwood Highway

R1

Fort Ross State
Historic Park

R1

*Napa Valley

Auburn

*Lake
Tahoe

Point Reyes
Nat. Seashore

*Sonoma

R2

*Sacramento

Placerville

Bodie State
Hist. Park

* Sausalito

*Berkeley

San Francisco

*Oakland

Yosemite
National Park
**

*Palo Alto

R3

*San Jose

R2

*Santa Cruz

*Mono Lake

** Monterey
Point Lobos *

**Carmel

* Mammoth
Lakes

Kings Canyon
National Park
**

Hearst Castle
**

Sequoia **
National Park

Death Valley
National Park
**

San Luis
Obispo

* Solvang

** Santa
Barbara

R3 **

*Channel Islands
National Park

Malibu **

R5

Calico
Ghost Town

R5

**Los Angeles

*Pasadena

R4

Barstow

Mojave
National
Preserve

* Santa Monica

**
Disneyland

*Palm
Springs

*Long
Beach

*San Juan
Capistrano

R6

*Joshua Tree
National Park

* Anza Borrego
Desert State Park

R6

**San Diego

©Baedeker

	Route 1
	Route 2
	Route 3
	Route 4
	Route 5
	Route 6

vine-growing valleys of **Napa** and **Sonoma**. You then drive via Fairfield through the fertile Sacramento Valley (fruit, citrus fruits) and the northern part of the Great Californian longitudinal valley between the Sierra Nevada and the Coast Range to the capital **Sacramento**. From there take the US 80 to **Auburn** and then the CA 49 to **Grass Valley** and Nevada City. Return to Grass Valley, on the CA 174 via Colfax to **Dutch Flat**. All these places were once gold-mining towns which still bear traces of their past. Continuing on the US 80 you come to Donner Lake and the Donner Memorial State Park (a memorial to the "Donner Party") and crossing the once important **Donner Pass**, the scene of a tragedy in 1846 when settlers were surprised by an early winter, you come to the pleasant winter sports resort of **Truckee**. Following the CA 89 southwards you arrive at the well-known **Lake Tahoe** one of the finest mountain lakes in the world, part of which is in the neighbouring state of Nevada. From here a short detour can be made to the casinos of Nevada.

From South Lake Tahoe first follow the CA 89 and then roads CA 89/US 50 and 395 (partially unmade) to Bridgeport and to the **Bodie State Historic Park**, a ghost town from the end of the 19th c. which has not been restored. The road continues beyond Lee Vining and the attractive **Mono Lake State Reserve** to the east entrance of the **Yosemite National Park**. You then take the CA 120 over the 3000 m (9846 ft) high Tioga Pass, the highest in California which can be crossed by cars, to Yosemite Village 120 km (75 mi.) further on in the centre of the national park. Leaving Yosemite on the CA 120 you reach Mariposa where can be seen the oldest Californian law court which is still in use and which dates from 1854. You now traverse the Merced Canyon (drive carefully) on the CA 49 to Chinese Camp, where in the 1850s thousands of Chinese prospected for gold, and reaches **Sonoro** which was founded by Mexican gold diggers. The road now continues through numerous gold prospecting places such as Mokelumne Hill, Jackson, Sutter Creek and Amador City, to **Placerville**, **Coloma** and the Marshall Gold Discovery State Park where in 1848 on the American River the first gold in California was discovered. The return journey is along the US 50 to Sacramento and from there the US 80 goes back to San Francisco.

3: San Francisco along the Pacific Coast to Los Angeles
(750 km (478 mi.))

Driving south from San Francisco on Highway 101 you first come to the university town of **Palo Alto**, the seat of the renowned Stanford University. Then you pass through the very fertile Santa Clara Valley, fringed by hills, which today is better known as **Silicon Valley**. You soon reach **Santa Clara**, one of the universities founded by the Jesuits, and **San Jose**, which is the fastest growing industrial town in the USA (micro-electronics), the population of which will soon exceed that of San Francisco. The CA 717 takes you south to **Santa Cruz** at the north end of Monterey Bay, a fishing port, market town (vegetables, fruit) and seaside resort. Continue along US 1 and CA 152 to Gilroy, from where you can make a short detour to the San Juan Bautista Mission (CA 156) and to the industrial and commercial town of **Salinas** (wine), the birthplace of John Steinbeck. It is only a few minutes drive along CA 68 to **Monterey**, the port on the south side of Monterey Bay (viniculture), which has a Spanish atmosphere and where there is a mission station.

From Monterey you can take a 17-mile drive around the picturesque Monterey Peninsula past Pacific Grove, Seal Rocks, Cypress Point, Pebble Beach and **Carmel**. The last named has a beautiful location and is popular with artists. The drive continues on the US 1 along the coast to **Point Lobos**, to the artists' colony of **Big Sur** and to **San Simeon** where the notable mansion of William Randolph Hearst is located. Via **Cambria** and **Morro Bay** you reach **San Luis Obispo**.

From this trading centre, lying a short way inland, you continue south on the coastal road 101 at first some distance from the sea. You come to Buellton from where the CA 246 branches off to **Solvang**, founded by the Danes and still having a Danish character, and to the Santa Ines Mission (**Mission Stations**). From Buellton continue south over the Gaviota Pass in the Santa Ynéz Mountains back to the sea. There is a view of Santa Barbara Island which is bounded on the south by the Santa Barbara Channel and which with Santa Catalina Island south of Los Angeles forms the Channel Islands (**Channel Islands National Park**).

On the CA 154 you drive to the trading and industrial town of **Santa Barbara** (electronics, computer manufacture) with its beautiful mission stations which, after a severe earthquake in 1925, were extensively rebuilt in Spanish and Mexican style. Now you pass the harbour towns of Carpinteria and Ventura, both of which have extensive beaches; from the latter you can make a detour along CA 33 to **Ojai** which attracts many visitors to California because of its sophisticated atmosphere. From Ventura or from **Oxnard**, a few miles further south, you are recommended to make a boat trip to the Channel Islands. From Oxnard continue along the US 101 direct to Los Angeles.

4: Los Angeles into Orange County (420 km (263 mi.))

You leave Los Angeles on US 5 going south through the industrial suburbs to **Buena Park** (Knott's Berry Farm) and to **Anaheim** (Disneyland), and via Santa Ana to **San Juan Capistrano** with its charming mission station of the same name. From here the tour continues on CA 74 (drive carefully, owing to the sharper curves on certain stretches), crossing the Cleveland National Forest to Lake Elsinore, another favourite excursion venue of the Californians. From here you continue on US 15 as far as the south of Temecula, through the most southerly vine-growing area of California, until you reach the intersection with CA 46 which leads west to Oceanside, near which is the huge Camp Pendelton, the largest base of the US Marine Corps. Continuing north on US 5 you pass several beaches before reaching San Clemente, a town in which many retired people have made their home. A few miles further north lies **Dana Point**, which was well-known as a port in the early history of California; now it is the surfing "capital". Here the US 1, also called the Pacific Coast Highway, begins again and runs past well-known coastal resorts, including **Laguna Beach**, **Newport Beach** and Huntington Beach, to **Long Beach** where the luxury liner "Queen Mary", now a hotel, lies at anchor. Beyond **San Pedro** – from where you can take a boat to **Santa Catalina Island** – are other coastal places, including Palos Verdes, Redondo Beach, Venice and **Marina del Rey**, before you reach **Santa Monica** and return to **Los Angeles** along the Santa Monica Freeway (US 10) and the Harbor Freeway (US 110).

5: Los Angeles into the desert (1150 km (717 mi.))

From Los Angeles you take the US 10 (now called the San Bernadino Freeway), drive east to **San Bernadino** and then take US 215 and US 15, passing the San Gabriel Mountains in the north and the San Bernadino Mountains (with Mount San Antonio 3072 m (10,082 ft) in the south, to Victorville, once the setting for many western films. Continue through the Mojave Desert with its dried-up salt lakes and sparse vegetation (yucca, cactus, juniper, wormwood) to **Barstow** and the neighbouring ghost town of Calico, an abandoned silver-mining town. You continue on US 15 to Baker, where you take the CA 127 to Shoshone; a few miles to the north you turn on to the CA 178 leading into **Death Valley** which you cross in a northerly direction. To reach the most important sights in this desert region which extends over an area of some 3000 square miles, it is necessary to make use of a number of by-roads.

You leave Death Valley on CA 190 and drive west; if you wish to see Scotty's Castle which lies to the north you will have to make a detour of about 100 km (62 mi.) CA 190 and CA 136 take you to Lone Pine, from where it is about. 20 km (12 mi) west to the foot of Mount Whitney, which at 4418 m (14,800 ft) is the highest mountain on the mainland of the United States.

The long return journey begins on CA 395 and CA 14, first to Mojave and then east on CA 58, and via Kramer Junction on CA 395, US 15 and US 215 to **San Bernadino**. From here you drive back to Los Angeles on US 10.

Because of the remoteness of many places – it is often 150 km (100 mi.) between filling stations – you must make sure that you have enough fuel, oil and water with you. Moreover, owing to the restricted accommodation facilities in several areas the trip must be planned with care and rooms reserved in good time. Advice

It should also be noted that hotels in Death Valley National Monument are closed from mid May to mid October. Because of the extreme heat in summer you should not attempt this tour during these months.

6: Los Angeles to San Diego (620 km (386 mi.))

This route also uses the US 10 from Los Angeles to **San Bernardino** – you can also make a short detour to **Pasadena** – and continues on the US 10 to Banning; about eight miles east of Banning you turn on to the CA 62 which takes you to Yucca Valley and Twenty-nine Palms, from where you traverse the very interesting **Joshua Tree National Monument** until you reach the US 10 and **Indio**, the "date" capital of the country, continuing to **Palm Desert** and **Palm Springs**. You return to Palm Desert, follow CA 74, CA 371 and CA 7 and then, south of Temecula, take US 215. This joins US 15 which leads direct to San Diego.

7: San Diego to the southern outskirts (410 km (255 mi.))

This trip begins on US 8 in San Diego and leads east as far as CA 54 and then follows CA 94 to Campo, close to the Mexican frontier. – 1.5 km (¾ mi.) from here lies Cameron Corners, where the county road S 1 leads back to US 8; shortly before reaching Descanso this crosses CA 79 which you follow as far as Julian. From here you take CA 78 to the **Anzo-Borrego State Park**. The county road S 3, a very attractive desert road, leads to Borrego Springs Oasis. You now drive west on S 22 as far as the CA 79 which you follow for about 6 km (4 mi.) to the CA 76 and continue along this road for about another 16 km (4 mi.) north-west to the S 7 which you follow to its intersection with the S 6. You take this road and reach the Palomar Obervatory (Pasadena). From here you drive 10 km (6 mi.) south along the S 6, then 8 km (5 mi.) west on CA 79 and then south again to Escondido, where a visit to the San Diego Wild Animal Park (**San Diego**) should on no account be missed. You take S 6 via Rancho Santa Fe to Del Mar, with its famous horse-racing course, and from there the S 21 and the North Torrey Pines Road to La Jolla, an exceptionally fine suburb of San Diego, and finally the US 8 back to the starting point. Speed should be kept well down on the mountain roads.

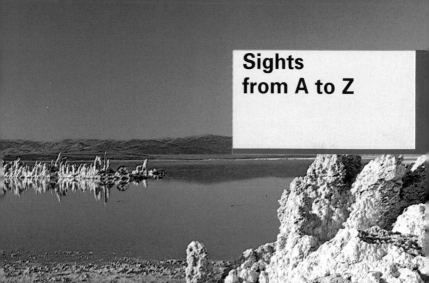

**Sights
from A to Z**

Sights from A to Z

Anaheim

Orange County
Altitude: 49 m (160 ft). Population: 267,000

Access

By air, Anaheim can be reached from Los Angeles airport (64 km (40 mi.)) away) and from John Wayne Orange County Airport (22 km (14 mi.) to the south). There are direct coach connections from both airports.

By car, you can drive to Anaheim from Los Angeles via Freeway No. 5 (Exit 78, Katella Ave. and Anaheim Blvd. lead direct to Disneyland).

Until about thirty years ago Anaheim was a rather unremarkable, sleepy place in the slowly developing Orange County, which takes in a 64 km (40 mi.) stretch of coastline, and reaches almost 40 km (25 mi.) inland. It was founded in the year 1857 by German immigrants, who decided to cultivate grapes and produce wine there – the name is derived from the river Santa Ana and the German word "Heim" (home) – and in a few years they succeeded in making Anaheim the leading wine-producing area of the United States. However, in the 1880s all the vines were destroyed by a leaf disease.

The cultivation of **citrus fruits**, especially oranges, proved so successful that this stretch of country became one of the most important orange-growing regions in the US. So it is not surprising that the county founded in 1889 – an offshoot of Los Angeles County – should be named "Orange County". However, Santa Ana (see entry) was nominated as the capital of the area, not little Anaheim.

In the year 1876 Anaheim attracted a group of Polish intellectuals, whose intention was to found here one of the many **"Utopian Communities"** found in the United States in the 19th c. The writer Henryk Sienkiewicz (later a Nobel Prizewinner for his novel "Quo Vadis") and the actress Helena Modjeska and her husband were at the head of the group. However, their dreams quickly vanished; only two years later the author returned to his homeland. Modjeska remained, however, and started a successful theatre career (there is even a town in Orange County which bears her name).

Development Not until 1955 when Walt Disney decided to choose Anaheim as the site for his Disneyland Pleasure and Leisure Park, did Anaheim develop rapidly into an industrial town. Since then the number of visitors annually has been in the millions. Hotels have mushroomed, some with over 1000 rooms, and there is also plenty of accommodation for meetings and congresses.

Sport Anaheim is the smallest of the 20 American towns which have a first – class baseball team. The Angels play there from the middle of April until the beginning of October; from August until December there are also matches involving the Los Angeles Rams, a football team, being played in the Anaheim stadium.

◀ *Bizarre limestone turrets in the picturesque Mono Lake*

★★Disneyland Resort

From Los Angeles the US 5 (Santa Ana Freeway) leads direct to Disneyland (exit Katella Avenue). By rail (Amtrak) from Los Angeles (Union Station) to Fullerton and then by no. 435 bus.   Access

Popularity When Walt Disney opened his first pleasure park in Anaheim in the year 1955 he could not have foreseen that others would follow some years later, namely, in Florida ("Disneyworld"), in Tokyo (opened 1983) and near Paris ("Euro Disney Resort", opened 1992). It celebrated its 40-year jubilee in 1995.

Disneyland itself has been constantly extended and adapted to the needs of the time. On many a Sunday in summer 70,000 people pass through the turnstiles of the park, and 50,000 to 60,000 on other days of the week, to enjoy Mickey Mouse and the other figures from Disney's fantasy world.

Scale In Disneyland, everything appears colossal: the size often confuses car drivers who, in spite of the good direction signs, cannot find their cars again on the giant car-parks (some with over 11,000 spaces). However, zealous officials in mini-cars always succeed in finding the vehicles, even with the barest of details. Tourists who have drifted away from their party can be reunited with it if they report to the City Hall in "Main Street USA", near the entrance to the park.

Large, too, are the **hotels** in the immediate vicinity, three of which can offer overnight accommodation to more than a thousand people: "Hilton", with 1600 rooms, "Disneyland" with 1174 and "Marriott" with 1043.

Annual Disney Parade

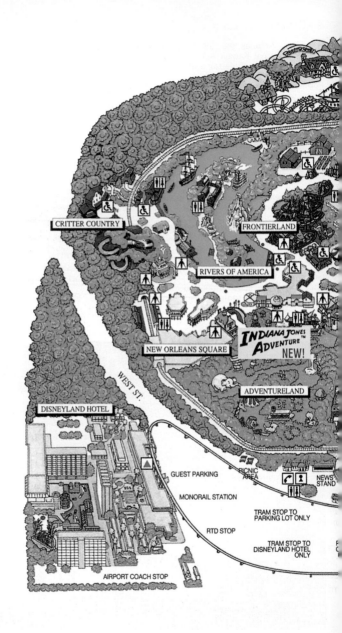

CRITTER COUNTRY

FRONTIERLAND

RIVERS OF AMERICA

NEW ORLEANS SQUARE

INDIANA JONES ADVENTURE™ NEW!

ADVENTURELAND

WEST ST.

DISNEYLAND HOTEL

GUEST PARKING

MONORAIL STATION

RTD STOP

AIRPORT COACH STOP

PICNIC AREA

NEWS STAND

TRAM STOP TO PARKING LOT ONLY

TRAM STOP TO DISNEYLAND HOTEL ONLY

Disneyland

MICKEY'S TOONTOWN

TOMORROWLAND

FANTASYLAND

STREET

LEGEND

✚ FIRST AID		⬚ BABY CENTER	
☎ TELEPHONES		🔒 LOCKERS	
♿ WHEELCHAIRS		△ TICKET BOOTH	
🚶 BE ABLE TO LEAVE WHEELCHAIR		● KODAK PHOTO SPOT	
🚼 STROLLERS		🚻 RESTROOMS	

KENNEL

GUEST RELATIONS

OTHS

CE

TTLE STOP

Ontario International Airport

Long Beach Airport

Los Angeles Int'l. Airport

Disneyland

Harbor Blvd.

Pacific Coast Highway

John Wayne Airport

MAP NOT TO SCALE

The pleasure park

Walt Disney and his successors (Disney died in 1966) have invested well over 200 million dollars in this project, which can prove fascinating to all age groups. Dozens of shops, from cheap souvenir stalls to elegant specialist stores, will suit all tastes. Every kind of food at all price levels is available, from fast food to French cuisine. There is only one thing you will not find in Disneyland, and which must not be brought in: alcoholic drinks.

A first **general view** of the park, which has already been visited by well over 100 million people, is obtained from the "Santa Fe & Disneyland Railroad", which passes through a diorama of the Grand Canyon. It is also worth taking a trip on the "Disneyland Alweg Monorail" (4 km (2½ mi.)).

How long a visit should last depends on the stamina of the visitors, their number and on the weather. However, a minimum of six hours is necessary to cover the total area of 31 ha (77 acres), and to view the most interesting attractions from the inside (the entrance fee includes, among other things, free visits to all roundabouts, rides, boats and film-shows).

Sectors

At the entrance on the right is **Main Street USA** built in the style of a small American town at the turn of the century, with horse-drawn trams, double-decker buses and a fire-engine; in the "theatre" old films are shown, including "Great Moments with Mr. Lincoln".

On the left lies **Adventure Land**, where you can go by boat on a "jungle cruise" through the jungle with its tropical animals (alligators, hippos, gorillas, water buffaloes and elephants).

In the so-called Tiki Room this exotic world is provided with background music in the shape of "South Sea Fantasies".

The latest thrill in this sector is the Indiana Jones Adventure, based on the George Lucas film trilogy. In the **Temple of the Forbidden Eye** visitors can follow in the footsteps of Indiana Jones. In the Indian jungle they can cross a swaying suspension bridge in a Second World War troop-carrier, while threatened by an avalanche or by a 50 tonne ball of granite.

Adjoining Adventure Land lies **New Orleans Square**, its streets typical of a French-influenced town of about 1850, with shops, restaurants, cafés and balconies. Boats (bateaux), such as are used in the swamps of Louisiana, ply from the square. On the trip you are treated to a colourful revue in the form of a battle between a pirate ship and a coastal fort ("Pirates of the Caribbean") and a ghost scene in an enchanted house, which is a copy of a public building in Baltimore.

From here it is possible to take a train ride to the last sector, Tomorrowland, or else you can walk to

Critter Country was not built until after Walt Disney's death, but is based largely on his characters, and its best attractions are an original bear revue, the "Country Bear Jamboree" Wild West Show, and a trip in an old-fashioned boat.

Since the summer of 1989 it has been possible to go on a canal trip ("Splash Mountains") through Critter County (previously Bear Country); at a speed of 40m.p.h., it is the fastest trip in Disneyland.

In the adjoining **Frontierland** you can get an idea of the gold-digging period of the Wild West: a mining-railway runs through the desert and the Rainbow Caverns; the paddle-steamer "Mark Twain" takes you back into the 19th c. On the reproduction of the "Columbia Redivina", the first

"Mickey's Birthday"

Snow White Fountain

American sailing vessel to circumnavigate the world at the end of the 18th c., you can either make a trip on the boat or be taken to visit a farm-house on Tom Sawyer Island.

In the heart of Disneyland is **Fantasyland**, where the familiar characters from Disney's productions are brought to life. These include Snow White and the Seven Dwarfs, Mickey Mouse and Alice in Wonderland. Since reconstruction of this section in 1983 the setting for Disney's fairytale world now includes a European village, an imitation of the Castle of Neuschwanstein and a steel-framed "Matterhorn" (sledge rides available). On festive summer nights firework displays add to the atmosphere of make-believe.

In **Mickey's Toontown** visitors can meet all the well-known characters from the cartoon films, such as Mickey Mouse, Goofy, Donald Duck and Daisy.

Tomorrowland adjoins Main Street USA. A 4 km (2½ mi.)-long cable rail-way ("Skyway") leads through the "Matterhorn", along the winding "Autopia" motor-racing circuit and the submarine-lake ("Submarine Voyage"). After passing the space travel control centre, a "Saturn" rocket-trip takes you into "space" for several minutes. Most impressive is the "Roundabout of Progress" (General Electric). In the circular Bell Telephone Theater ("Circle Vision 360"), you can experience "The Beautiful America", as in the present day, and the "Wonders of China".

Advice

The queues which form at the individual attractions in summer –

especially at week-ends – can best be avoided on week-days such as Tuesday and Wednesday when there are fewer visitors.

Open daily all the year round, with extended **opening times** in summer. Further information is available from:
Disneyland Guest Relations, P. O. Box 3232, 1313 Harbor Blvd., Anaheim, Ca. 92803–3232; tel no. (714) 7814565.

★Anza-Borrego Desert State Park   R/S 5

San Diego County
Altitude: 5–2370 m (16–7780 ft)

About 136 km (85 mi.) north-east of San Diego, and reached via Highways 8 and 79, is the entrance to the biggest state Park in California, which covers an area of about 242,200 ha (600,000 acres), and is one of the most beautiful desert landscapes in the state. Dunes, alluvial land, canyons, palm groves, flowers and cacti (which flower in March and April), as well as fantastic views, represent only some of the attractions of this area on the edge of the Colorado Desert.

The more than 805 km (500 mi.) of road are mainly unmetalled, and can be negotiated only in a cross-country vehicle. Apart from Route 78 (with some hotels) which runs past Borrego Springs, only the S2, S3 and S22 are made-up.

Information about the condition of the roads and informative brochures can be obtained from the Visitor Center west of Borrego Springs.

Wagons of the first pioneers in Anza-Borrego Desert State Park

Auburn: Fire-brigade House

Vintage car

The park was **named** after the priest Juan Bautista de Anza, who, in the course of 2½ months in 1774, crossed the Colorado desert with a small group from Sonora (Mexico) and reached the Californian mission stations (see entry).

The Spanish name "Borrego" (year-old ram) refers to the thick-horned sheep which at one time lived in this wasteland region, but which are seldom encountered today. The Anza-Borrego Desert State Park is open Oct.–May daily 9am–5pm, Jun–Sep. daily 10am–3pm.

Auburn   G 3

Placer County
Altitude: 395 m (1300 ft). Population: 11,000

Auburn, founded by inhabitants of the town of the same name in New York State in the year the gold rush started (1849), lies on the Transcontinental Highway 80, about 50 km (30 mi.) north of Sacramento (see entry). Its carefully restored old town, with houses from the middle of the 19th century – including an interesting fire-station and the oldest post-office in continuous use in California – reminds us of the gold rush era.

Of interest is the Placer County Museum (1273 Placer Street), in which the early times of this region are documented, for example by means of old gold-digging tools, as well as Indian and Chinese artefacts.
Open Tue.–Sun. 10am–4pm. In Bernhard House, which adjoins the museum, Victorian furniture and old photographs are on display.

Placer County
Museum

Baja California   off the map below S/T 3–7

Mexican State
Population: 2,300,000

The 1250 km (775 mi.) long and, on an average, 90 km (56 mi.) wide peninsula of Baja California (Lower California), which consists of two federal states, borders the USA (California) in the north. Its shores are lapped by the Pacific in the west and the Golfo de California in the east. The border between Baja California Norte and Baja California Sur runs along the 28th degree of latitude. The peninsula is a hot, dry area with mountain ranges and richly contoured coasts.

The most important chain of mountains is the Sierra de Pedro Mártir, running roughly from north to south, its highest peak being the Cerro de la Encantada (3080 m (10,100 ft) above sea level). The border with the state of Sonora is formed by the Rio Colorado, which runs into the northernmost point of the Gulf of California.

The peninsula, which obtained a north to south road connection with the building of the Carretera Transpeninsular in 1974, offers little that is typically Mexican, apart from some mission stations. As a result of its proximity to the USA and the great stream of tourists from the north, its towns and villages have largely assumed an American character. The tourist charm lies in the desert flora (cacti), the impressive silhouettes of the bare mountain regions and the endless coasts, with their mixture of sandy beaches, cliffs and lagoons. Apart from a few places overrun with tourists, in Baja California you can find barren, isolated countryside.

The original Indian population, made up of the Cucapá, Kiliwa, Pai-pai, Cochimí and Ki-nai tribes, numbers scarcely 1000 today.

Fauna Baja California is rich in varieties of animal life. On the peninsula still live the puma, coyote, fox, red deer, hare, wild goose, wild duck and sea-birds of all kinds; grey whales frolic in the sea and can be watched in the Bay of San Ignacio from December to February; sea-lions, seals, swordfish, dolphins, barracudas and tuna-fish also can be seen.

Archaeological sites Apart from some rock-paintings, such as those at San Boritja, San Ignacio and Calimalí, Baja California holds little of archaeological interest. Caves have been found in Caguama, Metate Comond£ and on the Isla de Cedros.

History Traces of settlements from pre-Columbian times, going back as far as 7500 BC, have been found. Almost nothing is known of the little developed culture of the early Indian tribes of the peninsula.

In search of a legendary Amazonian paradise ruled over by a black queen named Calafia, Hernán Cortés landed in the La Paz region in 1535. The Spaniards who followed later met with strong resistance from the Indios, and were unable to gain a foothold there. Embittered by their lack of success, they named the area "California", after the queen who had never been found.

Not until after 1697, when the Jesuit missionaries Francisco Eusebio Kino, Juan Maria de Salvatierra and Juan de Ugarte arrived, were they successful in colonising parts of the country. After the expulsion of the Jesuits in 1767, the Franciscans took over this task, until the Dominicans superseded them in 1772. In 1804 Lower California was separated from California, and during the war with the USA the peninsula was occupied by American troops in 1847/1848. In 1931 the division into northern and southern territories took place. Finally in 1952 Baja California Norte, and in 1974 Baja California Sur, were declared independent federal states.

A romantic bay in Baja California

Economy As well as a considerable tourist industry, the cultivation of cotton, maize, wheat, alfalfa, vegetables and fruit is carried on with the aid of artificial irrigation. The processing of agricultural and fishing products, and the mining of gold, copper, iron, silver and salt are worthy of mention. Fishing could be a good source of income but it lacks a strong fleet and processing facilities.

In addition to Tijuana (see entry), the most important destinations to aim for in Baja California Norte, which do not lie on the Carretera Transpeninsular, are Tecate, Mexicali and San Felipe (for all these see the entry for Tijuana).

Sights

The Carretera Transpeninsular from Tijuana to Cabo San Lucas

Baja California's largest town, Tijuana (see entry), on the border with the USA, is the starting point of the 1700 km (1056 mi.) long MEX 1 (Carretera Transpeninsular), which runs the whole length of the peninsula.

After 30 km (19 mi.), the first place you come to is El Rosarito. The next town of any size, after 80 km (50 mi.), is Ensenada (population 225,000). This fishing port, now a favourite tourist spot (water sports, deep-sea fishing), extends along the beautiful bay of Todos los Santos, which was discovered in 1542 by the Portuguese seafarer Rodríguez Cabrillo. After the separation of the northern part of the peninsula from the southern part, Ensenada was the capital of the northern part from 1888 until 1910, when Mexicali took over this position.

In addition to tourism, the town lives mainly from fishing and its deep-

Ensenada

Surf breaking in Baja California

water harbour. In the town is the biggest wine-cellar in all Mexico, the "Bodegas Santo Tomás".

La Bufadora

16 km (10 mi.) south of Ensenada, near Maneadera, a road branches off to the north-west to the tip of land known as Cabo Punta la Banda (22 km (14 mi.)), where you can witness a natural spectacle frequently found on the Pacific coast, in the form of "La Bufadora" (from "bufar" = to snort). The sea water is squeezed with terrific force through a narrow opening in the rocks, and hurled upwards with amighty roar to a height of 20 m (70 ft).

San Quintín

After returning to the main road continue along the 175 km (110 mi.) stretch to San Quentin; along this stretch you can visit some old mission stations, such as Santo Tomás, San Vicente and Vicente Guerrero, and Orte La Huerta and San Miguel, which are inhabitated by Cochimí Indios. The farming and fishing village of San Quintín, lying in a fertile valley on the flat bay of the same name has beautiful white beaches.

The road to the south leaves the coast near El Rosario and now runs inland. In addition to El Rosario, there are further mission stations along the road, including San Fernando, San Agustín and Cataviña, which lies in the midst of impressive, rocky scenery.

Bahía de los Angeles

The road leads past the Laguna Chapala and 50 km (30 mi.) further on there is a turn off to the left, which leads to the beautiful Bahía de los Angeles (Bay of Angels), about 70 km (43 mi.) away.

After returning to the MEX 1, the first place you will come to is Rosarito. Shortly before the Guerrero Negro, a 40 m (130 ft) high steel eagle (Monumento Aguila) marks the 28th degree of latitude, **the border** between the federal states of Baja California Norte and Baja California

Sur, and also the boundary between the time-zones Hora del Pacifico in the north and Hora de las Montanas in the south (+ one hour). In the vicinity of Guerrero Negro are huge salt-deposits caused by evaporation, which are among the largest in the world.

The quiet waters of the lagoons by the Bahía Sebastián Vizcaíno (Laguna **Grey whales**
Scammon, Laguna Ojo de Liebre) as well as the more easily accessible lagoon San Ignacio, south of the Sierra Vizcaíno, offer each year, from the end of December until March, the unique spectacle of the grey whales (Spanish "ballena gris") mating and bringing their young into the world. In and around Guerrero there are several points from which you can observe the whales. About 3 km (2 mi.) south of the town a road, marked with road signs showing symbols of grey whales, turns off to the nature park (Parque Natural de la Ballena Gris), which is about a further 27 km (17 mi.). Tourist visits by boat are at present very restricted.

The grey whales (eschrichtius gibbosus), weighing up to 25 tons and measuring 10 to 15 m (30 to 45 ft) in length, begin their long journey in the autumn, in the arctic waters of the Bering Sea. As grey whales have a gestation period of 13 months, the pregnant whales give birth while the other animals are preparing to mate. Two males and one female are involved in the mating. The dominant whale does the actual mating, while the other male helps the female into a suitable position. Having been seriously decimated by hunting, they have been a protected species since 1947.

From Guerrero Negro the road leads inland and, after about 126 km (78 **San Ignacio**
mi.), it reaches the pretty town of San Ignacio. With its Jesuit church, begun in 1728 and completed in 1786 by Juan Crisóstomo Gómez, it possesses the best preserved place of worship in Baja California. For those interested it is worth while making the three or four hour trip from here, under expert guidance, to see the cave paintings of Cueva de la Cuesta del Palmerito. These portray large impressions of animals and

Mexico
United Mexican States
Estados Unidos Mexicanos

Baja California Norte
Baja California Sur

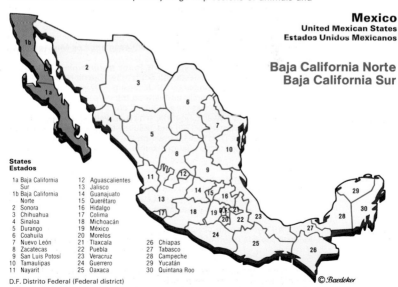

States
Estados

1a Baja California Sur	12 Aguascalientes
1b Baja California Norte	13 Jalisco
2 Sonora	14 Guanajuato
3 Chihuahua	15 Querétaro
4 Sinaloa	16 Hidalgo
5 Durango	17 Colima
6 Coahuila	18 Michoacán
7 Nuevo León	19 México
8 Zacatecas	20 Morelos
9 San Luis Potosí	21 Tlaxcala
10 Tamaulipas	22 Puebla
11 Nayarit	23 Veracruz
	24 Guerrero
	25 Oaxaca
26 Chiapas	
27 Tabasco	
28 Campeche	
29 Yucatán	
30 Quintana Roo	

D.F. Distrito Federal (Federal district)

© Baedeker

men, the origin and age of which have not yet been researched. Other caves in the vicinity should be visited only if, in addition to a guide, you have some days to spare and are suitably equipped.

On the left, on the road to the coast, stands the still active volcano Las Tres Virgenes (2180 m (7150 ft) above sea-level).

Santa Rosalía

74 km (46 mi.) further on from San Ignacio you come to the little port of Santa Rosalía (population 14,000). The little town was founded in the middle of the 19th c. The French, to whom the copper mines of the region previously belonged, built the church of Santa Rosalía, which was constructed of imported iron sections and was reputedly based on a design by Gustave Eiffel, the constructor of the Eiffel Tower. Further items of interest are the anthropological museum in the Casa de Cultura, and at the northern entrance a mining museum with an old train used for transporting ore. There is a ferry link to Guaymas (Sonora).

Caves of San Borjita

Continuing the journey from Santa Rosalía, after about 40 km (25 mi.) you come to a turning on the right to the Hacienda Baltasar leading by way of a track to the great caves of San Borjita (some 22 km (14 mi.)), where you can see colourful wall-paintings of hunting and warlike scenes. This trip can be made only in a vehicle suitable for cross-country work, and the last 2 or 3 km (1½ mi.) or so must be covered on foot. In the vicinity there are are a number of other caves (La Trinidad, San José de los Arce, El Coyote, La Esperanza) with similar but less impressive paintings.

Mulegé

The next place of any size is the little town of Mulegé (population 5000), on the Gulf of California, with the Jesuit mission of Santa Rosalía de Mulegé (1705). This is a copy of the Cananea Prison (Sonora) which has neither bars nor locked doors and which was made famous in folk-songs and street-ballads. There is a lovely walk along the river through the groves of date palms. The town also has several beaches and opportunities for fishing and boating.

★ Bahía Concepción

About 10 km (6 mi.) past Mulegé, in a particularly charming coastal region, stretches Bahía Concepción, with beautiful beaches such as Punta Arena, Santiapac, El Coyote, El Requesón and Los Muertos.

Loreto

135 km (84 mi.) from Mulegé you come to the picturesque little town of Loreto (population 11,000; fiesta: 8th September, Dia de Nuestra Señora de Loreto), which was founded by the Jesuits in 1697 when they built the now restored mission church, and is thus the oldest Jesuit foundation on the peninsula. Loreto was the setting-off point for the exploration and Christianisation of Lower California, which is well documented in the mission museum. Between 1776 and 1830 the town was also the capital of Lower California. This coastal town on the Gulf of California is popular as a base for trips to the offshore islands and for deep-sea fishing and diving.

San Javier

A detour from Loreto over 40 km (25 mi.) of mainly poor roads (cross-country vehicle neccesary) leads to San Javier, where you can visit the well-preserved mission church, dedicated to San Francisco Javier and dating from the first half of the 18th c.; it has a fine Baroque façade and guilded high altar.

26 km (16 mi.) south of Loreto, in magnificent natural surroundings, the new seaside resort of Puerto Escondido is developing.

Puerto Escondido

Some 40 km (25 mi.) out of Loreto the road again turns inland, and after 80 km (50 mi.) reaches the town of Villa Insurgentes. From here, a turn-off leads to Puert A. López Mateos, located on the long Bahía de Magdalena (Pacific coast). Like that of Sebastián Vizcaíno this bay is the place to watch the mating and breeding of the many grey whales, which winter here every year. An equally well located place to watch the whales from a boat is the little harbour town of Puerto San Carlos to the south, best reached by going 55 km (35 mi.) in a westerly direction from Ciudad Constitución. The Isla de Santa Margarita in the bay is inhabited by numerous sea-lions.

If you turn back near Ciudad Constitución onto the Carretera Transpeninsular it is then about a further 210 km (130 mi.) to La Paz.

From La Paz, MEX 1 leads via San Pedro (after 26 km (16 mi.)) there is a turn-off to Todos Santos and Cabo San Lucas) and El Triunfo (former mining town) to the fishing village and seaside resort of Los Barriles (104 km (65 mi.)). After a further 6 km (4 mi.) you come to Buenavista, visited mainly by sporting fisherman and sailors.

From Buenavista, via Miraflores, a former settlement of Pericúe Indians, now known for its beautiful leatherwork, it is another 75 km (47 mi.) or so to San José del Cabo (population 23,000; fiesta; 19th March, Día de San José). This old fishing and mission village is now an important agricultural centre for the region. In addition, it possesses several beaches, some with strong waves, and good facilities for fishing. In the Culture House is a small museum and a library.

San José del Cabo

South of San José del Cabo there are good opportunities for surfing at various points.

In another 35 km (22 mi.) you reach Cabo San Lucas, the terminus of the Carretera Transpeninsular.

Bakersfield   N 3

Kern County
Altitude: 124 m (407 ft). Population; 175,000

Popular attraction in Bakersfield is the Kern Country Museum

Bakersfield is easy to reach by road, along one of the great motorways of California, the US 5; it is 179 km (111 mi.) from Los Angeles and about 465 km (290 mi.) from San Francisco. Founded by Colonel Thomas Baker in the seventies of the last century, it first came to life in 1885, when – almost 40 years later than in the actual gold area to the north – gold was discovered in the Kern River Canyon. Major roles in the development of this town were played by the discovery of oil, by agriculture and wine production (about ¼ of the wine of the US is pressed here). However, in 1889 a fire destroyed the old town; the 1952 earthquake also caused great damage. Nevertheless, the population increased considerably in the years that followed; with an annual growth rate of some 3 per cent (ca 13.5 per cent between 1990 and 1994) Bakersfield stands at the head of all Californian towns.

Pioneer Village

About 5 km (3 mi.) east of Bakersfield, on the CA 99 (3801 Chester Avenue) and covering an area of about 6 ha (15 acres), stands Pioneer Village, with 60 restored houses from the second half of the 19th century. In its museum, the main branch of which is in Bakersfield, exhibitions alternating between natural and cultural history are held. Open weekdays 8am–5pm, weekends 10am–5pm.

Barstow   P 5

San Bernardino County
Altitude: 642 m (2100 ft)
Population; 22,000

Barstow lies north-east of San Bernardino, at the foot of the Calico Mountains and at the intersection of the US 15, US 40 and CA 58 highways. Founded in the year 1880, it did not attain economic importance until a decade later, when gold and silver was found in the hills. This upsurge was further fostered by the nearby military no-go area of Fort Irwin, with its weapon testing grounds, and by its favourable position as a setting-off point for expeditions and trips into Death Valley National Monument (see entry) as well as into the Mojave Desert (see entry; US 15).

Mojave River Valley Museum

In the Mojave Valley Museum (270 East Virginia Way) minerals from the Calico Mountains, archaeological finds, Indian artefacts and photos are on display. Open daily 9am–5pm; admission free.

Calico

The ghost town of Calico lies 17 km (10 mi.) east of Barstow, near the US 15. From 1881 to 1896 it was one of the most important US-American towns, from where thousands set off to prospect for silver in the nearby mountains. When the price of silver fell in 1895 the silver mines closed and Calico went into decline. In 1954 the ghost town was restored by the owner of Knott's Berry Farm. Open daily 9am–5pm.

Calico Early Man Archaeological Site

This museum lies 23 km (14 mi.) east of Calico, on the US 15 not far from the unmetalled Minneola Road. It was opened a quarter of a century ago by the renowned archaeologist Dr Louis Leakey, who excavated more than 12,000 stone-age implements dating back some 200,000 years. These are the oldest artefacts to prove the existence of man in the western hemisphere. Open Thu.–Sun. 8.30am–4.30pm, Wed. noon–4.30pm; tours each hour on the half-hour until 3.30pm except at 12.30pm.

Benicia   H 1/2

Solano County

Altitude: 2.5 m (8 ft)
Population: 25,000

Benicia lies on the north coast side of the road from Carquinez which connects San Pablo Bay with Suisun Bay. Founded in the year 1847 – before California became a member of the United States – Benicia is one of the oldest towns in the federation. However, the hopes of its founders to build a large harbour there, have not been been fulfilled; nevertheless, Benicia was the capital of the state between 1853/1854.

Here, too, the first Protestant church was built (1859), and the first Masonic Lodge in California came into being. Two camel stalls, a beautiful bell-tower and a Dominican cemetery bear witness to the early history of the town. It is also known that Jack London caught oysters in Benicia.

★Berkeley   H 1

Alameda County
Altitude: 46 m (150 ft)
Population: 103,000

At the northern end of the San Francisco-Oakland Bay Bridge are the outskirts of Berkeley which retains its small town character despite its considerable amount of industry and its 45,000 students.

History Founded on ranchland in 1866, it was planned from the first as a university town. It is named after the Irish bishop and philosopher George Berkeley, responsible for the saying "Westward the Course of Empire takes its Way".

In 1991 entire residential districts in Berkeley were destroyed by a catastrophic fire which fire fighting precautions introduced after a similar conflagration in 1923 proved powerless to prevent.

Worth seeing are Charles Lee Tilden Regional Park and Bancroft Way, with its pubs and shops much favoured by the students.   Sights

The main attraction, however, is the world-famous University of California. An excursion to Berkeley enables the visitor to appreciate the very special campus atmosphere of an American university.

A further attraction is provided by the University Art Museum, with a collection of paintings by 19th and 20th c. artists and an important film archive.

★University of California

In the eastern part, some 8 km (5 mi.) north-east of the bridge across the bay, lie the extensive grounds of the University of California (Telegraph Avenue and Bancroft Way), whose world reputation results not only from its numerous Nobel Prize winners, but also, inter alia, from the student unrest in the sixties which spread from here to the whole western world.

The symbol of the university is the bell tower known as **Sather Tower**, a 1914 reproduction of the St Marc's Tower in Venice (Open daily 10am–4.15pm). Being 94 m (308 ft) high, it towers over all the other buildings on the spacious and park-like university grounds. From the top (lift; entrance fee) there is a magnificent view of the campus, San Francisco Bay and the Golden Gate Bridge. Also worthy of mention is the peal of bells, which can be heard on weekdays at 7.50am, noon and 6pm (except during examination times), Saturdays at 6pm and Sundays at 2pm.

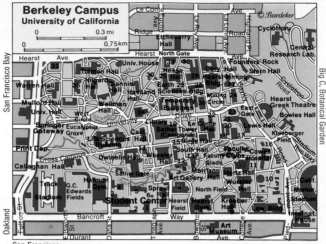

Berkeley Campus
University of California

1 Student Union (Visitor Center)
2 Eshleman Hall
3 Zellerbach Hall
4 Alumni House
5 Dining Commons (Mensa)
6 Ludwig's Fountain
7 Architects & Engineers Building
8 Barrows Hall
9 Lowie Museum of Anthropology
10 Calvin Laboratory
11 Minor Hall
12 Moses Hall
13 Stephens Hall
14 Durant Hall
15 Placement Center
16 Girton Hall
17 Hildebrand Hall
18 Gilman Hall
19 Bancroft Library
20 Glauque Hall
21 Latimer Hall
22 Campbell Hall
23 Physical Sciences
24 Stanley Building
25 McLaughlin Hall
26 Morgan Hall
27 Donner Laboratory
28 Davis Hall
29 Seismograph (Earth Sciences Building)
30 Leuschner Observatory
31 Biochemistry Building
32 Naval Architecture Building
33 North Gate Hall
34 Moffitt Library
35 Bechtel Building
36 Evans Building

Other buildings South-west of the bell tower stands South Hall, built in 1873 in the Tudor style, and the oldest building on the campus. Further south-west is the Sather Gate which together with the Plaza forms the centre of the student quarter.

The Earth Sciences Building, not far from the north gate, contains palaeontological and mineralogical collections, as well as an interesting seismograph on the ground floor. Open 8am–noon; admission free.

In the chapel of the Pacific School of Religion (1198 Scenic Avenue) can be seen one of the largest stained-glass windows in the world. Open Mon.–Fri. 8.30am–4.30pm.

The Cyclotron (particle accelerator) in the north-east and the California Memorial Stadium, a sports arena with more than 76,500 seats, in the south-east, are also of interest.

Something of a special nature which is worth a visit is the **Lawrence-Berkeley Laboratory**, in which the Nobel Prizewinner Ernest O. Lawrence pioneered new developments in the field of atomic research. His assistants included, among others, J. Robert Oppenheimer who did important preparatory work in developing the first atomic bomb. When Oppenheimer opposed the making of the hydrogen bomb investigations were made in 1953 on the grounds of his alleged Communist views, and President Eisenhower withdrew his permission for him to work on any further secret projects.

The symbol of the world-famous University of California – the impressive Sather Tower ▶

A guided tour through this extremely interesting research station is possible on Tuesdays at 2pm if a prior appointment is made by telephone (not on public holidays or during university vacations).

In addition to the University Art Museum, there are the following **other museums** on the campus:

The collection in the Judah L. Magnes Memorial Museum (2911 Russell Street; admission free) includes mainly Jewish ritual items. Two libraries adjoin it. Open Sun.–Thu. 10am–4pm.

The Lawrence Hall of Science (Centennial Drive) was named after the scientist E.O. Lawrence and attempts to simulate dinosaurs, space travel, laser beams, earthquakes and the structure of the brain. Open daily 10am–5pm.

The Phoebe Appenson Hearst Museum of Anthropology displays anthropological collections, mainly from California but also from Peru, Egypt and the Mediterranean region. Open weekdays 10am–4.30pm, Thu. to 7pm, Sat., Sun., noon to 4.30pm.

University Art Museum

Foundation This museum, located on the university campus, 2626 Bancroft Way (Open Wed.–Sun. 11am–5pm; admission free on Thur.) was built in 1970 to the design by Mario Campi, and in the following two decades has earned a good reputation. The surprisingly large stocks held by this young museum stem from works of art collected at the time the university was founded (1873).

The decisive impetus leading to the building of the museum came from the German painter **Hans Hofmann**, who lived in America from 1932 and had already held summer courses at the University of California in Berkeley from 1930 to 1931.

As a teacher (he opened his own art schools) he had a great influence on young American painters, such as Louise Nevelson, Helen Frankenthaler and Larry Rivers.

In 1963 he presented 45 of his paintings to the university and promised to donate money for the building of a museum.

Seven years passed before it was completed. Today, about a half of all Hofmann's works to be found here are displayed in one big hall, so that in no other museum can you get a better view of the work of this painter.

The museum also has a big collection of orientalia, as well as numerous paintings from the 19th c. Special exhibitions are often held, particularly of painters, sculptors and photographers of the 20th c.

The University Art Museum is also the home of the **Pacific Film Archive**, which continually offers interesting productions in its 200-seat auditorium. It possesses a stock of about 5000 films, including the greatest number of copies of Japanese films outside Japan; there are also numerous avant-garde and experimental US films, as well as a collection of 35 mm copies of Soviet silent films. Performances daily 7–11pm.

Big Bear Lake   Q 5

San Bernardino County
Altitude: 2059 m (6750 ft). Population: 5400

Big Bear Lake, on Highway 18, some 48 km (30 mi.) north east of San Bernardino in the San Bernardino Mountains, is located in the centre of an increasingly popular area for summer and winter sports (swimming in the lake is prohibited). Not far away is the start of the Gold Fever Trail, a car journey of some three hours through a number of places which still remain from the second Californian gold-rush in the years 1860 to 1875. A brochure giving more detailed descriptions is available free of charge from the Ranger Station, 6½ km (4 mi.) east of Fawnskin, on Highway 38.

Ski-slopes in the immediate vicinity are:

Snow Summit, 1.6 km (1 mi.) south of the lake, reached via a turn-off from Highway 18;

Goldmine, 3.2 km (2 mi.) south-east of the lake, reached via a turn-off from Highway 18.

Snow Forest, 800 m (½ mi.) away, on Pine Knot Avenue.

Big Sur   K 0

Monterey County
Altitude: 47 m (154 ft)
Population: about 1000

Big Sur – the name originates from Rio Grande del Sur, the biggest river in the South – is one of the most beautiful wooded coastal regions in northern California. It begins about 6½ km (4 mi.) south of Carmel (see entry) in Yankee Point, and stretches along the coast-road No. 1 as far as Salmon Cove, some 26 km (17 mi.) north of San Simeon (see entry). From Highway 1 there are splendid views over the picturesque coastal region. To the east, however, stretches a true wilderness; the Santa Lucia Mountains and Ventana Forests, with more than 350 km (220 mi.) of trails, are ideal for experienced walkers. The long-lasting dispute between those supporting further economic development of the area and the nature conservationists ended with the compromise that they would agree to the building of only 850 new houses here, none of which could be seen from the coast road. In addition, only small hotels with less than 300 rooms may be added to the 165 hotels already there. The main objective is to leave untouched the natural beauty of this region.

The name of Big Sur is linked with numerous **artists**; the writer Henry Miller lived in Big Sur in 1944 when it had only 60 inhabitants. At that time a friend of Miller's intended to set up a Henry Miller museum. John Kerouac, one of the "beat" literary figures, wrote the novel "Big Sur" about a "beat" leader who settled here. Robinson Jeffers immortalised the area in his poems; Joan Baez organised a festival here for many years called "Celebration at Big Sur"; since 1962 the Esalen Institute has had its home here; its aim is to help people to a new feeling of awareness by means of meditation and psychedelic insight.

In the close vicinity of Big Sur lies Pfeiffer-Big Sur State Park, with bathing facilities, the most southerly redwood grove in California, and further south the Julia Pfeiffer Burns State Park, a setting-off point for numerous walks in the Ventana Wilderness.

Pfeiffer-Big Sur State Park

Bishop   K 5

Inyo County
Altitude: 1264 m (4150 ft)
Population: 3700

Bishop lies at the north end of Owens Valley, between the two highest mountain chains in the state. From here, climbers set out on extended climbs in the eastern part of the Sierra Nevada; in particular, Bishop is the best starting point from which to reach the Bristlecone Pine Forest (Inyo National Forest), which has the oldest trees in California. One of these trees, which has been named Methuselah, is, according to the findings of Dr Louis Schulman of Washington University in St Louis, more than 4600 years old, and another, "Pine Alpha", bears this name because it was the first pine over 4000 years old which Schulman could definitely identify.

Pine groves To reach this rough terrain is far from simple: from Bishop you take Route 395 southwards as far as Big Pine, then turn east on to Route 168. About 20 km (13 mi.) from Big Pine, a wide road climbs up to a height of 3500 m (11,500 ft) into the Bristlecone Pines region. The total distance from Big Pine to Schulman or Methuselah Grove is 54 km (35 mi.), quite a difficult stretch, but you will not need a cross-country vehicle.

After a further 22 km (14 mi.) you come to Patriarch Grove, containing more examples of ancient Bristlecone pines. Only rarely do they exceed 7 m (23 ft) tall; the trunks are gnarled and shine from afar. In the raw climate, and in view of the low rainfall, they probably reach such a great age only because they do not have to share the meagre water supplies with animals or plants. From Schulman Grove it is possible to do a 6½ km (4 mi.) tour on foot; in view of the height and the rough climate great care should be taken. The best time for a visit are the summer months.

Sights Also worth seeing is the Laws Railway Museum, lying about 8.5 km (5 mi.) south-east on Route 6. Here the once bustling but now silent Laws Southern Pacific railway station dating from 1883, as well as a post-office more than 100 years old and other artefacts from that period have been lovingly restored. Open daily 10am–4pm; admission free.

Bodega Bay   G 1

Sonoma County
Altitude: 37 m (120 ft)
Population: 300

Little Bodega Bay is part of Point Reyes National Seashore (see entry) and lies roughly on the spot where Francis Drake dropped anchor in the year 1579. In 1809 Ivan Kusko of the Russian-American Co. established a settlement here for the purpose of growing wheat and catching otters. In order to halt the Russian advance the Mexican governor Vallejo gave three American sailors some land on the borders of the Russian settlement. After the Russians had withdrawn the land was sold to John A. Sutter.

Sights Bodega Bay, where Alfred Hitchcock shot the film "The Birds", is today an important fishing-port. The University of California also has a laboratory of marine biology here.

Bodie State Historic Park   J 5

Mono County
Altitude: 2600 m (8530 ft)

This ghost town, located 32 km (20 mi.) south-east of Bridgeport on Routes 395 and 270 (the final three miles are not made-up) once boasted 10,000 gold diggers, who were a particularly corrupt and disreputable bunch. Until about 1876 large amounts of gold were mined here; then the town fell into decay. The remaining 170 houses have not been fully restored, but were kept from further decay by the creation of a state park in 1964. As a result of the efforts to retain the gold digging atmosphere

Bodic a ghost town from the time of the gold diggers

of the previous century, it represents a place of interest unique in California.

In the winter months, the unmetalled stretch of the approach road is often barred to traffic.

Buena Park
P 3

Orange County
Altitude: 23 m (75 ft)
Population: 69,000

Buena Park is one of those towns on the US 5 Highway south of Los Angeles which follow one another without any clear boundaries, namely, Norwalk, Buena Park, Anaheim (see entry) and Santa Ana (see entry). This town, which has quickly shot up without any particular character, is typical of suburban development in the larger conurbations of California. In addition to Knott's Berry Farm, the oldest Californian pleasure park, Buena Park also offers other attractions.

8039 Beach Boulevard (3 km (2 mi.)) south of the US 5 on Route CA 39): in the year 1920 Walter Knott opened a fruit-stall here. Shortly afterwards he added a restaurant, in which at first he served only chicken dishes. The jams his wife made were a further speciality. In the course of time the farm developed into the present pleasure park to which new attractions are constantly being added. The emphasis here is on the re-awakening of the themes of the American past; the gold rush, a Spanish-American fiesta village, the "Roaring Twenties", a 19th century railway which runs round a large part of the grounds, a reproduction of the

★Knott's Berry Farm

89

Calistoga

Old railway engine at Knott's Berry Farm

Independence Hall in Philadelphia with its Liberty Bell in its original size, and roundabouts.

In the latest section ("Wild Water Wilderness") you take a white-water trip ("Big Foot Rapid") in original surroundings. Open Sun.–Thu. 9am–11pm, Fri. and Sat. 9am–midnight; closed Christmas Day.

Opened in 1995, the latest attraction is the longest roller coaster in the USA, which passes through the Temple of Jaguars, a Maya pyramid. The highlight of this breathtaking experience is the giant loop known as "Montezuma's Revenge".

Movieland Wax Museum

7711 Beach Boulevard: in this museum are more than 200 life-size wax figures of film and television stars, some in authentic-looking scenes, ranging from Charlie Chaplin to "Star Wars". There is also a fine collection of bioscopes (the first film projection equipment), props from old films, rare film posters and Hollywood photos. Open daily May to Sep., 9am–8pm; Oct. to Apr., 9am–7pm.

Calistoga   G 1

Napa County
Altitude: 110 m (360 ft). Population: 4500

Calistoga lies at the northern end of the Napa Valley, on Highways 29 and 128, some 120 km (75 mi.) from San Francisco. The town was founded in 1859 by Sam Brannan who sensed in the hot springs, the natural mud and the geysers the ideal requirements for building a spa.

"Old Faithful" geyser near Calistoga▶

Calistoga (the name is a combination of California and Saratoga, an important spa in New York State) reached its peak in the seventies and eighties of the last century. Since then vine cultivation has been the main source of income.

The hot springs and mud are today used for health treatments and mud-packs. Numerous health and beauty farms (named "Spa"), especially along the Silverado Trail (e.g., Calistoga Village Inn & Spa, 1880 Lincoln Avenue) offer relaxation and accommodation.

Sharpsteen Museum

In the main street of Calistoga (1411 Washington Street) is the Sharpsteen Museum, with photos, dioramas and other artefacts from the town's early days when it was still a spa. The wood cabin near the museum, which was built for those visiting the spa is another reminder of these days.

Open May to Oct. 10am–4pm, at other times noon–4pm.

Mount St Helena

About 13 km (8 mi.) north of Calistoga, on the CA 29, stands the extinct volcano Mount St Helena (about 1300 m (4270 ft)) where Robert Louis and Fanny Stevenson spent part of their honeymoon in 1880 (Robert Louis Stevenson State Park near Mount St Helena with a statue of the poet).

Old Faithful Geyser

Only 1.6 km (1 mi.) away between Routes 29 and 128 can be seen the "Old Faithful Geyser of California" which at regular intervals of 40 minutes sends water spouting 20 m (66 ft) into the air (occasionally its rhythm becomes disrupted). Open daily in summer 9am–6pm, at other times 9am–5pm.

Petrified Forest

Some 9 km (5 mi.) to the west by Petrified Forest Road you can see fossilised redwoods and a museum. Open daily in summer 9am–6pm, at other times 9am–5pm.

Cambria   L 1

San Luis Obispo County
Altitude: 20 m (66 ft). Population: 3100

Only 10 km (6 mi.) south of San Simeon (see entry), the site of the castle built by William Randolph Hearst, and not far from Highway US 1, lies the little town of Cambria, which offers a welcome change. It is built almost entirely in the English style, and because of its quiet atmosphere and its beautiful beach, numerous artists have chosen to live there. The short detour before going on to Morro Bay (see entry) and San Luis Obispo (see entry) is worthwhile, not least because of the many interesting shops. In an historical schoolhouse dating from 1881 the Cambria Allied Arts Association offers an insight into the work of native artists. Open daily noon–3.30pm.

Carlsbad   R 4

San Diego County. Altitude: 12 m (40 ft). Population: 62,000.

Although it bears no resemblance at all to the famous Bohemian spa of the same name (now Carlovy Vary), it must be explained that Carlsbad owes its name to mineral springs which are no longer used, but whose healing properties are every bit as good as those of Karlsbad. Established in 1889, Carlsbad has developed into one of the favourite water-sports resorts in southern California, where a lot of golf and tennis is also played.

A new attraction in the form of a leisure park of miniature Lego brick buildings, similar to Legoland at Billund in Denmark, was opened in 1999. This is the third of its kind, Legoland Park having been opened in Windsor Park, G.B., in 1996.

Legoland

★ Carmel

J 1

Monterey County
Altitude: 67 m (220 ft). Population: 4200

Carmel, a favourite resort of artists, is charmingly located south of San Francisco on the Monterey peninsula.

History The Spanish seafarer Sebastian Vizcaino named the river flowing past Carmel after the three Carmelite monks who in 1603 landed with him not far from the second Californian mission which was originally built in Monterey (see entry). On instructions from the Mexican viceroy, he pushed on from here to Monterey, the northernmost point of his journey. Carmel grew only slowly; at the beginning of the 20th c. it was still an unimportant village with cattle grazing nearby.

Carmel was then discovered by painters, writers and photographers, who chose to live there, but its fame had not yet spread beyond the borders of California. It did not fully develop into a mass-tourist attraction until after the Second World War. Today it is world famous, not least because in 1986 the film star Clint Eastwood was elected mayor for a time.

Tradition The long-lasting struggle between those advocating increased

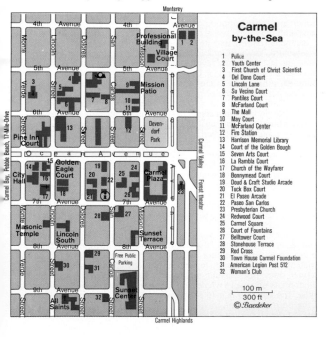

Carmel
by-the-Sea

1 Police
2 Youth Center
3 First Church of Christ Scientist
4 Del Dono Court
5 Lincoln Lane
6 Su Vecino Court
7 Pantiles Court
8 McFarland Court
9 The Mall
10 May Court
11 McFarland Center
12 Fire Station
13 Harrison Memorial Library
14 Court of the Golden Bough
15 Seven Arts Court
16 La Rambla Court
17 Church of the Wayfarer
18 Bonnymead Court
19 Doud & Craft Studio Arcade
20 Tuck Box Court
21 El Paseo Arcade
22 Paseo San Carlos
23 Presbyterian Church
24 Redwood Court
25 Carmel Square
26 Court of Fountains
27 Belltower Court
28 Stonehouse Terrace
29 Red Cross
30 Town House Carmel Foundation
31 American Legion Post 512
32 Woman's Club

100 m
300 ft
© Baedeker

Carmel: Serra sculpture

Carmel: shops

growth and those supporting the status quo finally led to a compromise, as a result of which Carmel changed only slightly and was able to retain its distinctive charm, with its houses clearly influenced by English village architecture. You will look in vain here for street lights or neon signs; there are still only very few pavements; the houses have no numbers (directions read "north of Ocean Avenue" or "west of San Carlos"); Monterey pines grow in the centre; no post is delivered (all the inhabitants collect it from the post office at the south-east corner of 5th and Dolores Street); there is a law against wearing high heels; eating in the street is forbidden; there are no parking meters, no large garages and no high-rise buildings; parking in the streets is restricted to one or two hours, and the streets are patrolled by 26 local policemen and policewomen.

Tourism Carmel has more than 50 restaurants (fast-food restaurants such as McDonalds and Kentucky Fried Chicken are not allowed), about 70 galleries and 40 real-estate agents. The total of some 1200 shops and service establishments are in a ratio of one to every four inhabitants, but are aimed at the large number of tourists who spend many millions of dollars here every year. In the high season especially – some 50,000 cars drive through Carmel in one day at the weekend – the stream of visitors is overwhelming.

This combination of cosy informality and mass tourism is Carmel's unique secret. The bulk of the visitors stay in the square mile of the town centre. Only a few venture out into the residential areas or on to the small but beautiful beach. In contrast to many other places in California, Carmel does not depend on outstanding individual attractions, but rather on its effect as a whole, and this is what makes a visit there worthwhile. The weather is mild all the year. 300 days of sunshine each year is the norm. However, there is often a morning mist in the months of July (21 days), August (22) and September (16).

Nobody should fail to visit the mission of San Carlos Borromeo del Rio Carmelo, where Peter Junipero Serra is buried (see entry for Mission Stations). The Bach Festival, which takes place every year in the second half of July, brings together prominent soloists and chamber music ensembles. You reach it via Seventeen Mile Drive which leads from Monterey (see entry) to Carmel.

San Carlos Borromeo del Rio Carmelo

Anybody who wishes to escape the mist in Carmel can pitch his tent in Carmel Valley, a few miles to the south-east (reached by Route G 16, a turn-off from the US 1). Located by the River Carmel, quite apart from its proximity to the town, Carmel Valley offers many sporting facilities, such as fishing and swimming. Here, too, you will find the largest Zen monastery in the United States of America. From Carmel visitors can also take the "Seventeen Mile Drive" around the Monterey Peninsula.

Surroundings

★Channel Islands National Park   O/P 1/2

The Channel Islands National Park is famous for its sea-lions, colonies of sea-birds and over 800 endemic plant varieties.

Of the eight islands forming this archipelago, five – Anacapa, Santa Barbara, San Miguel, Santa Rosa and Santa Cruz – have been declared a national park. They are located off the coast of South California between Point Conception, west of Santa Barbara (see entry) and Oxnard (see entry). Only two of these islands are accessible by ship from Ventura (see entry): Anacapa all the year round, and Santa Barbara only between the end of May and the beginning of September. A third island, Santa Rosa, was purchased a short time ago by the federal government, and should soon be accessible by boat (Island Packers Co. in Ventura).

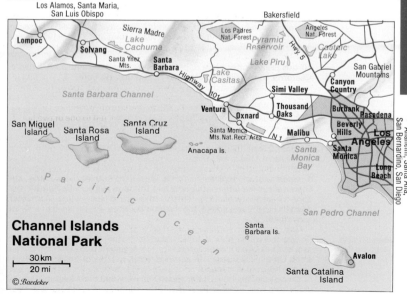

Before visiting the islands you are recommended to call in at the National Park Visitor Center (1901 Spinnaker Drive, Ventura), where you can see a half-hour film of the islands, photographs and other documents as well as utensils and ritual objects used by the Chumash Indians, the original inhabitants of these now almost uninhabited islands.

Anacapa Island

18 km (11 mi.) from the mainland is Anacapa, a group of three islands, connected only by boat. From Ventura you can get to East Anacapa. All three islands cover an area of about 290 ha (1 sq. mi.). Near the landing-stage is the start of a 2.4 km (1½ mi.) nature path, which opens up the beauties of the island. From January to March you can watch from here the migration of the grey whales from Alaska to Mexico. There is a camp-site on East Anacapa for which you must get a permit in advance from the park headquarters in Ventura.

Santa Barbara Island

Santa Barbara, the other island which can be reached by ship, is the southernmost one and, covering an area of 260 ha (640 acres), is the smallest island on the archipelago. It was not inhabited until the 1920s; prior to that it served as grazing land, but the vegetation was seriously damaged by fires and the mass invasion of wild hare. The island possesses tracks totalling 9 km (6 mi.) in length. A favourite setting-off point is Canyon View, south of the landing-stage. There is a camp-site here for which you need a permit. You must bring food and water with you. There is no shade on Anacapa or on Santa Barbara, so you must take precautions to protect yourself from the sun.

San Miguel Island

San Miguel (13 km (8 mi.) long and 6 km (4 mi.) wide) is a plateau about 120–150 m (400–500 ft) high. Here there is no public transport and no camp-site. If you wish to get there in your own boat you will need a special permit. This also applies to Santa Cruz – the biggest of the islands, which is 39 km (24 mi.) in length and covers an area of 96 sq. km (37 sq. mi.) – as well as to the 24 km (15 mi.) long and 16 km (10 mi.) wide island of Santa Rosa.

All five islands offer a rare opportunity of getting to know a small part of California in its original state, with rich fauna and flora.

Coloma   G 3/4

Placer County
Altitude: 275 m (900 ft)
Population: 1100

Coloma lies on Highway CA 49, between Auburn (see entry) and Placerville. This little settlement has found a place in California's history for one reason only: here is the actual spot where James W. Marshall (1810–85) found the first gold in the American River in the year 1848.

Marshall Gold Discovery Park

Today, the whole area in which Marshall, a partner of John A. Sutter, worked has been incorporated into the Marshall Gold Discovery State Park. On a hill stands a statue of Marshall, pointing a finger at the spot where the gold was found.

On instructions from Sutter a saw-mill was built there (about 80 km (50 mi.)) from Fort Sutter in Sacramento; see entry), a reproduction of which stands in State Park. Some of the older houses have been preserved.

The park is open daily 8am to sunset.

Costa Mesa   Q 3

Orange County
Altitude: 31 m (100 ft)
Population: 96,000

Costa Mesa forms part of the chain of middle-sized towns which lie one
after the other south-east of Los Angeles on both sides of the US 405,
the so-called San Diego Freeway. Costa Mesa, Huntington Beach,
Fountain Valley, Santa Ana and Newport Beach run almost imperceptibly one into the other. Costa Mesa takes precedent over the other
towns in Orange County because of its commitment to culture.

Here in 1986 the Orange County Performing Arts Center was first set up,
where the Los Angeles Philharmonic Orchestra and the New York City
Opera Company are regular guests, as well as numerous other orchestras and soloists. Rock concerts are no rarity here either. (600 Town
Center Drive.)

Orange County
Performing Arts
Center

In Costa Mesa, too, are the Orange County Fair Grounds, where in July
each year the Orange County Fair, which is worth a visit, is found. Within
the Fair Grounds stands the Pacific-Amphitheater where open-air performances are held all the year round.

Orange County
Fair Grounds

Costa Mesa is also notable in the theatrical sphere. The South Coast
Repertory Company (655 Town Center Drive), quite close to the Cultural
Center, is one of the best theatres in California. In its two auditoria, main
stage (seating 500) and second stage (seating 160), five to six premiäres
are presented every year (season tickets are obtainable). Californian
authors are often asked to speak here.

South Coast
Repertory
Company

Crescent City   A 2

Del Norte County
Altitude: 13 m (43 ft). Population: 4400

This town, located on the Pacific in the "High North" not far from the
border with Oregon, was founded by gold-seekers in 1851, and gets its
name from the horn-shaped bay. Point St George, the headland immediately north of the harbour, protects the town from the cold north winds.
The paddle-steamer "Brother Jonathan" sank off this coast in 1865 with
the loss of 265 lives. The victims of the catastrophe are buried in the
Brother Jonathan Cemetery (9th St, Pebble Beach). A further disaster, a
tidal wave, destroyed a large part of the town in 1964.

Redwood National Park, covering an area of 434,000 ha (1,070,000
acres), begins in Crescent City and runs south for 74 km (46 mi.), 48 km
(30 mi.) of which border the Pacific coast. As well as the beautiful redwood trees, the park offers numerous walks and picnic-sites. The headquarters of the park are in Crescent City (corner of 2nd and K Street),
where further information can be obtained.

**Redwood
National Park**

Inside Redwood National Park, which was created in 1868, lie three
State Parks, all on or near Highway 101: Jedediah Smith Redwoods
State Park, Del Norte Redwoods State Park and Prairie Creek Redwoods
State Park. The latter possesses the tallest redwoods; it lies about 53 km
(33 mi.) south of Crescent City.

Crescent City, with its seven motels (about 300 rooms), offers adequate accommodation, whereas near the US 101, also known as Redwood Highway (see entry), there is little to be found.

Dana Point   Q 3

Orange County
Altitude: 10 m (33 ft)
Population: 32,000

In the last few years Dana Point has developed into one of the major water-sports resorts between San Diego and Los Angeles, its proximity to the better known and often overcrowded Laguna Beach (see entry) being instrumental in this. During the 19th century Dana Point was one of the few natural harbours between San Diego and Santa Barbara; today this bay has a marina which can accommodate up to 25,000 motor-boats and sailing-boats.

The **name** Dana Point can be traced back to the sailor, writer and lawyer Richard Henry Dana who in 1834 as a simple seaman made the trip round Cape Horn to California and stayed here for sixteen months in the years 1835/1836. His adventures, including an act of heroism in the harbour later named Dana Point, are described in his novel, later to become a classic, "Two Years Before The Mast", which had a big influence on later travel literature. He thus became a champion of the rights of seamen, "that race of men with whom my fate was linked for so long".

Sights

From December to March Dana Point is an ideal spot from which to observe the whales migrating north. Here, too, can be found the Orange County Marine Institute, a reproduction of the ship "Pilgrim" which plied along the Californian coast, and the Dana Point Lighthouse with some interesting artefacts.

Davis   G 2

Yolo County
Altitude; 15 m (50 ft)
Population: 46,000

Davis, a suburb of Sacramento located on the US 80 going towards San Francisco, bears the name of its founder Jerome C. Davis who planted wheat, barley, vines and fruit trees on a 162 ha (400 acre) holding here. Today this now urbanised town still lies in the middle of a rich agricultural area.

University of California

The campus of the University of California can be traced back to an agricultural school founded in 1907, which for 15 years was transferred to Berkeley (see entry) as a branch of the University of California. In 1961 Davis obtained its own campus, whose total area of 400 ha (1000 acres) makes it the third largest site of the University of California, after Los Angeles and Berkeley (20,000 students), and which dominates the town. Davis has also made a name for itself in California through its energy-saving programme and its research projects in the sphere of solar energy.

★★Death Valley National Park   L–O 6/7

Inyo County
Altitude: 86 m (280 ft)–3368 m (11,050 ft).

Mighty lunar landscape in Death Valley

The valley can be reached from three sides: From Los Angeles it is   Access
480 km (300 mi.), via the US 15 Highway as far as Baker, then via the
CA 127 as far as the sign for Dante's View and thence to the Visitor
Center via the CA 190. From Las Vegas in Nevada, 224 km (140 mi.)
away, you take the US 15, then the 127 to Death Valley Junction and
the 190 direct to the Visitor Center in Furnace Creek. From Lone Pine
(see entry) on the CA 395, you drive direct to Death Valley on the CA
136 and 190.

Formerly known azs Death Valley National Monument and protected
accordingly, in 1994, following a government decree, it was declared a
National Park.

The Death Valley region, low in rainfall (land area 7770 sq. km (3000
sq. mi.), lies in central south-east California, extending slightly into
the US federal state of Nevada, and includes the 225 km (140 mi.)-
wide and 6–26 km (4–16 mi.)-wide desert valleys of the Amargosa
River and Salt Creek, as well as the surrounding chains of mountains
known as the Panamint Range in the west, and the Amargosa Range
in the east.

The impressive scenery of this geologically multiform desert (maximum temperature 56.7°C), with its wondrous rocky wastes and sand-
dunes, conceals numerous streams and a rich animal and plant life
including succulents of all kinds. 21 species of plants and trees found
here are unique to the valley.

Rock-drawings, hearths and supply trails have all been found, providing evidence of pre-historic settlements in almost all parts of Death
Valley.

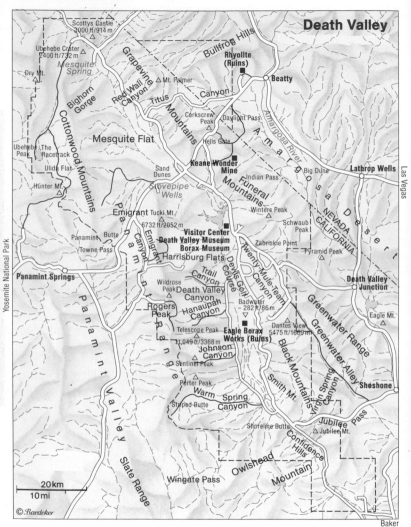

History

Death Valley is a harsh wilderness, with high mountain peaks and deep valleys, sand dunes like those in the Sahara, oases where date-palms grow, water courses below sea level, and a rich flora, especially in spring, which belies the name given to the whole region. Death Valley is also of great geological interest. Many years ago it was an inland lake; the mountains were formed as the result of mighty land eruptions, and the water evaporated under the merciless sun. The formation of the mountains was accompanied by a lowering of the valley bottom; the valley came into being not through erosion, as most did, but as a result of a shift in the earth's crust. Thus Telescope Peak was raised from 86 m (280 ft) below sea level to 3368 m (11,050 ft) above. What we see in many parts today is a world of rock in every colour imaginable which never fails to amaze the visitor.

This wonder of nature was **discovered** more or less by chance in 1849 when some adventurers, wanting to find their way as quickly as possible to the land of the gold-rush to the west, wandered into the unhospitable desert from which they escaped again only after considerable hardship and difficulty. They had to abandon their wagons and eat the oxen which pulled them in order not to starve – they also gave the area its present name. A few years later they were followed by men who believed they would find gold and silver. It is true that they found a few veins of these valuable metals but their labours were scarcely worthwhile and they soon moved on to pastures new.

Then, however, **"white gold"** was discovered in the desert – borax, an important chemical used in many branches of industry. At the start teams of two horses and eighteen mules (not just mules, as the legendary description of 20-mule teams would have us believe) had to pull their load over a distance of 264 km (165 mi.) to Mojave which took them ten days. Eventually, a railway was built. In 1881 Harmony Borax Works (near Furnace Creek), which is now partly restored and open to visitors, came into operation; others followed and the quantities of borax, which is still mined to some extent in Death Valley today, increased within a few years to hundreds of thousands of tons. Today borax is used mainly in the production of glass and glass-fibres, as well as in the soap industry.
    Although Death Valley has been a "National Monument" since 1933, borax can still be mined within its boundaries, but only underground. There are also still optimists who climb around in the deep canyons of Death Valley in the mostly vain hope of stumbling upon a vein of gold. However, the many thousands who come to Death Valley year after year (in the season, there are sometimes as many as 10,000 in one day) do so because of the unique scenery.

Sights

Can one "do" Death Valley in a day? It is possible if you arrive in the evening, stay there overnight (facilities only from the middle of October until the end of May), and then follow a definite plan. In Furnace Creek, the centre of Death Valley which lies below sea level, there is a hotel and a motel (for both it is essential to book in advance; tel. (800) 5286367). Here also there is a National Park Service information office, a post office and a filling station.

Furnace Creek

From Furnace Creek you should start the tour as early as possible the next morning, first going in a southerly direction for 6.4 km (4 mi.) to Zabriskie Point, from where there is a fantastic view of the western part of Death Valley and the Panamint Mountains. Here you are surrounded by gold-coloured rocks; in the foreground is Manly Bacon Peak, named after one of the men who were the first to cross the desert in 1849, the first white people to do so. Indians of the Shoshone tribe, who called the area "tomesha" or "fiery earth", had been there for 7000 years.

Zabriskie Point

From Zabriskie Point, return to the CA 190, and then drive a further 6.4 km (4 mi.) along a one-way road to 20-Mule-Team Canyon, a very winding stretch which is not easy to negotiate, then 30 km (19 mi.) up to the viewing platform Dante's View (an allusion to hell as described by the

Dante's View

Steam tractor in Furnace Creek

Italian poet. You are now at a height of 1669 m (5478 ft) and the temperature is considerably cooler than in Furnace Creek.

On the way, you will pass the still active Ryan Borax Mine. From here you can look down onto the lowest point of the American continent, Badwater, which lies 86 m (280 ft) below sea level. A mere 16 km (10 mi.) away you can see the 3300 m (10,380 ft) high Telescope Peak, which is often snow-capped until June.

Devil's Golf Course

Via East Side Road you now come to Devil's Golf Course, a giant flat area covered in sharp salt crystals. The nearest approach is Artist's Drive, a winding one-way road, the most beautiful part of which bears the description "Painter's Palette", because perhaps nowhere else in Death Valley do the rocks glow in so many colours as they do here.

Badwater

South of Furnace Creek, there only remains the drive to Badwater. It is not possible to reach the lowest point by car; you must be satisfied with going down to a depth of 85 m (277 ft). While it was about 20° cooler on Dante's Point and more windy than in Furnace Creek, here it is 6–8°C warmer. In Badwater there is a small salt lake which does not dry up even in the hot months, and which is surrounded by white salt. Only small insects and algae of various colours live in the sour, warm water.

Harmony Borax Works

From Badwater you should return to Furnace Creek for a rest and to recuperate, perhaps also have a refreshing swim in the pool which is fed by a stream, and then you are off again to see the sights to the north. The nearest is the Harmony Borax Works, which has already been mentioned; from there you can make a small detour to the sand dunes on the road leading to Stove Pipe Wells, which are most beautifully illuminated towards sunset.

Then it is northwards to the Ubehebe Crater, measuring about 1 km (½ mi.) wide and 122 m (400 ft) deep, one of the few craters in the area which resulted from a volcanic explosion. Directly adjacent to Ubehebe Crater lies Little Hehe Crater. About 50 miles away (north of Beatty, Nevada) can be found the giant Timber Mountain Caldera and Black Mountain Caldera.

So far in Death Valley you have only seen what nature has provided. Now, however, you come to Scotty's Castle, probably the strangest building you could expect to find in this part of the country. You can only visit it as part of a guided tour. It was built in the twenties by a Chicago businessman named Albert Johnson, about a decade before Death Valley was declared a national monument. At the time there were still no roads, and all building materials had to be obtained the hard way. In addition to the main house with its 15 m (50 ft) high living-room, in which the Johnsons only stayed for one month in the year, there are stables, a guest-house, a house for the staff, and a bell-tower, all maintained in the Hispano-Moorish style. The contents of the house are original; furniture, books and paintings are those owned by the Johnsons.

On the upper floor are the bedrooms and an unusual music room with a magnificent organ (1600 pipes) which is also fitted with self-playing musical cylinders as Mrs Johnson was not a very good organist. The house was never completed, however; before the garden, swimming pool and illuminated tiled courtyard could be finished, the Wall Street Crash of 1929 came and Johnson lost almost all his money. The house went to a religious institution from whom the National Park acquired it in 1970.

"Scotty's Castle" was the unofficial name for this strange building. It comes from "Death Valley Scotty", an adventurer who was also a confidence trickster and who bore the same name as the writer Walter Scott. Although not as much as one single brick belonged to him, he told anyone who would listen that the house was his and that Johnson was only his "banker"! In time people believed him.

Advice

Of course, anybody with more than a day to spare can see much more of Death Valley. Perhaps it is then a good idea to make use of one of the ten **camping sites**, the biggest of which is Sunset Camp with 1000 pitches (open only from November to April). Contrary to some other camping sites, you cannot book in advance in Death Valley; the maxim "first come, first served" applies here. With the exception of Furnace Creek camping site, where you can only stay for a maximum of 14 days, the period is 30 days on all the others.

Temperatures When should you visit Death Valley? If possible not in the months of June to September when the great heat does not make it an ideal holiday spot for people (or for cars). During these months the average maximum temperatures are 42–46°C, and some 6–8° hotter in the parts which lie below sea level. In Death Valley on one July day in 1913 the temperature was measured as 57°C (in the shade!), the highest ever recorded in the western hemisphere. In the other eight months, however, pleasant summer weather prevails with only very occasional rain (the average annual rainfall is only 50 mm (2 in.).

Rules Anyone wishing to visit Death Valley during the summer heat should take certain precautionary measures: you should take at least 4 l (1 gal) of water with you; do not switch the air-conditioning on in the car to avoid overheating the engine; wear a large hat with a brim and a long-sleeved white shirt which will reflect the sun; although there are several places in Death Valley where you can fill up with fuel (Furnace Creek, Stove Pipe Wells and Scotty's Castle), it is best to start with a full tank, as distances are fairly great; remember in summer especially never to stray from the made-up roads!

The **Visitor Center** in Furnace Creek is open every day. Guided tours are organised from there; from November to April slide-shows and other performances are given in the auditorium in the evenings.

Disneyland Resort

See Anaheim, Disneyland Resort

Donner Pass   G 5

This pass in the Sierra Nevada, west of Truckee (see entry), over which the Transcontinental Highway US 80 now runs, was the scene of a great tragedy in California's early history, and also the only authenticated case of cannibalism in the history of the US.

Trek to the west In April 1846 a group of 89 people from Illinois, led by the brothers Georg and Jacob Donner who probably originated from Germany, set off for California. The covered wagons, pulled by oxen, were supposed to follow a route which promised to be 560 km (350 mi.) shorter than those known at the time. However, they had to cross over

Beautiful mountain scenery and the picturesque Donner Lake – both can be found in the Donner Pass

high passes and a 57 km (36 mi.) stretch of desert. In the attempt some of their draught animals died and they had to abandon some wagons which was to cost them almost three weeks loss of time.

Natural obstacles It was the end of October before they reached the area now known as Reno, exhausted, embittered, demoralised and molested by Paiute Indians. After a short rest they continued their trek, but winter set in early at the beginning of November. The pass, which now bears the name of the Donner brothers, became snow-bound and they were unable to cross it. They had to pitch their tents on the lower shores of the lake, which now also bears their name and forms the centre of the Donner Memorial State Park. One of the members pressed on to Fort Sutter (now Sacramento; see entry). As he had to cover a rough stretch of almost 160 km (100 mi.) rendered almost impassable by heavy snow-drifts, it was March 1st before he could get back with the provisions they so desperately needed.

Cannibalism In the meantime some members of the Donner group had died of starvation. The others could stay alive only by eating the flesh of the dead men. Even after months of waiting, they could not all escape from this wilderness at the beginning of March; those left behind continued to starve. It is said that in April Louis Keseberg murdered Georg Donner's wife in order to get her money and consume the corpse. In all, 42 of those who had left Illinois perished, only 47 survived and settled in the Sacramento Valley.

In the Donner Memorial State Park can be seen the spot where the Donner group camped; this tragic episode in American history is remembered in the Emigrant Trail Museum two miles west of Truckee.

Donner Memorial State Park

Dutch Flat   G 4

Placer County
Altitude: 410 m (1346 ft)
Population: 800

The place name Dutch Flat derives from the "Dutch" which has been introduced into America as a phonetic form of "Deutsch" (German), but has no connection at all with the English word "Dutch". Today it is a forgotten former gold-mining town near the US 80, some 30 km (18 mi.) north-east of Auburn (see entry). It was founded in 1851 by German immigrants, the brothers Carl and Josef Dornbach.

Countless adventurers streamed to Dutch Flat, which developed into one of the richest gold-mining towns in the whole of the state and provided a home for one-tenth of the inhabitants of the whole of Placer County. In addition, some 2000 Chinese settled here to assist in digging for gold, initially as paid workers, but rapidly becoming almost slaves. The advertisements in the newspaper of the time, the "Dutch Flat Enquirer", show that at the beginning of the 1860s there were seventeen bars, two breweries, seven grocers' shops, three smithies, two banks, eight gents' clothiers, three hotels, a chemist, a Freemasons' lodge and an Oddfellows' lodge.

Today little remains of all that, even though Dutch Flat is not a ghost town in the true sense of the word. Nevertheless, thanks to the commitment of the village council, something of the original charm has been preserved; today men still search for gold in the nearby rivers with some success; a small museum has been set up in the village; at present, the only hotel still standing, albeit empty, is being renovated; the old chemists' shop has been changed into an antique shop, and the

Sights

Freemasons' and Oddfellows' lodges still exist – the latter in a house built in 1854 by the Hanoverian J. K. Hüdepohl.

Places like this are seldom found in California today. The authentic features of Dutch Flat have been preserved mainly because here, unlike so many other gold-mining towns, there has never been a major fire.

Not far from Dutch Flat, on the US 80, lies a town called Weimar which got its name not from the German town of the same name, but from the Indian chief Weimah who lived nearby. In 1886, some 30 years later and for no obvious reason, it was changed to Weimar.

El Camino Real   H–T 0–4

Literally translated, "El Camino Real" means "The Royal Road". The name came into being in the 18th c. and describes the road which begins in Baja California (see entry) and continues into Alta California and along which most of the mission stations (see entry) grew up.

In what is now California, it began in San Diego and ran past the mission stations of San Luis Rey de Francia, San Juan Capistrano and San Gabriel, then westwards via Los Angeles, Ventura, Santa Barbara, San Luis Obispo, Morro Bay, through the Salinas Valley, Monterey and San Francisco. The route taken by the Camino Real essentially corresponds to the present-day Highway 101 on which most of the mission stations are located.

★Eureka   B/C 1

Humboldt County
Altitude: 13 m (43 ft). Population: 27,000

This town on Humboldt and Arcata Bay was founded in 1850 as a port, and is today still the only port of any size between San Francisco and the mouth of the Columbia River in Oregon. It was given the Greek name "Eureka" ("I have found it"), which also appears in the coat-of-arms of the US Federal State of California. The importance of Eureka today lies in the shipping of wood, especially redwood, from the surrounding forests.

The town's early **history** has a few black spots. Here in 1853 Fort Humboldt was built on lands which belonged to the Wiyot Indians. In 1860 American troops carried out a fearful massacre of the Indian wives and children when most of the menfolk were out hunting. The exact number of dead has never been ascertained. 25 years later, as in so many other Californian towns, the Chinese were expelled by force. They were victims of the xenophobia emerging again and again in the United States.

Carson Mansion

From the same year (1885) dates what must surely be the most notable building in the town, Carson Mansion (143 M. Street), now a club. William Carson, a timber wholesaler and one of the richest citizens of Eureka, had this Victorian house built, mainly of redwood; its numerous pre-fabricated, almost Gothic-looking wood carvings and painted windows, together with its many interlocked sections, give it a unique appearance. Carson House stands on a raised plot and can be seen from afar when you approach it along 2nd Street (a visit is possible; see Culture and Art: Architecture).

Carson Mansion (Queen Anne style) in Eureka ▶

Sights

Fort Humboldt State Historic Park (3431 Fort Avenue) is the site of the former Fort Humboldt.

Also worth seeing is the little zoo situated within the precincts of the town in the middle of a redwood grove (Glatt and W. Street). The zoo is open every day except Monday. A bank building, designed like an earlier palace, in the centre of the partly-restored old town, houses the Clarke Museum which is particularly rich in Indian basketwork and other artefacts, as well as documents on the history of Eureka and Humboldt County (3rd and E. Street). Open Tue.–Sat. noon–4pm; admission free.

One-hour **boat trips** on Humboldt Bay from the pier at the bottom of C. Street daily from April to October, 1–8pm.

Ferndale   C 1

Humboldt County
Altitude: 30 m (98 ft). Population: 1300

Ferndale was founded by Danish farmers in the year 1860. It lies about 24 km (15 mi.) south-west of Eureka, and can be reached from there on the US 101 (8 km (5 mi.)) the other side of the Fernbridge intersection). Worth seeing are the numerous old houses built in the Victorian style – Queen Anne, Eastlake and Gothic revival styles – with an unusual number of art galleries and craft shops. In addition to the three parish churches the main places worth seeing are Shaw House (703 Main Street), today a small boarding house (tel. 786–9958), and Berding House (455 Ocean Avenue), both built in about 1854. More captivating than any of the individual highlights, however, is the overall impression made by this magical little town.

Fort Bragg   E 1

Mendocino County
Altitude: 23 m (75 ft). Population: 6100

This town, founded in the year 1884 and located on the US 1, is on the site of a fort built in 1857 to suppress the Indians. The fort was given up only ten years later and most of the land sold to woodcutters. The reason for the low population density of the coastal region is made clear when you realise that in spite of having only 5500 inhabitants it is actually the largest town between San Francisco and Eureka (see entry). The timber industry continues to be of importance. One of the many saw-mills, Georgia Pacific Mill, is open to visitors on weekdays.

Skunk Railroad

The biggest tourist attraction is undoubtedly "Skunk Railroad", as the 64 km (40 mi.) long railway line of the California Western Railroad to Willits is called. Pulled by an old diesel locomotive, it travels through redwood forests along the Noyo. The journey to Willits takes about two hours. There are two round trips each day from the end of June to the middle of Sept.; in the remaining months there is only one, to Northspur.

Mendocino Coast
Botanical Garden

Two miles south of Fort Bragg on the US 1 you come to Mendocino Coast Botanical Garden, about 20 acres of rhododendrums, fuchsias, native plants and trees. Restaurant and picnic sites nearby.

Wooden houses and well in Fort Ross

★Fort Ross State Historic Park   F 0/1

Some 80 km (50 mi.) north of San Francisco, on the US 1, lies Fort Ross
State Historic Park. From 1812 to 1841 the Russians who built the fort
settled here in the hope of being better able to provide Alaska with
wheat and other foodstuffs than they could from Russia itself.

Over 90 Russians, as well as Aleutians and Kodiaks, built their village
and the fort. Then they began to fish for otters and finally to trade with
Spanish California. It is open to debate whether they would have tried
later to have taken over more Californian land but the Spaniards had
decided in 1769 to occupy Alta California, in order to prevent a possible
Russian penetration into the almost uninhabited areas in the west of the
American continent. However, in 1812 the Spaniards had still not got
past San Francisco Bay towards the north. They first learned of the
arrival of the Russians when Fort Ross had already been built.

Inside the wooden fort were the commandant's house, the chapel and
two log-cabins – all carefully reconstructed in latter years. Two to three
dozen cannons were kept in the cabins.

The most interesting building is perhaps the **Russian Orthodox Chapel**,
originally built in 1824 and which remained standing after the Russians
withdrew until it collapsed in the great earthquake of 1906. It was rebuilt
in 1916/1917 and again four years later, but burned down in 1970. After
having been destroyed three times, it was given its present appearance
in 1974. The Russian bell, which had melted in the fire, was re-cast.

Changing owners Although they were never attacked, the Russians were
ordered back from Fort Ross by their Czar; the hopes they had had for
the colony were not fulfilled; the agricultural production was not

sufficient for the needs of the Russians in Alaska, and the otter population was almost completely wiped out. The area was to have been sold to the Mexican government, but when negotiations foundered the rich John A. Sutter from Sacramento (see entry) jumped in and bought the land from the Russians for 30,000 dollars.

Including the soldiers, the maximum Russian population must have been 700. In the period that followed Fort Ross changed owners several times, until in 1903 it passed to the state, who began to restore it. Fort Ross is open daily 10am–4.30pm.

Fresno   K 3

Fresno County
Altitude: 90 m (300 ft)
Population: 354,000

Fresno, the eighth largest town in California, lies 341 km (213 mi.) north of Los Angeles and 294 km (184 mi.) south of San Francisco, on the CA 99, roughly in the centre of the state. In the vicinity can be found the National Parks of King's Canyon (see entry; 90 km (56 mi.)), Sequoia (134 km (84 mi.)) and Yosemite (see entry; 146 km (91 mi.)). Fresno enjoys a mediterranean climate, with average annual temperatures of 20°C, and has 300 days of sunshine in the year. The town's name comes from the Spanish word "fresno" (ash-tree).

As it did at the start of its existence, the town's **economy** still depends largely on its agricultural products, especially grapes, nectarines, plums, tomatoes and peaches. As Fresno lies in the unusually fertile San Joaquin Valley the total value of its agricultural production can exceed 2 billion dollars per year.

In addition, one of the largest wine-producers in the country (Guild) and the world's biggest dried fruit firm (Sun Maid) are based here.

32,500 students in all are registered at the two **colleges** of California State University and City College. As soon as the extension work on the University of California planned for the 1990s is resumed Fresno will be the first town to contain a campus for California's major seat of learning. There are also 35 specialist colleges. Probably Fresno's most famous son is the writer William Saroyan (see Famous Personalities).

Population When it received its municipal charter in 1885, Fresno had exactly 3464 inhabitants, mainly Armenians, Volga Germans, Danes, Swedes, Irish, Scots, English and Portuguese, who had decided, on the basis of newspaper advertisements, to settle in Fresno. In the first decade of this century the town still had no more than 12,000 inhabitants; since then it has expanded rapidly; since 1980 alone the town has grown by over a third.

Sights

However, cultural development has not been able to keep pace with this population explosion. In Fresno you will find only one philharmonic orchestra, an opera company which performs only occasionally, several theatre groups and the Metropolitan Museum of Art History and Science (1555 Van Ness), better described as an extended museum of local history. Open Thu.–Sun. 11am–5pm, Wed. 11am–7pm. Also worth visiting are some parks on the edge of town, such as Roeding Park, with a variety of alpine and tropical plants. There is also a zoo, and Woodward Park with its Japanese garden open only at weekends.

Garberville   D 1

Humboldt County
Altitude: 162 m (530 ft). Population: 800

Garberville lies near the exit from Highway 101, by the first redwood forest to be found south of Eureka (see entry), Richardson Grove State Park. It is only a few miles from the southern end of the Avenue of the Giants, the old motorway to Eureka. This runs parallel to the US 101, and crosses a 52 km (33 mi.)-long redwood area, including, for example, Humboldt Redwoods State Park, 25 km (15 mi.) north of Garberville. Thanks to its location and its variety of hotels, motels and restaurants, Garberville is an ideal base for trips into the surrounding redwood groves.

Geyserville   F 1

Sonoma County
Altitude: 63 m (206 ft)
Population: 1000

Geyserville lies directly on Highway 101, about 33 km (21 mi.) north of Santa Rosa (see entry), in the north-east of Sonoma County. For the Indians who lived in this geothermal region Geyserville was a holy place. When the whites discovered it in 1847 they recognised the healing properties of these hot springs. Four years later they established the town and made it into a spa.

Not far from here is the Old Faithful Geyser (see Calistoga), periodically spouting 20 m (66 ft) or so into the air. Since about 1960 this geyser has served as a source of energy for the geothermic power station Pacific Gas and Electric Company which produces almost 1.2 million kilowatt hours of electricity.

Glen Ellen   G 1

Sonoma County
Altitude: 70 m (230 ft). Population: 1000

Located in the heart of the vine-growing region, Glen Ellen is the headquarters of numerous well-known wine producers. It lies on the CA 12, between Santa Rosa (see entry) and Schellville.

Only 1.6 km (1 mi.) away stretches Jack London State Historic Park, where the writer, who committed suicide is buried, and where the ruins of the house he built, Wolf House, are to be found; shortly before it was completed on August 22nd 1913 it was destroyed by fire, the cause of which was never discovered.

Jack London State Historic Park

In his novel "The Valley of the Moon", published in the same year, London provided a literary memorial to the region around Glen Ellen, and at the same time revived the old Indian legends, according to which the name Sonoma means "many moons" in the Indian language.

In 1919 London's widow had the "House of Happy Walls" built, and today this is the Jack London Museum, with many documents relating to the life of the author, his collection of South Sea Island artefacts, some of the furniture saved from Wolf House, as well as all the contents of his intended workroom (one of the 26 rooms in the destroyed house), tel. (707) 9385216.

Glen Ellen: ruins of Jack London's house

Grass Valley G 4

Nevada County
Altitude: 735 m (2412 ft). Population: 9000

Grass Valley, some 42 km (26 mi.) north of Auburn (see entry) on the CA 49, gets its name from the time it was founded in 1849 by the first settlers, who unexpectedly found plenty of fodder here for their cattle. They could not have suspected that under the meadows lay the biggest gold deposits in all California. The Empire gold-mine is today the centre of Empire Mine Historic Park and is open to visitors. In the 107 years of its existence nearly 6 million ounces of gold have been mined.

In Grass Valley also lived Lola Montez, the lover of King Louis I of Bavaria. The house in which she stayed for a time is to be converted into a museum.

Walking tours in the Empire Mine give the visitor a good impression of the working conditions in a gold-mine. You can go some 13 m (40 ft) down into the shafts, which are lit for a length of 45 m (150 ft), but which are 587 km (367 mi.) long altogether. On a model you can see the direction and depth of the individual veins.

Bourn Villa, the villa which belonged to the former owner of the mine, can also be visited. (10791 East Empire Street.) Open Apr.–Nov. 9am–6pm; in the remaining months until 5pm.

Healdsburg F/G 1

Sonoma County

Altitude: 32 m (105 ft)
Population: 9500

Healdsburg, on the Russian River and the US 101, 23 km (14 mi.) north of
Santa Rosa (see entry), lies in the middle of one of the fertile vineyard
areas of Sonoma County. The best known wine-cellars in and around
Healdsburg, all of which are open to visitors, are: Simi Winery, 16275
Healdsburg Avenue; Chateau Souverain, 5 km (3 mi.) north on the US
101; Geyser Peak Winery, 13 km (8 mi.) north on the US 101, exit Canyon
Road. The last has been in existence since 1880, and is thus one of the
oldest wine businesses in California.

There are around 50 further wine-cellars along the Russian River.
Details available from the Healdsburg Chamber of Commerce; tel. (707)
4336935.

Healdsburg is also a convenient starting point for a **canoe trip** lasting
several days along the American, Sacramento and Russian rivers
(Apr.–Oct.) as well as on the Colorado River (throughout the year).

Hearst San Simeon Historic Park

See San Simeon

Indio   R 5/6

Riverside County
Altitude: 4 m (13 ft)
Population: 37,000

Indio lies in the centre of the fertile Coachella Valley on the US 10,
about equidistant from Los Angeles and San Diego (160 km (100 mi.)).
Originally it was a work camp when the Southern Pacific Railroad
was under construction in 1876, and it was initially named Indian
Wells. Not until later did it receive its present name ("indio" is
Spanish for Indian); Indians had in fact inhabited the valley since the
11th c.

C. P. Huntington, president of the Southern Pacific Railroad, brought
back with him from a trip to Algeria some date-palm seedlings; these
formed the basic stock for the many trees which gave Indio the reputation of being the **"Date Capital"** of the United States. The "Date
Festival" has been held here every year since 1921, the highlights of
which are camel and ostrich races. 95% of all American dates are harvested in Coachella Valley, which is well irrigated by the distant
Colorado, thanks to the All American Canal. You may obtain information
regarding the history and cultivation of dates from a 25-minute slide
show in Shields Date Gardens (80–225 Highway 111.) Open daily
8am–6pm.

Inyo National Forest   J/L 5/6

This National Forest, extending along the US 395 and US 6 as far as
Nevada, covers an area of 763,000 ha (1,900,000 acres), and is divided into several wilderness regions, John Muir, Golden Trout,
Anselm Adams and Hoover. Within the whole area there are hundreds of lakes and rivers, as well as Mount Whitney (4418m (14,500

ft)), the highest mountain in the United States apart from Alaska. Moreover, it is only some 120 km (75 mi.) as the crow flies from the lowest point, Badwater in Death Valley (see entry for Death Valley National Monument), which lies 86 m (280 ft) below sea level. The Palisade Glacier on the border of Inyo National Forest and Kings Canyon National Park is the most southerly glacier in the United States.

For all **walks** in the forest region during the period from June 1st to September you must obtain permits, either in Lone Pine, Mammoth Lakes, Bishop (see entries) or in Lee Vining.

The National Forest is barred to visitors during the remaining months of the year. There is a visitors' centre for Inyo National Forest to be found south of Lone Pine, at the junction of the US 395 and CA 136 roads. Open daily in summer 8am–6pm, and during the rest of the year Mon.– Thu. 9am–5pm.

Irvine   Q 3

Orange County
Altitude: 63 m (207 ft)
Population: 110,000

Irvine, located on the US 1 north-east of Newport Beach, can claim to be the biggest community in the United States based on a "master plan". First established in 1971, in an area of 30,000 ha (75,000 acres), it underwent rapid development. In Irvine there are extensive industrial complexes and a campus of the University of California, with some 17,000 students, and living quarters occupied almost exclusively by whites (88%).

Irvine Meadows
Amphitheater

In the grounds of the former Lion County Safari Park (8800 Irvine Center) you will find the Irvine Meadows Amphitheater in which concerts are held from June to the end of September on Fridays, Saturdays and Sundays. The amphitheatre holds 10,000 people.

★Joshua Tree National Park   Q/R 5–7

Altitude: 300 to 1800 m (1000 to 6000 ft)

Formerly known as the Joshua Tree National Monument, this region was declared a national park in 1994.

Joshua Tree National Park covers an area of 2200 sq. km (850 sq. mi.) and lies within the desert regions of southern California at an altitude of 300 to 1800 m (1000 to 6000 ft). There are three main entrances: in the north (on the CA 62) at Twenty-Nine Palms, in the south (on the US 10) in Cottonwood Springs (40 km (25 mi.) east of Indio (see entry), and in the north-west the Joshua Tree entrance. There are also some minor entrances (including Indian Cove and Fortynine Palms), but these are not suitable for motor vehicles. The northern entrance is recommended. Maps and informative material can be obtained from the visitors' centres at the main entrances.

The **Joshua Tree**, which grows only in the Mojave desert, got its name from the Mormons who saw in its branches the outstretched arms of the praying prophet. The Joshua trees reach a height of up to 18 m (60 ft), and belong to the Yucca family, a type of lily bearing white flowers in April and May. Many of these trees are said to be several hundred years old.

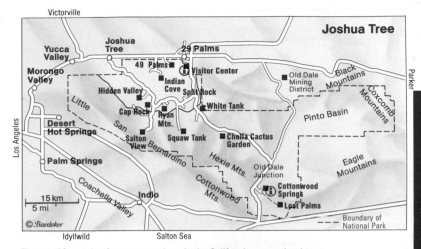

Flora and fauna As almost everywhere in the Californian wastelands you will find here a variety of plant and animal life, even though only a few animals are to be seen during the day. In this extremely dry climate the ground actually obtains the moisture it needs to support life from heavy thunderstorms during the summer months.

However, the flora and fauna have adapted to these inhospitable conditions. Thus the plants either spread their roots wide under the soil, in order to trap the water before it seeps away, or else they penetrate deeply down to the ground water. The leaves of some plants are coated with wax to prevent water loss. In the few oases grow palms, especially the famous fan palm or Washingtonia filifera. This was named after Colonel Henry Washington, to whom is attributed the discovery of the area in 1855.

By day the visitor will come across only a few species of animals, such as squirrels, dwarf antelopes and occasionally a coyote, the so-called prairie dog. Poisonous spiders and five different types of rattlesnake are native here; when it is very hot one must take great care in shady places, especially under rocks and bushes. When the temperatures are lower the snakes crawl out of their hiding-places to sun themselves.

Anyone whose main interest lies in Joshua trees should follow a course to the west, where the thickest clumps of trees are to be found in the **"Wonderland of Rocks"**. The interesting rock formations were shaped by the huge pressure and high temperatures under which the gneiss was forced up out of the earth many millions of years ago. There are also rocks of whitish and reddish quartz which, as magma, i.e. in a molten state, forced itself into the metamorphic rock and solidified.

Advice Several roads run through the territory – the two entrance points at opposite sides are only 60 km (37 mi.) from one another so deciding which to take is no great problem for the tourist. Only in summer must you be equipped for the heat, which often exceeds 40°C. Apart from the two entrances, there is water only in Indian Cove Ranger Station west of Twenty Nine Palms, and in Blackrock Campground not far from Yucca Valley in the extreme west of the park. There are no filling stations in the

The Joshua tree calls to mind the prophet's outstretched arms

whole of the Joshua Tree National Monument, but you can obtain fuel in the surrounding towns – Twenty Nine Palms, Joshua Tree, Yucca Valley and Indio.

In contrast to the rest of the park area, there are some motels and restaurants in these towns. However, as a precautionary measure you should take a supply of water with you.

In mild temperatures **walks** along the numerous trails and paths can be enjoyed. Especially worthwhile are walks in Hidden Valley, along the Cap Rock Natural Trail, and the 3 km (2 mi.) long path on Mount Ryan (beautiful view).

Laguna Beach   Q 3

Orange County
Altitude: 12 m (40 ft)
Population: 23,000

Laguna Beach, located on the US 1 below Newport Beach (see entry), stretches for more than 8 km (5 mi.) along the Pacific Ocean and must be one of the most beautiful places in California. There are bays, both small and large, lovely beaches, parks on the cliffs overlooking the sea, and a charming town centre with numerous boutiques, craft shops and interesting inns. In the sixties the hippies settled in Laguna Beach but soon disappeared from the scene. The disasterous fire of autumn 1993 (see History) reduced more than 300 of the town's buildings to rubble and ashes.

Many **events** are held here throughout the year, such as the six-week-long Festival of Arts and Pageant of the Masters in July and August, and the Sawdust Festival at about the same time (sale of objets d'art and craft items).

The regional museum, the Laguna Beach Museum of Art (307 Cliff Drive) houses a considerable variety of exhibits and paintings and sculptures by Orange County artists. Open Tue.–Sun. 11.30am–4.30pm.

The Laguna Moulton Playhouse theatre, 606 Laguna Canyon Drive, stages plays for almost the whole year.

★Lake Tahoe   G/H 5

Lake Tahoe, the larger part of which lies in eastern California and the smaller part in the US federal state of Nevada, is considered to be one of the most beautiful of mountain lakes and thanks to its immediate sur-roundings is one of the favourite winter sports regions. It covers an area of 518 sq. km (200 sq. mi.), lies about 1900 m (6200 ft) above sea level and is up to 490 m (1600 ft) deep. With a length of 34.5 km (21 mi.), and a width of up to 19 km (12 mi.), it is one of the largest lakes in California. Located about 320 km (200 mi.) from San Francisco, and 160 km (100 mi.) from Sacramento, you can reach it by taking the US 80 as far as Truckee (see entry), where you change to the CA 89 or 267 southbound, and in about 24 km (15 mi.) you come to the bank of the lake. The CA 28 leads around the north of the lake, and the US 50 around the south. From time to time, both roads offer splendid views of the lake. Lake Tahoe is com-pletely surrounded by mountains, from the Sierra Nevada in the west to the Carson mountains in the east. Many peaks are more than 3000 m (10,000 ft) high; thousands of mountain streams empty into the lake. The

The lovely Lake Tahoe in the Sierra Nevada is a popular holiday area all year round

Lake Tahoe in winter

best known is Eagle Creek, which plunges over the waterfall of the same name into Emerald Bay, 1460 m (500 ft) below in the south-west of the lake. A dozen public beaches as well as sailing and motor boats (to be seen in great numbers at weekends in particular) provide the visitor with many opportunities for recreation.

History The first white people to set eyes on Lake Tahoe in 1844 were Charles Frémont, later a Civil War general, and his German cartographer Charles Preuss. Frémont named it Lake Bonpland (in honour of a French botanist who had accompanied Alexander von Humboldt on his Latin-American expeditions). A decade later the name of the lake was changed to Lake Bigler; after a further decade it was changed yet again to Lake Tahoe. This comes from the word "da'au", which means "water" or "lake" in the language of the Washoe Indians. This change of name was not officially recognised until 1945, when a decree to that effect was issued by the Californian parliament.

The **climate** at Lake Tahoe is moderately warm in summer but extremely cold in the winter months. Average temperatures for the four seasons are: spring 3°C., summer 16°, autumn and winter 7°. While the annual rainfall amounts to about 25 mm (1 in.), the average annual depth of snow is some 5 m (16 ft).

The Resort On the north bank of the lake (in the townships of King's Beach, North Tahoe, Crystal Bay and Incline) no high-rise dwellings may be built; North Tahoe possesses an amphitheatre, where concerts are held and Shakespeare dramas performed every year in the second half of August.

On the west bank lie the townships of Tahoe City, Sunnyside and Homewood, whilst the south bank is taken up completely by South Lake Tahoe. This thickly populated district has the most motels, hotels and restaurants of all the lake-side places; it is only a stone's throw from here to Nevada.

The town of Stateline, which almost imperceptibly joins South Lake Tahoe, is the site of numerous hotels with 24-hour casinos (Caesar's, Harrah's and Harvey's). Here every day thousands of people throng round the gaming machines, colloquially known as "one-armed bandits". Watching is almost as much fun as actually playing.

Also in South Lake Tahoe you will find the Lake Tahoe **Historical Society Museum** (3058 US 50), with displays of artefacts, photos and documents reflecting the history of the area from early times onwards.

Tours Trips can be made round the lake on the "Tahoe Queen" from South Lake Tahoe and the "Dixie" from Zephyr Cove, Nevada; half-day trips in the big motor boats from Sand Harbor, and North Tahoe Cruises from North Tahoe. Cable-car trips from Heavenly Valley also start at South Lake Tahoe (from the US 50, turn into Ski Run Boulevard and look for the sign "Top of the Tram". From a height of 2540 m (8300 ft) you can enjoy a panoramic view of the lake, although the viewing platform is very small.

Winter sports Heavenly Valley is only one of the many ski-resorts near Lake Tahoe. The others are: Squaw Valley, 11 km (7 mi.) north-west of Tahoe City on the CA 89, from the middle of November to April; Alpine Meadows, 9.5 km (6 mi.) north-west of Tahoe City on the CA 89, from the middle of November to June; Homewood, 9.5 km (6 mi.) south of Tahoe City, on the CA 89, from November to April; Echo Summit, 13 km (8 mi.) west of South Lake Tahoe on the US 50, from mid November to mid April.

Somewhat further away lie Kirkwood, 48 km (30 mi.) south-west of South Lake Tahoe on the US 50, CA 89 and CA 88 roads, from November to May and Sierra Ranch, 19 km (12 mi.) south of South Lake Tahoe on the CA 89, from November to April. There are further winter-sports centres north-west of Lake Tahoe at Truckee (see entry).

★Lassen Volcanic National Park   D/E 4

This national park, located in the extreme south of the mountains with their waterfalls, and 427 sq. m (165 sq. mi.) in area, was founded in 1916 in order to protect Lassen Peak (3187 m (10,460 ft)), one of the few volcanoes in the USA which have become active in recent years (others being Mount St Helens in Washington State, and some in Alaska and Hawaii). As the southernmost link in a chain of mighty volcanoes, including Mount Baker, Mount Rainier, Mount Hood, the former Mount Mazama (Crater Lake) and Mount Shasta, it forms the impressive remains of the once higher, but now collapsed Mount Tehama, the cauldron of which has been filled by subsequent eruptions. Lassen Peak is named after its discoverer, the Danish pioneer and district governor Peter Lassen.

History Mount Lassen became active in May 1914, and continued to erupt sporadically until 1921. The biggest eruption occurred in 1915, when a mighty mushroom-shaped cloud rose to a height of 11 km (7 mi.). Lava spread to the south-west and north-east. On the south-west side of the mountain it flowed to a width of 300 m (1000 ft), cooled off and hardened. To the north-east, the lava flowed in great rivers and caused a lot of snow to melt. The flow, together with the remains of earlier eruptions, became an avalanche of mud, which rushed faster and faster down the valley. Fertile fields were buried under a blanket of mud up to 6 m (20 ft) deep. Three days later there was a fresh explosion,

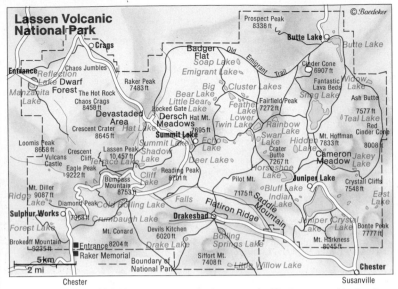

Chester   Susanville

which blew a new crater in the mountain. The lava poured in the direction of the avalanche of mud as it surged downhill. On its way it uprooted and crushed dozens of trees.

The most extensive and interesting **geothermal area** within the National Park is, without doubt, Bumpass Hell, below Lake Helen and reached by a footpath 1.6 km (1 mi.) in length. By means of easily negotiable wooden planks along a length of 1 km (½ mi.), you can observe from close quarters the land strewn with hot springs, volcanic gas-clouds (fumaroles) and bubbling whitish-grey mud-pots, over which an extremely intensive smell of sulphur pervades, and you can also feel it, for the high temperatures of some 100°C. heat up the whole area of Bumpass Hell. It got its name from its discoverer Kendall V. Bumpass, who walked into a thermal spring by mistake, and suffered such serious burns that he had to pay for his error with the loss of a leg.

Walks You can obtain information about the numerous tracks inside the park from the literature available in the Visitor Center. A favourite walk leads up to the peak of Mount Lassen, an easy route, but one completely lacking in shade, off the CA 89 near Lake Helen, with a climb of some 2600 to 3187 m (8500 to 10,500 ft). It will take about four hours to climb up and down. From the top of the mountain on a clear day you can see the 4317 m (14,168 ft)-high Mount Shasta to the north-west.

The entrance to the park, with a **Visitor Center**, is on the west side, not far from the junction of roads 44 and 89, and is about 70 km (44 mi.) from Redding (see entry). At the Visitor Center you can obtain plenty of literature and information about the places to visit.

The park is open only from the middle of June to the middle of October. The south entrance, which has no Visitor Center, remains open the rest of the year for access to the park's winter sports area only.

Seething mud in the Lassen National Park

★Lava Beds National Monument   C 5

In the extreme north-east of California in a thinly populated region seldom visited by tourists, extends the Lava Beds National Monument, founded in 1925 and covering an area of 186 sq. km (72 sq. mi.), with strange lava formations dating back thousands of years. It is only a few miles from the Oregon border and lies between the CA 139 and US 97. Barren heaps of ash, some more than 100 m (330 ft) high with steep craters, leave their mark on the landscape.

There are also more than 200 **caves** here, which provided hiding-places and also acted as small fortresses for the Modoc Indians in their last battles against the American army in the years 1872/1873. In spite of the far superior US forces, the Indians were able to hold out for six months. Some of the best-known caves bear descriptive names, such as Sentinel Cave, Catacombs Cave, Skull Cave (because so many skulls of mountain sheep were found there).

There is a camp-site in Indian Wells but no filling station inside the park. The **Visitor Center** is on the south side. Those wishing to explore the caves can do so with the aid of a plan. Torches are available from the Visitor Center free of charge and safety helmets can be hired for a small fee. There are slide shows in the Center during the Summer months.

Lompoc   N 1

Santa Barbara County

Lone Pine

Altitude: 32 m (105 ft)
Population: 40,000

Lompoc, not far from the mission station known as La Purissima
Concepcion (see entry for Mission Stations), lies in the valley of the
same name, which has its origin in the language of the Chumash Indians
who once lived there and, roughly translated, means "mussel mountain". Lompoc is only 16 km (10 mi.) from the Pacific coast, and can be
reached via the US 101.

Until a few years ago Lompoc was one of the important **flower-growing**
districts of California. Today the area used for horticulture has shrunk to
only 646 ha (1600 acres), as many individual houses have been built here
to accommodate the families of those employed at the Vandenberg air-
field only a few miles away. The flower festival is held in June every
year.

Lone Pine   L 5

Inyo County
Altitude: 1138 m (3740 ft)
Population: 1700

This little township, located on the CA 395, lies between Death Valley
Monument (see entry) 144 km (90 mi.) distant and the foot of Mount
Whitney, the highest mountain in North America, 21 km (13 mi.) away,
from where you can travel through the Alabama Hills (red sandstone
mountains of varying size). From Lone Pine – especially at sunrise –
there is a beautiful view of Mount Whitney and the neighbouring tall
peak of the western Sierra Nevada.
    In the previous century Lone Pine provided a living for the farmers
who had settled here, and later became the setting-off point for mountain tours. Conquering Mount Whitney, which was first climbed in 1873,
is a strenuous undertaking and takes at least three days, as the difference in level between Lone Pine and the Whitney peak is nearly 2000 m
(6500 ft).
    The Alabama Hills were the scene of fierce battles between Paiute
Indians, who were well able to hide out there, and the American troops.
Because of their colourful appearance these hills have provided the setting for many films.

Independence

The Eastern California Museum, in which can be seen Indian artefacts
and those from Lone Pine's pioneering period, is to be found in
Independence, the county town of Inyo County, some 26 km (16 mi.)
north on the CA 395 (open only Thu.–Sun.). Also in Independence can be
seen the so-called Commander's House, a beautiful Victorian building,
built for the commandant of Fort Independence (which no longer
stands), and was moved to its present site in 1889. It can be visited on
Sundays and on other days by prior telephone appointment.

★Long Beach   P/Q 3

Los Angeles County
Altitude: 9 m (30 ft). Population: 438,000

Bordering on Los Angeles to the south, Long Beach extends along San
Pedro Bay. The town was founded in 1881 under the name of Willmore
City by the Englishman W. E. Willmore as a summer resort for the inhab-

itants of Los Angeles. Its name was changed before the end of the nineteenth century to Long Beach, thus showing by its name that here there exists a beach averaging 150 m (490 ft) in width and over 9 km (5½ mi.) long.

With the construction of the harbour and the discovery of oil at the beginning of the 20th c., Long Beach became visibly urbanised, and today is the second largest town in Los Angeles County. Numerous important branches of industry have also become established here; particularly notable is the firm of aircraft manufacturers McDonnell-Douglas. A serious earthquake in 1933, which cost the lives of 120 people and caused damage amounting to 50 million dollars, slowed down development temporarily, but not for long.

Howard Hughes built the wooden flying boat which has a wing span of 298 ft (90 m) and is as high as a seven-storey block of flats.

Spruce Goose

As well as a large congress hall and museums, Long Beach can offer the visitor a sight of the legendary luxury line, the "Queen Mary", which has been converted into a hotel. After extensive restoration work the "Queen Mary", with its 365 cabins and three restaurants, has been made into a luxury hotel. Every half an hour a bus runs from the city centre to Pier J, where the ship lies at anchor.

★Queen Mary

The Aquarium of the Pacific at 310 Golden Shores, Rainbow Harbor, first opened in 1998. With more than 550 different species of fish and over 10,000 marine creatures from the Pacific it is one of the largest aquaria in the USA. An acrylic tunnel enables visitors to observe the fish at close quarters. Another tunnel leads through an artificial Alaskan glacier.

Aquarium of the Pacific

Also of interest is the Rancho Los Alamitos, dating from the year 1806 (6400 Bixby Hill Road), one of the oldest adobe-built houses in California. The furniture, however, is from a later date. Open Wed.–Sun. 1pm–5pm; admission free.

Rancho Los Alamitos

By the Pacific Ocean can be found the Long Beach Museum of Art (2300 Ocean Avenue Boulevard) with an impressive collection. Open Wed.–Sun. noon–5pm, admission free.

Long Beach Museum of Art

Trips round the harbour lasting 1½ hours leave daily from Pier J in the summer months. There are also **boat trips** to Santa Catalina Island (see entry).

At the bottom of Pine Street south of the Convention Center, a **harbour village** has been built along the coast in the style of the eighties of the previous century, with some 40 shops and restaurants.

Los Angeles P 3

Los Angeles County.
Altitude: 9,1530 m (30,5020 ft)
Population: 3,600,000; (Greater Los Angeles 15,500,000)

General

Los Angeles is the largest city in the federal state of California, and since 1984 the second largest in the United States, when it ousted Chicago from that position. This self-contained urban district, the sixth largest in the world, stretches for 160 km (100 mi.) from east to west 100 km (62 mi.) from north to south. It is located in the southern part of California and some suburbs are directly on the coast of the Pacific Ocean between the port of San Pedro and the San Gabriel mountain range on the landward side.

Expanse The city, which covered an area of 53 sq. km (20 sq. mi.) when it was legally constituted in 1850, has grown to 1200 sq. km (460 sq. mi.) in the course of 150 years, and thus in area is one of the largest cities in the world.

See map at end of book

Conurbation Greater Los Angeles incorporates more than 80 independent towns within the administrative district of Los Angeles County, ranging from the Santa Monica Hills in the west to Pomona in the east, and from the Tehachapi Mountains in the north to Long Beach in the south.

Megalopolis Los Angeles also includes Orange County in the south, Ventura County in the north as well as parts of Riverside County and San Bernardino County in the east. This socio-economic region is growing ever closer as a result of the continuous urbanisation of former agricultural districts.

The **administration** of this huge region is extremely complicated. In addition to the city corporation with a mayor elected every four years directly by the populace, and the assembly of city councillors, there is also the Board of Los Angeles County. This consists of five Supervisors, often called "five little kings", who are similarly elected every four years by an electoral district numbering 1.5 million inhabitants. They are responsible for public health, welfare institutions, building planning, fire brigade (but not the police), prisons and streets of the city as well as for the other 88 towns and the county's rural population numbering over two million.

Moreover, there is the largely autonomous Los Angeles **City School District** whose authority extends beyond the city precincts. Its members are directly elected and are independent of the other two administrative structures. Carrying out the decisions of the Board of Supervisors is the responsibility of a chief administrative officer nominated by this body.

Such a complicated bureaucratic structure pre-supposes a high measure of co-operation between those holding office, but conflicts are inevitable. One man who was successful for years in heading this multilayered conglomerate was the mayor **Tom Bradley**, a former black Los Angeles police chief. He was appointed mayor in 1976, and was re-elected four times. The present mayor is Richard Riordan.

Population

Like most Californian towns Los Angeles developed only slowly at the outset. In the year 1785, four years after it was founded, it had a total of 139 inhabitants, and even in 1890 there were only 50,000 compared with 300,000 in San Francisco. The number doubled by 1900 and again by 1905, when the census showed 200,000 people. In the following nine decades the population increased more than seventeenfold.

Growth In contrast to most other large towns and cities in the USA, the population of Los Angeles has continued to increase, mainly due to the influx of people into the suburbs, especially the San Fernando Valley. However, the decline in population in the inner city (Downtown Los Angeles) has been halted in recent years.

The city has received an influx of US citizens from other parts of the United States, attracted by the sun, the economic boom and the increasing prosperity.

Immigrants from neighbouring Mexico, from other Latin-American countries and Asia have also contributed to the population explosion. So today in Los Angeles you will find Buddhist temples and Chinese super-markets, Korean billiard halls and Armenian mamoul bakeries, Mexican clinicas and yerbarias (fruit and vegetable shops), Vietnamese acupunc-ture clinics and Guatemalan love-potions.

The 1990 population figures show that whites still make up just over a third (37.5%) of the total. The proportions of Latins (35.8%), who by the year 2000 will be the strongest population group, and Asians (about 12%) have risen dramatically while Afro-Americans remain the smallest minority (14.5%).

As in most US cities the various ethnic groups live predominantly in different quarters of Los Angeles – Latins Downtown and in districts east and south-east of the city centre, Blacks mainly in ghettos with a high rate of crimes of violence to the south and south-west of Downtown – the South Central district hit the headlines in 1992 as a result of the race riots there. Asians are found in Chinatown, Little Tokyo and Koreatown, and the majority of Whites in suburbs such as Beverly Hills, Pacific Palisades, Westwood or Santa Monica.

In line with the multiplicity of races, all **religions** are represented in Los Angeles. The city is the seat of a Catholic archbishop; the principal church in his diocese is the St Vibiani Cathedral (south Main Street, corner of 2nd Street). There are also several Greek and Russian Orthodox communities, the second largest Jewish community in the United States after New York, one of the biggest Mormon temples, with a 78 m (256 ft) high tower crowned by a gilded sculpture of an angel almost 5 m (16 ft) high (10777 Santa Monica Boulevard), as well as churches of all the Protestant sects represented in the USA.

Transport and communications

Los Angeles has no natural **harbour**. However, in San Pedro, 40 km (25 mi.) from Downtown Los Angeles, there was already a little harbour in the 1850s, providing an anchorage for sailing-ships. No start was made in extending it until the turn of the century, when a rail connection between Los Angeles and San Pedro came into being. When, following the merging of various districts, a land corridor developed between the harbour and Los Angeles, San Pedro was officially declared the port of Los Angeles in 1909. With neighbouring Wilmington and Terminal Island (where there was feverish ship-building during the Second World War) it developed into one of the five largest ports in the United States. Today it is the biggest fishing-port in the whole country.

Airports The International Airport at Inglewood, known as "LAX", is one of the largest in the country, used by more than 51 million passengers each year. Around 56 airlines, including British Airways, LTU and most American lines operate services to the airport.
Transport from the airport:

The municipal bus company Metropolitan Transit Authority (MTA) runs a number of buses to various parts of the Los Angeles conurbation.

Because of the distance from the airport to the city, a taxi is very expensive.

The hotels near the airport offer a free pick-up service with minibuses running all the time (from the hotel/motel – telephones available near the luggage reclaim).

A number of private transport companies also offer minibus services (Airport shuttles) to and from the city's hotels (reasonable prices). Details are obtainable from the "Ground Transportation" information desks run by particular airlines (keep an eye open for the signs once through the arrival gate!).

Los Angeles
International Airport *LAX*

All the major car-rental chains, such as Hertz, Avis, Budget, Alamo have a branch office at the airport (see Practical Information: Car rental).

In addition to the main LAX airport, there are a further six regional airports in the Greater Los Angeles area, namely in Burbank, Newport Beach (see entry: John Wayne Orange County Airport), Long Beach (see entry), Ontario, Santa Monica (see entry: Municipal Airport) and Van Nuys.

Rail As almost everywhere in the United States of America, railway traffic has lost much of its importance in Los Angeles. Apart from the daily rush-hour traffic from the suburbs into the city centre, the only line of any importance is to San Diego (see entry) and Oakland/San Francisco (see entry).

Long-distance services are available from the **Greyhound coach** station at 1716 E. Street in Downtown (the company also has stopping places in other parts of the city).

Buses Until the first section of the underground was opened between Downtown Los Angeles and Long Beach in 1990 (see below), all public transport in the city was by bus. At the latest count there were some 200 routes, running from Downtown to all the distant parts of the metropolitan district. The system of the MTA (Los Angeles County Metropolitan Transit Authority) bus company is so complicated that the tourist is unlikely to spend long enough in the city to become familiar with it.

Buses also run to the major tourist attractions nearby, such as Disneyland (see Anaheim), Universal Studios or Knott Berry Farm (see Buena Park). However, there are problems if the tourist is not setting out from the city centre because the buses all start in Downtown. In such a case you should obtain the timetables of the most important routes from, for example, the Greater Los Angeles Visitors and Convention Bureau (685 S. Figueroa Street. If in doubt telephone MTA direct, where you can obtain the information you require throughout the day and night (425 S. Main St., L.A., tel. (213) 6264455). You must have the right money ready, because the drivers cannot give change.

The **"Dash"minibuses** which ply within the city centre can be recommended without reservation. These little grey buses run at 5 to 20 minute intervals to places of interest, such as the Music Center, Little Tokyo, Chinatown, the Pueblo de Los Angeles State Historic Park and a number of hotels. The fare is only 25 cents. One disadvantage is that the minibuses run only on Monday to Friday until about 6.30pm.

Because of the distances involved, **taxis** are expensive and often difficult to find outside the Downtown area, so it is necessary to order one by telephone. There are plenty of taxis to be found at all places where there are a lot of people (airports, big hotels downtown, railway stations), as well as in Hollywood and Beverly Hills.

The first section of the planned 300 mile-long network of **underground** and tram services was opened in 1990 between Downtown and Long Beach (Blue Line). The Red Line stretch of the underground from Union Station in Downtown to Westlake/MacArthur Park (corner of Wilshire/Alvarado Boulevard) and Western Avenue is to be extended to Hollywood. It is planned to build a line to Universal Studios in the northern part of Hollywood in the year 2001. The Green Line runs from Norwalk in East Los Angeles to El Segundo near the international airport.

The subject of much controversy, the motorways, known as **"freeways"** in the USA, because there are no tolls to pay, are used by almost 4½ million people (not cars) in the course of 24 hours, and cover a total distance of approximately 925 km (580 mi.). Although traffic is extremely heavy in the rush-hours (7am–9am and 4pm–7pm), without the freeways it would be almost impossible to get around. The city has the ten busiest motorway junctions in the USA.

Downtown Los Angeles is surrounded by four freeways: the Santa Monica Freeway, which then becomes the San Bernardino Freeway and links Santa Monica in the west with San Bernardino in the east (US 110);

The Pasadena and Harbor Freeway, linking Pasadena in the north-east with San Pedro in the south (CA 11);

The Golden Gate and Santa Ana Freeway, which runs from Sacramento in the north to San Diego in the south (US 5);

The Hollywood Freeway, which is part of the great north-south coastal route, the US 101.

There are also the following freeways: Glendale (CA 2), Long Beach (CA 7), Ventura (CA 134), Foothill (US 210), Pomona (CA 60), Marina Del Rey (CA 90) and San Gabriel River (US 605). Completed in 1993, Century Freeway runs from L.A. International Airport east to Norwalk.

Before you use a freeway you should consult a map to ascertain the correct exit to take, in order to avoid having to use a road with a high crime rate.

Culture

At one time, the paucity of cultural life in the city gave rise to jokes, such as "What is the difference between Los Angeles and yoghourt?" Answer: "Yoghourt has an active culture!". This has now been rectified long since and after a late start Los Angeles has caught up with San Francisco, the traditional cultural capital of California, and is well on the way to overtaking it.

Today, Los Angeles possesses a **Music Center**, with three large auditoria, one for opera, musicals and concerts, the other two for theatre. Several concert halls were recently added. There are also fifteen to twenty smaller theatres in all parts of the city.

The **museums**, although mainly of recent date, have achieved world ranking thanks to donations from a number of prosperous citizens. In addition to the museums in Los Angeles, there are others in the immediate vicinity: the J. Paul Getty Museum in Malibu (see entry: the large

Getty Center museum complex at Brentwood Hills in Los Angeles opened in 1997), the Norton Simon Museum in Pasadena (see entry) and the Huntington Library and Gardens in San Marino (see entry for Pasadena).

Light entertainment is provided by a large number of cabarets, jazz and rock-bars. In addition, Los Angeles, together with Hollywood, is still the film capital of the world and numerous premières are screened here.

Los Angeles has about 30 **universities and colleges** within the city precincts. There are at least twice as many more in the neighbouring towns. The best-known institutions of higher education include the biggest university of the state, the University of California in Los Angeles (UCLA), together with its School of Medicine. There are also the University of Southern California, Occidental College, Los Angeles City College and Yeshiva University.

Because of the risk of earthquakes, **skyscrapers** were not built until quite recently. For many years the City Hall, built in 1932 with 27 storeys, was the tallest building in the city. Only after it became possible to erect earthquake-proof buildings did a real building boom take place. Nevertheless, as far as the number and height of skyscrapers is concerned, Los Angeles cannot compare with San Francisco, perhaps not even with San Diego. The tallest buildings, all located downtown, are:

First Interstate World Center (1989) – 305 m (1000 ft)
First Interstate Bank (1973) –257 m (843 ft)
Gas Company Tower (1991) – 221 m (725 ft)
Security Pacific National Bank (1973) – 222 m (728 ft)
Cocker Bank (1982) – (218 m (715 ft)
777 Tower (1991) – 215 m (705 ft)
Sanwa Bank Plaza (1991) – 214 m (702 ft)
Atlantic Richfield Towers (ARCO; 1971) – 210 m (689 ft)

Economy

In contrast to San Francisco Los Angeles, thanks mainly to the discovery of oil and the development of the aircraft industry, has become since the Second World War more of an industrial than a commercial city. Admittedly the skyscrapers of the banks dominate the downtown skyline – the old-established banks of Wells Fargo, Bank of America, Bank of California and United California have been joined in recent years by US branches of Japanese banks – but the stock exchange is of secondary importance. Los Angeles has noticeably become a city of service industries, thus creating new jobs in that sector. It is now the second most important financial centre in the USA.

As a result of the continuing building boom the construction industry has also contributed to keeping the unemployment rate low in spite of the many new immigrants.

The **film industry**, which employed about 100,000 people in 1950 (by 1995 there were about 150,000) and made Los Angeles – or, more exactly, Hollywood – the "film capital of the world", has lost out mainly to television. Today more television films than feature films are made in Hollywood, Burbank and Universal City. Nevertheless, there are still several hundred firms working in the field of producing and selling films, so that Hollywood remains the leading light in the entertainment industry worldwide.

History

On orders from the Mexican viceroy, the Portuguese Joan Rodriguez Cabrillo discovers California and lands in October at San Pedro, which today forms part of Los Angeles, and at Santa Monica.	1542

Gaspar de Portola, the first Spanish governor of California, names a river near where the city stands today El Rio de Nuestra Se nora La Reina de Los Angeles de Porciuncula. — 1769

22 men, 11 women and 11 children are the first inhabitants of Los Angeles, founded on 4th September, or, as it was named at the time, El Pueblo de Nuestra Se nora La Reina de Los Angeles de Porciuncula. — 1781

Los Angeles now has 185 inhabitants, mainly engaged in agriculture and cattle-raising. — 1785

The population has grown to 500. — 1786

Grapes and olives are planted for the first time, followed by hops ten years later. — 1795

A start is made on building a church on the plaza. It is finished in 1822. — 1816

Los Angeles has a population of around 1000 "gente de razon" (non-Indians, most of whom are mulattos and mestizos) as well as some 500 Indians. — 1821

Los Angeles is raised by the Mexicans to the rank of ciudad (city) and in a short time becomes the capital of Alta California. — 1835

On 13th August Governor Pio Pico surrenders in Los Angeles to the US forces under Robert F. Stockton and John Charles Frémont.
After both have left the city there is a revolt against the US military government, and the Americans are driven out. — 1836

Los Angeles is re-conquered; the capitulation in Cahuenga signals the defeat of the Californios and with it the ceding of Alta California to the United States. — 1847

The emergence of the state leads to the establishment of Los Angeles County. — 1850

"Los Angeles Star" is the first newspaper, appearing weekly. — 1851

The population has grown to 4485, and comprises 1% of the total population of the state. — 1860

The brothers Isaiah and Samuel Hellman from Bavaria found the first bank in Los Angeles (Hellman's First Bank). — 1865

Xenophobia leads to a massive attack on the Chinese; 15 Chinese are publicly hanged. — 1871

Introduction of obligatory elementary education.
Opening of the first high school (corner of Broadway and Temple Street). — 1873

The University of California is founded by the Episcopal Church on its present site.
   The population is almost 12,000 (compared with 233,000 in San Francisco). — 1880

Los Angeles

1881	The "Los Angeles Times" appears for the first time.
1885	The Santa Fe Railroad reaches Los Angeles.
1887	The Occidental College is set up by Presbyterian clergy and laymen. The oldest and most respected club in California, the California Club, is founded.
1889	Founding of Orange County, formerly a part of Los Angeles County.
1890	50,395 people live in Los Angeles.
1892	Edward L. Doheny discovers oil near Los Angeles, leading to an economic boom.
1893	Stephen M. White from Los Angeles is the first white man born in California to become a federal senator.
1895	Charles F. Lummis founds the Landmarks Club, with the aim of restoring the mission stations and other historic monuments.
1900	The population has risen to 102,000. Founding of the Automobile Club of Southern California.
1901	The founding of the Pacific Railway Company makes it possible to have a tram network in the county, by constructing tramlines to Pasadena, Long Beach and other places.

1906	Founding of Beverly Hills.
	  First film studio built.
	  First sailing-ship race (Los Angeles–Honolulu).

1909	The number of oil-drilling derricks has increased to 109. Through a merger of smaller firms, the Southern Californian Edison Co. is set up providing electric power to 14 counties.
1910	The population, numbering 319,000, is only 100,000 below that of San Francisco.
1911	Construction of the first film studio in Hollywood.
1912	One of the first museums, the Southwest Museum, is formed, dealing mainly with the history and culture of the Indians.
1917	The banker Hubert C. Eaton begins to lay out Forest Lawn Cemetery, the best known cemetery in California.
1919	Founding of the University of California in Los Angeles (UCLA) as a branch of the University of California.
1920	For the first time, the population of Los Angeles is higher than that of San Francisco (576,673 compared with 506,676).
1921	Simon Rodia begins to build the tower named after him in the Watts quarter of the city.
1922	Opening of the Hollywood Bowl. The building economy has a unprecedented boom creating sufficient living space for the population which is increasing by almost 100,000 people per annum.
1927	The "Los Angeles Open" golf tournament comes into being.

Regular air services between Los Angeles and San Francisco.

The Academy of Motion Picture Arts and Sciences awards the Oscar film prize for the first time. 1929

The population exceeds the million mark: 1,238,000 inhabitants are counted. 1930

Olympic Games in Los Angeles. 1932

A serious earthquake in Long Beach, which claims 120 lives and causes heavy damage, is also felt in Los Angeles. 1933

Heavy rainfall in one of the driest areas of North America causes serious flooding in Los Angeles and its surroundings. 1934

The first freeway comes into use (Pasadena Freeway); others follow in the next few years. The population growth is slowed down, but not stopped, by the economic slump felt throughout America. 1940

The number of workers employed in aircraft factories in and around Los Angeles increased twelvefold, from 20,000 to 243,000, in the years 1940–43. 1943

The demobilisation of thousands of soldiers and sailors, who fought on the Pacific Front and are now living in Los Angeles, leads to an unprecedented housing shortage until the wartime economy is converted to a peacetime one. 1946

The number of inhabitants has increased to almost 2 million (1,970,000). 1950

The Brooklyn Dodgers baseball team moves to Los Angeles. 1956

The population reaches the 2½ million mark. 1960

The Cultural Heritage Board is set up. Its task is to protect city buildings of historical or cultural importance by making them listed buildings. 1962

The Music Center, with the three auditoria named Dorothy Chandler Pavilion, Ahmanson Theater and Mark Taper Forum, is opened. 1964

Serious riots in the Watts quarter of the city; 34 dead, 1000 injured and almost as many arrests. Opening of the Los Angeles County Museum of Art. 1965

The population has increased to 2,809,000. 1970

A serious earthquake in the San Fernando Valley belonging to Los Angeles (6⁻6 on the Richter scale) claims lives and causes great damage. 1971

The second year without rain causes a very serious drought and leads to water rationing. 1977

Floods in and around Los Angeles and resultant landslides cause heavy damage. 1978

For the third time within a few years heavy rainfall in the months of January and February leads to floods. 1982

The Summer Olympics are held in Los Angeles for the second time. 1984

Under the law all buildings within the area of the geological faults along the Pacific Coast must be made earthquake-proof by 1990. 1986

The Museum of Contemporary Art opens near the Music Center.

1987   Opening of the first shopping centre in the inner city (Seventh Market Place, Figueroa Street, between 7th and 8th Avenue).

1988   Opening of the Gene Autry Western Heritage Museum in Griffin Park.
Permission to build a new concert hall, Walt Disney Concert Hall, in the Music Center.
Plans are drawn up for the complete restoration of the old town (Pueblo Historic Park).

1989   The US Environmental Protection Agency determines to make Los Angeles one of the cleanest cities in the world by 2008.
The package includes 120 individual measures (including the planting of two million trees within the next few years) and will cost 2000 dollars per head of the population. The number of cars should be reduced and the release of emissions which contribute to global-warming should also be reduced.

1990   The first stage of the city's planned Metro and urban rail network, a 22 mile-long stretch between Long Beach and Downtown Los Angeles, comes into operation. Meanwhile work progresses on a further two sections which should help reduce rush-hour traffic congestion in this "city of the automobile".
A short time before he dies, Armand Hammer opens the museum of art bearing his name, where the multi-millionaire's extensive private collection is displayed (10899 Wilshire Blvd.).

1992   The acquittal of the defendants – four white policemen – in the Rodney King trial, triggers violent racial unrest in South Central, Los Angeles's black ghetto. Riots leave many dead and injured as well as widespread damage to property. The trial follows an incident in the previous year when Rodney King, a black man, was beaten almost to death after being stopped by the accused for speeding.

1993   The city is threatened by bush fires which break out in the Los Angeles area.
The newly opened "Museum of Tolerance – Beit Hashoah" (Hebrew for "House of the Holocaust") provides a memorial to all victims of genocide, including the Armenians, Indians and Jews.

1994   Following a severe earthquake (measuring 6.6 on the Richter Scale), the city is declared a disaster area; gas pipes, expressways, motorway fly-overs and more than a 100 homes are destroyed. The soccer World Championships are held in the USA (Los Angeles) for the first time.

1995   A spectacular trial, which has held TV viewers spellbound for months, ends in September with the acquittal of the black football star O.J. Simpson following a charge of murdering his white wife in a fit of jealousy.

1997   The Getty Center, the world's most expensive museum having cost one billion dollars to build, is ceremonially opened in Westwood and now houses the legendary Getty Collection, formerly on view in Malibu.

Sights from A to Z

Academy of Motion Picture Arts and Sciences

The Academy of Motion Picture Arts and Sciences (8949 Wilshire Boulevard) was founded in 1927. This institution became famous as a result of the Oscar film award-giving ceremonies held there. Since Emil Jannings received an Oscar for his star rile in the film "The Way of All Flesh" it has been awarded annually in this building (see also Hollywood).

Temporary exhibitions are held continuously in the foyer. In addition, you can watch permanent showings of old films in one of the finest cinemas in the city; one of the most important film libraries is also available to the public. Open Mon., Tue., Thu. and Fri. 9am–5pm.

ARCO Plaza

One of the few shopping centres within the city proper, and also one of the oldest, is to be found very close to some large hotels (505 S. Figueroa Street). Here there are dozens of shops and restaurants. The shops are open daily 9.30am–5.30pm, the restaurants in the evening as well.

Worth seeing is the fountain sculpture, created by the Austrian architectural artist Herbert Bayer, which stands in front of the centre.

Armand Hammer Museum of Art

The billionaire Armand Hammer opened this art museum named after him (10899 Wilshire Road) shortly before his death in 1990. A large part of his private collection is on display, including works by Monet, Van Gogh, Constable and Picasso. After his death the collection came to the University of California, Los Angeles (UCLA). Open Tue.–Sat. 11am–7pm, Sun. until 9pm

Barnsdall Park

Located on a hill in eastern Hollywood surrounded by olive trees (488 Hollywood Boulevard), Barnsdall Park, measuring only 4 ha (10 acres) in area, offers some attractions such as the municipal art gallery and Barnsdall House, built in 1917 by the famous architect Frank Lloyd Wright for the oil heiress Aline Barnsdall, and typical of the building style of the period. Its ground plan resembles a flower. Guided tours: Tue.–Thu. 10am–1pm on the hour, Sat. noon–3pm also first three Sundays of each month.

Bel Air

Lying north of Westwood and west of Beverly Hills, having grown up during the twenties, Bel Air is one of the most elegant of urban districts, with very beautiful and expensive villas. The steeply climbing and winding roads can be negotiated only by car. In Stone Canyon Road stands the most expensive luxury hotel in Los Angeles, Bel Air. It is spaciously built in the Spanish mission style and stands in the middle of an idyllic park surrounded by the scent of bougainvillea, magnolias and avocado wood. The private atmosphere of this hotel, which has the appearance of a picturesque village with its arcades and colonnades, appeals to such famous guests as the Rockefellers and the Kennedys.

Beverly Hills

History Although an independent town with some 33,000 inhabitants, Beverly Hills is completely surrounded by the metropolitan area of the city of Los Angeles, and has grown so close to it that the tourist will

Los Angeles

Los Angeles Downtown

Hollywood — Dodger Stadium, Elysian Park

Mayan Theatre
Belasco Theater

CHINATOWN

Pasadena Freeway
Alpine St
College St
Broadway

Fort Moore Pioneer Memorial

EL PUEBLO

Pacific Stock Exchange

Music Center
Hall of Administration

Civic Center

Hall of Justice
Children's Museum

Union Station

Bunker Hill Towers
Walt Disney Concert Hall

County Court House

Hall of Records

World Trade Center

Federal Bldg.

Security Pacific Plaza

Museum of Contemporary Art

State Offices

City Hall

Atlantic Richfield Plaza

Wells Fargo Center

Wilshire Blv.

Wells Fargo Bldg.

California Plaza

Times & Mirror Square

Dep. of Transportation

Police Bldg.

Central Library

Grand Central Market

Crocker Plaza

Philharmonic Auditorium

Bradbury Bldg.

St. Vibiana's Cathedral

Japan. Village Plaza

Pershing Square

LITTLE TOKYO

Japanese Temple

Los Angeles Athletic Club

Embassy Auditorium

Bus Depot

Mayan Theatre/ Belasco Theater

GARMENT DISTRICT

Exposition Park, Coliseum, Convention Center

© Baedeker

500 m
0,25 mi

134

scarcely get the feeling that he is in a different borough. Located about 19 km (12 mi.) west of Downtown Los Angeles, Beverly Hills was first laid out in 1906 by a land speculator from Beverly Farms in Massachusetts (hence its name) in accordance with a plan whereby the streets would run at a 45° angle north from Wilshire Boulevard. However, the town developed only slowly, even after the Beverly Hills Hotel was built in 1912, and the census of 1920 showed the population to number only 674.

It was due entirely to the growing film industry that more and more film people settled in the wide tree-lined streets, and found it even more pleasing to possess plots of land in the hills at the foot of the Santa Monica mountains, where they built large villas. Pickfair (1143 Summit Drive), the house built by the husband and wife actors Douglas Fairbanks and Mary Pickford and where the actress lived in complete seclusion until her death in 1980, was from 1920 until 1935, when they separated, the social focal point of the film colony. Another particularly beautiful house is Greystone Mansion, which the oil millionaire Edward L. Doheny had built, and which for a time housed the America Film Institute.

Wealth Today, Beverly Hills is the richest town in America. 75 years ago the growing of beans brought it its first profits, then came the oil magnates and the film millionaires. The average annual income per family of £100,000 is four times more than the American average.

Beverly Hills is also the town of superlatives: here are the cleanest streets and the best-kept districts, the most modern fire-engines and most efficient waste disposal. 3000 private swimming pools, 250 private tennis courts, 140 jewellery shops, 214 first-class restaurants and a vast number of beauty salons, business and divorce lawyers and medical practices, mainly psychologists and psychiatrists, round off the picture of this town. The percentage of banks, saving banks and police is also higher than elsewhere in the United States.

Apart from the villas in the canyons and hills, the City Hall built in 1932 in the Spanish-Baroque style (corner of 450 N. Crescent Drive and Santa Monica Boulevard) and the nearby Beverly Hills Civic Center which is nearing completion, nowhere can one observe better the ambience of this town which simply radiates affluence than on Rodeo Drive, between Wilshire and Santa Monica Boulevards. In this, the most expensive shopping mile in the world and the meeting point of the international jet-set, can be found 50 or 60 luxury shops and restaurants.

Rodeo Drive

Beverly Hills has its own **laws**, which sometimes seem a bit strange. People walking through the villa-lined streets tend not to be viewed with favour. For one thing there are no pavements and, for another, a pedestrian looks suspicious. You must provide proof of identity when asked by the police to do so, to avoid being arrested for vagrancy. As an alternative to walking, some business-minded entrepreneurs offer jogging tours through the attractions of "Billionaires' Hill". Since 1987 smoking has been prohibited in all restaurants (except hotel-restaurants), although you can still continue to enjoy a cigarette a few streets away in the restaurants of Los Angeles.

The size of shop signs is also legally controlled, as everything which smacks of money – such as advertising posters which are usually so conspicuous everywhere else – is prohibited. There are also special regulations relating to car parking at night.

The Museum of Tolerance south of Beverley Hills (9786 West Pico Blvd.) first opened in 1993. Multimedia-based, interactive exhibits portray the history of racism, beginning with the persecution of the Jews under the Third Reich up to the Civil Rights Movement in the USA. The Hebrew name of the museum, "Beit Hashoah" (House of the Holocaust) serves

Museum of Tolerance

Panorama of Los Angeles

as a reminder of the murders not only of Jews but also Armenians and Indians. Open Mon.–Thu. 10am–4pm, Fri. 10am–3pm, Sun. 11am–4pm.

Biltmore Hotel

This hotel (506 S. Grand Avenue), built in 1923 and renovated several times since, the last time in 1986, is in the Renaissance style and has been a listed building since 1969. Although the immediate vicinity of the hotel, especially Pershing Square which is frequented mainly by the

homeless, no longer retains its former elegance, this has not damaged
the hotel's reputation, since in 1986 the main entrance was moved from
S. Olive Street, directly on Pershing Square, to Grand Avenue at the
back. The foyers preserved in the Spanish style are impressive as is the
Biltmore Bowl banqueting hall, seating 1500.

Bradbury Building

This house (304 South Broadway), commissioned by Louis Bradbury

The Plaza in the heart of Chinatown

in 1893 and today used as offices, has been a listed building since 1962. From the outside it appears quite plain. The interior, however, is a surprise with its open staircases and an interior courtyard of four storeys lit from above, thus illuminating the richly decorated wrought-iron banisters and beautiful wood panelling. A lift, the oldest of its kind in Los Angeles, is still in use. Open Mon.–Sat. 9am–5pm.

Broadway

The original cinemas of previous decades, several of which still serve their original purpose, have become places of entertainment for the growing Hispanic population (known in Los Angeles as "latinos"), with mainly Spanish and Mexican films. Today Broadway has become the main shopping street of the latinos. Consequently it is loud and lively here, especially on Sundays, when all the shops are open.

Sights

On Broadway you will find the interesting and very reasonable Clifton Cafeteria (608 S.), as well as more cinemas, the oldest of which are the Cameo (528 S.) and the Arcade (534 S.), both built in 1919. The Palace (611 S.) dates from 1913, the Rialto (810 S.) from 1917, and the richly decorated Million Dollar, in which Sid Graumann began his career, from 1918. All the others were built in the twenties and early thirties and are mainly typical of the American film palaces of the time both internally and externally. Examples are Loew's State (1921; 703 S. Broadway), the Orpheum (842 S.) and the United Artists (933 S.) both dating from 1926, the Tower (1927; 802 S.), the Los Angeles (1931; 615 S.) and the Roxie (1932; 518 S. Broadway).

The whole cinema district is under a preservation order.

Bunker Hill

Bunker Hill, not far from the present Civic Center, was where the well-to-do Angelenos lived in their Victorian houses at the turn of the century. In 1901 an open cable-railway, modelled on that in San Francisco, was constructed to make it easier for the residents to climb the eastern part of its hill, and which during the brief period of its existence earned the name "Angel's Flight".

As a result of the California Plaza building project this short steep stretch of railway came into operation again in 1996. In the fifties and sixties all the Victorian houses were demolished to make the land available for new purposes.

Since then several residential skyscrapers (the first in 1964) have been built on Bunker Hill near the Music Center and the Museum of Contemporary Art with two multi-storey office blocks in glass and granite, a block of apartments and an amphitheatre. In course of construction are a shoppong centre, restaurants and an underground railway station. At midday and sometimes in the evenings open-air concerts and other musical events are held on the California Plaza.

Dash minibuses run to Bunker Hill.

California Afro-American Museum

This very new museum in Exposition Park (600 State Drive, by the Harbor Freeway) offers numerous exhibits of the history, culture and art of the Afro-Americans and negroes in North and South America. Open Tue.–Sun. 10am–5pm.

California State Museum of Sciences and Industry

This museum, which is also located in Exposition Park (700 State Drive) houses a large number of exhibits which you can operate yourself – therefore a special favourite of children. Of particular interest is a newly installed earthquake exhibition which explains the causes and effects and the action to be taken. Films worth seeing are shown each day in the MAX Theater. Open daily 10am–5pm.

The famous Californian architect Frank Gehry designed the Californian Museum of Science and Industry **Aerospace Hall** (700 State Drive) in 1984. Of particular note are some historic aircraft.

Chinatown

There are neither as many Chinese living in Los Angeles as in San Francisco, nor is their quarter (in Block 800 of North Broadway, north of Downtown, and in the side streets) as interesting or as old as Grant Avenue in San Francisco. The Chinese, who could be found in Los Angeles as long ago as the fifties and sixties of the previous century, were initially domiciled in the area where Union Station now stands. When construction of the station began the district forming the present-day Chinatown was made available to the community.

The centre of Chinatown is the Plaza (951 N. Broadway) with restaurants, banks and numerous shops, some of which are built in the pagoda style. Many Vietnamese also live in Chinatown today and Vietnamese shop-signs are to be seen in many shopping centres.

The prosperous Chinese from Taipei and Hong Kong have turned their backs on Chinatown and moved to the suburbs, particularly to Monterey Park and Alhambra (both to the north of the city centre), where Chinese enclaves, with typical supermarkets, restaurants, bookshops and newsagents, have grown up.

★City Hall

When it was built in 1926–28, the City Hall (located in the middle of the Civic Centre at 200 N. Spring Street) was the first building to exceed the maximum height of thirteen storeys which was permitted at that time. As this building regulation was not revoked until 1957, it required a special public referendum before the City Hall could be built to a height of 27 storeys. The eclectic-monumental building style can be attributed mainly to its pyramid-shaped tower and the Egyptian, Greek and Roman elements. From the veranda of the 27th floor there is a beautiful view over Los Angeles and the surrounding mountains, especially when the weather is clear and smog-free; unfortunately, however, the 1994 earthquake caused considerable damage to the building and as a result there is no admission to the viewing platform at present. Upon entering the City Hall you are greeted by a hologram portrait of the former mayor Tom Bradley. Inside there is no lack of fine building materials. A tiled dome above the entrance rotunda and all kinds of marble pillars are examples of the luxurious way this building is furbished. Open daily from 10am–4pm.

Civic Center

In the Civic Center near the City Hall can be found the following administrative buildings: Hall of Records (320 West Temple Street), built in 1961 by the Viennese Richard Neutra (Open Mon.–Fri. 8am–5pm); the Criminal Courts Building (210 West Temple Street), built in 1925, the seat of several state and municipal courts (Open Mon.–Fri. 8am–4.30pm); the Federal Courthouse building (312 N. Spring Street), seat of the federal district court, built in 1940 in the New Functionalistic style of the period; the Parker Center (155 N. Los Angeles Street), built in 1955, and the Los Angeles police headquarters, named after a former police chief.

★El Pueblo de Los Angeles State Historic Park

The park is bordered by Alameda Street in the south, Sunset Boulevard and N. Spring Street in the east and north, and by the Hollywood Freeway in the west. Somewhere in the grounds – exactly where nobody knows – Los Angeles was founded by a small group of settlers at the behest of the King of Spain. It was not until 1953 that an effort was made to restore the 27 historic buildings. Eleven of them are open to the public, five were turned into museums.

Avila Adobe

Avila Adobe, the house of the mayor (alcalde) at the time, was built in the Adobe style in 1818. After being in the possession of his family for 40 years, it had a chequered history. After an earthquake in 1971 it was fully restored and fitted out to reflect the life style of a prosperous Spanish family of around 1840. Open Tue.–Fri. 10am–3pm, weekends 10am–4.30pm; admission free.

Church of Our Lady Queen of Angels

The Church of Our Lady Queen of Angels (535 N. Main Street) on the Plaza was built between 1818 and 1822, and today belongs to the archbishopric of Los Angeles. Originally constructed in the Adobe style, it has been restored and extended several times. Open 24 hours a day.

Masonic Hall

The Masonic Hall (416 N. Main Street) is one of the oldest temples of Freemasonry in the city (1858) and is still the meeting room of lodge no. 42. Nearby is a small museum. The single-storey building with a

Los Angeles: City Hall ▶

Over the "Moloch" by Helicopter

At Hollywood Burbank Airport we climb somewhat apprehensively into the twin-engined (safer!) helicopter belonging to KF Aviation (4411 Empire Ave., N. Hollywood; tel. (818) 2478687). The Burbank district of Hollywood at the entrance to the San Fernando Valley is today the headquarters of Warner Brothers and Columbia Pictures film studios and of the NBC television studio (all are open to visitors).

As soon as the doors are closed and we climb into the air the magic sounds of "Air Opera" drown the frightful noise of the propeller. It is a wonderful feeling to fly over L.A., the legendary city of artificial splendour. So many different assessments and prejudices circulate regarding this gigantic metropolis, the "Big Orange" in Southern California.

This conglomeration of over eighty individual towns, a veritable melting-pot of 14 million people of all cultures, has become an immense "moloch", ostensibly both faceless and heartless. On the horizon a sea of houses stretches way out of sight. The pall of haze which envelopes the city like a mysterious veil has given Los Angeles its nickname of "Smogville". Inverted weather conditions make the smog especially bad, and without the air-conditioning which operates round the clock during high summer it would be almost intolerable. The marked contrasts between rich and poor can also

be clearly seen from the air. On the hills to the west lie the magnificent villas with large park areas and swimming pools, owned by the "rich and beautiful" people living in the luxury suburbs of Beverly Hills and Bel Air. Here, too, the smog is not as oppressive as in the thickly populated downtown quarters. The social time-bomb which is ever present in these impoverished districts of the city last exploded in 1992 when serious racial riots broke out in the black ghetto of South Central.

With a total length of some 2000 km (1250 mi.), the ten-lane freeways wind their way like wide rivers through the urban landscape which covers an area larger than the Ruhr region of Germany. From the air the rolling columns of traffic look like a swarming anthill functioning in accordance with the Californian motto "motion is progress". To the city dwellers driving an automobile is both a pleasure and a passion in which they indulge for several hours every day covering the large distances involved. No wonder the new metro lines are poorly patronised.

The shadowy outlines of the ever-increasing numbers of skyscrapers in downtown L.A. tower in ghostly fashion above the sea of houses below. Office blocks up to 73 storeys in height, symbols of the massed power of financial and commercial enterprises, glisten in the late afternoon sun and remind one of the world of beautiful pretence as depicted by the film industry.

Other highlights spotted during the half-hour helicopter flight include Dodger Stadium, so popular with the fans of American football, the green oasis of Griffith Park with its observatory, Sunset and Hollywood Boulevards lined with palm trees and the sprawling Universal Film Studios.

wrought-iron balcony above is reminiscent of the Italian Renaissance.
Open Tue.–Fri. 10am–3pm admission free.

The Old Plaza Firehouse (by the Plaza) is a brick building dating from
1884, and at the time was an inn, boarding-house and shop. Today it
houses a museum, displaying fire-fighting equipment from the 19th c. as
well as photos of other old fire-stations. Open Tue.–Fri., 10am–3pm,
4.30pm at weekends.

Old Plaza
Firehouse

Pico House (430 Main Street) was built in 1869 by the last Mexican governor of California, Pio Pico, and is reminiscent in style of an Italian
palazzo. For many years it was the prime hotel in Los Angeles. It is now
a private house.

Pico House

Pelanconi House (17 W. Olvera Street) is one of the city's first brick-built
houses, and named after its second owner, the Italian Antonio
Pelanconi. This is also now a private house.

Pelanconi House

After the restoration of Old Los Angeles, Olvera Street was opened in
1930 as a Mexican market. In addition to market-stalls and shops, there
are many restaurants in the houses. The road bears the name of the first
judge in Los Angeles County, Agustin Olvera.

Olvera Street

El Pueblo de los Angeles Historic Monument

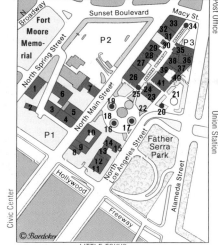

1 Brunswig Labo-
ratory (1924)
2 Beauty Bldg.
3 Brunswig
Annex (1897)
4 Vickrey/Bruns-
wig Building
(1883)
5 Plaza House
(1883)
6 Brunswig
Warehouse
(about 1912;
Juvenile Cours
Building)
7 Plaza Catholic
Church (1818
to 1822)
8 Masonic Hall
(1858)
9 Merced Theatre
(1870)
10 Pico House
(1869/70)
11 Garnier Building
(1890)
12 425 North Los
Angeles Street
(1898)
13 Turner Building
(1960)
14 Hellman/Quon
Building (1900)
15 Firehouse
(1884)

16 Founder's
Plaque
17 King Carlos III
of Spain
18 Plaza (1825 to
19 Felipe de Neve
20 Indian Garden
(1986)
21 Placita de
Dolores (1979)
22 Leo Politi Mural
(1978)
23 Biscailuz Building
(1926)
24 Plaza Metho-
dist Church
(1925/1926)
25 Olvera Street
Cross
26 Simpson/Jones
Building (1894)
27 Jones Building
(ca. 1880)
28 Machine Shop
(1910 to 1920)
29 Sepulveda
House (1887)
30 Pelanconi
House (1855
to 1857))
31 Hammel Building
(1909)
32 Siqueiros Mural
(1932)

33 Italian Hall
(1907/08)
34 Water Trough
(1930)
35 Path of Zanja
Madre
36 Old Winery (ca.
1870 to 1914)
37 El Pueblo Park
Offices (1914)

38 Old Winery (ca.
1870 to 1914) ;
El Paseo Inn)
39 Avila Adobe
(ca. 1818)
40 Park Offices
(Exhibits)
41 Plaza Sub-
station (1904)
P Parking

143

The **Visitor Center** is to be found in Sepulveda Building, which dates from the year 1887 (North Main Street. Here you can watch the film "Pueblo of Promise" about the early history of Pueblo. The Visitor Center is open Mon.–Sat. 10am–3pm.

★Farmers Market

The origin of the Farmers Market (Hollywood Freeway, Silver Lake exit) goes back to the year 1934 when, at the height of the economic depression, eighteen farmers got together and set up stalls on a piece of open land near Wilshire Boulevard (6333 West 3rd Street, corner of Fairfax Avenue) in order to sell their produce direct to the consumer. This experiment was so successful that Farmers Market kept on expanding. Today, in addition to more than 100 fruit, vegetable and food traders, there are no fewer than 20 restaurants and countless other specialist shops, some first class. Some days up to 40,000 people visit Farmers Market. Open Mon.–Sat. 9am– 7pm, Sun. 10am–6pm.

Forest Lawn Memorial Park

Scarcely any other city has so many "famous" cemeteries, and none is more famous than Forest Lawn (1712 South Glendale Avenue, Glendale), which is said to have more than a million visitors every year – a number exceeded by no other cemetery. Its founder Hubert Eaton acquired a small cemetery in 1917 and over the years converted it into a last resting place with the atmosphere more of a park than a cemetery. Leonardo da Vinci's "Last Supper" represented in a church window, can be seen in the "Memorial Court of Honor"; American history is conjured up in the "Court of Freedom", and a 5½ × 9 m (18 × 30 ft) mosaic repro-

duction of a famous painting shows the signing of the Declaration of Independence in 1776. You can see a copy of Michelangelo's larger than life sculpture of David, as well as a painting 29 m (95 ft) long × 13½ m (44 ft) wide of the "Crucifixion".

The graves are allowed to have only a simple plaque or sculpture, which must be passed by an art committee created specially for that purpose. In the words of its founder, "I want to establish a large park, without ugly monuments and other signs of death, but filled with tall flowers, the greenest of lawns, bubbling fountains and fine memorials".

Well-known film actors are buried here, including Clark Gable, Alan Ladd, W. C. Fields, Charles Laughton, Carole

Forest Lawn Memorial Park

Reconstructions of prehistoric animals from the tar craters of La Brea

Lombard, Jean Harlow, Errol Flynn, Humphrey Bogart, Spencer Tracy and Chico Marx, as well as numerous personalities from public life. Open daily 9am–5pm, in summer until 6pm. admission free.

Gene Autry Western Heritage Museum

This museum, opened in November 1988 in Griffith Park (4700 Zoo Drive, Ventura Freeway, exit to Victory Blvd./Zoo or Golden State Freeway, exit to Griffith Park Blvd.) contains over 14,000 artefacts on the history of the West or Wild West, and also has two galleries for temporary exhibitions. In seven galleries by means of rare old films such as westerns with Buffalo Bill, a reproduction of a Hollywood studio, and costumes and other exhibits dating from the time the wild west was discovered, you can see how Hollywood portrayed the wild west on film. Open Tue.–Sun. 10am–5pm.

George C. Page Museum of La Brea Discoveries

This steel-roofed museum, opened in 1977 (5801 Wilshire Boulevard) shows reconstructed fossils of prehistoric animals found in the giant tar-craters of Rancho La Brea, such as mastodons and mammoths, for which tar proved to be an excellent preserving medium. Throughout the years, hundreds of thousands of bone sections from some 420 different kinds of animals, 140 species of plants and even the 900 year-old skeleton of a woman have been discovered, which combine to provide valuable research material. From some animals a number of complete skeletons have been reconstructed. Visitors can watch the palaeontologists at work cleaning and cataloguing the fossils found in the tarcraters. Open Tue.–Sun. 10am–5pm.

★★Getty Center

At the end of 1997 the new Getty Center was opened at Brentwood Hills, not far from Westwood and the campus of the University of California. On a huge 40 ha (100 acre) site, which the Getty Foundation had acquired in the 1980s, an area of almost 10 ha (25 acres) was developed. As well as the museum complex there are administration and service buildings together with six institutes dedicated to the promotion of the arts and humanities. Designed by the top American architect Richard Meier, the building reflects expensive architectural tastes. About a billion dollars went into the project, making the Getty Center the largest and most expensive art centre in the world. It is expected to attract some 1,300,000 visitors a year.

From the **museum site** there are magnificent views of the skyscrapers in Downtown (unless they are wrapped in smog) and the Pacific Ocean and the San Bernardino Mountains. Clad in unpolished travertine panels, the façade contrasts with the smoothly-cut stone and tinted metal used on the rounded surfaces and upper parts of the building. The rotunda-like lobby is flooded with light and offers a view of a courtyard with a fountain, around which are arranged four exhibition pavilions. The way through the 54 galleries arranged in epochal order leads over glazed bridges or through terraces and provides views of the surrounding countryside. The inner rooms were styled by the interior designer Thierry Despont.

Admission to the Getty Center is free and it is open Tue., Wed. 11am–7pm, Thu., Fri. 11am–9pm, Sat., Sun. 10am–6pm. Two bus routes serve the museum. Visitors wishing to come by their own car (the museum has its own exit from Highway 405 into the San Fernando Valley) must telephone in advance, as permission to park a car depends upon the spaces available: tel. (562) 4407300 (parking fee). Visitors are then transported to the museum entrance in five minutes by an electric, driverless hovercraft. A full day should be allowed for the visit to the museum.

With the opening of the Getty Museum in the villa of the oil magnate J. Paul Getty (1892–1976) in 1954 the **Getty Collection** was made available to the general public for the first time. In 1973 the art collection was moved to Malibu (see entry). Initially it comprised only Greek and Roman sculptures, decorative art, principally French furniture and 15th to 18th c. European art.

Following Getty's death in 1976, and after the disputes regarding inheritance had been settled, the Getty Foundation, with its assets then valued at 4.5 billion dollars, was the richest foundation in the world; it found itself in a position where it was scarcely able to utilise the interest earned on its capital. In order not to lose its privileged tax status the Getty Foundation must spend 4.25% of its wealth on acquisition in three out of every four years. As a result, 5.7 million dollars were spent on Caspar David Friedrich's "Walk at Dusk" and more than 50 million on Van Gogh's "Irises". The latest acquisitions include illuminated medieval manuscripts bought from the German collector Peter Ludwig and several photographic collections, the only 20th c. items in the collection. Today the total value of the art collection is some 600 million dollars.

As a result of the many purchases made by the Getty Foundation the exhibition space available gradually became inadequate, and in 1997 all the exhibits were moved from Malibu (see entry) into the new Getty Center building. There are now plans to re-house the Greek and Roman art in Malibu from the year 2001.

Sculptures still form the most important part of the museum. One of the oldest pieces is a female figure from Cyprus, almost certainly four and a half thousand years old and standing about 40 cm (16 in.) tall and in a compellingly stylised form. There is a large collection of Greek and Roman sculptures, some in terracotta but mostly in marble, such as that of a seated man playing a lyre and accompanied by two sirens.

One of the highlights of the Getty Collection is the almost 2 m (6½ ft) tall marble **figure of Hercules** (Herakles) from the second c. AD. This larger-than-life figure holds in its left hand the club with which Hercules – according to legend – slayed the Nemean lion, and in its right hand the lion's hide. If this Hercules is compared with the sculpture of the "Victorious Athlete" from the early days of the Olympic Games (4th or 3rd c. BC) it can be seen that the athlete's left arm is hanging down, whilst his right hand points to his laurel wreath. Only a few bronzes of this kind have survived. There are also several busts and statuettes from the Roman era. Well-preserved Greek terracotta vessels, some with magnificent coloration (vases, amphorae and craters) are to be found in a gallery.

Scarecely any paintings have survived from ancient times, since the material on which they were painted disintegrated over the centuries. However, **mummy portraits** painted on wood were able to survive in the dry air of the Egyptian desert, as they were concealed in the layers of linen in which the mummies were wrapped. One example is the true-to-life portrait of a woman (Romo-Egyptian). Other less impressive paintings can be seen on shrines and sarcophagi. There are also examples of ancient silver and gold work in another gallery.

The collection of illuminated **manuscripts** from the time before the art of book-printing was developed is extensive, as evidence by the German, French, Italian and English exhibits on the upper floor. Nearly all the manuscripts are from the Ludwig Collection from Aachen.

Although Getty was never particularly interested in buying **paintings** he nevertheless did acquire in the 1930s a large number of major works by Rembrandt (including "Old Man in Knight's Armour"), Jan Steen, Jacob Ruysdaal, one of the 40 or so surviving paintings by Georges de la Tour, a Goya, a Gainsborough, two pictures from the Rogier van der Weyden school (including a "Descent from the Cross"), two Corots and works by the French Impressionists Pissarro, Monet and Degas, as well as works by the Post-Impressionist Gaugin and of the forerunner of the Art Nouveau style, Toulouse-Lautrec.

Also worthy of note are the **sketches and drawings** displayed on the upper floor, including works by Dürer and Hans Baldung (known as Grien), Raphael, del Sarto and Veronese, Rembrandt and Rubens, Poussin and Watteau.

The examples of **decorative art** originate mainly from France; the richly-decorated furniture includes a striking cabinet, probably made for King Louis XIV, above the door of which is a bronze medallion of the monarch surrounded by military trophies. Outstanding among the porcelain objects is a basket made in the Sèvres porcelain factory.

The **photographic collection** is dominated by numerous original prints from the 1840s. The two oldest items by unknown photographers can be dated to 1841. In addition to other 19th c. examples there are numerous prints by contemporary photographers, including Man Ray, Imogene Cunningham, Walker Evans and the German August Sandez.

Griffith Park

This park, located in the eastern part of the Santa Monica Mountains, and covering an area of 1620 ha (4000 acres), is the biggest state park in California. In the park is the Los Angeles Zoo, the Griffith Observatory and a planetarium, a Greek theatre with 4000 seats, a riding centre created for the 1984 Olympic Games, golf courses and tennis courts and lots more. Walks lasting several hours or drives into the mountains provide splendid views. The park bears the name of its founder Griffith J. Griffith who donated the greater part of the parkland to the city in 1896.

Los Angeles Zoo

Los Angeles Zoo (5333 Zoo Drive; tel. (323) 666–4090) has been in existence only since 1966, and thus is one of the newest zoological gardens in the USA. About 2000 animals, many grouped in their natural environment and according to their native habitat, roam around on the 46 ha (115 acres).

Among other things there is a reptile house, a section for aquatic animals and one for birds. The new koala-bear house and the children's zoo are very popular. Open daily, except Christmas Day, 10am–5pm and to 6pm in summer.

Observatory and planetarium

On a clear evening from 7–10pm the telescope of the observatory (2800 E. Observatory Road) gives a unique view of the star-lit sky. In the planetarium a big Zeiss projector shows natural manifestations such as eclipses of the sun and moon, the Northern Lights and star cycles.

In the Hall of Science astronomical phenomena are explained. In a "laserium" you will be completely surrounded by laser beams. Open summer daily 12.30–10pm; remaining months Tue.–Fri. 2pm–10pm, Sat. and Sun. 12.30–10pm.

Near the observatory stands a bronze bust of the late actor James Dean who, on this spot, shot the exciting motor-racing scene in the cult film "For they know not what they do".

Greek Theater

Greek Theater. In this open-air theatre (2700 North Vermont Avenue) jazz and rock concerts with very well-known soloists are held from May to October. The newspapers give details of the programme.

★Hollywood

Although Hollywood has become known worldwide, it is no longer an independent township as it has formed part of Los Angeles since 1910. It lies about 13 km (8 mi.) north-west of Downtown Los Angeles in the foothills of the Santa Monica Mountains, the so-called Hollywood Hills. Purchased more than 100 years ago (1887) by the Kansas real-estate broker Harvey Wilcox as cheap waste and arable land, Hollywood was named after the ranch of the same name and the holly trees which were to be found there in abundance at the time. From 1903 to 1910 it was an independent community of about 400 inhabitants. Business-minded film people, such as Samuel Goldfish (later Goldwyn) from Russia, Carl Laemmle from Baden-Württemberg and William Fox from New York, set up the first film studios in what had been horse-stables. At that moment was born the "film capital" of Hollywood, which offered ideal conditions – patent regulations, relating to Edison film cameras, could be more easily overcome here. From the daily treks of immigrants from the east of the USA – the novel "Grapes of Wrath" documents this trend – they could recruit cheap labour, including extras for the mammoth productions then becoming popular. In addition, there was the almost unbroken sunshine and the short escape route to Mexico – this latter possibility has to be borne in mind, for the venturesome film people did not enjoy a good reputation on account of their low moral standards.

Signs such as "No dogs or actors admitted" (golf course) were not rare by any means.

The famous Hollywood sign

On entering Hollywood you are welcomed by the famous **name-sign** in giant letters 16 m (50 ft) high, which is brightly illuminated on festive occasions. These letters, reminiscent of pop-art, were erected in 1923 on wooded scaffolding by real-estate brokers as an advertising gimmick. Since then they have won cult status, so that splinters and pieces which broke off when the sign was renovated in 1977 were sold as relics.

Hollywood Boulevard, Hollywood's main east–west axis, has been compared with New York Broadway because of its night-life, but instead of theatres Hollywood has only extravagant cinemas, such as the Chinese and Egyptian Theatres (6925/6704 Hollywood Boulevard) built originally by Sid Grauman in the twenties. The elegant shops which once lined Hollywood Boulevard have long since disappeared, the film stars having moved to other districts, particularly Beverly Hills (see also Mann's Chinese Theater).

Hollywood
Boulevard

Museums As well as countless curios and international gramophone records, the Guiness World of Records Museum at 6764 Hollywood Boulevard contains the prize valued at $30,000 awarded for Michael Jackson's album "Thriller". In the Hollywood Wax Museum (6767 Hollywood Blvd.) are figures of such famous names as Elvis Presley, Marilyn Monroe, Sylvester Stallone and Ronald Reagan.
   In the Max Factor Museum (1666 North Highland Avenue) Max Factor used to make up famous stars including Ginger Rogers, Marlene Dietrich, Bette Davis and Liz Taylor. In the wig room can be seen the wigs which were taken for the genuine hairstyles of Marlene Diedrich, Frank Sinatra or John Wayne.

Hollywood and the Oscars

The star of a star in Hollywood Boulevard

Hollywood with its main streets – Hollywood Boulevard, Sunset Boulevard, Melrose Avenue and Vine Street – now exists solely on its former glitter and the legends of its dream-factory. Since the first studio was set up followed by many others, Hollywood has become the very embodiment of films, even though none have actually been made there for some considerable time, the large studios having moved to other districts of Los Angeles such as Burbank and Universal City.

Instead of evoking what is in fact a rather faceless quarter of the city, the name "Hollywood" conjures up the American film industry itself, and above all a certain style of film-making in which technical skill and simple narrative forms are directed towards satisfying the need for escapism. The essential ingredient in this formula is the idolised "star" buffeted by one dramatic experience after another before the inevitable happy ending.

Over the years Hollywood has also become virtually synonymous with the "Oscars", the famous gold figurines which were awarded for the first time in 1929 by Douglas Fairbanks in the "Flower Hall" of the Roosevelt Hotel on Hollywood Boulevard.

Since then at least 22 Oscars have been awarded annually by the Motion Picture Academy (Academy of Motion Picture Arts and Sciences) in Hollywood or Downtown Los Angeles: two each for documentaries and short films and eighteen for the best individual performances in full-length feature films

(main and supporting roles), production, screenplay (original screenplay and literary adaptation), music (original song, original film score, musical adaptation) and film technique (camera work, décor, scenery and costume design, sound, film editing and special effects). There is also an award for the best foreign-language feature film. Most coveted of all however is the title "Best Picture of the Year", the award of which can quadruple a film's box-office takings. Many "Best Pictures", among them "Gone with the Wind" (1939), "Casablanca" (1943) and more recently "Dances with Wolves" (1990) and "The Silence of the Lambs" (1991), have become classics of the genre.

As a preliminary to choosing the actual winners – a process in which each Academy member casts their vote – a panel of experts nominates five candidates in every category, the sole condition being that the film in question should have been shown in a cinema in Los Angeles during the course of the year. For anyone employed in the film industry the award of an Oscar is the crowning point of their career, not least because it represents the judgement of their peers rather than of film critics or the public.

Only a few of Hollywood's beautiful Art Deco houses still remain; a present-day feature of the town is the number of good, some not too expensive, **restaurants**.

Coach tours are arranged by Gray Lines (1207 West 3rd Street), Starline Sightseeing Tours (6845 Hollywood Boulevard; Hollywood Fantasy Tours (6773 Hollywood Boulevard) and other companies.

Hollywood Bowl

Hollywood Bowl, located north of Hollywood Boulevard on Highland Avenue, is a natural amphitheatre which will accommodate up to 30,000 people (of whom 10,000 have to stand). From the beginning of July to the middle of September the Los Angeles Philharmonic Orchestra performs four times a week something which has become a permanent institution, namely, "Symphonies Under The Stars". These concerts enjoy great popularity and are directed by some of the world's leading conductors. The church service at sunrise on Easter Sunday is a long-standing tradition. The Bowl is open to visitors daily Jul.–Sep. 9am–sunset. Concerts Tue.–Sat. 8.30pm, Sun. 7.30pm.

In the grounds of the Hollywood Bowl, near the Patio Restaurant, you will find the Hollywood Bowl Museum (3201 Highland Avenue), which houses photographs and other exhibits relating to the history of the Bowl and its concerts, and where you can listen in small rooms to tape-recordings of some historic concerts. Open Jul.–Sep. 9.30am– 8.30pm.

Hollywood Bowl
Museum

Koreatown

One of the newer ethnic quarters, which has expanded even more in the last few years, is Koreatown. Some 100,000 Koreans now live in a district west of Downtown Los Angeles in about 200 streets. So far, however, the Koreans have preferred to keep to themselves and have made little attempt to attract tourists in the way that Chinatown and Little Tokyo (see entries) have done. Their houses border on Vermont Avenue, Pico Boulevard, 8th Street and Western Avenue. The Angelenos say that the district is scarcely recognisable anymore; the old houses have all been freshly painted and some converted, and everywhere there are Korean shops with signs only in Korean. There are acupuncture clinics, shops selling medical herbs, roast algae, kimchee (fermented white cabbage) and beautiful imported Korean articles such as porcelain musical-boxes. A Buddhist temple, Thal Mah Sah, stands in one of the main streets (3505 W. Olympic Boulevard). Not far away is the Sin Sae Kae department store (3150 W. Olympic). Korean restaurants are also to be found in abundance; however, the sharply spiced food is an acquired taste.

★ Little Tokyo

Little Tokyo, the Japanese enclave in Los Angeles, with its numerous new buildings is a clear indication of a thoroughly prosperous ethnic group. Located around 1st Street between Main and Alameda Streets, within walking distance of the City Hall, the Japanese Village Plaza quarter has developed, with a culture centre, dozens of Japanese shops and restaurants and a large shopping centre. The few 19th c. houses still remaining fit into the picture well. Today, more than 100,000 Japanese live in Los Angeles and the surrounding county; after the Japanese community had been decimated by internment after the war started in 1942, it is now bigger and probably richer than ever. Little Tokyo can easily be explored on foot.

Stone sculpture by Isamu Noguchi on the Plaza in Little Tokyo

Japanese
American Cultural
and Community
Center

Mention must be made of the Japanese American Cultural and Community Center, with a theatre in which from time to time Japanese Kabuki and Noh groups appear, as well as the Bunraku, puppet theatre, a gallery with temporary exhibitions of Japanese art, and a Japanese library, which includes books on Japanese–American relations. Open Tue., Wed., Thu., Sat. and Sun. 10am–5pm, Fri. 11am–8pm.

The **Plaza** in front of the Center was designed by the American–Japanese sculptor Isamu Noguchi, with a big rock sculpture dedicated to the "Issei", the generation of the Japanese immigrants (their descendants born in America are called "Nisei". Near the Center is a symbolic garden, half Japanese and half American, which is an oasis in the middle of the downtown concrete jungle (entrance through the basement of the Center).

Also worthy of note is the **Higashi Hongwanji Temple**, a Buddhist house of prayer dating from 1925 , built in traditional Japanese style.

The Little Tokyo Business Association arranges **tours** to the main places of interest.

Los Angeles Central Library

The main library (600 West 5th Street), which has 65 branches in Los Angeles, was temporarily closed following a serious fire in April 1986. At that time the whole patent collection was destroyed, as well as 400,000 of the 2.3 million volumes. Only 400,000 books remained undamaged.

The building, recently restored and modernised, was erected in the years 1922–26 and, with its pyramidal tower, it represents a mixture of Beaux Arts and various oriental styles. It is worth visiting the interestingly arranged internal rooms, some with murals depicting the history of California. The new Tom Bradley Wing has doubled the display area. Now the Central Library with its 2,100,000 books, 2,000,000 historic photographs and 10,000 magazines is the third largest main library in the USA.

Los Angeles Children's Museum

In this museum, designed specially for children (310 Main Street), young people are able to handle many of the things on display and even play with them. Active participation is expected of the young visitors, whether it involves the "City streets" department, the children's television station, the way an airline functions or trying to live in the world of the disabled. Open Jun.–Aug. 11.30am–5pm, Sat. and Sun. 10am–5pm.

★★Los Angeles County Museum of Art

Although this museum (5905 Wilshire Boulevard; tel. (213) 937/2590) first opened in 1965, its history goes back to the year 1913 when the Los Angeles County Museum of History Science and Art was dedicated. In addition to individual bequests, it possessed several collections which had been given to the museum over the years. As a result, it came near to bursting at the seams. However, it was not until 1954 that there was a real call for an arts museum on its own. Four years later the county gave

A museum with a world-wide reputation: Los Angeles County Museum of Art

153

Los Angeles County Museum of Art

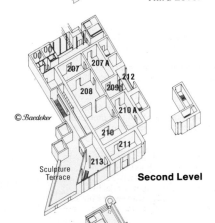

© Baedeker

Third Level

THIRD LEVEL
Parisian Cubism, German Expressionism, Russian Avant-garde, Bauhaus, DeStijl, Dada, Surrealism, Abstract Expressionism

Rooms 307–311 European art from 1900–1950
Rooms 312–314 Abstract Expressionism
Room 315 Contemporary art

© Baedeker

Sculpture Terrace

Second Level

SECOND LEVEL
American and European painting and sculpture since the Second World War, art from South California since the 50s, contemporary ceramics and glassware, Robert Graham, retrospective column

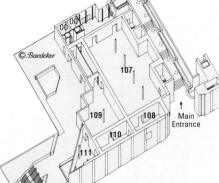

© Baedeker

Main Entrance

PLAZA LEVEL (FIRST LEVEL)
Temporary exhibitions of modern and contemporary art, Avant-garde, 'Machine Age', Gemini-(G.E.L.) prints, German Expressionism, works by David Hockney, Robert Longo and Frank Stella

Room 107 W. M. Keck Foundation Gallery

Plaza Level

its agreement, and after a further four years building work started and took three years to complete. The three original buildings cost twelve million dollars; the opening in 1965 was a huge success.

Buildings Since then the museum has, as a result of a large number of gifts donated in the interim, gained a worldwide reputation and should not be missed by any visitor to Los Angeles who is interested in art. It now consists of four separate buildings, connected with each other underground, and ranged around a large courtyard.

The Robert O. Anderson Building, erected as recently as 1986, has a new façade in the Babylonian style and provides adequate room for its important 20th c. art collection, including works from Europe and the USA.

In September 1988 an unusual pavilion was opened for the large stocks of Japanese art; from an architectural point of view this is without doubt the boldest undertaking this continually expanding museum has made. Its creator was the architect Bruce Goff, who died while the building work was going on.

Subsidy The museum is maintained by the county, not by the city; the individual buildings were financed by donations from private patrons. The cost of the Anderson Building, for example, amounted to 35 million dollars, and that of the Japanese Pavilion 12½ million. The other buildings which date from the beginnings of the museum bear the names of their chief sponsors: Howard Ahmanson, Armand Hammer and Leo S. Bing.

Art from the 20th c. is housed in the two upper floors of the Anderson Building, whilst the ground floor is used for temporary exhibitions. European works of art from 1900 to 1950 are displayed in galleries 307–311, including works belonging to such art schools as expressionism, cubism, Russian avant-garde, German expressionism, dadaism and surrealism. The German expressionists are well represented: Nolde, Meidner, Barlach, Schmidt-Rottluff, Kollwitz, Pechstein, Kirchner and Heckel. Schwitters holds a special place among the dadaists. Of those Americans who pay homage to abstract expressionism, works by Stuart Davis, Hans Hofmann, Mark Rothko, Morris Louis, Willem de Kooning, James Pollock and Frank Stella, to mention only the most important, are represented (galleries 312–14).

Anderson Building

On the **second floor** you can follow the development of American – especially South Californian – art of the last three decades; pop art and minimalism are particularly well represented. Also displayed here are works by contemporary potters and glass-blowers, as well as sculptures and new modern acquisitions. Works by retrospective contemporary artists such as Frank Stella, David Hockney, Robert Longo as well as other special exhibitions are to be found in the five galleries on the ground floor.

In the basement of this building are the offices and workshops of the museum's custodians.

Also with two floors, the Ahmanson Building has the most space for exhibits, having galleries placed around an atrium. Many art forms are represented – from the antiquarian to the 19th c. – and require maximum concentration from the visitor. Chinese and Korean art and Asiatic lacquer-work are to be found in the basement. On the ground floor you will find British decorative art (gallery 102A), British painting and sculpture (105), the unique Gilbert collections of Italian late Renaissance mosaics and large silver items (103 and 104), American painting, sculpture and decorative art from the 18th and 19th c. (106–113), African and South Sea art (114) and pre-Columbian art (115).

Ahmanson Building

On the **first floor** the tour begins with Egyptian art (201) and then continues with ancient western Asiatic art, including five reliefs from the second millennium BC from the palace of King Ashurnasir II in Nimrod, Assyria (201A). Then follows a newly-installed gallery of Iranian art, two 16th c. carpets being outstanding. Antique glass from various countries and civilisations is on show in galleries 203 and 219, Greek and Roman sculptures in gallery 205. Medieval and Renaissance art (205–208) and European paintings and sculptures from later epochs (210–217) are without doubt the main sections of the museum. Outstanding examples from this collection are pictures by Rembrandt ("The Raising of Lazarus" and "Man in a Black Hat"), Rubens ("Adoration of the Shepherds"), Frans Hals ("Portrait of a Man"), Fra Bartolommeo ("The Holy Family"), Canaletto, Georges de la Tour ("Magdalene with the Smoking Flame", one of the four representations of Mary Magdalene by the Frenchmaster) and one of St Andreas by El Greco. Of the German masters, Dürer, Hans Baldung (known as Grien), Lucas Cranach the elder, Riemenschneider and Schongauer are represented. There is also a good collection of works by French impressionists.

The **second floor** is devoted exclusively to Asiatic and Near Eastern art. The tour begins with Indian sculptures from the first millennium, mainly of sandstone, bronze and gilded bronze, and a representation of the dancing god Shiva dating from the 10th c. (301). Works of art from south-east Asia, Sri Lanka, Nepal and Tibet are to be found in galleries 302 and 303; many – including 15th c. Indian water-colours (304) – come from the collection by Frau Nasil Heeremaneck, who supported the museum in the seventies.

Islamic art – mainly textiles – from Iraq, Iran and Turkey can be seen in galleries 305 and 306. Costumes and textiles from various countries and epochs (307) complete this tour.

Hammer Building

In the two-storey Hammer Building only the upper floor is devoted to art. It contains a part of the important collection by the oil-industrialist Armand Hammer. Originally intended as a gift, it is today actually on loan, as Hammer fell out with the museum and is now thinking of building his own museum to house his whole art collection. On this floor, in addition to the Hammer Collection, are sketches, prints and photographs in three galleries. On the ground floor are offices and in the basement the museum shop and a gallery for special exhibitions.

Bing Center

The Bing Center houses a large auditorium, the Plaza Café and libraries which are accessible to the public only by prior arrangement.

Japanese Pavilion

The building of the Japanese Pavilion resulted from a gift. A collector was prepared to give the museum 300 screens and scrolls from the Edo period (17th c.) and as the museum did not have sufficient space for its now extended Japanese exhibits it was decided to build a special room for them. The collector Joe. D. Price had originally chosen the architect Goff to build the pavilion on his land in Oklahoma. However, Goff subsequently favoured housing the collection in a museum. His design was amended by another architect only to the extent that the building had to conform to the earthquake requirements and other building regulations laid down by Los Angeles. The roofs were supported by cables fixed to the curved beams, reminding one of Japanese gateways. The transparent walls are obviously meant to imitate Japanese shoji (paper screens). The curved interior of the pavilion contains cascades and pools.

The building consists of two parts: in one can be found prints, a Netsuke collection, ceramics, kimonos and sculptures, which were already in the museum's possession but only a part of which could be displayed. The second wing is fitted with ramps; this is where the screens and scrolls from the Price collection are displayed. As there is not sufficient room for everything, it is planned to alternate the exhibits.

The museum is open Tue.–Fri. 10am–5pm, Sat. and Sun. 11am–6pm. Admission free on the second Tuesday of the month.

Los Angeles County Museum of Natural History

When this museum, built in the Spanish Renaissance style (900 Exposition Boulevard, Exposition Park; tel. (213) 7443414), was opened in 1913 it housed the collections of the Los Angeles County Museum of Art, but in time this grew to such an extent that a special museum had to be built for the works of art. Since 1965 the 35 rooms and galleries have been available for natural history exhibits. The material on display includes sections for aquatic animals, birds, reptiles, fossils of mammals – including those of three dinosaurs – and also an extensive section for minerals, semi-precious and precious stones. Open Tue.–Sun. 10am–5pm, in summer until 6pm.

Mann's Chinese Theater

Very often hundreds of people are to be found in front of Mann's Chinese Theater (6925 Hollywood Boulevard) – still the great sensation of Hollywood. This cinema was built in 1927 and opened with Cecil B. De Mille's film "King of Kings". Like the Egyptian Theater on Hollywood Boulevard and the Million Dollar on Los Angeles' Broadway, the Chinese Theater is also a creation of Sid Grauman, who had a predeliction for exotic cinema palaces. Now it is run by Ted Mann, who named it after himself. Both the inside and the outside incorporate numerous Chinese features. The entrance is guarded by two giant Chinese heavenly dogs,

In the forecourt of Mann's Chinese Theatre some 200 film stars have left their mark by foot and hand prints.

to keep away evil spirits. The foyer is fitted with thick oriental carpets; large vases and urns, the statue of a Chinese philosopher and the three wax figures in the corner, clothed in exotic Chinese robes, emphasise the Chinese character of this room.

Movie Stars' Homes Tour In front of Mann's Chinese Theatre tickets can be bought for a rather unusual excursion, namely, a coach tour leading past the houses of the film stars.

In the forecourt you can see the largest **"autograph collection"** in the world: foot and hand-prints of more than 150 film personalities, together with their signatures. It is said that it was the silent-film actress Constance Talmadge who first – by mistake – walked on the wet cement and inspired Grauman to this original undertaking. There is still enough space left for the foot and hand-prints of actors, directors and producers to last for another thirty years.

Mayan Theater

The Mayan Theater (1040 Hill Street, near 11th Street) opened in 1927 with George Gershwin's musical "Oh, Kay!" reflects the pre-Columbian Maya style. It was commissioned by the oil millionaire Ed Doheny.
   The façade is covered with well-preserved stone figures – including the mighty Maya god Huitzilopochtli – and geometric mosaics, copies of those found in the Yucatan cities of Uxmal and Chichen Itza.
   The glazed tiles in the foyer were made specially for the Mayan Theatre by a Mexican artist, and are reproductions of tiles found in a sun-temple in Guatemala.
   As the Mayan Theatre is located in a run-down area (1040 Hill Street, near 11th Street) and for years has been used only to show porno-graphic films, the auditorium is nearly always kept dark, so you can see very little of what is described as a very beautiful room. It is said that the lights are not even switched on during the intervals between performances.

As a second theatre building, the **Belasco Theatre**, stands in the immedi-ate vicinity of the Mayan Theatre, one gets the impression that the other-wise unattractive Hill Street was once part of a theatre district. However, the Belasco Theatre, named after the actor, producer, theatre director and playwright David Belasco, who was born in San Francisco, has been a church for years.

On the side-wall of the house opposite the Mayan Theatre (1031 S. Hill Street; best seen from the car-park) is a painting, over 20 m (65 ft) long, by the well-known **mural** artist Kent Twitchell. It depicts the painter Ed Ruscha.

★Museum of Contemporary Art (MOCA)

This museum (250 South Grand Avenue), was founded in 1979 as "a private museum with a public conscience", but the main building on Bunker Hill, designed by the Japanese Arata Osozaki, which was expected to be opened in time for the Olympic Games in Los Angeles in 1984, was in fact not ready for occupation until December 1986.

Outside Mann's Chinese Theatre not only tourists, but also stars ▶
and starlets can sometimes be seen

In the meantime the administrators used a storeroom provided by the city, which was very skilfully converted into a number of galleries by the well-known architect Frank Gehry.

It became known as the **Temporary Contemporary** (152 North Central Avenue) and was so well received that it has continued in use as a kind of permanent branch of the main museum.

Until this museum was founded Los Angeles was without a collective home for art which is exclusively contemporary, not just modern. The main building was erected on the last piece of vacant land on the California Plaza, a giant complex of offices and apartment buildings, shopping centres and restaurants, between the City Hall and the actual city centre.

Pontus Hulten, former manager of the Centre Georges Pompidou in Paris, was chosen as the first director of the museum, but he withdrew from the post before the two buildings were inaugurated, and his deputy Richard Koshalek was appointed in his place.

The museum was set up so that there would be a home in Los Angeles for contemporary art, and the many native collectors could be catered for. It is hoped that one day it will acquire what is probably the most important private collection of contemporary art, that of the industrialist Frederic R. Weisman.

Exhibits In the meantime two important collections have been donated to the museum: 80 works that were in the possession of the Italian Count Guiseppe Panza di Biumo (mainly of abstract impressionism and pop-art), as well as 64 from the estate of the collector Barry Lowen (minimalists from the sixties and seventies, neo-expressionists, post-minimalists from the eighties).

Together with gifts of individual works, the museum has a stock of

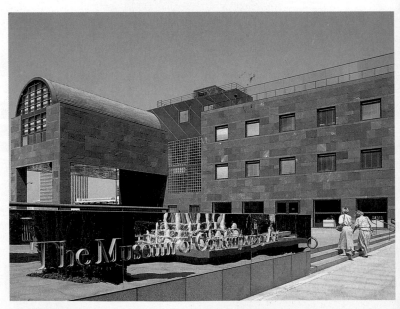

Outdoor exhibition at the Museum of Contemporary Art

over 400 paintings, sculptures, prints, sketches, photos, installations and other works, and it is still in the building-up phase.

The natural **lighting conditions** of the Isozakis Museum, built of red sandstone, are extremely advantageous, thanks to its pyramidal superstructures, cubes and cylinders which give the low building the appearance of being at the same time higher and yet firmly anchored to the ground. The same applies to the "Temporary Contemporary"; the division of the old storeroom into small and large galleries, with ramps and staircases, provides many possible arrangements for exhibitions.

Both museums are open on Tue.–Sun. 11am–5pm (Thu. until 8pm).

Music Center

The Music Center (135 N. Grand Avenue), located on the summit of Bunker Hill, was built from sandstone in the years 1964–67, and is similar in many ways to the Lincoln Center in New York, dating from about the same period. At the time, the total cost of the three buildings amounted to 34 million dollars, half of which came from public collections made by Mrs Dorothy Chandler, the mother of the publisher of the "Los Angeles Times". A plaza links the three buildings which, were it not for the giant sculpture by Jacques Lipchitz, would have a somewhat desolate appearance.

In the **Dorothy Chandler Pavilion** concerts (Los Angeles Philharmonic Orchestra), operas (Los Angeles Music Center Opera) as well as musicals and solo performances take place. The 3200 seats are filled almost every evening. The opera company, performances by which are held in

Concerts and musical entertainments take place in the Dorothy Chandler Pavilion

Lipchitz sculpture in front of the Mark Taper Forum

the months of October, December, February, April and May, has a modern repertoire by American standards. The Joffrey Ballet also appears here, mainly in the spring.

Four musicals and stage plays are presented each season in the **Ahmanson Theater**, as well as guest performances by the New Yorker Broadway Theater, and also some of their own productions by the Center Theater Group (2100 seats).

In the semi-circular **Mark Taper Forum** (740 seats) the Center Theater Group presents contemporary plays, including premières, large numbers of which have found their way to Broadway. Thus it has become one of the most successful regional theatres in the United States.

The **Walt Disney Music Hall** was completed in 1997, and was built in accordance with plans drawn up by the Californian architect Frank Gehry. It is to be the permanent home of the Los Angeles Philharmonic and seats 2400.

Pacific Palisades

This district, part of Los Angeles, lies north-west of the city, high above the Pacific Ocean. It was founded in 1921 by the Southern Conference of the Methodist Episcopal Church, and thought of as a kind of spiritual centre of the sect. Since then Pacific Palisades has developed into an elite part of the city, the inhabitants of which have the highest average income in Los Angeles.

It has also been the exile home of some prosperous German writers, such as Thomas Mann (he had a house built here at 1550 San Remo Drive), Emil Ludwig and Lion Feuchtwanger, whose house went to the University of Southern California after the death of his widow in 1987.

Pacific Coast Exchange

The stock exchange known as Pacific Coast Exchange (233 S. Beaudry Avenue) came into being in 1957 as a result of the merger of the previously independent Los Angeles and San Francisco exchanges, and today is the second largest in the country after that of New York. The Los Angeles Stock Exchange was founded in 1889, and that in San Francisco in 1882. Only about 10% of the shares traded here are issued by Californian companies, the rest are also handled on the New York Exchange or the American Stock Exchange (also in New York and some other American cities).

From a gallery, where there are some historic artefacts, you can watch what is going on in the stock exchange. Open Mon.–Fri. 6.30am–1.30pm.

At present **Pershing Square** is mainly the haunt of the homeless, drug-dealers and their customers. In order to attract pedestrians back to this now run-down district Pershing Square is to be renovated and converted into a pleasant park.

West of the La Brea Museum lies the latest museum to be built on Miracle Mile (6060 Wilshire Boulevard), the Peterson Automotive Museum. It emphasises the close links between Los Angeles and the automobile. As well as 200 vintage cars, some lent by their owners, there are numerous motor-cycles and other vehicles. Open Tue.–Sun, 10am–6pm.

Peterson
Automotive
Museum

San Pedro

San Pedro, 40 km (25 ml.) from the city centre, is indeed a part of Los Angeles, but is often regarded as an independent district. A start was made on developing this natural harbour in the 1880s. It was completed towards the end of the century, but not until 1909 did it form a part of Los Angeles with which it is linked by a narrow corridor.

In San Pedro can be found the Cabrillo Marine Museum (3720 Stephen White Drive; tel. (323) 548-7662), housed in the enclosed 70-year-old public-baths and in several small houses in which the aquaria are located. Open Tue.–Sun. 10am–5pm; admission free.

Cabrillo Marine
Museum

The Los Angeles Maritime Museum (pier 84, bottom of 6th Street), houses items and photographs relating to the history of the port. Open Tue.–Fri. 9am–4pm, Sat. and Sun. 10am–5pm; admission free.

Maritime Museum

The Villages at Ports O'Call complex is laid out like a port of New England on the east coast of the United States. Here you will find shops, some with an international flavour, and restaurants. From here, too, you can watch the activity in one of the world's biggest harbours, Worldport LA (Los Angeles). Open 11am–9pm, restaurants until 10pm.

The Villages at
Ports O'Call

Trip to Santa Catalina Island From San Pedro you can go by boat or helicopter to Santa Catalina Island (see entry). The helicopter flies every day given sufficient demand (departing from Pier 95).
    Boat leaves from piers 95 and 96.
    Bus no. 446 (Fermin/San Pedro), change to bus no. 147.
    By car: Harbor Freeway in southerly direction, Harbor Boulevard exit.

★Simon Rodia (Watts) Tower

The tower, named after its builder Simon Rodia, stands in East 107th Street No. 1765, and you can reach it via the Harbor Freeway, exit 14, Gage Avenue.

In 1921 Simon Rodia, an immigrant builder and carpenter from Naples, began to build "his" four towers from cement, steel poles and wire-netting, clad with something like 70,000 mussel-shells and glass, tile and mirror fragments. In 33 years of work he completed four towers, two of which are 34 m (112 ft) high, and represent perhaps the most complete example of folk-art today.

Simon Rodia was certainly no trained architect, but – scorning all help – created buildings with an almost Gothic effect, which can best be compared with the architecture of the Spaniard Antonio Gaudi. When the towers were completed in 1954 he made a present of them to a neighbour, moved to Martinez, a town near San Francisco, and never returned to Watts.

In 1959 the towers were bought by two young people. Their efforts to prevent their demolition were crowned with success when after four years the sculptured complex was declared a **cultural monument**. However, this did not prevent the towers from being damaged by vandals. The interior can be visited on only four days in the year.

Guided tours Sat. and Sun. noon–4pm.

Southwest Museum

Founded in the year 1907 by the Southwest Society, the Southwest Museum opened on its present site in 1914. Located at 234 Museum Drive, it is reached via the Pasadena Freeway, exit 43rd Avenue. This building in the mission-house style lies in the Highland Park area of the city, high above the Pasadena Freeway, north-east of the city centre. Today, the museum owns one of the best collections of Indian art and culture; exhibits come from as far apart as Alaska and Tierra del Fuego on the southernmost tip of South America. Its founding was attributable to the initiative of Charles F. Lummis, who applied himself at an early stage to preserving Indian culture, and set up the Southwest Society for that purpose. Over the years the stock of North American Indian artefacts increased, mainly as a result of the acquisition of the Poole Collection, including among other things Navaho carpets and basket-work. The building contains a well-stocked museum shop, as well as a library with works on Indian culture. A festival of Indian art is held in October each year.

Museum and library open Tue.–Sat. 11am–5pm.

Union Station

This station, built in the Spanish mission-house style between 1934–39 (800 North Alameda Street), proved to be one of the last large city railway stations of its kind in the United States. It was a communal project by three private railway companies, Southern Pacific, Santa Fe and Union Pacific. Particularly worth noting are the waiting-room, over 15 m (50 ft) high and with a ceiling of wooden beams, the marble floors and the numerous arcades. The Union Passenger Terminal became less important with the decline in long-distance travel. At the present time it is being converted to a regional transport junction of Greater Los Angeles (see Facts and Figures: Transport).

Union Station, one of the oldest in the USA

★★Universal Studios

One of Los Angeles' most important sights, the Universal Studios (Hollywood Freeway, exit Linkershim Blvd.), was created in 1915 by the German-American film pioneer Carl Laemmle on the site of a chicken farm. At that time the part of town now known as Universal City was still wild, hilly countryside. Initially Laemmle built only two sets, on which the first silent films were made in the open air.

As an advertisement for the new film industry he arranged **tours of inspection** for 25 cents, when he explained to the visitors how films were made.

Today, such trips are considerably more expensive and last a lot longer, but are every bit as good as the Disneyland Pleasure Park (see under Anaheim). Since the new tours were introduced over 30 years ago many millions of people have been taken around the 16 ha (40 acre) film studio, the biggest in the world, for a glimpse behind the scenes of film making. You can see King Kong, almost 10 m (33 ft) tall, as well as the shark from the film "Jaws", fitted with internal mechanism. You also pass by sets where special effects conjure up, for example, the skills of Fred Astaire dancing on the ceiling, or the secrets of making a bicycle appear to fly through the air.

Natural catastrophes take place before the onlooker's very eyes: avalanches in the Alps and an earthquake in an underground station (8.3 on the Richter scale). You can experience the Battle of Galactica portrayed with laser beams, pass by Alfred Hitchcock's "Psycho House", and witness films actually at the production stage. After the 45 minute tour you can also pay a visit to the show in the Entertainment Center.

The latest spectaculars include the high-tech film "Back to the Future",

165

where visitors can race through time in a sports car surrounded by three-dimensional pictures. The authentic backdrops from Steven Spielberg's "Jurassic Park" have been on view since late 1996.

On entering Universal Studios you pass the **Universal City Walk**, a shopping street with restaurants. Since 1992 this has been the site of the new Museum of Neon Art, the most striking exhibit of which in the Mona Lisa portrait (Mona in Neon).

Opening times The Universal Studios are open every day in the summer months 8am–6pm, the rest of the year 9am–3.30pm, weekends 9.30am–3.30pm; the Entertainment Center stays open longer. Groups of more than 20 are advised to make arrangements by telephone in advance.

University of California, Los Angeles (UCLA)

With almost 35,000 students, this high college (405 Hilgard Avenue, Westwood) is the largest constituent of the University of California. Having originated from a so-called Normal School founded in 1882, it began to expand when it acquired its present campus site in the Westwood area of the city. In the year 1929 the college institute, laid out in the form of a rectangle, was re-opened. To these four buildings, based on an Italian model, have been added 80 more in the last six decades. The 160 ha (400 acre) campus is today one of the most beautiful in California.

The campus Its numerous gardens are noted for their exotic plants. A botanical garden situated in a canyon, 1½ ha (3¾ acres) in area (open weekdays 8am–5pm, weekends 8am–4pm), is laid out like an unusual woodland landscape. Royse Hall, one of the four original buildings, has a large auditorium in which numerous concerts take place. The adjoining Haines

Universal Studios

Universal Studios: in action

Hall houses the Museum of Cultural History, with temporary exhibitions. In Schoenberg Hall (named after the composer Arnold Schoenberg who worked at the UCLA for a number of years) unusual concerts are often given. There is a large gallery in the Dickson Art Centre.

Advice Cars are allowed only on the main roads of the campus, so you must find the places of interest on foot. Guided walks are available on Mondays to Fridays 10.30am–1.30pm, starting from the Visitor Center, Ueberroth Building, corner of Le Conte & Broxton Avenue.

University of Southern California

This private university was established on its present site (3551 University Avenue, Harbor Freeway, exit 9th Exposition Avenue) two years before the UCLA, and in the interim has grown to have over 31,000 students (53 students registered in its first year). The present campus covers an area of some 60 ha (150 acres), on which stand nearly 90 university buildings. The better known include the Schoenberg Institute, housing the works bequeathed by the composer (Open Mon.–Fri. 10am–4pm), the Hancock Memorial Museum (with the furniture from the 19th c. house, since pulled down), the Fisher Gallery (in which temporary exhibitions are held), the Norris cinema and the Bing Theater, in which public performances are given.

Guided tours of the campus: most buildings are open 9am–5pm.

Watts

Watts, one of the smallest parts of Los Angeles, lies south-west of the centre of the city and is inhabited mainly by negroes and Mexicans. One week in August 1965 the tension prevailing there exploded, 34 people met their death, over 1000 were wounded and enormous damage was caused. Unemployment, poor living conditions, friction with the police and a general feeling of frustration were the root causes of the riots. They were triggered off by the arrest of a negro by a white police officer for allegedly being drunk in charge of a vehicle. Shops owned by whites were plundered, cars set on fire and occasional shots fired. As the police were unable to control the situation the armed National Guard was called in, but even it could not restore order until the sixth day. Since then Watts has calmed down again, but tensions remain and bands of youths still make trouble there. You should therefore take due care when visiting Watts (see also Simon Rodia Towers).

Wells Fargo History Museum

Like the museum of the same name at the big Californian bank in San Francisco, this museum (333 South Grand Street) also describes, by means of artefacts and photos, the bank's history and its contribution to the development of the West and of California in particular. Slides and videos are shown in a small projection-room. Open all banking days 9am–5pm.

Westin Bonaventure Hotel

This Downtown hotel, near the freeways (400 South Figueroa Street, with a second entrance on Flower Street), is one of the most unconven-

Roller skating is practised on the promenades all along the California coast as here at Venice Beach (see Baedeker Special p. 29)

tional buildings designed by the hotel architect John Portman of Atlanta. The five free-standing round towers, with lifts going up and down on the outside, dominate the skyscraper scene of Downtown Los Angeles like no other building. Around the inner atrium, in the building of which much concrete was used, are numerous shops and restaurants. The hotel, built in 1978, has 1500 rooms.

Los Gatos   I 1

Santa Clara County
Altitude: 117 m (384 ft). Population: 27,400

Los Gatos, established about 1850, is protected by two mountain peaks: El Sombroso (the Shady One) and El Sereno (the Nightwatchman). It lies south of San Francisco Bay, at an intersection of the CA 17, and owes its name to the wild cats which once roamed the area (los gatos = the cats). Until the start of the Second World War it was a small community, the inhabitants of which made a living mainly by growing fruit. Today, Los Gatos forms part of the catchment area of Santa Clara and Santa José (see entries).

Los Gatos offers the tourist a museum of history and natural history (Main & Tait Street; open daily except Mon. 1–4pm; admission free) and an old town district with restored houses of Spanish and Victorian origin, shops, restaurants and workshops (50 University Avenue; open Tue.–Sun. 1–4pm).

Sights

Los Padres National Forest   M/N 1/2

Los Padres National Forest, lying west and east of the CA 33 and US 5 highways and east of Santa Barbara (see entry), covers a total area of 750,000 ha (1,875,000 acres), and rises in places to a height of 2700 m (8860 ft). Within its boundaries are several wild parks, such as Ventana, San Rafael and Santa Lucia, as well as two areas where the condor is a protected species. This largely unspoiled wilderness admittedly with few trails suitable for walks, is served mainly by unmade-up roads, and possesses no visitor centre or information offices of any kind. Originally created as long ago as 1903, the area has been extended several times, finally reaching its present official boundaries in 1936. In that same year it received its name, in memory of the Franciscan monk who set up eight mission stations in the immediate surroundings.

Malibu   P 3

This community, which still belongs to Los Angeles, lies between the Santa Monica Mountains and the Pacific coast, along the CA 1, and possesses some of the most beautiful Pacific beaches in Los Angeles. Like the neighbouring Pacific Palisades, Malibu, with a population of some 10,000, is one of the most well-to-do parts of the city. Scholars differ regarding the meaning of its name; although it is certain that "Malibu" can be traced back to the Umalibo ranch belonging to the native Chumash Indians, the actual meaning of the word is uncertain, although it could well be the name of a person.

Advice In the interests of the residents, parking is prohibited on the streets of Malibu and Pacific Palisades.

The Getty Museum in Malibu built in the style of a Roman villa

Worthy of mention are the **beaches** running from south to north, seven of which are maintained by the city of Los Angeles: Topanga Beach, originally a private beach; Las Tunas Beach, quite narrow even at low tide; Malibu Pier, used mainly by anglers; Surfrider Beach, chiefly the domain of surf-riders; Corral Beach, 1.5 km (12 mi.) long, inaccessible at high tide; Paradise Cove, particularly good for swimming; Pirate's Cove, barely 200 m (650 ft) long; Zuma Beach, where you should watch out for giant waves, and Nicholas Beach. Further north lies Leo Carrillo State Park, which also has an especially beautiful beach.

★★ J. Paul Getty Museum

The main place to visit in Malibu is the J. Paul Getty Museum (17985 Pacific Coast Highway). It was opened in 1954 in the oil-magnate's villa in Pacific Palisades, and moved to Malibu in 1973. The style of building is reminiscent of the Roman villa buried when Vesuvius erupted in the year AD 79.

The building stands on a wooded hill above Santa Monica Bay, about 400 m (1320 ft) from the Pacific Coast Highway. The narrow road up to the museum is lined with tall eucalyptus trees and leads directly to the underground garage. From the garage a lift goes up to a loggia with Corinthian pillars, from where you have your first view of a 100 m (330 ft) long garden around a elongated pond. On both sides of the garden area there is a colonnade. Only after walking along this 100 m (330 ft) stretch do you come to the villa, an exact copy of a building from Pompeii almost 2000 years old has been perfectly achieved.

Removal to Getty Center With so many acquisations being made by the Getty Foundation it was inevitable that the collection would one day outgrow the available exhibition space and an extension to the museum

Picture of an Egyptian woman

Statue of Hercules (Herakles) ...

would be necessary. A few years ago 43 ha (107 acres) of land on a hill in the Santa Monica Mountains, not far from Westwood and the campus of the University of California in Los Angeles (UCLA), were acquired. At the end of 1997 the new Getty Center (see p. 145) was opened; as well as exhibition rooms it houses research institutes and the art library. At present the Getty Museum in Malibu is closed. When restoration work is completed in the year 2001 it is intended that the villa will be devoted solely to ancient Greek and Roman art. There will also be a new amphitheatre in which stage plays from the ancient world will be performed.

★ Mammoth Lakes   J 5

Mono County
Altitude: 2377 m (7800 ft). Population: 5000

Mammoth Lakes is more than 600 km (370 mi.) from Los Angeles (approached via the US 10, US 15, CA 395 and CA 203 highways) and almost 500 km (310 mi.) from San Francisco (via the US 80, US 50, CA 395 and CA 203). Although Mammoth Lakes and the surrounding countryside, including the 3680 m (12,080 ft) high Mammoth Mountain 6 km (4 mi.) away, can be enjoyed at any time of the year, it is one of the best winter sports resorts in the country, where you can ski from the end of November until the beginning of July. With 17,000 skiers finding their way here on one working day – there are correspondingly more at weekends and on public holidays – Mammoth Lakes, although perhaps less well-known than Vail (Colorado) and Squaw Valley, is the busiest ski resort in the United States. This region, south-east of Yosemite National Park, lies within the Inyo National Forest (see entries). By taking the

Mountain panorama with a sculpture of a mammoth at Mammoth Lakes

cablecar (which continues in operation throughout the summer and is reached from Mammoth Lakes village by following the signs for Devils Postpile National Monument) it is possible to enjoy the magnificent panoramic view gained from the summit.

Devils Postpile National Monument

The Devils Postpile is a 20 m (65 ft) high vertical rockface formed of basalt columns. Another feature worth seeing in the National Park is the 30 m (98 ft) high Rainbow Fall on the San Joaquin River. A shuttle-bus service operates between the cablecar station and Devils Postpile from July to September.

During the snow-free months a visit to Mammoth Lakes can be combined with highly recommended **detours**; for example to the John Muir Wilderness Area (many footpaths), Yosemite National Park, Mono Lake (see entry) and Bodie (see Bodie State Historic Park).

Access There are flights to and from Los Angeles, Oakland and San Jose. Local bus services operate in Mammoth Lakes as well as to the ski slopes.

Mendocino   E 1

Mendocino County
Altitude: 38 m (125 ft). Population: 1000

Mendocino lies on the CA 1 running parallel to the Pacific coast, and is some 240 km (150 mi.) from San Francisco (US 80, CA 116, CA 1). Originally known as a port for shipping timber, some of its early houses have been well preserved and lend a colourful appearance to this little

Façades in Mendocino

coastal town. Many artists settled here after the Second World War. Today Mendocino boasts a number of galleries, the best known of which is the Mendocino Art Center (45200 Little Lake Street), where exhibitions, concerts and theatrical productions are held, and instruction is also given in various branches of art.

An unusually large number of boutiques in Main Street and in the side streets complete the shopping facilities. Of the many pubs built for the lumberjacks and port workers – Mendocino is said to have had no fewer than 22 in the second half of the 19th c. – only a few remain, such as Dick's Place near the Mendocino Hotel on Main Street (built in 1878 and worth seeing). One of the oldest houses, Ford House on the side of Main Street facing the sea, dates from 1854; it is now an information bureau. Also worth a visit are Kelly House, built 1861 (45006 Albion Street), now a local museum and library, and MacCallum House, dated 1882 (45020 Albion Street). In spite of a tendency to modernise, Mendocino has succeeded in retaining its village character. It shows no signs of urbanisation in the way that Carmel (see entry) does. An interesting stroll is along the cliffs high above the sea.

Sights

Merced   J 3

Merced County
Altitude: 52 m (170 ft). Population: 56,000

Merced lies in the fertile agricultural region of the San Joaquin Valley where in addition to rearing cattle, peaches, tomatoes, almonds and alfalfa are grown; it is well-known because of its location on the approach road to the western entrance to Yosemite National Park (see entry) which is scarcely 100 km (60 mi.) away.

Lake Yosemite State Park

Only some 12 km (7 mi.) north-east of Merced lies the charming Lake Yosemite State Park (boats for hire, fishing and water-sports facilities).

★Mission Stations

In accordance with normal American practice, the simple term "Mission" is used in the text. This actually means the particular mission station concerned.

Origin When the Spanish King Carlos III had cause to fear that the Russians or the British (the latter had just annexed Canada) would attempt to seize the unexploited lands in Alta California, he managed to forestall them; he instructed the Franciscan monks coming from Mexico to build mission stations in Alta California, as he believed that in this way it would be easier to control the surrounding land. The Fathers were to convert the native Indians to Christianity and also initiate them into the secrets of husbandry. However, he clearly overestimated his abilities, and this ambitious undertaking, to acquire land on the one hand and save souls on the other, was doomed to failure from the start.

Living witnesses to this period are the 21 mission stations which were built in the course of 54 years (1769–1821) along the Pacific coast from San Diego to Sonoma. This almost 960 km (600 mi.) stretch of the California Highway No. 1 has been called **"El Camino Real"** (see entry) since Mexican times. The Spanish word "real" has two meanings: "really, actually" and "royal, splendid". So it is up to you how you wish to interpret the roadsign: "Road to Reality" or "The Royal Road".

Today After their secularisation under Mexican rule only a few mission stations remained in their original condition, as fire, earthquake and malicious damage led to their destruction. Almost all have been restored and are accessible to visitors, but only a few still serve their true, religious purpose.

Tourism The peace to be enjoyed in the well-kept gardens will provide the visitor with a welcome change from the busy Californian towns and cities. All mission stations can be visited. They are listed below in order of the date when they were built.

Mission of San Diego de Alcala (1769)   S 2

Mission Valley, 10 km (6 mi.) from the San Diego catchment area; a well-signed diversion off Highway 8 leads to it. Open daily 9am–5pm.

History The Spanish military governor Gaspar de Portolo took possession of the land near San Diego Bay on behalf of Spain. In 1769 the Spanish Franciscan Father from Majorca, Junipero Serra, founded the mission stations, the first of which was built in San Diego. A few years after it was founded, however, it was moved 10 km (6 mi.) inland, because disputes had arisen between the Spanish troops and the Indians. In 1775 the Indians set fire to the new mission; the Fathers sought refuge with the army and it was 1777 before they built a new mission station with the help of the Indians. However, it quickly became dilapidated following secularisation. All that remains is a church with a bell-tower, declared a basilica in the seventies, a beautiful garden and a small museum.

Entrance front of the Carmel Mission

Mission of San Carlos Borromeo de Carmelo   J 1

3080 Rio Road, Carmel. Located about 8 km (5 mi.) from Monterey, on the southern edge of Carmel. Open weekdays 9am–5pm, Sun. 10.30am–5pm.

History Because of its architecture and its location on Monterey Bay, the Carmel Mission, as it is generally known, is one of the most beautiful of the mission stations. When it was founded it formed the northernmost point of Spanish dominance. Here, too, soldiers and priests soon separated; Serra moved the mission station some 8 km (5 mi.) into a valley by the Carmel river. It remained Serra's headquarters until his death, by which time there were already nine mission stations. Here you can still see the spartanly simple room with its wooden bed and writing table, from which Serra supervised the mission stations and watched over the baptism of more than 5000 Indians.

From 1934 onwards the mission and the church, built in 1797 in the Moorish style by a Mexican stone-mason, were restored in their old form. It is one of the few mission stations to retain its square inner court-yard. Here, too, lies the tomb of Serra, who was canonised by Pope John Paul II on September 25th 1988.

Mission of San Antonio de Padua (1771)   K 1

Located near the village of Jolon, about 66 km (40 mi.) south of Soledad and 58 km (36 mi.) north of San Miquel; turn off the 101 Jolon Road or Fort Hunter Ligett Military Reservation. Open weekdays 9.30am–4.30pm, Sun. 11am–5pm.

History This mission fell into decay so quickly after being secularised in

1834 that no buyer could be found for it when it was advertised for sale eleven years later. Everything that was not nailed or screwed down was stolen, and the interior demolished. It was 1907 before a start was made on restoration, especially of the church and the inner courtyard, and this was not completed until the fifties. A small museum houses some interesting artefacts from long ago. The rural character of the isolated valley gives the mission its special charm.

Mission of San Gabriel Arcangel (1771) P 3/4

537 West Mission Drive, San Gabriel, reached via turn-offs from San Bernardino Freeway (1–10), exits Atlantic or Rosemary Ave. Open daily 9.30am–4.15pm; tel. (818) 2825191.

History This mission's church, which still serves as such today, was built by the Franciscan Antonio Cruzado in 1806, using as a model the Moorish cathedral at Cordoba, with some notable modifications. The bell-tower fell victim to an earthquake in 1812 but the church remained standing. North America's first grape-vines were cultivated on its land and, although others followed its example, San Gabriel's area of cultivation remained the biggest and its mission themost prosperous. Serra had brought some cuttings from Spanish vines with him in 1769 so as not to be dependent on imports from Spain for his communion wine. At the beginning of the 19th c. up to 50,000 l of wine were produced here each year.

At the San Gabriel mission, where some 1000 Indians – called Neophytes – lived and worked, soap, leather and tallow were produced as well as barley, maize, beans, peas and lentils. More than 2000 orange, lemon, fig, apple, peach and pear trees were planted.

Sights

The museum with its parchment scrolls and old and valuable books going back to the 15th c. is well worth a visit. On the mission land is a cemetery where more than 6000 Indians are buried, mainly victims of epidemics. At the beginning of the 19th c. about 100,000 of North America's 900,000 Indians must have lived in California.

Mission of San Luis Obispo de Tolosa (1772) M 1

At the corner of Monterey and Chorro Street, San Luis Obispo, about halfway between Monterey and Los Angeles; tel. (805) 5436850.

History Little remains of this mission station, once a flourishing cattle centre. Today its ruins lie in the town centre of San Luis Obispo. After secularisation the mission was stated to be the property of the Indians; cattle could be taken away unhindered; the church and other buildings quickly fell into decay. At a public auction in 1845 the mission station was sold for only 510 dollars. A hotel sprung up directly opposite. More than 100 years ago the church was "modernised" in the New England style, when the bell-tower was given a totally unsuitable spire.

Mission of San Francisco de Asis (Mission Dolores: 1776) H I

16th and Dolores Street, near Market Street, San Francisco. Open daily 9am–4.30pm in summer, 10am–4pm in winter.

History The mission, located in the southern part of Downtown San Francisco, still displays its former size and importance. It was built near the Dolores Stream which flowed into a lake no longer there (it reached

Exterior of the Dolores Mission

from 16th to 23rd Street). The outside of the church is less notable than the Baroque altar inside, which came from Mexico. The patio (inner courtyard), common to almost all mission stations, has also long since disappeared and a basilica erected in its place.

In a cemetery lie the remains of 5500 Indian victims of an epidemic, as Indians in this region showed themselves to be particularly prone to disease.

★Mission of San Juan Capistrano (1776)   Q 3/4

This mission station lies near Junction 1–5/Pacific Highway, about 6 km (4 mi.) from Dana Point. Los Angeles is 100 km (60 mi.) away. Open daily 7.30am–5pm.

History The San Juan Capistrano mission, shrouded in romance, is a favourite with tourists; its church is also worthy of attention. Its construction was not started until 20 years after the founding and took until 1806 to complete. Its name goes back to the Italian jurist and later Franciscan crusading priest John of Capistrano (14th/15th c.), who was canonised at the end of the 17th c. This mission, dedicated by Serra, is the only one in Orange County, south of Los Angeles. The church with its twelve domes was badly damaged by earthquakes in 1812 and 1918 and, like other buildings forming part of the mission, only partially repaired. Since the church could not be used as a result of the earthquake a mere six years after completion – 40 Indians had been buried in the ruins – services were held in a little adobe-built church.

This mission station is one of the few remaining which are fully preserved.

There is a romantic **legend** concerning these ruins. It is said that the swallows which nest in the stonework set off each year on their migration south on October 23rd (the day on which John of Capistrano died in 1456), and return on St. Joseph's Day, March 19th. This legend is immortalised in a 50-year-old hit tune "When the Swallows Come Back to Capistrano", and still lives on – even though the dates do not exactly agree.

Mission of Santa Clara de Asis (1777)   I 1

This mission is scarcely 5 km (3 mi.) from Pueblo San José, on the CA 82, between Franklin and Bellamy Streets. It has the same opening times as the university, i.e. until 8pm in the summer months and until 11pm in the remaining months.

History After the founding of the Santa Clara de Asis mission almost half a century passed before the church was built, and today we see only a 1929 copy – four earlier churches were destroyed by earthquake or fire. This one is the most successful as far as fulfilling the aims of the missions is concerned; more Indians – 8536 to be precise – were baptised here than in any other mission station.
    After secularisation in 1834 it was handed over to the Jesuits, and formed the nucleus of the first of California's colleges, the University of Santa Clara. Today the mission forms part of the campus.

Mission of San Buenaventra (1782)   O 2

211 E. Main Street, Ventura, from Highway 101 turn into Main Street via California Street. Open weekdays 10am–5pm, Sun. 10am–4pm; tel. (805) 6434318.

History One of the last of the mission stations to be founded by Father Serra, little now remains of San Buenaventura except the church which, like so many others, suffered damage in the 1812 earthquake. The gardens which once surrounded the church have long since given way to buildings of all kinds, principally because of their location in the centre of the present-day town. At the time when the mission stations were built this region was inhabited by Chumash Indians, said to have been the most highly developed tribe in California.

★Mission of Santa Barbara (1786)   O 2

2201 Laguna Street, corner of Oliveros Street, Santa Barbara. Approached from Downtown via the well-signed Santa Barbara Street. (Open weekdays, 9am–5pm, Sun. 1pm–5pm.)

History The "Queen of the Mission Stations", as Santa Barbara is generally called, was the only one to remain with the Franciscans after being secularised and to be preserved by them in its original condition to the present day. However, this applies only to the buildings, for the large estates which once belonged to the mission were lost after 1834.

The **church**, completed in 1829 after the original had been destroyed by earthquake in 1812, is the work of Father Antonio Ripoli. It has a Roman temple façade and was built by the obviously extremely skilled Chumash Indians. In the library Ripoli discovered the Spanish translation of a work by the Roman engineer and military technician Vitruvius Pollio, dating from the year 27 AD. The drawings by Vitruvius of Doric columns and Roman temples inspired Ripoli's design; a French visitor said of the church that "he had not expected to find such luxury in this

"Queen of the Mission Stations" in Santa Barbara

country, so far away from all the beauties of Europe". It is the only mission with two towers, and had to be rebuilt in earthquake-proof construction after the 1925 eruption which laid waste the whole of Santa Barbara. Today it serves as a parish church.

In the buildings of the mission station you will find a **museum** with objets d'art from the colonial period and many interesting artefacts, as well as the archives of the Californian Franciscans. Until 1968 the seminar of the Franciscan Province of California was also held here. Especially worth seeing are the garden, and the cemetery in which many prominent early Spaniards as well as 4000 Chumash Indians found their last resting-place.

Near the mission you can see the remains of the extensive **irrigation system**, part of which is still in use today.

★Mission of La Purisma Concepcion (1787)   N 1

The best route to the mission, the ruins of which can still be seen and which forms part of the town of Lompoc, is via the US 101 and CA 246 (Buellton exit). Open daily 9am–5pm.

History This mission station is the only one located in the State Historic Park and is located in a charming valley surrounded by the Santa Ynez Mountains. After the first mission building had been completely destroyed in the 1812 earthquake, the Fathers moved their mission somewhat further north, but there too, not far from the old Camino Real, they were still pursued by misfortune. A disastrous drought, a fire and finally in 1824 an Indian rising crushed by Spanish troops did not allow

◀ *Fountain outside the Mission Church of San Buenaventura*

the original building plans to come to fruition. La Purisma is the only mission without an inner courtyard. Secularisation further affected it, until finally there was little left but ruins.

In the 1930s La Purisma was restored from the ground up by the Civilian Conservation Corps, a body formed by the Roosevelt government, with the result that no other mission gives such a good insight into life in the mission stations. In addition to the church, a monastery, military barracks, a tannery, a soap factory, various workshops and the water-reservoir have been rebuilt in their old authentic form, so that visiting them is essential for a real understanding of days gone by.

Mission of Santa Cruz (1791)   I 1

Corner of Emmet and High Streets, Santa Cruz. The reproduction stands on Mission Hill; tel. (408) 4265686.

History Practically nothing is left of this mission, and no attempt has been made to restore it. In 1825 an earthquake demolished the building, and scarcely had makeshift repairs been carried out when the foundations were weakened by the spring tide of the Santa Cruz river. In 1857 another earthquake destroyed what was left and looting added to the devastation. Near the original site can be seen a smaller reproduction of the church, and a little museum in a wing of the monastery is open to visitors.

Mission of Nuestra Señora de la Soledad (1791)   K 1

Ft. Romie Road, about 5 km (3 mi.) north-west of Soledad, the site of a state prison, not far from the US 101. Open Tue.–Sun. 10am–4pm; tel. (408) 6782586.

History Little remains of the Nuestra Señora de la Soledad mission. Its Spanish name means "Our Lady of Solitude". The Franciscan Fathers thought they recognised the Spanish "soledad" in the name the Indians had given it.
  One is still haunted today by this feeling of solitude, and can well understand why the Fathers tried to flee from this oppressive isolation. In scarcely four and a half decades 30 Fathers took on the leadership. Epidemics and floods occurred frequently; in 1831 the church collapsed, and a storehouse had to be converted quickly into a chapel. Secularisation did the rest. Only this chapel and a wing of the inner courtyard have been restored.

Mission of San José de Guadalupe (1797)   I 1

Fremont, 43300 Mission Boulevard, at the junction of the CA 238 and Washington Boulevard. Open daily 10am–5pm; tel. (415) 6571797.

History This mission was set up about 23 km (14 mi.) from the present town of San José, on a slope of the Diablo Mountains (the town was not established until 1851) and was intended as a base for expeditions against hostile Indians and also as a place for baptisms. Only one wing of the inner courtyard has been restored, and this houses a museum with artefacts from the mission period and some Mexican sculptures. Shortly after it was secularised the mission leader of many years' standing, Father Narciso Duran, founded an orchestra made up of Indians who had been taught to play western stringed instruments. After secularisation the church served initially as a parish church. It was finally

Church of the Santa Cruz Mission

destroyed by a serious earthquake in 1868. There are plans for the old mission church to be restored.

Mission of San Juan Bautista (1797)   J 1

2nd and Mariposa Street, San Juan Bautista, 5 km (3 mi.) south of the US 101 on the CA 156. Open daily 9.30am–5.30pm, Mar.–Oct. 9.30am–4.30pm rest of year; tel. (408) 6234528.

History Like the Santa Barbara mission, that of San Juan Bautista – located in the centre of the town of the same name, in the middle of a state park – was used only occasionally, and today serves as a parish church for the predominantly Mexico-American population. The damage caused by the 1906 earthquake was not put right until 70 years later. As it lies directly on the San Andreas Fault the mission was particularly at risk from earthquakes. However, during the 1906 earthquake it stayed more or less on its foundations. As in the San José Guadalupe mission, music received special attention; Father Esteban Tapis formed a choir and an orchestra. He also drew up a notation system based on colours, which made it easier for the Indians to read the notes.

The **church** stands on the west side of the square and is the only mission church to have three aisles. The painted altar is by Thomas Doaks, a sea-farer from New England stranded in Monterey, and apparently one of the first "Yankees" to come east. He undertook to do the painting work in return for board and lodging.

Mission of San Miguel Arcangel (1797)   L 1

The mission lies on the US 101, about 9 mi. (15 km) north of Paso Robles and 53 km (33 mi.) north of San Luis Obispo. Open daily 10am–5pm, the museum 10am–4pm.

History This mission, located in the extreme north-east of San Luis Obispo County, over 60 km (37 mi.) north of the town of the same name, has – in contrast to most of the others – a church (the third one, and completed in 1821) which has withstood the rigours of time rather better, so that in 1901 and 1928 it had to be merely renovated, not rebuilt. As a result of secularisation the mission lost its estates, which extended as far as the Pacific Ocean 50 km (30 mi.) away, and during the 1850 gold-rush it was a favourite place for fortune-seekers to stay. By the end of the 19th c. there was a bar in the monastery!

The **church**, however, was not adversely affected; it remains intact and is one of the best-preserved examples of mission architecture. The interior is richly painted; Indians worked under the artist Estevan Munras from Monterey and succeeded in producing some interesting "trompe l'oeil effects" (French for "deceiving the eye"). Above a statue of its founder is an all-seeing Eye of God, supposed to exert a hypnotic effect upon believers. In the nearby museum you can see interesting items from the mission period.

Mission of San Fernando Rey de Espana (1797)   P 3

15151 Mission Boulevard, San Fernando, at the junction of the Golden State (I–5) and San Diego Freeway (I-405), easy to reach from Pasadena and Downtown Los Angeles. You can also take bus no. 24 from 11th and Main Street in Los Angeles. Open weekdays 9am–5pm, Sun. 10am–5pm.

History Although this mission bears the name of a secular ruler, that of King Ferdinand III of Castille, he was nevertheless canonised after his death. He founded the University of Salamanca, and he also fought successful wars against the Moors. The mission lies west of the town of the same name, about half-way between the San Buenaventura and San Gabriel mission stations. The largest of the buildings fell victim to the 1812 earthquake; only one monastery wing about 80 m (260 ft) long remains standing. The symptoms of decline which followed secularisation were rectified between 1879 and the 1930s, so that now not only the monastery but also the church, the bell-tower, and various workshops have been restored to their original condition. Eight years after secularisation the mission had to endure a kind of gold-rush itself because some of the precious metal was discovered on one of its properties. This was still seven years before the actual gold-rush at the Sacramento River, but the finds were so unimportant that interest soon waned.

In the restored **monastery** made of adobe – one of the longest of its kind – can be found the workshops, where the handiwork of the time is documented. Here, too, pilgrims walking along the Camino Real could rest. Particularly beautiful, being stocked with exotic plants of all kinds, is the cemetery, where thousands of Shoshone Indians, as well as many Franciscans, are buried. This mission was the last of four to be built in twelve months; never before had so many new missions been established within a single year.

★Mission of San Luis Rey de Francia (1798)   R 4

4050 Mission Avenue, Oceanside, from which place it is 8 km (5 mi.)

away on the CA 76. From San Diego the distance is 53 km (33 mi.). Open weekdays 10am–4pm, Sun. noon–4pm; no admission during mass.

History This mission is also named after a canonised monarch, Louis IX of France, who was admitted into the band of the saints because of his crusades against the heathens in 1297. It is the last of ten mission stations built by Father Fermin Francisco de Lasuen and lies in the far south between the San Diego and San Juan Capistrano missions, some 8 km (5 mi.) east of the present town of Oceanside. It was Father Antonio Peyri who in the years 1811–15 supervised the building of this mission church which holds 1000 people. The Moorish style and the tower with its red-painted window-sills, gables and pilasters give this church its very unusual appearance. Adjoining the church is the interior courtyard with a monastery; on one side of the church was the Indian village, on the other stood a military barracks which were found in every mission station. Below these buildings were a garden and a laundry.

After the usual neglect of the secularised buildings, a start was made in 1893 on restoring the mission, which had meanwhile become the property of the Catholic church. Today it serves as a seminary.

This, the largest and most beautiful mission station, possesses an interesting **museum** in the former monastery and in the workshops, where some paintings and wood sculptures from Mexico are well worth seeing. In the magnificent garden with its cloister is the first mastix tree (also known as the pepper tree, from Peru) to be planted in North America, as well as an Indian cemetery. The French visitor who had admired the Santa Barbara mission in 1840, considered that from an architectural point of view the mission of San Luis Rey de Francia was the most impressive and symmetrical in the whole of California.

Mission of Santa Ines (1804)   N 1

1760 Mission Drive, Solvang, via the CA 154 about 53 km (33 mi.) north of Santa Barbara or via the US 101 about 70 km (43 mi.). Open weekdays 9.30am–4.30pm, in summer until 5pm; Sun. noon–5pm.

History Only after a long pause in what had been a hectic period of building activity did the 19th mission appear, roughly on the site where the Danish township of Solvang is today. The name comes from St Agnes (Spanish Santa Inés), and appears in its Spanish form in the naming of the Santa Ynez mountain chain and of the valley of the same name. The original building was a victim of the 1812 earthquake. Subsequently, a second building went up in the years 1813–17, but was damaged in the Indian uprising kindled in the mission of La Purisma Concepcion 40 km (25 mi.) away. Restoration started in 1904 but was restricted to the church, bell-tower and a part of the inner courtyard. Santa Ines is one of the smallest mission stations; perhaps this is where its special charm lies.

Mission of San Rafael Arcangel (1817)   H 1

1104 Fifth Avenue South, corner of Court Street, San Rafael, only three blocks from the US 101 (Central San Rafael exit), 19 mi. (30 km) north of San Francisco. Open daily 11am–4pm except Sun. 10am–4pm; tel. (415) 4546141.

History This mission was originally intended as a hospital for the Dolores mission, as there was a desire to keep away from the latter the many Indians suffering from epidemic illnesses. The actual reason for building the 20th mission, some 13 years after the 19th, was in fact quite different: the Russians had set up in Fort Ross a base for otter-catching, and the Spaniards wanted at all costs to prevent a further Russian advance southwards. Basically the mission was nevermore than a kind of sanatorium and monastery; it was pulled down in 1870 but was rebuilt in the same style in 1949.

Mission of San Francisco Solano (1823)   G 1

Near the plaza in Sonoma. From San Francisco, 38 mi. (60 km) away, it is easily reached via the US 101, CA 121 and 12. It is part of the Sonoma State Historic Park and houses the Jorgensen collection of water-colours of Missions of California; tel. (707) 9381578.

History The last of the mission stations and the only one to be built during the period of Mexican rule, it bears the name of one of the Spanish missionaries in Peru. After secularisation General Mariano Guadalupe Vallejo went to the trouble of nominating the governor Figueroa commandant of North California as a precautionary measure against the Russian advance. At the same time Figueroa became administrator of the mission and was to maintain it as a buffer against the Russians. For reasons which are not known the church collapsed. In its place was built a parish church, which was also destroyed but was rebuilt in the years 1911–13. The nearby monastery built in 1825 survived, and is thus the oldest building in Sonoma. It houses a museum. The annual celebrations held by the wine-producers begin here.

Modesto   I 2

Stanislaus County
Altitude: 27 m (88 ft). Population: 165,000

Located on the Tuolumne River, in the north-east of the San Joaquin Valley, Modesto has made a name for itself through its processing industry: conserve factories, dairies, slaughter-houses and wine-producing form the most important industries of the town, which has more than doubled its population since 1970. Its name can be traced back to a San Francisco banker, who "modestly" (Spanish "modesto") declined the suggestion that the town be named after him.

Modesto, established in 1870, possesses a row of Victorian houses dating from that time, a natural history museum (1100 Stoddard Avenue), a post- office decorated with murals from the depression years (1125 I Street), a museum of local history (1402 I Street) and a railway station built in the Spanish mission style, now used only for freight (J & 9th Street). A two-day balloon festival is held in the middle of September. In the immediate vicinity of Modesto are numerous lakes, offering extensive facilities for water-sports (Modest Reservoir, Turlock Lake, Lake Don Pedro). The town was also the scene of the well-known film "American Graffiti", the director of which, George Lucas, hails from Modesto.

Sights

Surroundings

On Highway 99 south of Modesto lies the town of Merced (pop. 56,000) in the fertile agricultural region of the San Joaquin Valley, where cattle are reared and peaches, tomatoes, almonds and alfalfa is cultivated. It is well known because of its location on the CA 140 approach road to the Yosemite National Park (see entry) some 100 km (60 mi.) away.

Merced

Lake Yosemite State Park

About 12 km (7 mi.) north-east of Merced lies the charming Lake Yosemite State Park, where boats can be hired and there are facilities for fishing and water-sports.

Mojave Desert   J–R 3–8

The Mojave Desert (pronounced "mohárvee") is a barren stretch of land running south of the Sierra Nevada and north of the San Bernardino and San Gabriel mountains, covering an area of 38,850 sq. km (15,000 sq. mi.), its eastern boundary being formed by the states of Nevada and Arizona. Although the main parts of the desert are very hot and dry, attempts at agricultural cultivation in the extreme west, Antelope Valley (Los Angeles County), have been crowned with success. Originally, the Chemehuevi and Mojave Indians lived here.

Solar technology As the sun pours down on many days of the year (over 3000 hours), the average air-humidity is very low (thus protecting the steel in the modern industrial plant from rust) and vast land-areas are for the most part unused, the Mojave Desert offers ideal conditions for the production of regenerative energy. In this region of America most energy is consumed around midday, for the Californians switch on their air-conditioning punctually at twelve o'clock. In all, there are seven solar power stations at three sites, the main one being that of Dagget on Highway No. 1; the eighth solar power station is nearing completion.

In Dagget they are experimenting with different systems: the economically unprofitable solar-tower power station and the "solar-dish", standing on a single foot and made up of several individual mirrors. The latest technology is based on **solar fields**: with so-called "low-tech", the sun's energy is trapped by means of parabolic mirror channels, up to 100 m (330 ft) long and over 5 m (16 ft) wide. Using conventional power-station techniques, steam and resultant energy is produced by means of oil which is heated in the channels.

Edwards Air Force Base

In the south-western part of the Mojave Desert is the Edwards Air Force Base with a concrete landing-strip for NASA space-shuttle flights.

★Mono Lake State Reserve   J 5

Lake Mono, located close to the CA 395, is about 23 km (14 mi.) south-east of the eastern entrance to Yosemite National Park (see entry) and about the same distance south of Bodie (see entry for Bodie State Historic Park). This salt-water lake, 1900 m (6240 ft) above sea level, is 21 km (13 mi.) wide and 13 km (8 mi.) long. Although several rivers flow into Lake Mono, it has no outlets, and is one of the oldest lakes in the world, having been formed perhaps 700,000 years ago. In the water, which has a higher salt content than most lakes, only a few life forms can exist, mainly single-cell algae; these provide food for the salt-water flies and crabs, which in turn are eaten by 70 kinds of migratory birds which reside on Lake Mono in spring and summer. These are mainly phalaropes (wading birds), grebes and Californian gulls. It is estimated that each year a million of these three species alone nest by Lake Mono at various times. About 90 per cent of all Californian gulls are hatched on Lake Mono – especially on its volcanic island of Paoha and the Negit peninsula, which is linked to the mainland by a dam.

Sinter turrets in the Mono Lake ▶

Phenomena of a special kind are the **limestone turrets**, most of which are to be found on the south bank. They are formed when the chalky spring water from the bed of the lake mixes with the very alkaline lake water. This forms limestone, and over the course of centuries curiously shaped turrets are formed where the springs enter the salt-water. This chemical process takes place only in the lake itself; when the water level falls and the turrets poke out of the water they cease to grow. Limestone turrets can be seen high above the present bank, and their age has been estimated at up to 13,000 years.

In the last 50 years the **water-level** of the lake has fallen by over 12 m (40 ft) since Los Angeles began to tap four of the seven rivers which flow into Lake Mono. At the same time the salt content has doubled. In order to put a stop to any further danger of emptying the lake and completely changing the ecological system, legal steps have been taken after the city of Los Angeles had refused to listen to all compromise proposals. The effects of the struggle for water here in California can be seen at first hand.

The **Visitor Center** of the committee which is active in preserving the lake is in the neighbouring town of Lee Vining.

★★Monterey   J 1

Monterey County
Altitude: 12 m (40 ft). Population: 32,000

As well as being beautifully located on Monterey Bay, on the peninsula of the same name, Monterey has an interesting past. From 1770–1822 it was the capital of Spanish California (Los Angeles, San Francisco and the present capital Sacramento did not exist at that time) and, after Mexico had broken free from Spain, it remained the provincial capital for a further 24 years. Thereafter it quickly lost its political importance.

Economy The tourist trade now constitutes the main source of income as the fishing industry declined following the disappearance of sardines from the Monterey waters.

Climate As far as weather is concerned, the months of September to June are the best time to visit the peninsula; (however, rain can be expected in January and February), but the three summer months often mean fog and low clouds.

Sights

Places of interest include houses from the Spanish and Mexican periods, a fishing-port, which is not as busy as it once was, as well as Cannery Row, made famous by John Steinbeck's novel of the same name (1945). This once industrial street was converted some years ago into a complex of restaurants, shops, cafés and art-galleries, so that only the walls of the buildings remain as a reminder of that which Steinbeck described in his novel. For instance, the unique Monterey Bay Aquarium has been opened on the site of an old canning factory.

Monterey State
Historic Park

In Monterey State Historic Park the following houses are worth a visit (all are open daily 10am–5pm).
   Casa del Oro, a restored grocery shop dating from 1845, at the corner of Scott and Oliver Streets (closed Mon. and Tue.).
   Casa Soberanes, an adobe-built house with walls 1 m (3 ft) thick, dating from 1842, now a museum of the history of Monterey 1830–1970. (Corner of Pacific and Del Monte Streets.)
   Custom House, built in the adobe style in 1827 at the time of Mexican dominance, now houses an historical exhibition covering the period

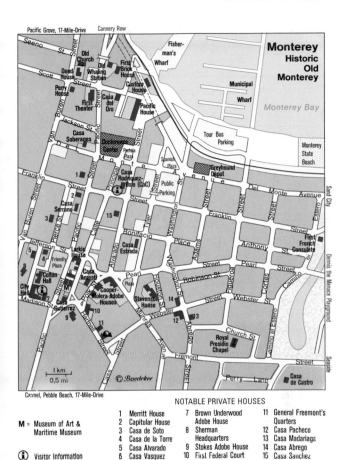

NOTABLE PRIVATE HOUSES

M = Museum of Art & Maritime Museum

(i) Visitor Information

1 Merritt House	7 Brown Underwood Adobe House
2 Capitular House	8 Sherman Headquarters
3 Casa de Soto	9 Stokes Adobe House
4 Casa de la Torre	10 First Federal Court
5 Casa Alvarado	11 General Freemont's Quarters
6 Casa Vasquez	12 Casa Pacheco
	13 Casa Madariaga
	14 Casa Abrego
	15 Casa Sanchez

1830–50. Two of the famous Monterey cypress trees are growing in a garden in front of the house.

First Theater on Custom House Plaza is California's oldest theatre and was originally a boarding-house and inn (also built in the adobe style). Theatrical performances have been regularly held here since 1847; now on Wednesday to Saturday in July and August and on Friday and Saturday in the remaining months. (Corner of Pacific and Scott Streets.)

First Theater

Historic houses Larkin House, dating from the 1830s, served Thomas Larkin as the American Consulate Bureau in Mexico (510 Calle Principal, Main Street; closed Tue.).

Pacific House, dating from 1847, today a museum of Californian history, with an Indian exhibition (Custom House Plaza).

Robert Louis Stevenson House, where the English poet lived for four months, when visiting his future wife. Numerous Stevenson memorabilia are on display, including many documents (530 Houston Street; closed Wed.).

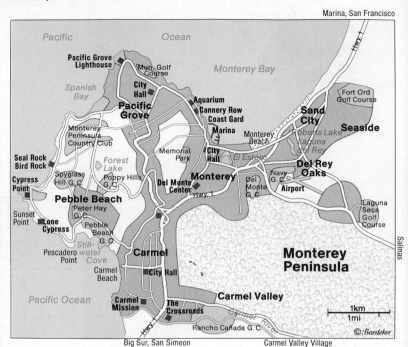

Marina, San Francisco

Pacific Ocean

Monterey Bay

Spanish Bay

Pacific Grove Lighthouse

Mun. Golf Course

City Hall

Pacific Grove

Aquarium
Cannery Row
Coast Gard
Marina

Fort Ord Golf Course

Sand City

Seaside

Monterey Peninsula Country Club

Monterey Beach

Roberts Lake

Laguna del Rey

Seal Rock Bird Rock

Forest Lake

Memorial Park

City Hall

El Estero

Del Rey Oaks

Cypress Point

Spyglass Hill G.C.

Poppy Hills G.C.

Del Monte Center

Monterey

Del Monte G.C.

Navy G.C.

Airport

Pebble Beach

Peter Hay G.C.

Hwy 1

Laguna Seca Golf Course

Sunset Point

Lone Cypress

Pebble Beach G.C.

Still-water Cove

Carmel

Monterey Peninsula

Salinas

Pescadero Point

Carmel Beach

City Hall

Carmel Valley

1km
1mi

Pacific Ocean

Carmel Mission

The Crossroads

Carmel River

Rancho Canada G.C.

©Baedeker

Big Sur, San Simeon

Carmel Valley Village

Presidio

Presidio of Monterey, now the home of the Defense Language Institute, has artefacts and dioramas on the history of Presidio Hill from the times of the Indians, Mexicans, Spaniards and Americans. (Pacific Street, near Scott Street; admission free.)

The Royal Presidio Chapel is the only one still in existence in California, and in continuous use since 1795. Note the richly-decorated façade. (San Carlos Cathedral, 550 Church Street; admission free.)

Monterey possesses two **museums**, the Monterey Peninsula Museum of Art, with Californian, Indian and Asiatic art as well as temporary exhibitions of photographs (559 Pacific Street), and the Allen Knight Maritime Museum, displaying material relating to the history of ships in the region. (550 Calle Principal.)

★★Bay Aquarium

The most important place to visit in Cannery Row (No. 886) is the Monterey Bay Aquarium at the end of the road. It is the biggest marine aquarium in the USA, with the emphasis on displaying more than 6000 living things (from otters to sharks, octopuses and wolf-eels) and their biosphere in Monterey Bay, an extraordinarily rich marine biotope.

The visitor is offered many opportunities of viewing coastal formations, marine plants, fish and other aquatic animals, as well as coastal and sea birds, through glass-walled pools, telescopes, macroscopes and microscopes and also underwater video cameras which you can operate yourself by remote control. Also to be seen on three floors are algae

Seal in the Monterey Bay Aquarium, the largest in the USA ▶

Former warehouse of the Monterey Canning Company

forests, marine mammals, coastal bird-life and much more. Open daily except Christmas Day 10am–6pm.

On the main floor a "Habitat Path" leads to the many **sections** of the aquarium. The most impressive are called "Monterey Bay Habitats" (a 27.5 m (90 ft) long cross-section through the bay), "Kelp Forest" (a giant pool 8.5 m (28 ft) high containing 1.26 million litres of water), or "Great Tide Pool".

In the "Marine Mammals Gallery" are models of numerous marine mammals native to the bay, especially whales, dolphins, sea-lions and seals. In a two-storied special aquarium frolic sea-otters, threatened with extinction and being bred here.

In "Mexico's Secret Sea", a new section opened in 1989, you can wonder at the colourful underwater world of the Gulf of California, with over 300 strange life-forms, such as eels and scorpion-fish.

Also opened in the same year, the "Jewels of the Pacific" section shows a spectrum of marine animals and underwater formations from the Pacific Coast. Particularly attractive to children is the "Touching Pond", where visitors can touch ray-like fish and observe them through a microscope.

Cannery Row

Other buildings in Cannery Row which are worth seeing are:

No. 851: Kalisa's Lak Ida Café built in 1929, a brothel from 1936 (immortalised by Steinbeck), a coffee-house since the mid-fifties.

No. 835: opened in 1918 as a Chinese Wing Chong grocery shop (Won Yee, who lives on the top floor, appears as Lee Chong in Steinbeck's "Cannery Row"; the novel begins with a description of the shop). Today keepsakes of the author are to be found here.

No. 800: The Pacific Biological Laboratory, near Steinbeck Western Biological Laboratory, where the author spent much time from 1930–35.

No. 799: The site of Flora Wood's "Lone Star Café", which Steinbeck called Dora Flood's "Lone Star Café/Real Flag Restaurant", another brothel from 1923–41. The present concrete building houses an antiques warehouse.

No. 711: Once this was the storehouse for the Monterey Canning Co.; now there are shops and a fish restaurant.

Nos. 650 and 654: On this site were located Monterey's second Chinese restaurant and the hotels of Messrs. Wu and Sam, replaced years ago by the elegant Spindrift Inn.

No. 400: Where once stood a magnificent villa, almost completely destroyed by fire in 1924, and later a fish-canning factory, there now stands the luxury hotel Monterey Plaza.

No. 242: Here too, where the Enterprise Canning Factory once packed sardines, stands one of Monterey's many luxury hotels, the Monterey Bay Inn.

Nearby Pacific Grove, a town with almost 15,000 inhabitants, boasts **Pacific Grove** numerous Victorian houses, a natural history museum and the Asilomar Conference Center. There is also Ocean View Boulevard, 6 km (4 mi.) long and very suitable for walkers, offering views of the rocky coast. South of Monterey lie Pebble Beach and Del Monte, both with almost palace-like villas and golf-courses which are among the finest on the Monterey peninsula.

Only a few miles from Monterey, on the south side of the Monterey peninsula, lies Carmel (see entry). The many charms of the countryside make it worthwhile going the long way round, the **"Seventeen Mile Drive"**. This begins at Pacific Grove Gate and then goes along the Pacific coast and for part of the way through the Del Monte Forest, where there is a number of large villas. The forest is impressive by reason of its rich abundance of cypress trees and the Monterey pines. You will also drive past picturesque beaches, isolated cliffs, the "Lone Cypress", the Pebble Beach Golf Course and the "Lodge at Pebble Beach" Hotel, where rooms cost 300 US dollars. Many kinds of gulls live in the Seal and Bird Rocks. Often you can spot sea-lions and seals there too. Cypress Lookout offers a particularly beautiful view north and south along the Pacific coast.

You have to pay a toll to use this private road.

Morro Bay   L/M 1

San Luis Obispo County
Altitude: 61 m (200 ft)
Population: 9700

This peaceful bay, about halfway between Los Angeles and San Francisco, was discovered in 1769 by the same Spanish expedition under Father Juan Crespi which had earlier founded the first mission in San Diego (see entry). It is dominated by the 170 m (560 ft)-high volcanic rock known as Morro Rock ("morro" is Spanish for a rock rounded at the top). The township itself did not come into being until the second half of the 19th c. A large fishing fleet is based here.

South of the town, on the CA 1, lies the Morro Bay State Park, an area of **Morro Bay State** almost 600 ha (1500 acres), with a golf course, picnic and camping sites, **Park** as well as an important natural history museum and a small aquarium with about 300 aquatic animals (595 Embarcadero). Short trips round the harbour start from house no. 1205 Embarcadero, and on Saturdays and Sundays during the season there are evening trips with refreshments available.

A volcanic rock dominates the idyllic Morro Bay

Mother Lode County   G–J3/4

Mother Lode County describes the region from Mariposa in the south, near the western entrance to Yosemite National Park (see entry), as far as Georgetown, some 16 km (10 mi.) north of Coloma (see entry), where the first gold was discovered in 1848. It is about 192 km (120 mi.) long and its width varies from a few hundred metres up to 3.2 km (2 mi.).

Mother Lode County probably did not receive its name until 20 years after the discovery of rich deposits of gold-quartz. It was wrongly assumed that there were only a few quartz veins containing **gold**. In fact, however, there were other important mines north of so-called Mother Lode. Placerville can act as a setting-out point for trips through Mother Lode County. Those who wish to search for gold in one of the brooks and rivers, under the guidance of an experienced gold-digger. You can drive to that area along the CA 49, passing uninhabited ghost-towns, once flourishing gold-mining townships.

Mount Shasta   C4

Siskiyou County
Altitude: 1083 m (3550 ft). Population: 2900

Situated not far from Redding in the Shasta Trinity National Forest on the US 5, this little town is the starting point for water-sport trips to Siskiyou Lake, 4 km (2½ mi.) away, and for climbing the 4317 m-high (14,168 ft) mountain of the same name, Mount Shasta. For a time the peak was called Shatasia or Sastise. These are variations of the spelling of the name of the Shasta Indians who originally lived there. A somewhat lower peak stands west of Mount Shasta and bears a similar name, Mount Shastina. Mount Shasta was first climbed in 1854. Covered with five glaciers, it is a dormant volcano which last erupted in 1786. Only the hot springs serve to remind one that it was once active. Today the mountain is a popular skiing region which can be climbed even in summer by means of a ski-lift.

Muir Woods National Monument   H1

From San Francisco, take Highway 101 via the Golden Gate Bridge as far as the CA 1 turn-off, which takes you direct to Muir Woods. At the weekend it is also possible to take the ferry from San Francisco (Ferry Building) to Larkspur.

Access

The tallest trees in the world are the so-called redwoods or mammoth trees (see entry for Redwood Highway, Redwoods), which thrive only in California and South Oregon, including those in Muir Woods National Monument some 24 km (15 mi.) north of San Francisco. Since 1908 the park has been controlled by the National Park Service, which has a Visitor Center (tel. (415) 3882595) at the entrance where detailed information can be obtained.

This 223 ha (550 acres) area of forest, named after the famous naturalist and founder of the Sierra Club, John Muir, contains large numbers of **redwoods**, the botanical name of which is sequoia sempervirens. The tallest trees in Muir Woods reach a height of 73 m (240 ft). In the first 100 years they grow 30 cm. (12 in.) each year, then the rate of growth slows down. The oldest mammoth tree (now dead) was 2200 years old; the average age is 400–800 years. The trees' root systems spread out sideways to about 46 m (150 ft), but the depth never exceeds 2 m (6½ ft).

In Muir Woods there are about 10 km (6 mi.) of well-signed **trails**. As it is often cool and damp even in summer, you should take warm clothing.

Napa   G1

Napa County
Altitude: 5 m (16 ft). Population: 62,000

Situated at the southern end of the valley of the same name, some 85 km (52 mi.) from San Francisco, Napa is one of the largest Californian towns north of San Francisco. It was founded in 1848 and bears the name of the long extinct Napa Indians. Today it is the main despatching point for the wines produced in the Napa Valley as far as Calistoga (see entry). In addition, there are a number of light industries and electronic firms. The western boundary is formed by the Napa Mountains; further to the west lies the other famous wine-valley, Sonoma (see entry), in Sonoma County. The Howell Mountains form the eastern boundary of Napa County and they also protect the valley from storms.
    For several years now wine producers in the Napa Valley have been threatened with heavy losses as a result of an outbreak of vine pest. It will cost at least $1 billion to eradicate the problem.

The most important **wine production** takes place along the stretch from Yountville to St Helena (see entry), near Oakville and Rutherford: names such as Mondavi, Beaulieu, Inglenook, Heitz and

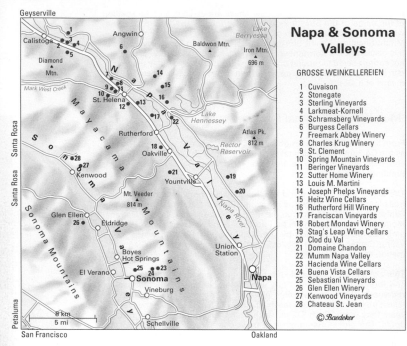

Geyserville

Calistoga

Angwin

Baldwon Mtn.

Iron Mtn.
696 m

Diamond
Mtn.

Mark West Creek

St. Helena

Santa Rosa

Santa Rosa

Rutherford

Lake
Hennessey

Atlas Pk.
812 m

Rector
Reservoir

Oakville

Kenwood

Yountville

Mt. Veeder
814 m

Glen Ellen

Eldridge

Boyes
Hot Springs

Union
Station

El Verano

Sonoma

Napa

Vineburg

Petaluma

8 km
5 mi

Schellville

San Francisco

Oakland

Napa & Sonoma Valleys

GROSSE WEINKELLEREIEN

1 Cuvaison
2 Stonegate
3 Sterling Vineyards
4 Larkmeat-Kornell
5 Schramsberg Vineyards
6 Burgess Cellars
7 Freemark Abbey Winery
8 Charles Krug Winery
9 St. Clement
10 Spring Mountain Vineyards
11 Beringer Vineyards
12 Sutter Home Winery
13 Louis M. Martini
14 Joseph Phelps Vineyards
15 Heitz Wine Cellars
16 Rutherford Hill Winery
17 Franciscan Vineyards
18 Robert Mondavi Winery
19 Stag's Leap Wine Cellars
20 Clod du Val
21 Domaine Chandon
22 Mumm Napa Valley
23 Hacienda Wine Cellars
24 Buena Vista Cellars
25 Sebastiani Vineyards
26 Glen Ellen Winery
27 Kenwood Vineyards
28 Chateau St. Jean

© Baedeker

Louis Martini have a good reputation in America. North of St Helena, on the CA 128, you pass the wine lodges belonging to the Beringer Brothers, Christian Brothers and Charles Krug (the latter is one of the oldest in the valley), and still further north are those of Hans Kornell and Schramsberg, one of the few American champagne producers.

In recent years some 50 Californian wine-producing concerns have passed into the hands of overseas owners, or share-holdings in them have been acquired by foreign firms. These include Inglenook and Beaulieu (British) and Beringer (Swiss). In the last 20 years the number of wine-producers in the Napa Valley alone has grown from 30 to 200. As the bigger firms in particular offer guided tours, the valley is becoming more and more tourist-orientated (about 2.5 million tourists each year).

Wine trains Since 1989 it has been possible to become acquainted with the Napa Valley wine-producing district by travelling in authentic Pullman saloon coaches (George Mortimer Pullman built the first luxury saloon and sleeping-cars in Chicago in 1858), visiting vineyards and taking part in wine-tastings. On the 58 km (36 mi.) round trip from Napa to St Helena gourmet dishes are served in the elegant dining-car.

Balloon flights over the Napa Valley in the early morning, when the thermals are peaceful, have become increasingly popular. The colourful hot-air balloons climb almost imperceptibly into the sky and provide a magnificent view over the whole wine-producing area. After the gentle landing visitors are taken by the organisers "Balloons Above the Valley" (P.O. Box 3838, Napa, CA 94558; tel. (800) 6466824) to a champagne breakfast at the Domaine Candon vineyard.

The best way to reconnoitre the Napa Valley is by hot air balloon

The Silverado Museum (1490 Library Lane) received its name from the silver mine which was once worked nearby. Dedicated to the author Robert Louis Stevenson, the museum contains first issues of his books, manuscripts, photos and letters. Open Tue.–Sun. noon–4pm. Admission free.

Silverado Museum

One of the major wine-producing sites in the Napa Valley, there being six large vineyards here or nearby. These are those of Beaulieu, Beringer, Inglenook, Hans Kornell, Charles Krug and Louis M. Martini. (see entry).

St Helena

About 20 km (12½ mi.) east of St Helena lies the artificial Lake Berryessa, made following the building of the Monticello Dam. The total length of its banks is 265 km (165 mi.), with ample water-sports facilities.

Lake Berryessa

Newport Beach   Q3

Orange County
Altitude; 8 m (26 ft)
Population: 67,000

Newport Beach, often likened to Cannes on the French Riviera, does indeed have a beautiful sandy beach over 8 km (5½ mi.) long, but it is extensively urbanised. Newport Beach includes Balboa, Balboa Island, Corona Del Mar, Newport Heights, Lido Isle, Harbor Island, Bay Shores and Linda Isles. There are luxury hotels with hundreds of rooms, as well as magnificent villas, elegant shops and first-class restaurants. Sunning themselves in Newport Beach will be found the rich from Orange County and Los Angeles, which is less than 60 km (37 mi.)

197

Entrance to a wine lodge in the Napa Valley

away on the CA 1 coast road. Not far from Newport Beach lies the campus of the University of California of Irvine – the whole region once formed part of the Irvine Ranch, the rural character of which has long been lost.

Sights

Newport Beach possesses an excellent museum with temporary exhibitions as well as its own permanent exhibits (850 San Clemente Drive; Open daily except Mon.). About 8 km (5 mi.) to the south, near the coast road, you will find the Sherman Library and Gardens, also a charming garden with exotic flora (Open daily). The marina, with berths of 9000 sailing craft and motor boats, is one of the largest on the Pacific coast. The Marina Village and eight other shopping centres can meet the needs of every customer. There is a pleasure park called "Fun Zone" on Balboa Boulevard, above Balboa Pier, from which there are boat trips of various kinds.

★Oakland   H1

Alameda County
Altitude: 13 m (43 ft)
Population: 372,000

Oakland, connected with San Francisco by the San Francisco–Oakland Bay Bridge, and situated only 12 km (8 mi.) east of the metropolis on the west bank of the great bay, was where the lumberjacks lived who discovered the big oak-forests near the bay and the beautiful redwood stands in the nearby hills, very little of which remain today. Then came the gold-diggers, and in 1852 the town named after its oak trees was

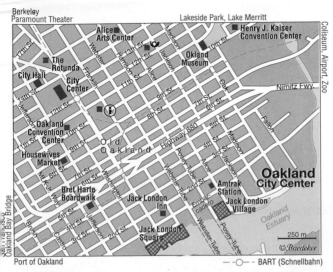

founded. Oakland grew in importance in 1869 when it was made the terminus of the transcontinental railway; in the same year the mayor of the day laid out in the centre of town the Merritt salt-water lake which bears his name. The construction of piers and a ship-canal confirmed the important role which Oakland was to play as a traffic junction.

Economy After the devastating earthquake of 1906 which left Oakland relatively unscathed, the town received such an influx of people from San Francisco that its population doubled between 1900 and 1910. In the twenties industry gained a foothold and larger office buildings appeared. The Second World War brought additional changes: the port facilities were improved, and in the fifties Oakland, more farseeing than San Francisco in that respect, was reorganised to take container freight traffic and soon overtook San Francisco to become the biggest container port on the west coast with several large shipyards and about 1600 factories. This, in turn, resulted in more than 1000 road-transport companies setting up their headquarters in Oakland.

Oakland also proved attractive to many black people from the south, who by 1970 constituted about a third of the population. In 1966 Bobby Seale and Huey Newton founded the Afro-American group known as the **"Black Panthers"**. Their radical demands resulted in a number of clashes with the police. Gradually, however, the organisation adopted a lower profile.

Of the writers who lived in Oakland in their youth, Bret Harte and Jack London (see Famous Personalities) are the best known. **Bret Hart Boardwalk** got its name from the former, and the latter gave his name to Jack London Square at the end of Broadway where a life-size statue of the author stands.

"Heinhold's First and Last Chance Saloon" is where Jack London not only drank his whiskey but also wrote many of his short stories. Nearby stands the rebuilt Klondike cabin in which London spent a winter. The

★Jack London Square

The picturesque yacht harbour of Oakland near Jack London Square is a short way from San Francisco

leisure complex by the harbour with numerous restaurants and bistros is particularly colourful on Sundays from 10am to 2pm when the farmers from Central Valley offer their produce for sale.

At the end of Clay Street (FDR pier near Jack London Square) lies the luxury yacht which belonged to the form US president Franklin D. Roosevelt (1882–1945). It has been restored at a cost of $5 million. In the "Potomac", the **"Floating White House"**, the president is said to have held numerous conferences which may have altered the course of the world's history.

Once a month 1½ hour cruises can be made (departure 10.30am and 1pm) on board the "Potomac" from San Francisco Bay to the Golden Gate Bridge (for reservations tel. (510) 8397533).

East of Jack London Square at the bottom of Alice Street is **Jack London Village**, with souvenir shops, restaurants, a marina and the Jack London Museum with memorabilia of the writer.

The authoress **Gertrude Stein**, born in neighbouring San Francisco, also spent a part of her youth in Oakland. In the early 1880s she lived on a farm with her parents. Her famous saying, "When you get there, there's no there there", now often used to refer to Los Angeles, was said to have expressed her disappointment at the fact that, after forty years' absence in Europe, the house of her youth in Oakland was no longer standing.

Lake Merritt

In the centre of town lies Lake Merritt, a 64 ha (160 acres) salt-water lake, on which you can take boat trips.

Not far from the lake, which is surrounded by Lakeside Park, a fairytale park and a Japanese garden have been laid out. There are also a botanical garden, picnic-sites and footpaths. At the south-west end of the lake stands the Oakland Museum, with its large open-air exhibition grounds.

The first theme park in the USA, Children's Fairyland (1520 Lakeside Drive), opened in 1950 and served as the inspiration for Walt Disney to found "Disneyland" in Anaheim in 1955. Children's Fairyland (open Tue.–Fri. 10am–4.30pm, Sat., Sun. 10am–5.30pm) symbolizes the best-known fairy tales (for children under 10).

Children's Fairyland

Oakland Museum, situated at the south-west corner of Lake Merritt (1000 Oak Street) contains interesting collections of the natural history, history and folk-art of California (extensive grounds). It is the only museum devoted to California's history and culture as well as exclusively to works by Californian artists.

★ Oakland Museum

The origins of this museum go back to the year 1910 when the Oakland Public Museum was built, followed a few years later by the Oakland Art Gallery. The present museum, a largely subterranean building, was designed by the well-known architect Kevin Roche.

This limitation to one theme was dictated largely by economic necessity, for Oakland was unable to compete with other museums for more expensive paintings.

Exhibits The top floor – through which you enter the museum – is devoted to the works of Californian painters.

Below that you will find a large exhibition room on the history of California. On the bottom floor (the word floor is not quite right, because the levels are arranged terrace-wise one below the other) the theme is the state's natural history. There is also an auditorium.

In addition to Californian painters, photographers are also well represented, including Anselm Adams, Dorothea Lange, Edward Weston and Edward Muybridge.

By means of topographical models visitors can go on a "tour" of California's various regions – the coastal zone, coastal mountains, Central Valley, Sierra Nevada and the desert.

Open Wed.–Sat. 10am–5pm, Sun. noon–7pm. Guided tours by arrangement.

Another park, Joaquin Miller Park, is also named after a Californian writer who lived in Oakland.

J Miller Park

Preservation Park In the heart of Oakland lies a complex with some lovingly restored offices and conference rooms, which make a charming contrast to the modern town centre.

11 km (7 mi.) south of the town centre is a **zoo** which you can reach by the US 580 road (open daily).

Anyone who happens to be in Oakland on the first or third Saturday in the month should not fail to visit the Paramount Theater of Arts, one of the last of the Art Deco cinema palaces remaining in the USA, where at 10am there are guided tours through the building which was designed by the architect Timothy L. Pflueger. The Oakland Symphony Orchestra now performs here.

Paramount Theater of Arts

Leaving Oakland on Highway 880 towards the airport the Western Aerospace Museum can be found at 8260 Boeing Street. The museum contains numerous veteran aircraft and is housed in an aircraft hangar which was built in 1939 on North Field and used as an instruction centre by the firm of Boeings during the Second World War. The main attraction is the "Flying Boat", a 1946 reproduction of

Western Aerospace Museum

Victorian Houses and modern town architecture in Oakland

the famous British craft, the Sunderland. Open Wed.–Sun. 10am–4pm.

Ojai   O2

Ventura County
Altitude: 227 m (650 ft)
Population: 7600

Ojai (pronounced "oohigh"), founded in 1874, lies in the valley of the same name where cattle are reared and citrus fruits cultivated. Originally named after the Californian writer Charles Nordhoff, it received in 1916 the name of the valley which had been taken from the language of the Chumash Indians (meaning "moon"). The town impresses the visitor because of its remoteness (take the US 101 and turn off onto the CA 150 south of Carpentaria), and the harmony of the architecture, unusual in Californian townships of this size.

Countless artists, musicians and writers have lived here, either permanently or temporarily, including the conductor Leopold Stokowski and the Indian mystic Krishnamurti. Each year a music festival is held at the end of May/beginning of June, and a Shakespeare festival at the end of June. At the end of April Ojai is the venue for a tennis tournament which claims to have been the first held anywhere in America. In 1937 Frank Capra filmed "Lost Horizon" in Ojai, based on the novel by James Hilton; not too far away from Hollywood, it seemed to him to be the most fitting arena, his "Shangri-La" (perhaps also because the name sounded somewhat similar).

Oroville   F3

Butte County
Altitude: 53 m (175 ft)
Population: 12,000

This town, 100 km (62 mi.) from Sacramento and 245 km (154 mi.) from San Francisco (via the US 80 and CA 70), was established at the time of the gold-rush around 1850, and amongst its first settlers it must have had some gold-diggers who were well versed in the Bible and who named it Ophir City (after the legendary Old Testament land from which Solomon's fleet brought back gold and other precious items). Only six years later it was re-named Oroville by its inhabitants who were obviously Latin scholars.

At that time the region was still inhabited by the **Yahi Indians**, who were to be wiped out by the whites in the decades which followed; the last member of this tribe was discovered, half-starved, in a slaughterhouse near Oroville, and spent the last five years of his life in the Museum of Anthropology of the University of California in Berkeley (see entry), where he, as the last surviving wild Indian, was transplanted from stone-age culture into the 20th c. His biography appeared under the title of "Ishi", and contains interesting pointers to earlier Indian culture.

Oroville, situated on the northern and central arm of Feather River, today offers few clues to its former **gold-rush** period. Only Miner's Alley and a Chinese temple dating from 1863 (Open Mon.–Thu.) remain, even though Oroville's Chinese quarter is California's second largest after San Francisco's Chinatown.

Some 16 km (10 mi.) north-east of Oroville (CA 162 and Canyon Drive) the 235 m (775 ft)-high Oroville Dam has been constructed, forming the lake of the same name; with banks totalling 269 km (170 mi.) in length it is an important part of the California State Water Project, which was begun in the sixties to bring water from the north of the state down to the central regions and the south.

Oroville Dam

Oxnard   O2

Ventura County
Altitude: 16 m (50 ft)
Population: 143,000

Oxnard, on the CA 1 south-west of its junction with the US 101, first came into being towards the end of the 19th c., but developed quickly, thanks to its agricultural hinterland and two fleet installations to the south, Port Hueneme and Point Mugu. It owes its name to the owner of a sugar-beet refinery, one of the first pioneers to come here. From Channel Islands Harbor, at the end of Peninsula Road near Channel Islands Boulevard, there are direct connections to Channel Islands National Park (see entry), the offices of which, however, are to be found in Ventura (see entry). From Oxnard it is only 17 km (11 mi.) to the nearest island, Anacapa.

The Carnegie Cultural Arts Center (424 South C. Street) owns works of art, an important archaeological collection and artefacts on local history (Open Tue.–Sat.; admission free; tel. 9844649). Previously the building served as a library and town hall.

Carnegie Cultural
Arts Center

Palm Springs: an oasis in the desert

★Palm Springs   Q5

Riverside County
Altitude: 142 m (470 ft)
Population: 40,000

Palm Springs is less than 180 km (113 mi.) from Los Angeles, via the US 10 and CA 111 roads. Together with its sister towns of Palm Desert, Rancho Mirage, Cathedral City, Desert Hot Springs, Idyllwild and Indian Wells it has grown together into what is really one single holiday haunt and winter resort for the richest Americans. Although it lies in the Colorado Desert there are, as the name suggests, springs and numerous palm trees. Palm Springs was discovered as long ago as 1774 by Spaniards, who named it Agua Caliente (hot water), after the hot springs frequently found in this tectonic region. Cahuilla Indians lived there, and today they own a reservation covering almost 12,500 ha (31,000 acres), nearly one-fifth of which lies within the town of Palm Springs, so that the 150 members of the Agua Caliente Group of the Cahuilla are the biggest land-owners in Palm Springs.

Town of VIPs One hundred years later, Palm Springs was still just a sleepy railway town with a few shops and several hut-like houses. Not until the thirties of this century was it "discovered" for a second time, this time by important figures from Hollywood, including Frank Sinatra, Bob Hope and, somewhat later, Elvis Presley and Liberace. They were followed by politicians: Presidents Eisenhower, Kennedy, Johnson, Nixon, Ford and Reagan.

   Palm Springs also became a popular place of retirement for prosperous people from America's north-east states seeking to escape the cold winters; it draws others like them from the cities and towns of California itself for holidays and at weekends.

Shopping It goes without saying that there are very many high-class shops in every part of Palm Springs, such as in the new Desert Fashion Plaza, Palm Springs Mall, Palm Desert Town Center and on El Paseo Drive.

In order to beautify the barren wasteland, some 50,000 **palm trees** were planted and irrigation channels laid, thus making it possible to establish gardens and build swimming pools, which none of the houses lack.

Since the Second World War giant palace-like **hotels** have been built, the biggest of which, Marriott's Dessert Springs Resort and Spa, has almost 900 rooms, 16 tennis courts, a golf course and a big open-air swimming pool on a 140 ha (350 acres) site (opened in 1987). In the season from the middle of December to the end of May the prices reach dizzy heights, such as 1400 dollars for a suite for one night.

Tariffs at the once expensive hotels, built originally for congresses, conferences and company holidays, have fallen sharply as Palm Springs attempts to attract an increasing number of tourists to fill rooms which in recent years have tended to remain vacant.

Out of season, when it gets very hot in Palm Springs and the surrounding country (up to 45°C in the summer months) but remains quite dry, most of the prices are halved when the temperatures double.

However, the months of June, September and October are quite bearable in Palm Springs (particularly in view of the lower prices!), while in November it often rains.

Golf and tennis are the order of the day; there are no fewer than 70 **golf** courses in the vicinity, and in many of the hotels you can relax after physical exertions in fresh, bubbling spring water.

Sights

In addition to touring the town and seeing the houses of the VIPs, anyone spending several days in this domain of the rich and super-rich can book a whole series of other excursions.

The Desert Museum (101 Museum Drive) houses beautiful displays of western art and Indian artefacts, as well as natural history exhibits. Open mid-Sep.–May Tue.–Fri. 10am–4pm, Sat. and Sun. until 5pm.

Desert Museum

Moorten Botanical Garden (1701 South Palm Canyon Drive) contains countless species of desert flora, placed in order according to where they were found and with detailed descriptions on the signposted pathways. Open Mon.–Sat. 9am–4.30pm, Sun. 10am–4pm.

Moorten Botanical Garden

Living Desert Wild Animal Park and Botanical Gardens is a 480 ha (1200 acres) open space with birds, birds of prey, mammals and reptiles in their natural surroundings, as well as desert plants, a palm-oasis, tracks leading into the hills and canyons. Open daily 9am–5pm; closed mid-Jun.–Aug. Address: 47–900 Portola Avenue, 3 km (2 mi.) south of the 111 road, in Palm Desert.

Living Desert Reserve

A special experience is offered in the form of a ride by cable-car up the 2600 m (8600 ft) Mount San Jacinto. The valley station is on the northern edge of Palm Springs. The railway, built in Switzerland in the early sixties, winds its way up the difference in altitude in fourteen minutes, during which time you pass through several climatic zones. Even if it is a hot day in the valley it is cool on the peak.

Mount San Jacinto

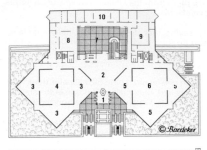

**Palm Springs
Desert Museum**

1 Entrance area
2 Orienteering centre
3 Art gallery
4 Gallery for temporary exhibitions
5 Natural History gallery
6 Gallery for temporary exhibitions
7 Sculpture courtyard
8 Members' room and loan gallery
9 Offices
10 Library and Administration

A Communications centre (auditorium))
B Stage
C Green Room
D Art classroom
E Classroom for Natural History
F Foyer
G Store
H Sales kiosks
J Store

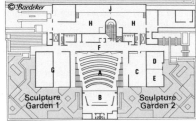

Trips at least every half hour Mon.–Fri. 10am–8pm, weekends and public holidays 8am–8pm; last trip down to the valley 11.45pm. How to get there: 111th Street, turn into Tramway Road, then uphill for 5 km (3 mi.).

Palm Canyon

Palm Canyon, about 10 km (6 mi.) south of the centre of Palm Springs at the end of South Palm Canyon Drive, is a 25 km (15 mi.) long canyon wilderness belonging to the Agua Caliente Indians; it is covered with some 3000 fan-palms and there are fantastic views of the canyon, to which an easy footpath leads. You can also view the neighbouring Andreas and Murray Canyons. Open daily Sep.–May 9am–4pm.

★Palo Alto   I1

Santa Clara County
Altitude: 7 m (23 ft)
Population: 56,000

The town of Palo Alto lies 47 km (29 mi.) south of San Francisco on the US 101. The Spanish name means "tall tree" and can be traced back to a centuries-old redwood tree (the Spaniards named it "palo colorade"), under which the Spanish governor camped with his expedition when they were searching for San Francisco Bay. The trunk of the tree is still there, by the San Francisquito brook, at the junction of Palo Alto Avenue and Camino Real. A century later Governor Leland Stanford revived the name by calling his ranch (where Stanford University now stands) Palo Alto. This name was also used when the town was founded in 1892. A year later a railway station of the Southern Pacific Railroad was built here; by absorbing other districts the town then extended as far as the bay of San Francisco. The part which reached as far as the Santa Cruz Mountains, however, was intentionally not built on.

The large forecourt of the Memorial Church

Thanks especially to the university, Palo Alto has become an important home of the American electronics industry, with numerous small firms having been set up by university graduates. The biggest company established here is **Hewlett-Packard**. Its premises cover such a large area that it is as big as a town, with 25 car parks, a large swimming-pool and a municipal golf-course (see Baedeker Special: Silicon Valley).

However, Palo Alto owes its fame mainly to the fact that in 1891 the college, originally called Leland Stanford Junior University, came into being with 559 students (one being the future president Herbert Hoover). Stanford established the college in memory of his precocious son who, before he died in Rome at the age of 16, had undertaken archaeological expeditions on his own.

★Stanford
University

The original site covered an area of 3300 ha (8250 acres), the driveway lined with palms and the rest of the parkland being the creation of Frederick Law Olmsted (known especially as the designer of Central Park in New York). By way of Palm Drive you come to the inner courtyard, bordered on one side by arcades and on the other by the Memorial Church; its stylistic forbears are to be found in the Romanesque and the Californian mission style.

Although the 1906 earthquake caused considerable damage to the slowly developing campus, including the collapse of the Memorial Church, this could not stop the growth of the university which, in its relatively short period of existence, showed itself equal to those eastern universities which were centuries older (especially Harvard and Yale), and in some disciplines, such as medicine, engineering and English literature, it even outstripped them.

After the First World War the university became the home of the library now known as the Hoover Institution, the nucleus of which was formed by the Hoover Collection and which is devoted mainly to the

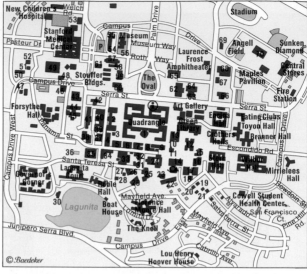

© Baedeker

1 Memorial Church
2 Physics Lecture Hall
3 Skilling
4 Durand
5 Mitchell
6 Building 550
7 Building 530 – 540
8 Building 520
9 Building 500
10 Clock
11 Placement Center
12 Meyer Library
13 School of Education
14 Bookstore
15 Sweet Hall
16 Center for Educational
   Reserach (CERAS)
17 School of Law
18 Kresge Auditorium
19 Rogers
20 Muriposa
21 The Bridge
22 Braun Music Center
23 Dinkelspiel Auditorium
24 The Nitery (Bldg. 590)
25 Tresidder Mem. Union
26 Bowman Alumni House
27 Black House
28 Harmony House
29 Faculty Club
30 Elliott Program Center
31 Old Fire House
32 Building 570
33 Press Bldg., Storke Bldg.
34 Terman Engineering Center
35 Roble Gym
36 Roble Pool
37 Noble
38 Hepl End Station

Stanford University
Palo Alto

39 Salvatori Applied
   Electronics
40 Electronics
41 Hansen Labs
42 Sequoia Hall
43 Center for Integrated
   Systems
44 Applied Physics
45 Ginzton Lab
46 Cogen Facility
47 Ventura Hall
48 Fairchild Center
49 Center for Molecular &
   Genetic Medicine
50 Medical School Office
   Building
51 Mayer Cancer Research
   Laboratory
52 Psychiatry Building
53 Falk CVR Building
54 Anatomy
55 Health Research & Policy
   Building
56 Rodin Sculpture Garden
57 Keck Science Building
58 Organic Chemistry
59 Old Chemistry Building
60 Herrin Hall & Labs
61 Mudd Chemistry Building
62 Graduate School of
   Business
63 Memorial Hall
64 Little Theater
65 Littlefield Center
66 Old Pavilion
67 Department of Athletics
68 Encina Gym
69 Track House
70 De Guerre Pools & Courts

themes of war, revolution and peace. It is housed in the 85 m (280 ft) tall Hoover Tower. Another landmark of the university is the library tower (Green Library).

The students, numbering some 15,000, attend lectures by 1200 professors. These include or have included no less than ten Nobel Prize winners and 75 members of the National Academy of Science.

The campus includes the Stanford University **Museum of Art**, also built in memory of the young Leland Stanford and opened three years after the university was established. The building, based on the National Museum in Athens, was not completed until 1905. Of outstanding importance are the oriental department (which has now grown to 7000 exhibits, only a fraction of which can actually be displayed), and the Egyptian department. An important collection of Indian funerary objects, many examples of Cypriot sculpture and, more recently, numerous European works of art from the last two centuries, form the highlights of this important university museum. Also worth seeing is the sculpture garden, laid out only in recent years on the south side of the museum, devoted exclusively to bronzes by the French sculptor August Rodin – 20 works in all – including the "Gates of Hell", the group-sculpture "Adam and Eve", "The Spirit of Eternal Rest" and several male figures.

Opening times The museum is open Tue. to Fri. 10am to 5pm, at weekends 1–4pm; admission free. It is closed during the university holidays, approximately from the beginning of July to the end of August. Guided tours lasting one hour, covering the whole campus, start from the arcades at 11am and from the Visitor Center at 2pm. On these tours you will also see the Hoover Institution (the library is open 8am–5pm). By booking in advance it is possible on Thursday afternoons to have a free visit to the Stanford Medical Center.

★★Pasadena   P3

Los Angeles County
Altitude: 264 m (866 ft)
Population: 132,000

Founded in 1875, the town can be reached from Downtown Los Angeles in less than 20 minutes, along the Pasadena Freeway (exit Orange Grove/Arroyo), or by bus no. 434; the town's melodic name is not in fact of Spanish origin, but comes from a Chippewa Indian word meaning roughly "grown of the valley".

In its early days Pasadena was a kind of winter spa resort, mainly for visitors from the Middle West of the United States; the first hotels appeared in the 1880s, but only the Huntington Sheraton, originally named the Wentworth, still remains. It opened its doors again in 1989 following a complete refit.

Increasing numbers of well-to-do Americans from other parts of the country settled in Pasadena in order to spend their retirement years in the agreeable climate. Particular mention should be made of the houses built by the brothers Charles and Henry Greene in an interesting mixture of Oriental and Art Deco styles, which dominate whole streets in Pasadena to this day.

The Throop Polytechnic Institute was founded in 1891. In 1920 it was given its present name, California Institute of Technology. This private college employs 780 teachers for its 1800 students. It also runs the almost 2000 m (6600 ft) high observatory on Mount Palomar in the north of San Diego County, while the scarcely less well-known observatory 1700 m (5600 ft) up on Mount Wilson near Pasadena is directed by the

California Institute of Technology

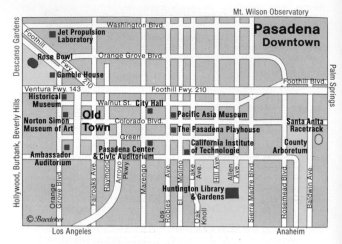

Carnegie Institution. One department of the California Institute of Technology is the Jet Propulsion Laboratory, which has made important technological contributions to the scientific expeditions to the moon and other planets.

Worth seeing is Pasadena's **Old Town**, reached by turning into Raymond Avenue off the main street Colorado Boulevard. On the way you will pass single or two-storied houses not more than 8–16 m (25–50 ft) wide, the ground floors of which are now occupied mainly by shops. A few years ago the old town was beautifully restored and now, with its fine restaurants, street cafés and boutiques, it is a perfect place for a stroll. Old Pasadena is one of the few districts in Los Angeles where one can walk around until late in the evening in complete safety.

Many tourists come to Pasadena to visit two **museums**, the Norton Simon Museum in Pasadena and the Huntington Library and Art Gallery in neighbouring San Marino.

*Norton Simon Museum of Art

The Norton Simon Museum of Art (open Thu.–Sun. noon–6pm) was founded in 1924 as the Pasadena Museum of Modern Art, and erected on its present site (411 Colorado Boulevard, corner of Orange Grove Boulevard) in 1969. In 1974 it was reorganised under the supervision of the industrialist Norton Simon, rebuilt and re-opened a year later as somewhere to display his own impressive collection. Larger works of contemporary art for which there is no room in Pasadena are on permanent loan to Los Angeles County Museum of Art (see entry under Los Angeles).

Exhibits The museum contains important works from almost all periods. The Italian masters represented include Filippino Lippi, Raphael ("Madonna and Child with Book") and Tiepolo ("Victory of Virtue and Steadfastness"), to name only some of the more important. From the Dutch and Flemish masters you will find Rembrandt (a "Titus" painting, a self-portrait and the "Bearded Man with the Broad-brimmed Hat"), as well as numerous etchings; there is also a Rubens, a particularly beauti-

Vincent Van Gogh: "Portrait of a Peasant"

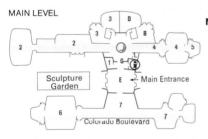

MAIN LEVEL

Pasadena
Norton Simon Museum

MAIN LEVEL
1 Rodin
2 European painting
3 20th c. art
4 European Renaissance
5 Early Italian art
6 Art from India and
  south-east Asia
7 19th and 20th c. art

B Bookstalls
E Entrance area
G Cloakroom

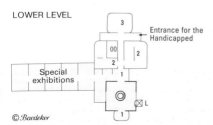

LOWER LEVEL

LOWER LEVEL
1 Degas
2 Dutch and Flemish painting
3 Art from India and
  south-east Asia

L Lift (elevator)

00 Toilets

© Baedeker

211

Norton Simon Museum of Art: exterior

ful Mernling ("Jesus Blessing") and a portrait by Franz Hals. The Spaniards are represented by the painters Murillo, Zurbaran and Goya; you will also find a number of graphic works by Goya.

The widest display is devoted to the various periods of **French art**; ranging from Rigaud, Poussin, Chardin and Watteau (17th and 18th c.) to Degas, Monet, Manet, Rousseau, Seurat, Cézanne, Renoir, Gauguin and Matisse (19th and 20th c). The collection could be described as an almost panoramic vista of French art. The "Portrait of a Farmer" by van Gogh hangs in this department. In a special gallery in the basement you will find 88 examples of the work of this Impressionist, including countless models for his little bronze figures. Cubist works by Picasso, Braque and Juan Gris lead on to painters who worked in Germany, including the American Lyonel Feiniger, the Russians Jawlensky and Kandinsky and the Swiss Paul Klee.

19th and 20th c. **sculptures** can be seen both inside the museum as well as outside in the gardens; these include Rodin's "Burghers of Calais", a Henry Moore, a Henri Laurens and an interesting artistic presentation by the contemporary American John Mason of an oven for baking bricks. Particularly worthy of note, however, are bronzes of the Indian Chola period (10th c.) as well as stone-sculptures from India, Tibet and Nepal.

★★Henry E. Huntington Library and Art Gallery

From Los Angeles the way to this museum complex (1151 Oxford Road, San Marino) is via the Pasadena Freeway (exit for Altadena/Arroyo), or by taking bus no. 432, but this service is not very frequent.

As unusual as the museum itself is its history. Like so many others,

Priceless art treasures can be seen in the Huntington Gallery

... and in the Huntington Library in Pasadena

Collis Huntington, a small shopkeeper in Oneonta in New York State, left the town of his birth in 1849 to go in search of gold in distant California. However, it was not gold which made him a very rich man, but the fact that he went into railway construction at the right time. A large part of his fortune went directly to his nephew Henry, who also inherited the rest through marriage – he married Arabella, his uncle's widow. With this money Henry bought a 200 ha (500 acres) ranch in San Marino – today it is a township of elegant villas with about 13,000 inhabitants – and in the years 1909 to 1911 he built his palace-like villa with its huge garden. While Arabella concerned herself mainly with the acquisition of European, especially English, works of art, Henry devoted himself completely to the library, which today boasts one of the most important manuscript collections of English and American history in the world, and to laying out the garden. Henry Huntington was no idler; he founded the Pacific Electric Railway Co., which ran the whole tramway network in Los Angeles and the county and as the result of clever purchases he became the biggest landowner in southern California. By the time of his death in 1929 he had considerably increased the fortune he had inherited.

In 1919 he donated the whole of his land and estates in San Marino to the library, gallery and garden. At the same time he founded an ancillary research institute with an initial capital of 10½ million dollars.

Literary art treasures, such as the Ellesmere Manuscript from Chaucer's "Canterbury Tales" dating from 1410, and, in the same display cabinet, numerous superbly illuminated books of hours dating from the Middle Ages, are unique. You can then admire a two-volume Johannes Gutenberg bible, printed on parchment in 1455. Not far away can be

Huntington Gallery

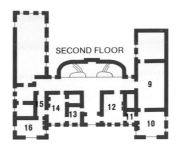

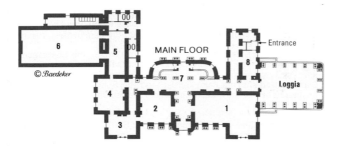

© Baedeker

MAIN FLOOR
Room 1: Gobelins (including sketches
   by François Boucher, 17th c.
   tapestries)
Room 2: Paintings by Gainsborough,
   Reynolds, Romney and Turner;
   French furniture
Room 3: Paintings by Constable,
   English and French applied art
Room 4: Paintings (including portraits)
   by William Hogarth, Geoffrey Kneller,
   and Gilbert Stuart (portrait of
   Washington)
Room 5: English miniatures (17th &
   18th c.)
Room 6: Paintings by Thomas
   Gainsborough (including the "Blue
   Boy") and Thomas Lawrence
   ("Pinkie")

Room 7: Sculpture by J. A. Houdon,
   Roubillac, and P. Warren; 18th c.
   Chelsea porcelain
Room 8: Bronze statuettes
   (Renaissance)

SECOND FLOOR
Rooms 11–15: Temporary exhibitions
   (including English watercolours and
   drawings, European prints, etchings
   by Dürer and Rembrandt; English
   silverwork)
Room 16: Artistic representations of
   sport, hunting scenes and life in the
   country, including paintings by Ben
   Marshall, George Morland and
   George Stubbs

seen some manuscript pages from Benjamin Franklin's autobiography,
which he wrote between 1771 and 1790, leaving a half of each page
empty for later amendments and corrections. Also displayed are the
completely illegible "Forests" manuscript by Henry Thoreaus, letters by
George Washington and Mark Twain, the Shakespeare Folio Edition, a
copy of the large-format original edition of Audobon's "Birds of
America" and much more. There are reading and work rooms available
to academics, who have the choice of nearly four million items.

The works of art are no longer housed solely in the villa, but also in a
new building erected specially for the purpose, the **Virginia Steele
Scott Gallery**. The superb collection is devoted mainly to American art,
but also includes important English works of art of the 18th and 19th c.,
including "Blue Boy", Thomas Gainsborough's most famous painting,
and the scarcely less famous "Pinkie" by Thomas Lawrence. Sir Joshua

Reynolds, George Romney, Sir Henry Raeburn are all represented, as well as works by the French artists Fragonard, Houdon, Baptiste Greuze and François Hubert Drouais; particular mention should be made of the pictures of children which were obviously Arabella's favourite.

The Arabella Huntington **Memorial Collection**, containing predominantly French sculptures from the 18th c., tapestries, porcelain and furniture from the same period, is housed in the west wing of the library.

If the treasures in the museum and gallery were the only things to see, they would be quite sufficient to fill the three and a half hours allowed to visitors each day. However, the beauties of nature displayed in the **gardens** easily match the aesthetic pleasures experienced inside the building. Each of the gardens, here blended into a whole, will attract its own admirers. Most visitors, however, make for the Japanese garden which, with its red bridge, traditional Japanese five-roomed house, the Ikebana house, traditional Bonsai trees and little Zen Garden, inspires them just to sit and meditate.

Other parts of the grounds are: the Herb Garden, the Shakespeare Garden with plants such as existed in the poet's time, the Desert Garden and – in direct contrast – the Jungle Garden, the Rose Garden and two Camellia Gardens, the Palm Garden and the Subtropical Garden and finally, just behind the mausoleum where the Huntingtons lie buried, the Orange Grove.

Opening hours Tue.–Fri. 1–4.30pm, Sat. and Sun. 10.30am–4.30pm. You are recommended to arrange Sunday visits by telephone because the crush is particularly heavy on that day. There is a guided tour through the Botanical Gardens every day at 1pm.

Petaluma   G1

Sonoma County
Altitude: 4 m (13 ft). Population: 43,000

This town, situated on the US 101 about 60 km (37 mi.) north of San Francisco, was founded in 1852, and even before that it was already providing the rapidly growing metropolis with agricultural products. To an immigrant Canadian, Petaluma – the Miwok Indian word for "flat back" – appeared to be an ideal place for chicken farming; he imported white Leghorn chickens, and in 1878 invented the incubator. Chicken farming reached its peak in 1920 when Petaluma, often called the egg-capital of the world, despatched 22 million eggs.

Today there is nothing left of the chicken farms, even though the buildings of historic Petaluma have been amazingly well preserved, and its earlier importance as a river port for trade with San Francisco is still clear to see. Petaluma also possesses a shopping centre with 30 shops and two restaurants.

Pinnacles National Monument   K1

This national monument, created by the federal government in 1908, lies in the Gabilan Mountains on the CA 25, south-east of Salinas (see entry). It is an area of 8 sq. km (3 sq. mi.) of volcanic origin, which has been eroded by wind, rain, frost, heat and chemical reactions of various kinds, producing interesting rock formations with cliffs and pinnacles. It is assumed that a volcano was formed as the result of earth eruptions 23 million years ago; its remains can be seen in Pinnacles Monument. Beyond the actual peak district (6 km (4 mi.) wide and 11 km (7 mi.) long), the National Monument includes a further area of 52 sq. km (20 sq. mi.), as well as numerous caves.

Advice It is possible to walk through the whole area, but some of the paths are difficult. The west entrance leads via Soledad to the US 101 and the east entrance via the CA 25.

Pismo Beach   M1

San Luis Obispo County
Altitude: 10 m (33 ft)
Population: 7700

This little town, right by the Pacific Ocean south of San Luis Obispo (see entry) on the US 101, stands out because of its 35 km (22 mi.) of beach, where several kinds of edible mussels can be dug up at any time of the year, and all kinds of water sports can be pursued.
   Pismo Beach – the name comes from the language of the Chumash Indians and means "tar" – is also known for being (at the time of going to press) the last place close to the sea to allow cars to drive on ramps right on to the beach. Known for its extensive sand dunes, vehicles are prohibited in the Dunes reserve.

Placerville   H4

El Dorado County
Altitude: 570 m (1880 ft)
Population: 8400

Placerville, only a few miles from where the first gold was found in Coloma (see entry), still lies in the gold-region, at the junction of Mother Lode Street (now the CA 49) and the main highway from Sacramento to the Comstock silver mine in Nevada (now the US 50). Originally the town was named Dry Diggins; this was later changed to Hangtown, because so many unruly gold-diggers were hanged in order to maintain law and order. On a house in Main Street where the gallows stood, a life-sized figure of a "hanged man" can still be seen today. Little of its wild past remains in Placerville. Today it lies in the middle of a fruit-growing area, where a big "Cherry Carnival" is held in the middle of June, and where the apple harvest is celebrated from September to December, during which period 45 farmers welcome visitors.

Three **famous Americans** began life in Placerville: Mark Hopkins, a grocer who became a railway magnate and one of San Francisco's rich-est men (a hotel bears his name), the butcher Philip Armour, founder of one of the largest meat processing companies still in existence, and the coach-builder John Studebaker, one of the first important motor-car manufacturers in Detroit.

★Point Lobos State Reserve   J0

This unusual coastal region in the south of Carmel Bay lies only a few miles from Carmel (see entry), and the harshness of its granite cliffs and

Rugged cliffs and wild vegetation on the Pacific Coast draw the visitor to walk to Point Lobos

caves forms a stark contrast to the civilised township. As a result of the constant movements of the waves over many millions of years a gradual erosion of the rock has taken place, producing some strange formations. Along sign-posted trails through this 500 ha (1250 acre)-tract, declared a nature reserve since 1933, (more than half of which lies under water), you can admire its beauty from close quarters: the numerous rocks lying off the coast, the caves, the rock-enclosed ponds which continually re-form, the fish in the clear waters and – with luck –sea-otters and sea-lions.

Walks Point Lobos is also a good point from which to observe the whales swimming not too far from the coast, on their way north or south, depending on the time of the year. You can cover the whole area, but this rather difficult stretch, almost 10 km (6 mi.) long, starts at the entrance to Point Lobos on the CA 1 and will take some three to five hours.

If you have less time to spare you should at least walk along the Cypress Grove Trail (many Monterey cypresses) and the North Shore Trail.

Opening hours Point Lobos State Reserve is open daily, 9am–5pm, often longer in the summer months.

Point Loma

See San Diego

Cove in Point Lobos State Reserve

★Point Reyes National Seashore G/H0/1

Only 48 km (30 mi.) north of San Francisco on the CA 1 you will find Point Reyes, declared a "National Seashore" in 1962 and now forming part of the Golden Gate National Recreation Area which starts in San Francisco. The British landed on this peninsula 41 years before the Pilgrim Fathers at Plymouth. In 1579 Sir Francis Drake dropped anchor here and took possession of the land for the British Crown, but his homeland did not concern itself unduly with the west of the newly-discovered continent. 24 years later, on January 6th 1603, the Spanish seafarer Don Sebastian Vizcaino landed on the peninsula and – as it was the Feast of the Epiphany – named it La Punta de los Reyes (the Point of the Kings).

Point Reyes lies at the end of the San Andreas Fault, which was responsible for the devastating earthquakes of 1906 and 1989 which have struck San Francisco. From the Bear Valley Visitor Center starts a so-called **"Earthquake Way"**, about 1 km (3300 ft) in length, along which can be found seismographic evidence of earthquake movements, such as parts of a fence which formed one unit prior to the earthquake and which are now five metres apart.

Wildlife Numerous sea-birds spend the winter in this protected coastal terrain; several species of deer live in the forests, as well as foxes. Recent attempts have been made to re-introduce the elk.

In the months of December and January the Californian **grey whale** can be observed on its migration from the north to Baja California. As there is more fog in Point Reyes than at any other point along the Californian

Point Reyes National Seashore

coast, a lighthouse was built in 1870. From here you get a splendid view of the whales as they swim past. They can be seen again in the months of April and May when they return to the Arctic.

From the Bear Valley Visitor Center more than 120 km (75 mi.) of **trails** suitable for walking and riding lead into all parts of this coastal nature reserve. Information regarding the length and condition of these trails, as well as maps, can be obtained from the Visitor Center.

Nearby can be found a reproduction of a Miwok Indian village (the Miwoks were the original inhabitants of the region). The **Visitor Center** is open only Thu.–Mon.

Red Bluff   D/E3

Tehama County
Altitude: 94 m (310 ft). Population: 12,000

The town gets its name from the red sandstone and gravel cliffs in the surrounding countryside. Situated on the upper reaches of the Sacramento River, at the junction of the US 5, CA 99 and CA 36, Red Bluff, in the middle of the 19th c. was mainly a stopping-off place for gold-diggers who often went back there when they realised that the soil was favourable for growing wheat and fruit. Its position on the Sacramento River made Red Bluff a centre for private and commercial shipping. Timber and agriculture remain the chief sources of revenue even today.

Redwood Empire: Avenue of the Giants ▶

W.B. Ide Adobe State Historic Park

Only 3 km (2 mi.) to the north-east on the US 5 (Wilcox Road exit), you will find the William B. Ide Adobe State Historic Park, with the restored adobe residence (built 1846; tel. 8954303) of the only president of the short-lived Republic of California. In the town itself stands a beautiful Victorian house with its original furnishings. In the Kelly Griggs House Museum (311 Washington Street) you can see a collection of Chinese and Indian artefacts. Open daily 8am–sunset.

Redding   D3

Shasta County
Altitude: 170 m (560 ft). Population: 67,000

This town, founded in 1872 and situated on the upper reaches of the Sacramento River and on the edge of the Sierra Nevada, is particularly important because of its favourable position as a starting point for numerous excursions into nearby districts: Lake Shasta (its famous caves are only 25 km (16 mi.) away), the 4317 m (14,170 ft) high Mount Shasta (about 10 km (6 mi.) away), Whiskeytown Shasta Historic Park with its gold-digging past (10 km (6 mi.)) and Shasta Trinity National Forest. Redding is also well-placed traffic-wise being at the junction of several highways: the US 5, which runs south to San Diego via the county capital of Sacramento, the CA 299 to the Pacific coast via Eureka and the CA 44 to Lassen Volcanic National Park (see entries).

Museum & Art Center

The town's main place of interest is the Museum & Art Center (1911 Rio Drive) with Indian and pre-Columbian artefacts as well as documentation on the history of Shasta County (open Jun.–Aug. Tue.–Sun. 10am–5pm; remaining months Tue.–Fri. and Sun. noon–5pm). The museum stands on the northern edge of the town in beautiful Caldwell Park, right on the shores of the Sacramento River (various water-sports).

To cater for the tourists who stream into the charming countryside to the west, north and east of the town, Redding possesses more than 20 **hotels and motels**.

★★Redwood Highway   A–D 1/2

Redwood Highway is the name given to that 480 km (300 mi.) stretch of the US 101 which passes through the terrain where about 97% of all Californian Redwoods grow, most of them between Leggett and the Oregon border. Humboldt Redwoods State Park runs along both sides of the highway. Before this road was built the Avenue of the Giants – parallel to it – was the main route from Philipsville in the south to Pepperwood in the north.
   Redwoods also grow in Grizzly Creek Redwoods State Park, a few miles east of the US 101 on the CA 36 south of Carlotta, and in Redwood National Park between Orick and Crescent City (see entry), on the Oregon border, to which the Del Norte Coast Redwoods State Park belongs. Almost everywhere where Redwoods grow you will come across stalls selling wood-carvings, ranging from little boxes to larger-than-life legendary figures.

North Coast Daylight

Part of the Redwoods and many other natural beauty spots along the north Californian coast which are difficult to get to can also be enjoyed by taking a ten-hour train ride on the North Coast Daylight from Willits to Eureka (see entry). On this journey you will pass through no fewer

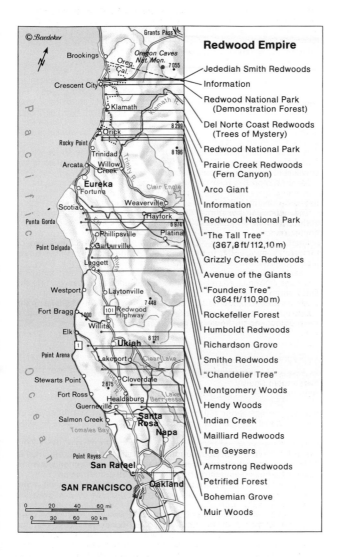

© Baedeker

Redwood Empire

Jedediah Smith Redwoods

Information

Redwood National Park
(Demonstration Forest)

Del Norte Coast Redwoods
(Trees of Mystery)

Redwood National Park

Prairie Creek Redwoods
(Fern Canyon)

Arco Giant

Information

Redwood National Park

"The Tall Tree"
(367,8 ft/112,10 m)

Grizzly Creek Redwoods

Avenue of the Giants

"Founders Tree"
(364 ft/110,90 m)

Rockefeller Forest

Humboldt Redwoods

Richardson Grove

Smithe Redwoods

"Chandelier Tree"

Montgomery Woods

Hendy Woods

Indian Creek

Mailliard Redwoods

The Geysers

Armstrong Redwoods

Petrified Forest

Bohemian Grove

Muir Woods

than 25 tunnels and over 29 bridges. (Information: North Coast Daylight, Box 3666, Eureka CA 95502.)

All the **information** and brochures you require on the "Redwood Empire" in California can be obtained from the Redwood Empire Association, 1 Market Plaza, Spear Street Tower, San Francisco CA 94105.

Riverside   Q4

Riverside County
Altitude: 262 m (860 ft). Population: 227,000

Riverside is the capital of the county of the same name, and is to be found south-east of Los Angeles on the CA 60 and 91 close to the US 10. Established about 1870, it was initially a silkworm-breeding centre, but within a few years had developed into an important agricultural area, concentrating mainly on growing navel oranges which had been cultivated by mutation in Brazil in 1873. Most navel oranges still come from here today, although Riverside has experienced rapid growth since 1950 and is now an important commercial and industrial town.

A citrus experimental station was the nucleus of the University of California in Riverside. With some 7500 students, the campus is the smallest of the nine university sites.

March Airport lies near the town.

Sights

Riverside has the following places which are worth a visit:

The municipal museum (37220 Orange Street), exhibiting historical, anthropological and natural history items. Open daily except Mon.; admission free.

The California Museum of Photography, which has been in existence for over 15 years, and is to be found in a new building in the Main Street Mall. Open Wed.–Sun. noon–5pm.

The historical Mission (3649 7th Street), where Spanish antiques, paintings, 900 bells, etc. are on exhibition. Guided tours daily at 11.30am and 2.30pm.

Mount Rubidoux Memorial Park, at a height of 400 m (1300 ft) on the western edge of town, with the Serra Cross in honour of the founder of the mission, and the Tower of World Peace.

★Sacramento   G/H2/3

Sacramento County
Altitude: 8 m (27 ft). Population: 400,000

Sacramento lies about 150 km (93 mi.) north-east of San Francisco on the US 80, and has been the capital of the federal state of California since 1854.

History John A. Sutter (see Famous Personalities) founded the town in 1839, and named it after the nearby river. The old fortification known as Sutter's Fort has been restored and is now a tourist attraction.

In the early fifties the town suffered from several floods as well as frequent fires. The old town (Old Sacramento), cheek by jowl with the Sacramento River, with plenty of shops and restaurants, was restored around 1980. In 1856 the first Californian railway was opened between Sacramento and Folsom, and was later connected to the Transcontinental Railway line running between the east and west coasts.

Sights

Big Four Building

The Big Four Building is named after the four most influential men in the Californian railway industry. They all lived in Sacramento before moving to the larger and more important San Francisco: they were Charles Crocker, Mark Hopkins, Collis B. Huntington and Leland Stanford. (Address: I Street, between Front and Second Street.)

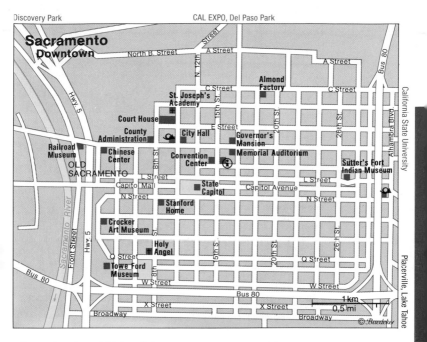

Discovery Park — CAL EXPO, Del Paso Park

Sacramento Downtown

North B Street — A Street
North B. Street — A Street — A Street
Hwy 5
N 12th Street
C Street — Almond Factory — C Street
St. Joseph's Academy — 15th St
Court House — E Street — 20th St — 26th St
County Administration — City Hall — Governor's Mansion
Railroad Museum — Chinese Center — Convention Center — Memorial Auditorium — Sütter's Fort Indian Museum
OLD SACRAMENTO — 8th St
L Street — L Street
Capitol Mall — State Capitol — Capitol Avenue
N Street — N Street
Stanford Home
Crocker Art Museum
Holy Angel — 15th St — 20th St — 26th St
Q Street — Q Street
Towe Ford Museum
W Street — W Street
Bus 80
X Street — X Street
Broadway — Broadway
1 km
0,5 mi
© Baedeker

Sacramento River — Front Street — Hwy 5 — Bus 80

California State University — Alhambra Blvd — Placerville, Lake Tahoe

Comprehensive exhibition of documents on the history of Sacramento and California. (Address: 1020 O Street). Open Mon.–Fri. 8am–5pm.

California State Archives

The old neo-classical Capitol, with its 70 m (234 ft)-high dome, was built between 1861 and 1869; extensions were added later. A complete restoration of the old Capitol (cost: 68 million dollars) was completed in 1982. Since then the marble mosaic floors and many chandeliers again shine as they did in the old days, and make the Governor's official seat and the parliamentary chambers (which can also be visited when parliament is not sitting) interesting and attractive to tourists. (Address: 10th Street and Capitol Mall; open daily 9am–5pm; admission free.)

★California State Capitol

The colourful **gardens**, extending over several blocks and with tall palms and numerous other species of trees and plants, make the building the most beautiful Capitol in the United States.

Since December 1988 a bronze group **sculpture**, the Vietnam War Memorial, has stood in the north-east part of Capitol Park (L and 15th Street); its construction was entirely funded by donations, and it commemorates those who sacrificed their lives in the longest war involving the United States of America.

Californian State Capitol **Museum** Seven historic rooms in the old Capitol, with furniture and other accoutrements from the beginning of the 20th c., provide the visitor with a glimpse of the past. Films are also shown. Open daily 9am–5pm. Information available in the Capitol Building, Room 124.

Sacramento

California State Railroad Museum

With a floor area for exhibits of over 10,000 sq. m (100,000 sq. ft)., the California State Railroad Museum is the world's largest railway museum. It houses 21 restored locomotives and railway coaches of all ages, as well as 46 other items. Almost all the wagons can be viewed inside. Open; daily 10am–5pm, except for Christmas and New Year. With the same admission ticket you can also visit the old "Pacific" railway station. (Address: 125 I Street, in Old Sacramento State Historic Park.)

Sacramento's oldest railway station, **Central Pacific Railroad Station**, dates from the 19th c., and has been opened up to visitors as a branch of the Californian State Railroad Museum.

In the completely restored station building you will find the Central Pacific **Passenger Depot**, where you will be transported back to the second half of the 19th c. In the summer months you can travel to Miller Park in historic trains. (Address: Front Street, near the Railroad Museum.)

Old Sacramento

Crocker Art Gallery

Crocker Art Museum

A reconstructed Victorian building, originating from 1873, houses the oldest art museum in the western United States. It has been extended several times. In addition to paintings and drawings by Californian artists (from Sacramento in particular), the exhibits include European, East Asian and recently also some contemporary works of art and photographs. (Address: 216 O Street.) Open Wed.–Sun. 10am–5pm, Thu. till 6pm.

Hastings Building

The Hastings Building, dating from 1853, was originally a bank; today it is a museum where you will find a reproduction of California's first Supreme Court, as well as the Pony Express Museum and the Wells Fargo Museum. (Address: 2nd and J Street.) Open Tue.–Sun. 10am–5pm; admission free.

Historic Governor's House

This magnificent Victorian villa, built in 1878, served as a residence for thirteen Californian Governors, the last being Ronald Reagan, who lived there from 1966 to 1975. (Address: 16th and H Street.) Open daily 10am–5pm; guided tours on the hour every hour 10am–4pm.

★ Old Sacramento

About 10.5 ha (26 acres) of Sacramento's old town, between I and M Street and also 2nd and Front Street, have been restored in the style of the years 1849–70, including the cobbled streets (buggy rides available). At weekends, at 11.30am and 1.30pm, guided walks through the old town are organised starting from the Central Pacific Passenger Depot.

Eagle Theater

In the old town stands the Eagle Theater, built in 1849; performances on Friday and Saturday evenings. (Address: 25 Front Street.)

Schoolhouse

The Old Sacramento Schoolhouse is a reproduction of a school of 1880.

Sacramento: Californian State Capitol

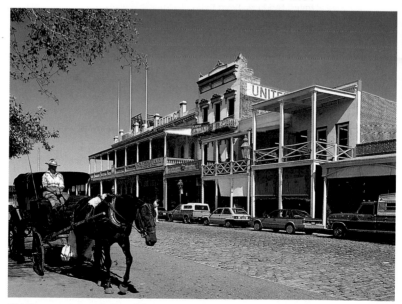

Old Sacramento: reminders of the past

Vintage car in front of an old fashioned filling station in the Towe Ford Museum

(Address: corner of Front and L Streets.) Open Mon.–Fri. 9.30am–4pm, weekends noon–4pm.

Old harbour district

Sacramento is carrying out a project to restore the old harbour district to what it looked like in days gone by. A start has been made on the east bank of Sacramento River, between I Street Bridge and Tower Bridge.

Since 1989 "Delta King", the ship which used to ply between Sacramento and San Francisco from 1920 to 1941, has been laid up; it could hold 1000 passengers and 2000 tonnes of freight. In the Second World War it served as a hospital ship, and has now been converted to a floating hotel, with 44 single cabins, 12 restaurants, function rooms for a total of 200 people, as well as a museum and theatre.

Discovery Museum

The Sacramento History Center is a modern museum with four galleries:

The information centre introduces the visitor, by means of a 9-minute film and a computer system, to the way the gallery has been built up (ground floor).

The Topomorphology Gallery describes the changing environment and the interaction of man and geology in the Sacramento Valley (first floor).

The Community Gallery presents the sometimes conflicting social forces in the community known as Great Sacramento (first floor).

On the ground floor also there is a gallery of agricultural technology and one for exhibitions held on a rota basis. (Address: 101 I Street.) Open daily 10am–5pm.

★Sutter's Fort

Where Sutter's Fort Museum stands today was once the site of the first outpost of the white man in California, set up by the German-Swiss immigrant Johann August Sutter in 1839. The adobe house built in the same year has been restored in the original style, and today houses

Sutter's Fort: first outpost of the white man in California

relics of the pioneering and gold-rush period; there are also items on show to remind us of the town's founder, whose estates reached as far as the other side of the American River near Coloma (see entry). After gold was discovered Sutter was literally overrun by gold-seekers, so that he was forced to flee. (Address: 27th & L Street.) Open daily 10am–5pm; last guided tour begins at 4.15pm.

The Indian Museum nearby offers an insight into the life-style of California's original inhabitants. (Address: 2618 K Street.) Open daily 10am–5pm.

Indian Museum

The Towe Ford Museum was first set up in 1987 and contains a collection of 150 Ford cars, with an example from each year of manufacture and at least one model from each of the years 1903–53. (Address: 2200 Front Street.) Open daily 10am–5pm.

Towe Ford Museum

St Helena   G1

Napa County. Altitude: 78 m (256 ft). Population: 5000

Some 60 km (37 mi.) north of San Francisco lies St Helena, one of the important wine-producing towns in the Napa Valley, with six big wine firms operating in the town or nearby: Beaulieu, Beringer, Inglenook, Hans Kornell, Charles Krug and Louis M. Martini. Not far away the 1300 m (4300 ft)-high Mount St Helena looks down over the Napa Valley. It forms part of the Mayacamas Mountains (named after the old Indian village of Miyakmah, near Calistoga – see entry).

Salinas

Silverado Museum

The Silverado Museum (1490 Library Lane), named after a former Mount St Helena silver mine, is dedicated to the writer Robert Louis Stevenson; as well as first editions of his works it has numerous manuscripts, photographs and letters. Open Tue.–Fri. noon–4pm; admission free.

Lake Berryessa

About 20 km (12 mi.) east of St Helena, you will find the artificial Lake Berryessa, formed as a result of the building of the Monticello Dam; its banks are 265 km (165 mi.) in length, and there are numerous opportunities for water sports.

Salinas   J1

Monterey County
Altitude: 16 m (53 ft). Population: 109,500

Salinas is to be found some 80 km (50 mi.) south of San José, in the middle of a fertile agricultural region, where mainly lettuce, sugar-beet and fruit and vegetables of all kinds are grown, and some canning is done as well. Founded in 1856, its name comes from the salt-marshes at the mouth of the river of the same name; it became well-known as the birthplace of John Steinbeck (see Famous Personalities).

Several of **John Steinbeck's** works are set in Salinas or the Salinas Valley, for example, "Tortilla Flat" (1935), "East of Eden" (1952) and "Of Mice and Men" (1937). The house in which Steinbeck was born (132 Central Avenue, corner of Stone Street) is an imposing building, which now houses a restaurant on the ground floor. The house is not open to visitors. However, you can see some Steinbeck memorabilia in the John

John Steinbeck's birthplace in Salinas

Steinbeck Library (110 W. San Luis Street.) Open Mon.–Thu. 10am–9pm, Fri. and Sat. 10am–6pm; tel. 7587311.

Salton Sea   R/S6

The Salton Sea, situated some 200 km (124 mi.) north-east of San Diego, can be reached via US Highway 15 to Escondido, then CA 78 eastwards to its junction with CA 86, where head further north.

Origin An ancient dried-up bed of a lake became an actual "sea" again in 1905. Having broken through an irrigation canal in Imperial Valley, the Colorado River flooded over into the old bed and filled it to a depth of 25 m (82 ft) and a diameter of almost 75 m (250 ft). The river continued to flood until 1907; the resultant lake (now 48 km (30 mi.) long and 13–23 km (8–14 mi.) long and 13–23 km (8–14 mi.) wide, with a surface of 74 m (235 ft) and lying below sea-level) has no outlets, apart from some ditches dug to lead water away.

The Salton Sea State **Reservation Area** has been created on the northern bank. This area, covering 6672 ha (16,680 acres), provides 175 well-equipped camping sites, which are especially popular with fishermen and water-sport enthusiasts (water-skiing, boats) and naturalists (walks, bird-watching).

San Antonio de Padua

See Mission Stations

San Bernardino   P/Q4

San Bernardino County
Altitude: 320 m (1050 ft). Population: 165,000

San Bernardino, the capital of the largest county in the USA, lies on the Barstow Freeway (US 215) and on the CA 66, some 90 km (56 mi.) east of Los Angeles, 170 km (106 mi.) north-east of San Diego and 725 km (450 mi.) south-east of San Francisco; it is 25 minutes by car from Ontario International Airport. The town occupies a position surrounded by mountains, fertile valleys and deserts, and is one of the fastest growing parts of California.

Development The Franciscan Fathers of the San Gabriel Mission (see entry for Mission Stations) founded a hospital here in 1810, but it was pillaged several times by the Paiute Indians. As it was founded on the name day of San Bernardino of Siena it was named after that saint. Four decades later Mormons settled here, and laid the town out in the manner of Salt Lake City. However, the Mormon leader Brigham Young recalled them after only six years. Nevertheless, the town developed without further hindrance, and today is one of California's orange-growing centres.

The CA 18, also called "Rim of the World", is a very famous highway. It leads to Lake Arrowhead (water-sports), Big Bear Lake, Baldwin Lake and other popular destinations. The 62 km (38 mi.)-long road, which winds and twists its way up to a height of 2200 m (7220 ft), provides plenty of picturesque views. The most beautiful panoramic view, however, is from the highest point, known as Lakeview Point.

Rim of the World Drive

San Buenaventura

See Mission Stations

★★San Diego   R/S3/4

San Diego County
Altitude: 13 m (43 ft)
Population: 1.17 million (Greater San Diego 2.5 million)

San Diego is situated some 120 miles/200km south of Los Angeles. The town's southern boundary is also the border with Mexico. Being on two protected bays, San Diego Bay, which is separated from the sea by Point Loma and by Coronado Island/North Island, and the multi-lobed Mission Bay north of the San Diego River, San Diego has become an important port. It is the biggest American naval base after Norfolk. The equitable warm and dry climate and the beautiful and fertile surrounding countryside (oranges, tomatoes, avocados, fruit and vegetables) make San Diego a popular place in which to live.

See map at end of book

Conurbation San Diego has become an important port. It is the biggest American naval base after Norfolk. The equitable warm and dry climate and the beautiful and fertile surrounding countryside (oranges, tomatoes, avocados, fruit and vegetables) make San Diego a popular place in which to live.

The town is a favourite centre for seminars and conventions, as well as being important in the research sphere (space travel, oceanography, electronics and three universities). This is where the "Atlas" rockets used in space flights were developed.

Population San Diego is the oldest town in California and – from its foundation in 1769 – the one where development was the slowest. Early in the Second World War (about 1940) San Diego had barely 150,000 inhabitants. Since then its attractions have increased to such an extent that it has become the second town in California, after Los Angeles, to have a million people.

Since 1980 the number of people living in San Diego has increased by a third. With the exception of Houston in Texas and Phoenix, the capital of Arizona, no other large American town has experienced such a high percentage increase.

Leisure San Diego offers the visitor an enchanting natural beauty and a climate with plenty of sunshine: the 565 ha (1410 acres) Balboa Park, with perhaps the world's finest zoo; more than 110 km (68 mi.) of beaches in town and county; countless opportunities for water sports (including sailing and motor-boats); excursions into the nearby waste-lands or – by tram – to Mexico. It has more public and private golf courses than any other American town. There are also several stud-farms.

Climate The weather is exceptional. The sun is nearly always shining, and the drop in temperature extremely small, certainly smaller than any-where else in California. Average temperatures are 16°C in spring, 21°C in summer, 19°C in autumn and 14°C in winter. Fluctuations from these are rare; very hot summer temperatures occur only now and again, and temperatures below freezing point are unknown. Like everywhere else on the Pacific coast, in the summer months there are sometimes early morning mists and low cloud, and the sun often does not get through before 10am or noon. There are occasional showers only between November and February.

History

As long ago as 1542 a Spanish expedition under Juan Rodriguez Cabrillo had sailed into San Diego Bay and discovered what was later to be known as California. On his voyage along the Californian coast 60 years later Sebastian Vizcaino entered the bay and gave it the name of his flagship, St Didacus de Alcala. Didicus (Diego in Spanish) was a 15th c. Franciscan monk who was canonised after his death as a reward for his fantastically strict regime of penitence. In 1769 an expedition came from the governor of Baja California, Don Gaspar de Portola, to Alta California with some Franciscan monks on board, including Father Junipero Serra, beatified in 1988, who started to build the first of 21 mission stations (see entry) on July 16th 1769 which is also the date when San Diego really came into being. The present-day Mission of San Diego de Alcala is to be found some 10 km (6 mi.) inland from its original site.

19th century It was not until 1820 that a plaza was built, surrounded for the next 20 years by about 40 adobe houses. At that time, no more than 200 Mexicans and Spaniards lived there. The first North Americans came around 1803. However, when in 1846 during the Americo-Mexican war the town was occupied by American marines, there was merely a handful of white men living in the Old Town. San Diego changed owners several times in the following five months; only after the Battle of San Pasqual, east of the present Escondido, did it finally fall into American hands.

Balboa Park: lily pond outside Botanical Building

With the acceptance of the federal state of California into the Union in 1850 San Diego County came into being, and the town was given its charter. At first this did not speed up its development in any way. Only when, in 1885, the Santa Fe Railroad arranged for San Diego to be connected to the transcontinental railway network was there a noticeable upswing. Shortly after the population had increased to 40,000, however, the first crisis occurred and the hoped-for economic boom failed to materialise.

Furthermore, the extension of the harbour which was now underway proved insufficient to break the predominance of San Francisco and the new San Pedro Harbor of Los Angeles.

Early 20th century The town's real upswing began to take place after three major events: first the completion of the Panama Canal in the autumn of 1914; secondly, the Panama-Californian Exhibition held in Balboa Park in 1915/1916, which directed the world's attention towards San Diego; and thirdly, the moving of an army and, in particular, a naval base to San Diego during the First World War.

When the town was redeveloped in 1868, Balboa Park was saved – thanks to a far-sighted city father – and this extensive green area still exists today.

Present-day The town is expanding on all sides, and now covers an area of 800 sq. km (310 sq. mi.); in the south it reaches as far as Point Loma and nearly to the Mexican border in the suburb of Chula Vista, in the north to La Jolla, and in the west to La Mesa and El Cajon. Whether, in view of the many facilities offered to residents in the suburbs, the authorities will succeed in breathing life back into the town centre and avoid what has happened in Los Angeles, remains a fateful question for San Diego.

Economy and culture

After the Japanese attack on the Pacific naval base in Honolulu in December 1941 when the United States were considering a new base, the choice fell on San Diego. Since then the 11th Naval Squadron has been stationed here; it is also the headquarters of the Pacific Fleet. This military presence is of the greatest importance to San Diego's **economy**. The second most important economic factor is the aircraft industry (the Convair works are the biggest employers), and the third is tourism. The building of space-rockets, oceanic and bio-medical research, electronics and higher education (especially the University of California at San Diego in La Jolla) also play a decisive rôle in the town's economy.

Unfortunately San Diego's **cultural development** has lagged behind its economic progress. One of the main reasons is that potential patrons of the arts were somewhat late in deciding to settle in the town. As public subsidies are rare, the town's cultural pursuits depend mainly upon private sponsorship. As a result, San Diego has no adequate museum and is outclassed by San Francisco and Los Angeles in the musical sphere as well. Only the theatre has recently gained in importance.

Transport

San Diego can be the beginning or the end of a trip through California. Its **airport**, only a few miles from the centre of town (Lindbergh Field), is to be moved further out into the county in the foreseeable future. It serves thirteen airlines, including American, American West, Continental, Delta, TWA and United Airlines, with direct flights from the east coast.

Routes When coming from the north by car along the US 5 or 15 and the

CA 163 turn-off past the Miramar Naval Air Force Base, you drive straight into town. Another road which leads through the town from north to south is the US 805. You approach from the east along the US 8, CA 125 (east of La Mesa) and CA 94, which then merges with the US 5. Greyhound and Trailway buses operate a service to downtown San Diego.

It is worth taking the two and a half hour **train** ride from Los Angeles to San Diego or vice-versa; Amtrak Station in San Diego is situated on Broadway and Kettner Boulevard.

In San Diego – like almost anywhere in the USA – the **car** is the best form of transport. Most of the places of interest described in this book will be found quite near to the freeways, and there is generally adequate parking space. If you come by car you should, whenever possible, choose a motel or hotel with an underground garage. You should also note that most streets in the town centre are one-way.

Public transport (buses and trams) are normally time-consuming for the tourist because they go all round the town, do not use the freeways and stop frequently. (Time-table information from the San Diego Transit Company.)

★Balboa Park

Most of the town's museums are to be found on this 565 ha (1412 acres) site. It is therefore advisable to park your car on the big car-park in front of the zoo and visit the places of interest on foot. The time required to see the park depends on where your interests lie. Experience suggests setting aside one full day for the museums and another for the remaining sights. Between 10am and 4pm (5.30pm in summer), there is a free tram service from the car-park to seven stops in Balboa Park.

The lily pond filled with gold fish in front of the Botanical Building was used during the Second World War as a swimming pool by patients at the US naval hospital. The building itself is another reminder of the past – the steel framework was actually made for a station belonging to the Santa Fe Railroad but was purchased by the managers of the exhibition. Inside there are more than 500 species of tropical and sub-tropical plants to be seen. Open Tue.–Sun. 10am–4pm.

Botanical Building

The fifteen bungalows of the House of Pacific Relations, reminiscent of the Mexican colonial period, were each intended for one of the Latin-American countries participating in the exhibition. They have retained their purpose to this day. Viewing of the interiors of the houses is restricted to Sun. 12.30–4.30pm and the fourth Tue. of the month noon–3pm; admission free. Folk-concerts and dances are also held during these hours.

House of Pacific Relations

The exhibits in the Museum of Man were collected by the Smithsonian Institute in Washington from the Indian Pueblos in the south-west of the United States; further excavations were made at the ruins of the Aztec and Maya settlements in Latin America. Among other things, they illustrate the early history of the human race by portraying prehistoric man. Today thousands of artefacts make up the exhibits displayed in this ever-expanding museum, which also mounts exhibitions alternating on a rota basis. Open daily except on important public holidays 10am–4.30pm.

Museum of Man

The relatively new Museum of Photographic Arts is housed in the arcades of the Casa de Balboa and presents exhibitions of black and white, and colour, photographs on specific themes or by well-known photographers, as well as video and film programmes from its own archives. Open daily 10am–5pm, Thu. 10am–9pm.

Museum of Photographic Arts

Skyline of San Diego at twilight

Old Globe Theater

This theatre, also built in 1935/1936 for the California Pacific International Exposition and based on Shakespeare's Globe Theatre in London in the style of the 15th c., was destroyed by fire in 1978, but was re-built and is now the home of the San Diego Repertory Company.

Directly next to it are to be found two further units of the Simon Edison Center for the Performing Arts: a theatre for contemporary plays (225 seats), named after the famous 19th c. Shakespeare director Cassius Clay, and the Lowell Davies Festival Theater, an open-air stage with over 600 seats, where the Shakespeare Festival is held in summer.

Reuben H. Fleet Space Theater and Science Center

The Reuben H. Fleet Space Theater is a planetarium and cinema combined which, by means of a 23 m (75 ft) long, hemispherical dome-projector, gives you the impression that you are floating in space. In the adjoining Science Center you may handle as well as look at the items on display. The demonstrations in the Space Theater (55 mins) take place eight times a day in the summer months and seven times in winter (Sun.–Thu. 9.45am–9.30pm, Fri. and Sat. 9.45am–10.30pm).

San Diego Aerospace Museum

In this museum, a round building dating from 1930, aircraft from the earliest days right up to NASA missiles are displayed, including a replica of the "Spirit of St Louis", the aeroplane in which Charles A. Lindbergh made the first solo transatlantic flight (the original is in the National Aerospace Museum in Washington). The International Aerospace Hall of Fame in the same building shows photographs and memorabilia of the pioneers of flight. Open daily 10am–5pm.

San Diego Museum of Art

The San Diego Museum of Art, originally called the Fine Arts Building, is a copy of the 17th c. University of Salamanca in the so-called Platero style (i.e. finely-chiselled terracotta and silversmith work). Busts of Spanish painters adorn the façade, and their works hang in the museum's collection. The main interest lies, perhaps, in the pre-

Renaissance paintings and those by Flemish masters, as well as 19th and 20th c. art, and a large department housing American, Chinese, Japanese and other oriental works of art, including Indian and Persian miniatures. There are also some contemporary sculptures.

Next to the museum a sculpture-garden has been constructed which, although small, boasts some exquisite works by contemporary sculptors, including Alexander Calder, Barbara Hepworth, Juan Miró, Henry Moore and Louise Nevelson. The museum also presents exhibitions on a rota basis. Open Tue.–Sun. 10am–4.30pm. Guided tours on the hour, 10am–2pm, Tue., Wed. and Thu., on other days at 1pm and 2pm.

The Natural History Museum, established more than 100 years ago, has been housed in its present building since 1932, and displays southern Californian fossils, birds, reptiles, mammals, insects, plants and marine animals. Several life-size dioramas are dedicated to the fauna and flora of the Californian desert. Open from Jun.–Apr. daily 9.30am–5.30pm, Thu. till 9pm, otherwise 10am–4.30pm.

San Diego Museum of Natural History

More than a quarter of Balboa Park is taken up by the San Diego Zoo, one of the largest in the country and certainly one of the most beautiful. Its reputation as a unique place of interest has grown with the years. Its beginnings go back to the Panama Pacific Exhibition, when animals were put on show in San Diego for the first time; it has occupied its present site since the early twenties but is continually being extended, for example by the 1 ha (2½ acres) Tiger River rain forest which was first laid out in 1988, complete with lush vegetation, waterfalls and artificially-produced mist. Here you can see exotic plants and more than 800 animals in their natural surroundings, including majestic tigers from Sumatra, mysterious tapirs from Malaysia, water-dragons, koala bears from Australia, kiwis from New Zealand, rhinoceroses and other exotic creatures. The sub-tropical climate here is not very different from that in San Diego.

★★San Diego Zoo

Because of the gradient of the canyon, the visitor must be prepared to face some steep winding climbs, but will be rewarded by impressive sights which will stay in the memory. Immediately after passing through the turnstile you will be greeted by rose-pink flamingos, succeeded by giant tortoises which are native to the Galapagos Islands; then come the koala bears, which cling to branches of eucalyptus trees in their native Australia, and the golden monkeys. You can also go into the bird-houses with their hundreds of birds, some of which are very rare.

The zoo is laid out rather like a botanical garden, in which many exotic plants grow and mutli-coloured attraction for the youngsters, who can admire the young animals and also stroke some of them.

In 1995 the zoo acquired two pandas from China, the funds generated being used for the protection of this endangered species. Other new developments include an expanse of artificial rain forest with a rhino in its river (Hippo Beach), and an area of African rain forest with brightly coloured tropical birds, gorillas, waterfalls and a plantation house.

Advice Those who find walking difficult can take a 5 km (3 mi.) bus trip through the canyons and over the hills. By this means they will be able to see a great many of the animals and have the benefit of expert commentaries. There is also a cable-railway which travels over the tree-tops at a height of about 50 m (115 ft), from which you can have a bird's-eye view of the zoo. The zoo is open from 9am to 5pm in July, August and the first week in September, and from 9am until 4pm in the remaining months of the year.

Wild Animal Park	See Excursions from San Diego.
Spreckels Organ	This massive open-air organ, was a gift made to the town in 1915 by the sons of Adolph Spreckels, an immigrant from Hanover in Germany, who became a multi-millionaire in America. Since then, except during the Second World War, a concert has been held every Sunday afternoon at 2.30pm. The organ has some 4400 pipes, the smallest being 4 cm. (1½ in.) and the largest almost 10 m (33 ft) in length. When the organ is not being used it is protected by a metal curtain weighing 12 tonnes.
Timken Art Gallery	The Timken Art Gallery, built in 1965 on the Panama Plaza, houses an important collection of Russian icons from the 16th to the 19th c., works by Italian, French, Spanish and Dutch painters, as well as American art from several centuries. Open Tue.–Sat. 10am–4.30pm; guided tours Tue.–Thu. 10am–noon.
Spanish Village Arts and Crafts Center	In a number of low-built houses in the Spanish Village and Arts Center artists and craftsmen (potters, painters, sculptors, gold and silversmiths, photographers and weavers) can be seen at work. The articles and works of art they produce are on sale. Sometimes artists erect their easels in the courtyard where you can also watch them at work. Open daily 11am–4pm, except on Jan. 1st; admission free.

Coronado

Access	From downtown you can reach Coronado in a few minutes by crossing the Coronado Bridge off the US 5. If you are in no hurry you can go on the ferry which starts from Broadway Pier in San Diego, but must then walk a short distance to the hotel.

The garden town of Coronado (pop. 2,000) is situated on a peninsula. Whilst it has its own town council, it is nevertheless regarded as a suburb of San Diego, to which it is linked by the bridge over San Diego Bay and by the ferry. It was named after the islands of Los Coronados which lie off the shores of Baja California (see entry). Because of its

San Diego: Hotel del Coronado

majestic beauty it is also known as Crown City, although when he named the islands in 1602, the seafarer Viczaino wished to honour the three Romans who were crowned as martyrs.

Coronado's only building of interest, but one which is well worth seeing, is the Hotel del Coronado, built in 1888. Its mixture of Spanish and Mexican styles is unique in America today since, in spite of its wooden construction, it is still used as a luxury hotel (almost 700 rooms including those added on).

★ Hotel del Coronado

Predominantly Chinese workers with no previous knowledge of building techniques completed the hotel in less than eleven months. The main four-storey building, over 100 years old, has had no structural alterations of any kind during that period, although the guest-rooms have been renovated several times. It was the largest building outside New York to be fully served by electricity at that time. Thomas Edison himself supervised the electrical installation.

No fewer than thirteen American presidents, film actors, Charles Lindbergh, and many other VIPs have been guests in this famous hotel. Numerous films have also been made here, including "Some Like it Hot" with Marilyn Monroe, Jack Lemmon and Tony Curtis.

Perhaps the most interesting room in the hotel is the 9 m/30 ft-high dining-room, in the construction of which not a single nail or any kind of supporting beam was used; the pine ceiling is held together by wooden dowels.

Gaslamp Quarter

Adjacent to Horton Plaza, Gaslamp Quarter lies in the centre of the inner town between Broadway and San Diego Bay. The sixteen or so blocks of houses built between 1880 and 1910 comprise most of the Victorian

239

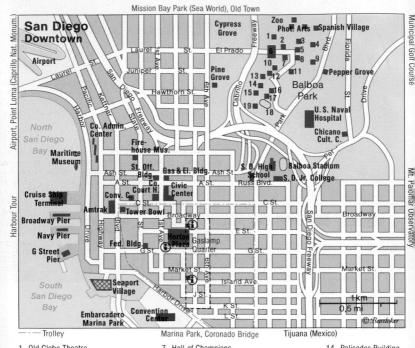

houses still preserved in San Diego, as a result of which it has been declared an historic (listed) district. Most worth seeing in the 14 ha (35 acres) quarter is Fifth Avenue, between E and F Streets, where houses nos. 832 and 840 are particularly deserving of attention. Some of the streets have already been re-surfaced in red brick.

Villa Montezuma

Not very far from Gaslamp Quarter stands Villa Montezuma (1925 K Street), built in 1887, an unusually luxurious Victorian house constructed when San Diego was enjoying its first brief economic boom between 1886 and 1888. Well worth seeing are the stained-glass windows (more than 20), some rooms restored in their original style, as well as alternating exhibitions in the house which now functions as a museum. Open Tue.–Sun. noon–4pm.

Horton Plaza

Horton Plaza also lies downtown between Broadway and G Street, 1st and 4th Avenue. From an architectural point of view it is one of

San Diego – Horton Plaza, downtown shopping centre

California's most interesting shopping centres. The name is derived from one of San Diego's pioneers, Alonzo Horton, who in 1867 bought for only 265 US dollars some 400 ha (100 acres) of land in what was then a village. This included practically the whole of the downtown district of today. Horton Plaza boasts some 140 shops, including four department stores (Nordstrom, Robinson's, The Broadway and Mervins), numerous restaurants, a cinema and a theatre. The bright colours and avant-garde architecture, together with the open-air displays, make it all most attractive.

★★La Jolla

La Jolla (pronounced "la hoya") extends along a 11 km (7 mi.) curved strip of coastline, 22 km (14 mi.) north of Downtown San Diego (take the US 5 and then the Ardath Road exit). It has rich vegetation and enjoys mild weather all the year round, but, like all places on the coast, it is plagued with mists in summer.

Although the name translates as "jewel", the original name of La Hoya (as still recognisable from the pronunciation) comes from a geographical word for "cave".

Today La Jolla has about 40,000 inhabitants, the numbers having increased appreciable during the last decade.

Autonomy Even though La Jolla forms part of San Diego and is the seat of the University of California at San Diego, it functions quite independently, so that most visitors consider it more of a village enclave than a suburb of San Diego. It has in fact been able to preserve its idyllic atmosphere. Mail posted there is stamped "La Jolla", not "San Diego". The abundance of elegant shops in Girard Avenue is a distinguishing feature.

241

As a result of the university and other research institutes being here, many academics, budding artists and writers have made their homes here. This intellectually active life has produced numerous galleries and, in particular, a museum of contemporary art.

The town The heart of La Jolla is best explored on foot, especially Girard Avenue, mentioned above, and the main street, Prospect Street, with the town's finest hotel, Hotel Valencia. You should also take a stroll along the coast road, the north-eastern extension of Prospect Street, beginning at the junction of Park Row and Prospect Place. You will pass the famous La Jolla Cove (small bay) and Ellen Browning Scripps Park, some 30 m (100 ft) below Prospect Street, with shallow steps leading down to it.

Another somewhat longer walk will take you to the scientific institutes and past many modern houses. The following are the most important places to look out for:

University of California

The University of California at San Diego came into being in the year 1912. This branch of the central Californian university, with some 16,000 students, has made a name for itself in a number of spheres, especially in that of medicine. The campus is well worth a visit, mainly because of the interesting architecture of some of the newer buildings, such as the library. There are many modern sculptures to be seen on the campus. Guided tours by prior telephone arrangement.

Scripps Aquarium

The Scripps Aquarium belongs to the Institute of Oceanography founded in 1903 and an integral part of the University of California since 1912. This oldest and biggest American marine institute employs a staff of 1000 scientists and other personnel. Its library is one of the most important of its kind. The aquarium, which has 300,000 visitors every year, portrays marine life in the coastal waters. Progress made in oceanography is displayed in 22 tanks. (Address: 8602, La Jolla Shores Drive; tel. (619) 5343474.) Open daily 9am–5pm.

Salk Institute

The Salk Institute lies north of the university campus, on a canyon overlooking the Pacific. It was founded in 1960 by Dr Jonas Salk, the discoverer of the polio vaccine, and is devoted exclusively to bio-medical research. The 500 people who work there include four Nobel Prizewinners who are aiming at a better understanding of cancer illnesses, birth defects, alcoholism and brain functions. The building, designed by the well-known architect Louis Kahn, must be one of the most unconventional in La Jolla. (Address: 10010 North Torrey Pines Road, on Torrey Pines Scenic Drive.)

Torrey Pines State Park

On the boundary between La Jolla and Del Mar you will find Torrey Pines State Park, where one of the rarest species of pine in the world grows on the rocky subsoil of the cliffs and canyons by the Pacific. Apart from La Jolla, the Torrey pine (*pinus torreyana*) thrives only on the island of Santa Rosa, 50 km (30 mi.) south-west of Santa Barbara (see entry). It was identified as long ago as 1850 and bears the name of a famous contemporary American botanist.

The park covers almost 400 ha (1000 acres) of land: canyons, mesas (plateaux), many footpaths and a sandy beach almost 5 km (3 mi.) long. Here you can also watch sail-planes and glider. (Information: tel. (619) 7552063.)

Museum of Contemporary Art

Originally built as a villa for Ellen Browning Scripps, who contributed much to La Jolla's development, the Museum of Contemporary Art was first arranged into a centre for local artists in 1941, and then converted into a museum. Its extensive collections include southern Californian works of art, minimalist, pop-art, installations and other forms of modern

Aerial photograph of the beautiful coastline at La Jolla▶

art; there is also a department dedicated to the development of the modern chair. Temporary exhibitions are also arranged. (Address: 7000 Prospect Street.) Open Tue.–Fri. 10am–5pm, Sat. and Sun. 12.30pm–5pm.

Mission Bay

The Mission Bay section of the town lies north-west of Downtown and south of La Jolla. With its many small coves Mission Bay, covering some 1800 ha (4500 acres), is a convenient and beautiful holiday resort for the citizens of San Diego. Every conceivable kind of water sport is practised here and thanks to the constantly warm climate can be enjoyed practically all the year round. The beaches are almost 43 km (27 mi.) long; there is also a yacht club, a marina from which you can take steamer trips round the bay, half a dozen luxury hotels for permanent guests, as well as several golf-courses, one of which is even floodlit at night.

If you drive west along the US 5 as far as the exit to East Mission Bay Drive you will find an information counter where you can get all the details you require.

Mission San Diego de Alcala

See Mission Stations

Old Town

State Historic Park

To get to San Diego's Old Town take the US 5 and the Old Town Avenue exit, or the US 8 and the Morena Boulevard exit.

The Old Town San Diego State Historic Park, the very core of the old part of town, takes the visitor through the town's Mexican and early American history. It was probably founded in 1820 by demobilised Mexican soldiers who had done their military service at the Presidio or in the fort on Presidio Hill (both part of the old town today). Many of the historic buildings, including numerous adobe houses, have been repaired in recent years. The houses, which are now open to visitors, date from 1827 to 1869, roughly comparable as regards building date with the houses in El Pueblo de Los Angeles State Historic Park (see entry for Los Angeles).

In the Old Town State Historic Park you will find:

Casa de Estudillo

This fairly large restored adobe dwelling, Casa de Estudillo (1829), today houses Spanish-Mexican and early American relics and furniture. (Address: 2645 San Diego Avenue.) Open daily 10am–5pm.

Pendleton House

Pendleton House (1854), situated behind Whaley House, is fitted out with authentic furniture from the period at which it was built. Open Wed.– Sun. 10am–4.30pm.

San Diego Union Museum

The "San Diego Union" (1868) newspaper first saw the light of day in this house. The interior still retains the appearance of a newspaper office of more than 100 years ago. (Address: 2626 San Diego Avenue; tel. 2972119.) Open Tue.–Sun. 10am–5pm; admission free.

Seeley Stables

The Seeley Stables (1869) originally served the American mail; today you can see various horse-drawn wagons, including the covered wagons in which the first settlers came to California. (Address: 2648 Calhoun Street.) Open daily, 10am–5pm.

Casa de Lopez

Casa de Lopez (1834), once a candle-maker's workshop, is today a museum with candles from all over the world. (Address: 3890 Twiggs Street; admission free.)

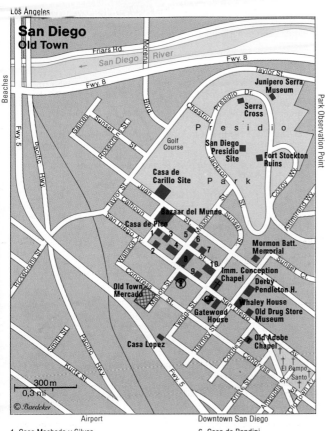

San Diego
Old Town

Los Angeles

Friars Rd.

San Diego River

Fwy 8

Taylor St.

Junipero Serra
Museum

Beaches

Presidio Dr.

Serra
Cross

Chestnut

Park Observation Point

P r e s i d i o

Golf
Course

San Diego
Presidio
Site

Fort Stockton
Ruins

Jackson St.

Casa de
Carillo Site

P a r k

Cosoy Wy.

Juan

Bazaar del Mundo

Casa de Pico

Mormon Batt.
Memorial

Imm. Conception
Chapel

Old Town
Mercado

Derby-
Pendleton H.

Whaley House

Gatewood
House

Old Drug Store
Museum

Casa Lopez

Old Adobe
Chapel

El Campo
Santo

300 m
0,3 mi

© Baedeker

Airport

Downtown San Diego

1 Casa Machado y Silvas
2 Machado y Stewart Abobe
3 Casa Racine & Laramie
4 Mason Street School
5 Machado y Smith Abode

6 Casa de Bandini
7 Seeley Stables
8 Casa de Estudillo
9 Casa de Pedrorena
10 San Diego Union Hist. Restoration

Junipero Serra Museum stands on the site of the first mission to be built in Alta California. Today it contains artefacts connected with the mission's history and the origin of San Diego. (Address: 2727 Presidio Drive; tel. (619) 2973258.) Open Mon.–Sat. 9am–4.45pm, Sun. noon–4.45pm.

Junipero Serra
Museum

Whaley House (1856), the oldest brick-built house in southern California, was once a private residence, then the home of a theatrical troupe, and the court-house for San Diego County until 1871. It has been restored to its original condition and equipped with furniture from the middle of the last century. A reproduction of the old village apothecary's shop has been built in the grounds. (Address: 2482 San Diego Avenue.) Open Wed.–Sun. 10am–4.30pm.

Whaley House

Adjoining the plaza, the hub of community life in old Pueblo and now at

Bazaar del Mundo

weekends the scene of frequent dances and concerts, stands the modern Bazaar de Mundo with many shops and restaurants in an arcade with an interior courtyard. Here there is music and dancing.

Point Loma

On this peninsula west of Downtown San Diego, stretching from San Diego Bay to the Pacific Ocean, will be found the Cabrillo National Monument, erected to commemorate the discovery of California by the Portuguese seafarer Juan Rodriguez Cabrillo in September 1542, only three months before he died.

Linked to the peninsula by causeways are Shelter Island and Harbor Island, from where you get a fine view of the skyscrapers of San Diego.

On Point Loma peninsula there is also a station for naval exercises, as well as one of the country's largest naval cemeteries (Rosecrans National Cemetery).

Cabrillo National Monument

The best way to get to the Cabrillo National Monument – situated right at the end of Point Loma, 16 km (10 mi.) from San Diego – is to go via North Harbor to Rosecrans Street, then turn into Cannon Street, Catalina Boulevard and Cabrillo Memorial Drive.

When visibility is good, the National Monument provides a panoramic view as far as La Jolla to the north, the Pacific to the west, Mexico to the south and San Diego County to the east. From mid-December to mid-February it is also a good point from which to observe the whales on their migration south.

A brief visit to the well-equipped Visitor Center with its little museum will provide by means of brochures and a slide-show information about the origins of the National Monument and the history of the discovery of California. Not far away stands the Cabrillo Monument, erected by a compatriot of Cabrillo, the Portuguese Alvaro de Bree. The Cabrillo National Monument is open daily 9am–5.15pm; in the summer months until 7.45pm.

A short walk takes you to the old **lighthouse** which was in use from 1855 to 1891. It was then replaced by a new lighthouse with stronger lights, which still serves shipping to this day. The old lighthouse has meanwhile been restored. Numerous footpaths lead down to the shore of the peninsula. On the Bayside Trail and Sylvester Road you will find a strange mixture of desert and coastal vegetation. All the animals and plants are protected species.

★ San Diego Maritime Museum

The San Diego Maritime Museum, established in 1948, consists of three ships which have been restored to their original condition and are lying alongside Harbor Drive, between Ash and Laurel Streets.

The three-master **"Star of India"** is a sailing ship which was built in the Isle of Man in 1863 and sailed round the world several times. It plied between England and New Zealand as a passenger and cargo ship, and often had on board as many as 400 British passengers who were emigrating to New Zealand. From 1901 to 1923 it was in service for America on the Alaska route before coming to San Diego. The ship, which is still seaworthy, last went to sea on the occasion of the celebrations to mark the bi-centenary of American Independence on July 4th 1976.

The others are the ferry-ship **"Berkeley"**, built in 1898 and which plied between San Francisco and Oakland, and the luxurious 1904 motor-yacht **"Medea"**, which still occasionally makes trips round the bay.

San Diego Maritime Museum: The three-master "Star of India" ...

Killer whale in the Sea World Pleasure Park

The San Diego Maritime Museum is open daily 9am–8pm.

★Seaport Village

Seaport Village leisure resort is, like that in San Pedro, Los Angeles (see entry), a shopping and restaurant centre in the form of a large village. On a 5 ha (12½ acres) site close by San Diego Bay 28 houses have been built, now occupied by more than 60 shops, boutiques, galleries and several restaurants. (Address: 849 West Harbor Drive.)

★★Sea World

Near Mission Bay will be found a counterpart to Disneyland (see entry Anaheim), the Sea World Pleasure Park (1720 South Shores Road). From San Diego take the US 5 (exit for Sea World Drive). Penguins in their hundreds, dolphins, sea-lions, otters and whales have been trained here to show off their newly-learned skills in more than 30 different performances. Water fantasies, hydrofoil boat trips, cable railways and much more are features of this maritime leisure park. There are similar parks in Orlando (Florida), San Antonio (Texas), Aurora (Illinois). Until they were sold at the beginning of 1989 they represented the most profitable branch of the Harcourt Brace Iovanovich publishing firm.

Among Sea World's newest attractions are a tropical play paradise for children (Shamu's Happy Hour), a killer whale show (Shamu: World Focus), a dolphin basin (Rocky Point Preserve) and an observation tunnel through an aquarium populated with sharks, rays and tropical fish. Open 9am–5pm, in summer until sunset; entrance fee.

Wild Animal Park

From San Diego follow the CA 163 and US 15 to the junction with the CA 178, driving eastwards on the latter as far as the Via Rancho Parkway exit.

The Wild Animal Park, a 700 ha (1750 acres) game reserve situated about 50 km (30 mi.) north of San Diego, was opened some years ago by the Zoological Society of San Diego (which also manages the zoo with its more than 5000 animals). An almost hour-long safari through the park provides the opportunity to watch some 3000 animals native to Africa and Asia (800 species in all) in a natural environment.

Here too is found the most extensive planted area of bonsai trees in the American West. The Baja Garden in the Kupanda Botanical Centre features succulents and cacti native to Baja California.

In 1995 a small area of coniferous forest was transformed into **"Dinosaur Mountain"**. Eighteen dinosaurs (reconstructions thereof) roam the mountain, the primitive, computer-simulated cries of these prehistoric creatures echoing scarily through the forest. At the entrance to Dinosaur Mountain is a small theatre where visitors can experience in virtual reality life on mysterious Dino Island, with volcanically-active valleys, lava flows, prehistoric vegetation and dinosaurs.

The Wild Animal Park is open 9am–4pm (6pm in Jul., Aug. and beginning of Sep.).

Excursions

There are plenty of tours available from San Diego, including some to Tijuna (see entry) and other places in Mexico by bus or boat, into the

Anza Borrego Desert (see entry), along the 84 km (52 mi.) "Scenic Drive" from within San Diego to as far as La Jolla, and trips round the harbour.

★★San Francisco   H1

San Francisco County
Altitude: 19 m (62 ft)
Population; 790,000 (Greater San Francisco 6.2 million)

San Francisco is the third largest city – after Los Angeles and San Diego – in the state of California, and lies at the north end of a hilly peninsula, 48 km (30 mi.) long and 10 km (6 mi.) wide, which separates the Pacific Ocean from San Francisco Bay, one of the world's best natural harbours. On its north side it is bounded by the Golden Gate, the 1.5 km/1 mi.-wide and 116 m (380 ft)-deep entrance into San Francisco Bay. Artificial earth-banks, especially on the east side of the peninsula, have extended the area of the city.

Conurbation San Francisco extends over 332 sq. km (128 sq. mi.), of which 120 sq. km (46 sq. mi.) are land and 212 sq. km (82 sq. mi.) water, with small outlying areas in the Californian counties of Tuolumne, San Mateo, Kern, Fresno and Monterey.

See map at end of book

The metropolitan area of the city incorporates the surrounding counties of Marin (north), San Mateo (south), Alameda and Contra Costa (both east).

The city has a central **administration** which is headed by a Mayor who comes up for selection every four years.

The Mayor is aided by a Chief Executive Administrator, the counter-part, albeit with lesser powers, of the City Managers found in many other American cities. The Board of Supervisors, the equivalent of a single chamber for local government, consists of eleven elected members.

The city's current constitution dates from 1931 but has been subject to over 400 amendments which makes it some 110,000 words long.

Climate A particular feature of San Francisco are the mists which form along the coast in summer; the heat from the hinterland then forces them through the Golden Gate into the bay. Warm outer garments are advisable, especially in the afternoons when a strong sea-wind blows.

Its situation on a tectonically unstable section of the earth's crust around the Pacific Ocean (the San Andreas fault) means that, after the serious **earthquakes** of 1906 and 1989, there is always the possibility of further seismic movements (often followed by "microquakes"). The three penultimate earthquakes occurred on August 8th 1989 (5.2, 4.2 and 4.5 on the Richter Scale), and were felt as far away as San Luis Obispo to the south (358 km (222 mi.)) and Sonoma to the north (96 km (60 mi.)). For more on the subject of earthquakes see Baedeker Special page 12.

Cityscape San Francisco is one of the most popular destinations in the United States, indeed in the whole world, because of its unique rural pos-ition, its cosmopolitan atmosphere and endearing reminders of days gone by, including the cable-cars along the ultra-steep streets. Unconventional modern high-rise buildings such as the pyramid-shaped Transamerica Building and the skyscraper of the Bank of America, the biggest bank in the United States, give the city a new and unfamiliar silhouette.

Population

The population of San Francisco originally grew very slowly and in 1846, which saw the end of Mexican rule, amounted to barely a thousand. This

The skyline of San Francisco seen from Alamo Square

dropped to a few hundred in the years that followed – in 1847 the count was actually 459.

The 1849 Gold Rush sparked off a population explosion; only one year later the total was estimated at 25,000. After reaching 342,000 in 1900 the figure fell back after the 1906 earthquake, to 175,000. The numbers peaked at 775,000 in 1950, then fell to 679,000 in 1980 as a result of people moving to the surrounding rural areas. The subsequent upward trend – 714,000 were counted in 1985 – is due mainly to the influx of coloured people, as the number of Whites plummeted from 700,000 in 1950 to less than 450,000.

In addition to its 100,000 Afro-Americans, San Francisco has a higher proportion of Asians among its population than any other American city: 85,000 Chinese, 30,000 Filipinos, 14,000 Japanese, also Koreans, Vietnamese, Samoans, Malaysians and others. There are also smaller groups of British (10.3 per cent), Irish (8.5 per cent), Germans (7.5 per

cent), Italians (5.7 per cent), Mexicans (5.3 per cent), Russians (2.8 per cent) and French (2.5 per cent).

Originating in the 1950s, the **Beatnik Movement** was a revolt against the dollar-chasing, consumer mentality. Many of its followers congregated in the North Beach district, meeting in its bars and bookshops and philosophising. Leading literary exponents of the movement were Allen Ginsberg, William Burroughs and Jack Kerouac. Later the Beatniks moved to Haight Ashbury, their numbers being swelled in the mid Sixties by the Civil Rights Movement and opponents of the Vietnam war. At this point the **Hippies** arrived on the scene: long hair, beards, drugs, communal living, free love, Love not War. Some 6000 full-time hippies were joined at weekends in the "Summer of Love" of 1967 by a further 20,000, drawn by rock concerts and other such events. But the hippy environment attracted criminals and drug dealers; violence became

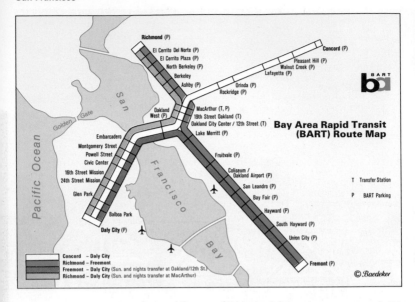

Bay Area Rapid Transit (BART) Route Map

BART

T   Transfer Station

P   BART Parking

Concord – Daly City
Richmond – Freemont
Freemont – Daly City (Sun. and nights transfer at Oakland/12th St.)
Richmond – Daly City (Sun. and nights transfer at MacArthur)

© Baedeker

commonplace and the peaceful hippies left to set up communes in the country, enter the student scene at Berkeley or simply return home.

San Francisco has become home to many homosexuals of both sexes. The rainbow flag of the **Gay Community**, who today account for about a sixth of the city's population, is mainly seen flying in the Castro district. The arrival of AIDS brought a fundamental change in the city's gay scene, the formerly carefree existence giving way to militant demands for more public money to fight the disease and counter discrimination against those infected. A network of organisations now focus on prevention, research and care of the sick.

In the city of multifarious ethnic backgrounds there are churches for almost all the **religions** practised in the USA (including two Russian Orthodox cathedrals). The largest Lutheran congregation is that of St Mark's near St Mary's Cathedral. The city is also the seat of a Catholic Archbishop and of the Episcopalian Bishop for the whole of Northern California.

The city has long been a hotbed for religious sects, of which the most famous was the People's Temple under Jim Jones. In the early 1970s Zen Buddhism gained its first foothold in the States in San Francisco, mainly through the books of Alan Watts, a former Anglican priest.

Transport

San Francisco's natural harbour, once America's principal **port** for trade with the Far East, has in recent years lost much of its importance.

Nowadays many of the 46 piers stand empty or out of commission. Container traffic has drastically declined, having been taken over as long ago as 1969 by Oakland on the opposite side of the bay. The San Francisco fishing industry has also declined considerably.

The **airport**, 23 km (14 mi.) south of the city, was opened in 1927 as Mills Field which, with expansion, changed its name to San Francisco Airport and finally to San Francisco International Airport. Today it is one of the largest in the United States and serves over 28 airlines. There is another large airport at Oakland on the east side of San Francisco Bay.

Like many American cities, **rail** transport in San Francisco has become almost insignificant, with only one station handling the commuter traffic of the Southern Pacific Railroad. The Amtrak trains that run along the Pacific Coast leave from Oakland and passengers get there by shuttle bus from the Transbay Transit Terminal.

San Francisco is served by a large number of local and long-distance **bus lines** and has two main bus stations, the Greyhound Terminal and the Transbay Transit Terminal.

The bus network serving virtually every part of town is San Francisco's most important form of public transportation. There are 57 routes altogether and the fixed fare includes transfers between the different forms of transportation in the Municipal Railway Company (**MUNI**) system, which also covers the streetcars (trams) and cable cars.

San Francisco does not have an underground system as such, but in 1981 the four streetcar lines that ran along Market Street were moved underground. In 1972 the first line of the Bay Area Rapid Transit (**BART**) of California was opened, connecting the centre of San Francisco with the surrounding counties.
There are 31 stations on the 120 km (75 mi.) network, eight of them in San Francisco itself. The 5.5 km (3 mi.) stretch that runs under the waters of the bay between San Francisco and Oakland is the longest of its kind in the world.

Fisherman's Wharf and the island of Alcatraz can be seen from the cable car along Hyde Street

Except for New Orleans and Sacramento, the capital of California, San Francisco is the only city in the USA to have retained its **trams**, or street-cars as they are called in the States. It has five streetcar lines, part of them underground, as well as three cable car lines, a service that dates back over 100 years.

The **ferries** that were needed to cross the bay before the bridges were built have by now almost all gone out of business, but passenger ferries still operate to the bay communities of Sausalito and Larkspur as well as to Tiburon (from Ferry Building) and to Angel Island and Alcatraz (from Fisherman's Wharf).

Highways From San Francisco Highway 101 is the fastest route to Southern California and the other main roads are Interstate 180 and State Highway 1 along the coast.

Going northwards, Highway 101 crosses the Golden Gate Bridge to Northern California, the north-west of the United States, and Canada, with Coastal Highway ` branching off to follow the Pacific coast.

Interstate Highway 80 runs east over the San Francisco–Oakland Bay Bridge to State Highway 17 and Interstate 680 to the south; State Highway 24 and Interstate Highway 680 also lead north and Interstate 580 proceeds east.

Culture

Until 1960 San Francisco was the undisputed cultural centre of California but has since had to share this distinction with Los Angeles, which is five times its size.

Today San Francisco has four large theatres and a number of "little" theatres. It has its own opera company, the San Francisco Ballet

"Victorian" houses in a steeply sloping road

(America's oldest ballet company), a symphony orchestra and some first-class art museums – the M. H. de Young Memorial Museum, the Asian Art Museum, the San Francisco Museum of Modern Art and the Palace of the Legion of Honor, as well as the important natural science museum of the California Academy of Sciences and others.

At the end of March and in early April each year a Film Festival is held in the Palace of Arts and Science and the Castro Theater. Started in 1927, it was the first of its kind to be held in America.

Three large **universities** – the Catholic University of San Francisco founded in 1855 (7000 students), the state University of California in Berkeley (30,000 students) and Stanford University (12,000 students) in Palo Alto – make San Francisco an important academic and research centre. The University of California Medical Center in San Francisco, incorporating the University Hospital, is also of considerable importance. Other important colleges are the San Francisco State University, the Hastings College of Law, Lincoln University and the San Francisco Art Institute.

Architecture

San Francisco's architectural face is characterised by the skyscrapers in the city and the mainly 19th c. wooden houses in the residential quarters which are described as Victorian houses because of the period when they were built.

Do not attempt to take photographs in Alamo Square (serious offence).

Although the finest of the **Victorian houses** built between 1879 and 1906, especially those on Nob Hill and in Van Ness Avenue, were destroyed in the earthquake, there are still over 13,000 such houses in the Bernal Heights, Duboce Triangle, Eureka, Glen Park, Haight-Ashbury, Mission District, Noe Valley, Potrero Hill and Western Addition areas.

Between 1870 and 1880 many houses with blind windows were built in the **Italian** style, so called because much of the detail was based on Roman ornamentation.

In the 1880s the vertical style known as the **San Francisco Stick** was in vogue; it was so called to distinguish it from the simple "stick" buildings along the East Coast and in the Middle West. The architecture emphasises the vertical structure, with the outside decoration resembling a bundle of sticks.

In the 1890s the **queen Anne** style was developed. These were expensive, mainly detached houses adorned with towers and cone-shaped caps, high gables and massed-produced ornaments. All these houses were built with redwood which was abundant around San Francisco, and which is cheap, weather-resistant and resists fire and termites.

San Francisco does not have many so-called **cast-iron** houses, the distinguishing features of which are the stanchions on the outside as well as the inside. The best known is the 1907 Columbus Tower, the green colour of which makes it stand out against the surrounding low buildings. Because of the contrasting styles, people like to photograph it with the Transamerica Pyramid in the background.

San Francisco's ten tallest buildings are all to be found in the financial quarter. No **skyscrapers** may now be built outside that area of the city, and it is questionable whether council planning consent will in future be granted even in the financial quarter for a building taller than Transamerica Pyramid. The three tallest building are:

Transamerica Pyramid, 600 Montgomery Square (260 m (860 ft))
Bank of America, 555 California Street (232 m (765 ft))
California Center, 345 California Street (217 m (715 ft))

Economy

Banks Unlike Los Angeles, with its oil industry and high industrialisation, and other parts of Southern California, San Francisco has never been in the forefront of industrial cities. It owes its importance much more to services and tourism. Foremost among its service industries are its banks, which include America's biggest bank, the Bank of America, as well as the Bank of California, the Wells Fargo Bank and the Crocker Bank.

Business sector The city is also noted for its insurance companies, to the largest of which it owes its latest landmark, the Transamerica Pyramid. In the Pacific Stock Exchange San Francisco also has the most important trading exchange in the American West.

Tourism Its many hotels and restaurants are of incalculable value to the city's economy. The city is such a magnet that every year it attracts five times as many visitors as the resident population, with almost a third of these three million visitors coming to San Francisco for conventions.

Industry centred on the port, once the most important sector of San Francisco's economy, has been declining for many years and will probably never recover its earlier importance – the same is true of the city's fisheries and canneries.

Many industrial corporations, including Chevron and McKesson, have their headquarters in San Francisco but their factories in other parts of California.

History

1542	Juan Rodriguez Cabrillo sails into the waters of what is now known as San Diego Bay and six weeks later sights in San Francisco Bay the Farallon Islands which have been part of the city since 1872.
1579	Sir Francis Drake is the first European to land on the coast of Northern California, probably on the opposite side of the bay from San Francisco in what is now Marin County. He names the land "Nova Albion" and claims it in the name of Queen Elizabeth I.
1595	Sebastian Rodriguez Cermenho lands in a bay on the Marin coast which he calls La Bahia de San Francisco (now Drake's Bay). This is the first use of the name which was given to the city.
1769	The present San Francisco Bay is discovered by Gaspar de Portola and his troops approaching from the landward side. Portola, later to be the first Governor of Spanish California, is leading a "Holy Expedition" northwards from Sonora in Mexico in conjunction with Father Junipero Serra, founder of the mission.
1776	A group of 250 Spanish soldiers and civilians, led by Juan Bautista de Anza decide on the site for the San Francisco Presidio. Consecration of the first "Mission Dolores", originally San Francisco de Assisi.
1835	President Andrew Jackson offers the Mexicans, who had cast off

Spanish rule in 1821, 500,000 dollars for the bay of San Francisco. In the same year William Richardson, an English whaling captain (married to a Mexican, and a convert to Catholicism) founds the village of Pueblo Yerba Buena.

Yerba Buena now numbers some 350 souls – Americans, Indians, Dutch and Spanish.   1845

On July 9th Yerba Buena becomes part of the United States when 70   1846
marines from the US frigate "Portsmouth" land there and hoist the Stars
and Stripes in the village square. Three weeks later a ship arrives bringing 238 Mormons in search of their promised Zion; they find themselves
back in a different part of the United States, the country from which they
were trying to flee.

Yerba Buena's first American "alcade" or mayor, Lieutenant Washington   1847
A. Bartlett, announces on January 30th that henceforth the town is to be
called San Francisco. At this time it has a resident population
(Americans, Indians, Dutch and Spanish), excluding military and naval
personnel, of 459.

While building a windmill for John Augustus Sutter, James Marshall dis- 1848
covers gold on January 24th at Coloma in the foothills of the Sierra
Nevada. His discovery sets the seal on the future of San Francisco. When
news reaches the outside world, prospectors set out in their thousands
for San Francisco which serves as the setting-off point for the gold fields
on the Sacramento River.

San Francisco's population has grown to 25,000 and it becomes a city. A 1850
few months later California becomes the 31st State of the Union.

Opening of the telegraph line direct to New York.   1862

Following smaller earth tremors, San Francisco suffers its first major   1865
earthquake on October 9th, followed by a second quake on October 23rd
which causes considerable damage to the city.

The Central Pacific Railroad completes the building of the railroad from 1869
the East Coast to San Francisco, an event that is enthusiastically celebrated in the city.

The City Government decides to build the Golden Gate Park.   1870

On August 2nd the cable-car, Andrew Hallidie's brainchild, makes its first 1873
trip over the 100yd-stretch of Clay Street between Kearny and Jones
Streets.

Opening of the Pacific Stock Exchange.   1875

The Southern Pacific Railroad completes construction of the line from   1876
San Francisco to Los Angeles.

July sees the first serious rioting against the Chinese. A Citizen's Safety 1877
Committee restores law and order.

February 5th goes down in history because it was the only day on which   1887
snow covered the whole of San Francisco.

Fifteen new banks are opened within a month; the following year sees   1903
the founding of the Bank of America, now the USA's biggest bank.

A serious earthquake on April 18th destroys four-fifths of the city.   1906

Even worse than the force of the earthquake (8.25 on the Richter Scale) is the raging fire which follows and which the fire-fighters cannot quench because the water-mains burst. Some 28,000 houses were destroyed, 500 people killed. During the rapid reconstruction many buildings are designed in the Neo-Classical style, influenced by the Chicago Exhibition of 1893.

1907   A plague epidemic is successfully brought under control after several months.

1912   James Rolph begins 19 years in office, thereby becoming the city's longest-serving Mayor.
The city's first streetcar line commences operations in Geary Street.

1915   The great Panama-Pacific International Exposition is opened in Lincoln Park a few months after the first ship to take the new route through the Panama Canal docks in San Francisco.
Dedication of the present City Hall.

1921   Opening of the M. H. de Young Memorial Museum in Golden Gate Park.

1933   The island of Alcatraz off San Francisco becomes a Federal Penitentiary.

1934   A general strike paralyses San Francisco for weeks.

1936   November 12th: The San Francisco–Oakland Bay Bridge is opened to traffic.

1937   May 27th: Dedication of the Golden Gate Bridge constructed by Joseph B. Strauss.

1945   April 24th: Opening of the inaugural assembly of UNO in the War Memorial Opera House, followed by the signing there two months later of the original charter.

1951   September 18th: Yoshida, the Japanese Prime Minister, signs the Treaty marking the ending of hostilities between Japan and the USA in the War Memorial Opera House.

1963   March 23rd: The penitentiary on Alcatraz is closed down. A year later the island is occupied by Sioux Indians who lay claim to Alcatraz, but they are forced out in 1971.

1967   April 15th: One of the first big peace marches protesting against the Vietnam War takes place in Market Street. Others follow at regular intervals.

1978   Mayor George Moscone and Harvey Milk, one of the eleven Supervisors, are gunned down in City Hall by an ex-colleague who had been fired by Milk and whose sentence to seven years in jail had resulted in protest demonstrations. A week later Dianne Feinstein, Chairman of the Board of Supervisors, is named as Moscone's successor. She is the city's first woman Mayor.

1983   Dianne Feinstein is re-elected Mayor with an overwhelming majority.

1984   After two years' closure the cable cars come back into service on June 21st.

1986   The Nobel Peace Prizewinner, Mother Teresa, builds a convent in San Francisco.
At the seventh attempt the electorate votes for the restriction on building in downtown San Francisco. In future not more than 4.4 ha (475,000 sq. ft) of building can be started annually.

Whereas the townscape was changed in the early eighties by several new skyscrapers, there are now more than half a dozen new hotels which have changed the appearance of the district around Union Square. Some 16% of available office space is empty; rents are falling for the first time.   1987

After ten years as Mayor, Dianne Feinstein is replaced in office by Art Agnos.   1988
    When digging foundations for a new bank building at the corner of Kearny and Sacramento Streets artefacts are discovered which point to Chinese having settled in San Francisco prior to 1850.

For reasons of economy, the Pentagon decides to close the Presidio. This infuriates the citizens and results in protests.   1989
    On October 17th at 5.04pm (during the rush-hour) San Francisco is struck by the worst earthquake (6.9 points on the Richter Scale) since that of 1906. The Marina quarter is the worst affected: a lot of houses are set on fire as the result of gas leaking from burst mains. A 2 km (1¼ mi.) section of the San Francisco–Oakland Bay Bridge collapses, burying numerous cars.

June: Serious fires, some started deliberately, cause widespread devastation in southern Californian.   1990

Two new museums, the Friends of Photography (Ansel Adams Center) and the Museum of the City of San Francisco, open.   1991

In January the new San Francisco Museum of Modern Art, designed by Swiss architect Mario Botta, opens. In December violent rain storms cause extensive damage; in the Golden Gate Park more than 250 trees are uprooted and Alcatraz Island, the former penitentiary, is cut off.   1995

Sights A to Z

Alcatraz Island

The former penitentiary of Alcatraz, located 2.4 km (1½ mi.) north east in San Francisco Bay, is one of the most fascinating places to visit. The first Spaniard to land there, Ayala, named it Isla de los Alcatraces ("Island of the Pelicans"), because he found vast numbers of these birds nesting on the sandstone island.

History As this rocky island, covering an area of some 5 ha (12 acres) and rising to a height of 41 m (135 ft), has no springs, it remained uninhabited for years. In 1853, during the Californian gold-rush when the number of ships visiting the foggy bay increased considerably, a lighthouse was erected. Soon afterwards the island was fortified and became a military prison during the Civil War (1861–65). From 1933 to 1963 it became the most infamous and feared of all federal prisons in the USA. Even the most incorrigible jail-breakers hardly ever succeeded in escaping.
    In the course of its 30 year existence the penitentiary received a total of 1576 convicts. There were never more than 250 at any one time, even though there were 450 cells measuring about 3 x 1.5 m (10 x 4 ft). At times the number of guards, etc. was greater than that of the convicts.
    After the prison was closed the island was virtually forgotten for six years until it was taken over by Indians who squatted there for seven years. Although the island has been open to visitors since 1973 only emergency repairs have been made to the run-down buildings.

Advice Ship departures: Pier 41 (Fisherman's Wharf). It is necessary to book in advance. Ferry services: in summer daily 9am–5pm autumn to spring daily 9am–3pm, with 1½ hour guided tours.
    As the island is frequently shrouded in mist and the wind is almost always strong, visitors are recommended to wear warm clothes.

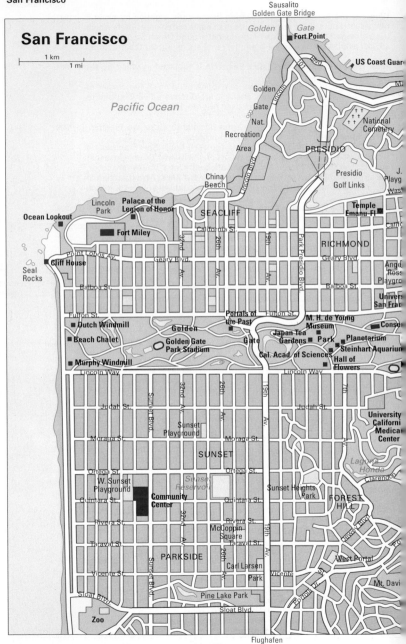

San Francisco

1 km
1 mi

Sausalito
Golden Gate Bridge
Fort Point

US Coast Guard

Golden Gate Bridge

Pacific Ocean

Golden
Gate
Nat.
Recreation
Area

National
Cemetery

PRESIDIO

Presidio
Golf Links

J.
Playg
Was

China
Beach

Lincoln
Park

Palace of the
Legion of Honor

Temple
Emanu-El

Ocean Lookout

SEACLIFF

California St.

RICHMOND

Cali

Fort Miley

Geary Blvd.

Geary Blvd

Cliff House

Point Lobos Av.

Anga
Ross
Playgro

Seal
Rocks

Balboa St.

Balboa St.

Univers
San Frai

Fulton St.

Portals of
the Past

Fulton St.

M. H. de Young
Museum

Conse

Dutch Windmill

Golden

Japan Tea
Gardens

Park

Planetarium

Beach Chalet

Golden Gate
Park Stadium

Gate

Cal. Acad. of Sciences

Steinhart Aquarium

Hall of
Flowers

Murphy Windmill

Lincoln Way

Lincoln Way

Judah St.

32nd
Av.

26th
Av.

19th
Av.

Judah St.

University
Californi
Medica
Center

Sunset
Playground

Moraga St.

Moraga St.

SUNSET

Lago
Honda

Ortega St.

Ortega St.

Clarendon

W. Sunset
Playground

Sunset
Reservoir

Sunset Heights
Park

FOREST
HILL

Community
Center

Quintara St.

Quintara St.

Rivera St.

Rivera St.

McCoppin
Square

Taravat St.

Taravat St.

West Portal

PARKSIDE

Carl Larsen
Park

Vicente St.

Vicente

Mt. Davi

Sunset Blvd.

Sloat Blvd.

Pine Lake Park

Sloat Blvd.

Zoo

Alcatraz

Gas House Cove

Marina Green Park

Fisherman's Wharf

Pier 39

Aquatic Park

San Francisco Bay

Marina orium

Nat. Marit. Museum

The Cannery

Ghiradelli Square

North Point St

Bay St

MARINA

Bay St

Art Institute

Coit Tower

Funston Playground

Lombard St

Lombard St

Stockton St

TELEGRAPH HILL

St. Peter & Paul

Union St

California Hist. Society Bldg.

NORTH BEACH

Broadway

Oakland, Berkeley

PACIFIC

Broadway

Lilienthal House

Washington

CHINA TOWN

Ferry Building World Trade Center

LaFayette Park

Grace Cathedral

California St

Trans America Pyramid

Alta Plaza

PACIFIC HEIGHTS

Pine St

Pine St

Market St

Pacific Medical Center

NOB HILL

Union Square

Transbay Transit Terminal

Geary Blvd

Winterland Auditorium

Geary Blvd

Japan Center

Yerba Buena Gardens

MOMA

Federal Office Bldg.

Moscone Convention Center

WESTERN ADDITION

State Bldg.

City Hall

Turk St

Old Mint

SOUTH OF MARKET

Alamo Square

Opera

Civic Center

Southern Pacific Terminal

China Basin

Fell

Oak

Market St

Howard St

Folsom

Hall of Justice

Mission Rock Terminal

US Mint

Hwy 101

na Vista Park

Bryant

Stewart

Central Basin

Corona Heights

Market St

Mex. Museum

16th St

Franklin Square

Jackson Park

Eureka Playground

Mission Dolores

Mission Park

South Van Ness AV

McKinley Square

Freeway

EUREKA VALLEY

Guerrero St

Dolores St

Valencia St

POTRERO

Potrero Hill Playground

3rd Street

MISSION

Clipper St

Garfield Square

Army ST Terminal

Douglas Playground

Army

Army

Islais Creek Channel

Hunters Point

DIAMOND MOUNTAINS

BERNAL HEIGHTS

Bayshore

James

Wholesale Produce Market

Bayshore

Southern

BAY SHORE

GLEN PARK

Holly Park

San Jose AV

St. Mary's Park

Boswroth St

© Baedeker

The Anchorage

Situated in Leavenworth Street, this shopping and leisure centre is one of San Francisco's latest attractions. There are nearly 50 shops and restaurants on various levels, as well as an hotel in a delightful architectural setting.

The centre of the complex is an inner courtyard, where buskers from all parts of the city perform in a mini-amphitheatre.

Angel Island State Park

Angel Island lies north of the city in San Francisco Bay. It has an area of 300 ha (750 acres). In the course of the last hundred years it has been used as a quarantine station for Asian immigrants and also as a coastguard station, becoming a prisoner-of-war camp and anti-aircraft site during the Second World War. The uninhabited island is now a municipal park where some 200 red deer are allowed to roam free.

Motor **vehicles** are banned from the island but it is a favourite spot for excursions from the city as there are pleasant cycle tracks and paths for pedestrians as well as large picnic sites.

Moorings: Pier 43½ (Fisherman's Wharf). Ferry services: in summer daily; autumn to spring Fri.–Sun. to Ayala Cove.

Bank of America

The marble skyscraper belonging to the Bank of America, between Pine Street and California Street, is 52 storeys high and rises 237 m (778 ft). Built in 1969, it is the headquarters of the biggest private bank in the world, with assets of about 30 billion dollars. The building was designed by two eminent firms of architects, Wurster, Bernardi & Emmons and Skidmore, Owings & Merrill, with Pietro Belluschi as consultant. The material used is reddish South Dakota granite.

Bank of California

The Bank of California (400 California Street) is the oldest bank on the West Coast. The first bank building, which was erected here in 1867 on the site occupied by the present Banking Temple, was in the Neo-Renaissance style. It was pulled down just before the earthquake of 1906. The second head office, at the corner of Sansome Street, takes the form of a granite temple with pillars on two sides.

The **Museum of Money of the American West** in the basement is not very large but is an important source of information about the history of the American West. Here may be seen gold quartz from the time of the Gold Rush, and nuggets of gold and silver. There is also a collection of gold coins and banknotes from the second half of the 19th c.

The interesting collections of the museum also include weapons which are historically important, some of them having been used in duels by famous personalities of the past.

★★Cable Cars

History Inventor and manufacturer of the cable cars was Andrew Hallidie, an engineer born in London. He conceived the idea of replacing the horse trams, which found the steep streets of San Francisco difficult

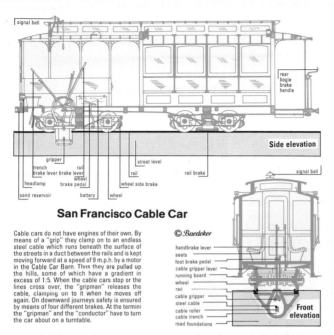

signal bell

rear bogie brake handle

Side elevation

gripper

trench brake lever · rail brake lever

headlamp · wheel brake pedal

sand reservoir · battery

street level

rail

wheel · wheel side brake

rail brake

signal bell

San Francisco Cable Car

Cable cars do not have engines of their own. By means of a "grip" they clamp on to an endless steel cable which runs beneath the surface of the streets in a duct between the rails and is kept moving forward at a speed of 9 m.p.h. by a motor in the Cable Car Barn. Thus they are pulled up the hills, some of which have a gradient in excess of 1:5. When the cable cars stop or the lines cross over, the "gripman" releases the cable, clamping on to it when he moves off again. On downward journeys safety is ensured by means of four different brakes. At the termini the "gripman" and the "conductor" have to turn the car about on a turntable.

© *Baedeker*

handbrake lever
seats
foot brake pedal
cable gripper lever
running board
wheel
rail
cable gripper
steel cable
cable roller
cable trench
road foundations

Front elevation

Cable Car Barn – the control centre

Panoramic view from the observation terrace of the Hotel Westin St Francis in Union Square

to negotiate safely, with a more modern transport system. Without any power of its own, the cable car is suspended with the aid of a "grip" on an endless cable housed in a trench under the street and is thus pulled up the steep slope (gradient up to 21 per cent). When the cable cars stop or the lines cross over, the "gripman" releases the cable, clamping it on again when the car moves off. Four powerful braking systems ensure safety when going downhill (the speed of the cars, which always have right of way, is a steady 15 k.p.h. (9½ m.p.h.). At the termini the "gripman" and "conductor" together – often with the help of the passengers – turn the car round on a turntable.

The first stretch was opened in 1873. By 1880 there were eight lines in operation covering a total network of 180 km (110 mi.). Today only 17 km (11 mi.) remain. Since 1964 the system has been declared an historic monument.

Cable Car Barn

This red-brick building at the corner of Washington Street and Mason Street was erected in 1887 as the control centre for the three cable car lines still in existence. From an observation gallery it is possible to see just how the cable cars work. Open Apr.–Oct. daily 10am–6pm, Nov.–Mar. daily 10am–5pm; admission free.

Day passes are available for the cable cars, offering worthwhile saving.

The little **museum** shows three of the first vehicles which plied in Clay Street, equipment such as gripping and braking mechanisms, cables 3.5 cm. (1½ in.) in diameter, gas lanterns and warning-bells, photographs and models of all the types of cable car ever put into service. There is continuous screening of a film lasting a quarter of an hour about the cable cars and how they operate. (Admission free.)

California Palace of the Legion of Honor

California Palace of the Legion of Honor

On the extreme north-west outskirts of San Francisco, in a most picturesque situation on a hillock in Lincoln Park, stands the Neo-Classical museum building known as the California Palace of the Legion of Honor, a copy of the Palais de la Légion d'Honneur in Paris. It was built in 1915 as the French pavilion for the Panama-Pacific Exposition. While the original intention was that the museum should be devoted exclusively to French art, it became endowed in the course of time with works by artists of other nationalities. During closure for restoration some of the collection is being displayed at the De Young Museum (see Golden Gate Park) and in other Californian galleries.

Thanks in particular to the munificence of three married couples – the Spreckels, the Huntingdons and the Williams – as well as other benefactors, the museum boasts a comprehensive **collection** of European (mainly French) art. Among the French painters represented are Claude Lorrain, Nicolas Poussin, Jean-Antoine Watteau, Louis David, Gustave Courbet, Camille Corot, Edgar Degas, Edouard Manet and Claude Monet.

A further attraction is the **Foundation for Graphic Arts**, a collection of 100,000 graphic works dating from the 15th to the 20th c., presented to the city by Mr Moore Achenbach and his wife Sadie.

★ The Cannery

On the south side of Fisherman's Wharf (see entry) an interesting

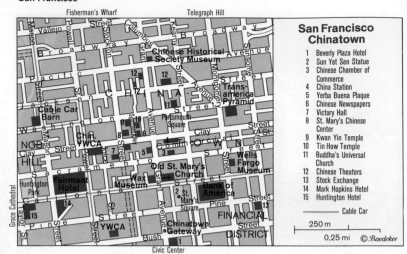

Fisherman's Wharf · Telegraph Hill

San Francisco Chinatown

1 Beverly Plaza Hotel
2 Sun Yat Sen Statue
3 Chinese Chamber of Commerce
4 China Station
5 Yerba Buena Plaque
6 Chinese Newspapers
7 Victory Hall
8 St. Mary's Chinese Center
9 Kwan Yin Temple
10 Tin How Temple
11 Buddha's Universal Church
12 Chinese Theaters
13 Stock Exchange
14 Mark Hopkins Hotel
15 Huntington Hotel

—— Cable Car

250 m
0,25 mi © Baedeker

Civic Center

complex with fashion houses, food shops, boutiques, art galleries, restaurants and leisure facilities has developed since 1968 on the premises, now nearly 90 years old, of the redundant Del Monte fruit canning factory. Open-air concerts, poetry readings and other shows are put on here. Musicians and actors perform in an inner courtyard among the old olive trees. In Cannery Casuals there is a Byzantine mosaic ceiling. There are similar developments at Ghirardelli Square and Pier 39.

★Chinatown

The largest Chinese city outside Asia is in San Francisco on Grant Avenue between Bush Street and Columbus Avenue. The people are the descendants of Asians, mainly railway workers, who settled here from 1850 onwards, just after the Gold Rush. With ever-increasing immigration from Asia in the last 30 years, Chinatown has experienced its greatest period of population growth. Since 1950 the Chinese population has increased from 30,000 to 100,000.

Almost completely destroyed in the 1906 earthquake, Chinatown was rebuilt entirely in the Chinese style and was soon even more attractive than before the disaster. Now with its temples, theatres, workshops, small businesses, stores, antique and souvenir shops, teahouses and pharmacies with their odd nostrums, Chinatown has become one of the major sights of San Francisco.

Chinese Six Companies

The headquarters of the Chinese Six Companies (843 Stockton Street) is perhaps the most important institution in Chinatown. In the 19th c. it recruited Chinese labourers, the so-called "coolies" – the word means roughly "hard labour" – to build the Transcontinental Railway. Later it functioned as a sort of arbitrator to sort out quarrels between the Chinese. Today it has lost something of its former prestige but is still of considerable social significance.

Fidelity Savings Bank

The Fidelity Savings Bank at 845 Grant Avenue near Washington Street was built in 1971 in the most extravagant Chinese style. The roof is covered with gilded tiles.

Temple of the Buddhist Tin How

This building was erected in 1977 on the corner of Clay Street and Stockton Street. It is the head office of the oldest Chinese friendly society in America, the Kong Chow Benevolent Association. Visiting times for the temple which bears the same name are posted on its doors.

Kong Chow Benevolent Association and Temple

The central post office for Chinatown is housed on the third floor.

This museum devoted to the history of the Chinese in America can be found in Adler Place branching off near 1140 Grant Avenue. The collections are primarily of objects, photographs and documents relative to the role of the Chinese during the Californian Gold Rush. The museum also has important material about later periods. Every exhibit is labelled in Chinese and English. Open Tue.–Sat. noon–4pm; closed on public holidays.

Chinese Historical Society Museum

Chinatown Gateway stands on the corner of Grant Avenue and California Street. It is a gate of characteristic Oriental construction, decorated with dragons and other beasts.

Chinatown Gateway

Old St Mary's Church, on the corner of Grant Avenue and California Street, is the oldest Catholic church in San Francisco. It was built in 1845 and badly damaged in the 1906 earthquake and again by a serious fire 60 years later. It has been restored in its original style. Originally a cathedral, it is now simply a parish church.

Old St Mary's Church

From Old St Mary's Church there is a view of St Mary's Square. On the square stands Rafael Bufano's statue of Dr Sun Yat-Sen, the first president of the Republic of China (January 1st 1912–February 14th 1912). Early in the 20th c. he spent several years of political asylum in San Francisco.

St Mary's Square

Dick Young House

On the spot where Dick Young House now stands (823 Grant Street) the first human habitation of Yerba Buena, as San Francisco was originally called, was erected on June 25th 1835. In fact it was a tent which was replaced by the first timber house a few months later. A plaque has been fixed to the wall of Dick Young House to commemorate the event.

Tin How Temple

Tin How Temple is on the top floor of 125 Waverly Street (between Washington and Clay Streets). It is relatively easy for non-Buddhists to visit the temple. It was founded in 1852 on another site, and bears the name of Tin How, the Buddhist Queen of Heaven. Open daily 9am–5pm and 7pm–9pm.

Street scene in Grant Avenue

Bank of Canton

This pagoda-like building on the corner of Grant Avenue and Washington Streeting is at present occupied by the Bank of Canton. It was originally built in 1909 as the Chinatown telephone office.

Buddha's Universal Church

Buddha's Universal Church, the largest Buddhist temple in America, was built in 1961 on the corner of Washington Street and Kearny Street by members of the Pristine Orthodox Dharma, a strongly Americanised modern offshoot of Buddhism. On the roof may be seen, in addition to a lotus pool, a Bodhi tree, said to be a shoot from the tree under which more than 2500 years ago the Buddha arrived at enlightenment (Bodhi). Visits are allowed only if notified in advance by telephone.

Chinese Theater

In and around John Street there are three Chinese theatres. A visit is particularly interesting because of the simple style of staging, the dissonant music, the exotic audience, the wonderful costumes and the apparent lack of event in the plots of the plays, the performance of which used to go on for days and weeks on end, and in which even the women's roles were formerly taken by men.

★Civic Center

The Civic Center is located in the south-west part of the city centre, surrounded by Market Street, Van Ness Avenue, and McAllister Street. No other city in America has such a magnificent official and administrative centre as San Francisco. Its focal point is Civic Center Plaza, a square around which the following buildings are grouped:

City Hall

On the west side of the square stands the City Hall, built between 1912 and 1915, and the fifth that San Francisco has had. The Californian archi-

City Hall in the Civic Center

tects John Bakewell and Arthur Brown jnr. conceived a building on the lines of a French Renaissance château. It is nearly 120 m (400 ft) long and 90 m (300 ft) wide. Its offices are round an enclosed courtyard over which a dome has been built. The latter is 93 m (300 ft) high, appreciably higher than the Capitol in Washington.

The Main Public Library, the headquarters of the city's library services, stands on the east side of the square, opposite the City Hall. The building was constructed in 1917 by George Kelham in Beaux-Arts style; the steel magnate George Carnegie provided financial support. The library has a stock of some 1.8 million books, not to mention a considerable collection of newspapers and manuscripts, and also houses temporary exhibitions on the 2nd and 3rd floors.

Main Public Library

The Civic Auditorium, the oldest building in the Civic Center, is on the south side of Civic Center Plaza. It was designed in 1915 by the architect Arthur Brown jnr. for the great Panama-Pacific Exhibition and now, together with Brooks Hall, built alongside it in 1958, it serves as the city's conference centre.

Civic Auditorium

The War Memorial Opera House, also in the Civic Center, was built in 1932 by Arthur Brown jnr. together with the Veterans Building opposite the City Hall.

War Memorial Opera House

The United Nations was inaugurated in the War Memorial Opera House and the Veterans Building. The Charter founding the world organisation was signed by the representatives of 43 nations on the stage of the Opera House on June 26th 1945. This event is commemorated by the square known as United Nations Plaza.

Until 1980 performances were given here by both the San Francisco Opera (founded in 1923) and the San Francisco Symphony. Now, how-

269

Embarcadero Center – office blocks and shopping precinct

ever, the Symphony Orchestra is able to use the recently built Louise M. Davies Symphony Hall.

★ Louise M. Davies Symphony Hall

The opening of this concert hall in September 1980 was the fulfilment of a long-cherished ambition of music-lovers in San Francisco; at last the Symphony Orchestra had a home of its own. The building, designed by the New York firm of architects Skidmore, Owings & Merrill, with the collaboration of Pietro Belluschi, was required to blend with the rest of the Civic Center (see above) while yet being modern in conception (there was no question of imitating the Art Deco style of the other buildings).

Cow Hollow

In the years following the Gold Rush the part of present-day Union Street west of Van Ness Avenue was a green valley. People used to call it "Cow Hollow" and the name has remained.

The area began to be developed about a century ago, and there has been a genuine example of urban renewal here in the last 25 years. The numerous Victorian houses have been restored, some being converted for commercial purposes. Now there are fashion boutiques, antique shops, galleries, restaurants and some of the best-known singles bars and cafés.

Octagon House

The long section of Union Street between Van Ness Avenue and Steiner Street, incorporating eight blocks of houses, is worth a visit to see the large number of Victorian dwellings. An undoubted curiosity is Octagon House (2645 Gough Street, corner of Union Street), built as the result of a short-lived vogue for octagonal houses in the late 1850s. It serves now as the headquarters of the National Society of Colonial Dames of

The Museum of Modern Art designed by Mario Botta was opened in 1995

America. The house is also a museum, and the exhibits date from the American colonial period. Admission free; guided tours on the second Sunday and the second and fourth Thursdays of each month, noon–3pm.

At 2963 Webster Street, on the corner of Filbert Street not far from Union Street, stands the striking Vedanta Temple. It was built in 1905 by the architect J. A. Leonard in collaboration with Swami Trigunatitananda, the founder of the Vedanta Society of North California which is still in existence.

Vedanta Temple

With its grotesque mixture of various styles – Queen Anne, Colonial, Oriental, Moorish and mediaeval – the building is supposed to symbolise the Vedanta concept that all religions are but ways of approaching the one God. Vedanta is the highest of the six systems in the Hindu philosophy of religion.

★Embarcadero Center

Situated between Embarcadero, Battery and Clay Streets, this shopping and leisure centre must be regarded as one of the most interesting and original examples of urban renewal. The six buildings – five skyscrapers with between 32 and 43 storeys and the 20 storey Hyatt Regency Hotel – are the work of the Atlanta architect John Portman. Four skyscrapers are linked by means of footbridges which give access to more than 175 shops and restaurants. The plazas between the buildings are on different levels; in several places sculptures by various artists are exhibited.

Exploratorium

This outstanding science museum, situated west of the Marina district (at 3601 Lyon Street; near the Golden Gate Bridge), is housed in the Palace of Fine Arts, the sole survivor from the 323 large structures erected for the Panama-Pacific Exhibition of 1915. Opened in 1969, the Exploratorium was one of the first interactive museums in the USA. Virtually all the more than 650 exhibits can be activated by visitors (a bonus in particular for children), greatly facilitating an understanding of natural processes.

Open Tue.–Sun. 10am–6pm, Wed. until 9pm. Admission free on the first Wed. in the month.

Ferry Building

At the foot of Market Street, east of Embarcadero Plaza, stands Ferry Building, built between 1986 and 1903 and once the real symbol of San Francisco with its Neo-Romanesque façade and its 70 m/230 ft-high tower, modelled on the campanile of Seville Cathedral.

Until the building of the San Francisco–Oakland Bridge and the Golden Gate Bridge the area around Ferry Building was the place where all roads met.

Every day 170 ferries kept up a shuttle service to the other side of the bay. Now there are just a few boats serving Sausalito, Larkspur and Tiburon.

Museums The building now houses both the Port Authority and the California State Division of Mines Museum containing a valuable collection of stones and minerals, as well as the World Trade Center with its exhibition of products from all parts of the globe. Open Mon.–Fri. 9am–3pm; admission free.

*Fisherman's Wharf

The Embarcadero ends near Fisherman's Wharf, a picturesque harbour on the North Waterfront with some 200 fishing boats. At one time there were Genoese feluccas (two-masted sailing ships), then came Chinese junks, to be followed by boats owned by Neapolitans and others from southern Italy, who gave this quarter its Italian atmosphere.

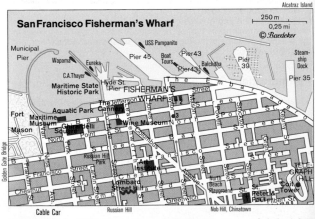

1 Ripley's "Believe it or Not" Museum   2 Wax Museum   3 St. Francis Statue

Pier 39 at the picturesque Fisherman's Wharf has many tourist attractions

Lombard Street, newly surfaced, is now a pedestrian only street

Now the harbour is more like a fairground with many shops and restaurants. However, there are still some fishermen who will take tourists out with them for a fee; their boats are moored near the block between Jones Street and Leavenworth Street. Most of their daily catch, including crayfish and crabs, is delivered to the many local restaurants.

Museums The "Believe it or not" Museum (175 Jefferson Street) has some 2000 curiosities from all corners of the globe. Open every day 9 or 10am–10, 11pm or midnight.

To the east is the Wax Museum at Fisherman's Wharf, with over 200 wax figures imported from England on show. Open 9 or 10am–10pm or midnight.

Ghirardelli Square

Ghirardelli Square (900 North Front Street) was inaugurated in 1964. It was the first of a number of projects designed to give new life to abandoned factory complexes. (Others that have been completed as shopping and leisure centres are The Cannery, Pier 39 and The Anchorage; see entries.) The Italian Domenico Ghirardelli's old red-brick chocolate factory has been turned into a centre for shoppers, art-lovers and those in search of entertainment or a good meal. Its belfry (built in 1916) is modelled on that of the Château de Blois in France. Later additions are rose gardens decorated with fountains (for example, Rose Court with its concrete fountain by Lawrence Halpin, the garden-designer of Ghirardelli Square) and terraces with fine views.

★★Golden Gate Bridge

The Golden Gate Bridge passes over the Golden Gate, the strait between the San Francisco Peninsula and Marin Peninsula. As well as being one of the largest bridges in the world, the splendid scenery all around makes it undoubtedly the most beautiful. The bridge was inaugurated on May 28th 1937. It had taken four years to build (1933–37), and the director of the project was Joseph B. Strauss. Construction proved very difficult on account of the strong cross-currents, and there were some fatal accidents. At the date of its completion it was the longest suspen-

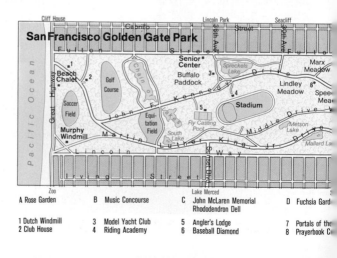

A Rose Garden	B Music Concourse	C John McLaren Memorial Rhododendron Dell	D Fuchsia Gard
1 Dutch Windmill	3 Model Yacht Club	5 Angler's Lodge	7 Portals of the
2 Club House	4 Riding Academy	6 Baseball Diamond	8 Prayerbook C

Golden Gate Bridge (in the foreground Fort Point)

sion bridge in the world. For years it was the symbol of San Francisco, though this distinction is now claimed by the Transamerica Pyramid.

The bridge, which is illuminated in the evening, is nearly 2.7 km (2 mi.) long and 27.5 m (90 ft) wide; it stands 67 m (220 ft) above normal water level. The supporting towers are 227 m (740 ft) high.

Every week 25 painters use about two tons of red-lead paint ("International Orange") to keep the paintwork in good condition. This

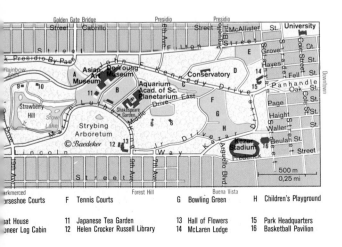

	F	Tennis Courts		G	Bowling Green	H	Children's Playground

	11	Japanese Tea Garden	13	Hall of Flowers	15	Park Headquarters
	12	Helen Crocker Russell Library	14	McLaren Lodge	16	Basketball Pavilion

275

remarkable fact is another reason why the golden Gate Bridge is known all round the world. A toll is payable only when travelling from north to south.

In spite of the heavy traffic, the superb views make a walk across the bridge well worthwhile. There is a wire-netting screen to deter potential suicides who contemplate leaping over into the water – there have already been 600. At the end of the bridge stands a monument to its builder, J. B. Strauss from Cincinnati. He constructed more than 400 major steel bridges all over the world including one in Leningrad.

Fort Point

Fort Point lies below the bridge and was built between 1853 and 1861 to protect San Francisco from attack. It is one of the earliest military buildings in the American West. For the most part it was never used, but served as a construction base while the Golden Gate Bridge was being built. In 1970 it was declared an historical monument.

Golden Gate
National
Recreation Area

This large leisure park in San Francisco and Marin County, covering an area of some 1600 sq. km (620 sq. mi.), was created in 1972 in order to prevent the coastal area from being used for industrial purposes or being built up.

Golden Gate Park

Golden Gate Park, in north-west San Francisco, is 5 km (3 mi.) long and 800 m (½ mi.) wide. Originally there were just arid dunes here; in 1887 the Scottish botanist and landscape gardener John McLaren planted over 5000 different kinds of flowers and trees (originally mainly eucalyptus, acacia, spruce and oak) to make it one of the most splendid parks in the USA, with reserves for several species of deer, including Wapiti, and bison.

★California
Academy of
Sciences

The California Academy of Sciences was founded in 1853 with its museum (open daily, 10am–5pm; admission free on the first Wed. of each month) built in 1916, lies in the east of the park.

Its collections are mainly devoted to natural history. In the west wing are displays of minerals, fossils, mammals and birds of North America. The east wing has an African department and rooms for space travel, anthropology, natural history and botany.

The Morrison Auditorium is here, as well as the Morrison Planetarium, the first "Theatre of Stars" that was not imported from Germany but constructed in the United States in 1951–52. 3800 star patterns are projected on to a dome 20 m (65 ft) in diameter.

The Steinhart Aquarium at the end of the courtyard is one of the largest of its kind, boasting a collection of over 14,000 aquatic creatures. Some 250 tanks teem with fish, dolphins and reptiles (alligators), etc.

★M. H. de Young
Memorial
Museum

The M. H. de Young Memorial Museum (open Wed.–Sun. 10am–5pm; on the first Sat. in the month 10am–noon. Admission free on the first Wed. in the month) is located in a building erected on the initiative of the newspaper publisher Michael H. de Young at the time of the California Midwinter Exposition in 1894. While art from the first half of the 19th c. features strongly in the collection, the museum's 40 or so galleries contain a wide range of works (some donated by William R. Hearst, Samuel H. Kress and Roscoe and Margaret Oakes) from Egypt, Greece and Rome, from the Middle Ages and the Renaissance, from North America and Europe. Folk art from Africa, the South Seas and America is represented by first-rate pieces. There are many paintings by Rembrandt (including two portraits), Rubens, El Greco (John the Baptist), van Dyck, Frans Hals, Fra Angelico, Titian, Verrochio, Cellini, Tiepolo, Goya, Gainsborough, Watteau and Monet. The interior has rooms fitted out in

Japanese Tea Garden - a secluded little place to linger a while

period style from Spain, France, England and Germany which are well worth seeing.

★ Asian Art Museum

Occupying the two-storied west wing of the M. H. de Young Memorial Museum is the Asian Art Museum (Avery Brundage Collection; Open daily 10am–5pm). Its exhibits are mainly the private collection, donated in 1966, of Avery Brundage, president from 1952 to 1972 of the International Olympic Committee. There are now nearly 10,000 sculptures, paintings, bronzes, jade-carvings, ceramic objects and architectural pieces from Japan, Korea, China, India, Iran and other Asiatic cultures.

The examples of Chinese lacquerwork and ebony carving are exceptional, as are the Chinese scrolls and bark paintings. The chief attraction of the museum is the Jade Room. With about 1200 works of art in jade it is the largest collection in any western country. It covers virtually all the Chinese periods, but the emphasis is mainly on the Ming and Ching periods (about AD 1400–1900). There are also a Japanese Department and a library with 12,000 volumes on art in the Near and Far East. As special exhibitions are often held, only some 10 per cent of the total collections can be displayed at any one time. The museum is due to be rehoused in the Civic Center (in what is now the Main Public Library) by 1998.

★ Japanese Tea Garden

South-west of the museum lies the charming Japanese Tea Garden, with its curved bridges (the Moon Bridge is a special attraction), little waterfalls, a gaily coloured pagoda and a tea-house. It is particularly beautiful in early April when the cherry-blossom is out (about 200 trees).

Strybing Arboretum

At the side of the road opposite the Japanese Tea Garden lies the Strybing Arboretum with 6000 species, mainly bushes and trees from Asia.

The oldest museum in San Francisco, the M.H. de Young Memorial Museum, also contains the Asian Art Museum

Conservatory of
Flowers

North-east of the Academy of Sciences is the Conservatory of Flowers, a large hot-house containing palms, chiefly from South America and the islands of the South Pacific. This is the oldest building in the park and one of the best examples of Victorian architecture. It was brought by freighter from England to San Francisco and re-erected here in 1879. It is now a protected building.

In the conservatory may be seen, as well as a tropical garden, orchids, ferns and other plants, and displays of various varieties of flowers – arum lilies, begonias, chrysanthemums and many others – according to the season.

Jackson Square

To the north behind the Transamerica Pyramid lies Jackson Square, one of the most interesting parts of San Francisco from an historical point of view.

Contrary to what the name suggests it is not a square, but just a few streets. In 1972 it was the first part of San Francisco to be declared an area of historical interest; a considerable number of the 19th c. business establishments largely survived the 1906 earthquake and, following restoration, have been listed as protected buildings. These include No. 472, one of the oldest and, in its simplicity, most handsome office buildings in San Francisco of the years 1850–52; between 1865 and 1875 it housed the French Consulate.

Today Jackson Square is a **shopping** and wholesale centre for interior design materials and arts and crafts.

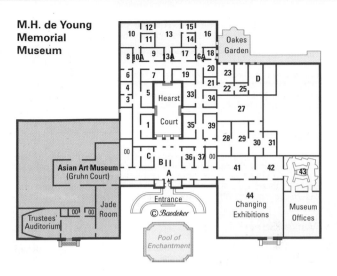

M.H. de Young Memorial Museum

| | | | | |

A Cloakroom   B Telephone   C Bookshop   D Café   00 Toilets

Room 1	Old World
Rooms 3–5	England: furnishings, paintings
Room 6	Salon from Massachusetts (1805)
Rooms 7–19, 27, 33, 35, Art from USA	
Room 7	17th and 18th c. paintings
Room 8	Late 18th c., early 19th c. paintings
Room 9	18th c. interiors and paintings
Room 10	Early 19th c. painting and artwork
Room 10A	Tapestries, chairs
Room 11	19th c. sculpture
Room 12	19th c. Shaker folk art
Room 13	Painting and furniture mid 19th c.
Room 13A	Temporary exhibitions
Room 14	Late 19th c./early 20th c. sculptures
Room 15	Art of the American West
Room 16	Impressionist and emigrant painting.
Room 16A	Late 19th c. painting
Room 17	Genre painting mid 19th c
Room 18	Trompe l'œil and still-life
Room 19	Genre painting late 19th c.
Room 20	Hearst Art Education Room
Room 21	Visitor's information
Room 22	Textiles from the museum collections
Room 23	Conference room
Room 25	16th c. drinking vessels; F.W. and S. Sichel glass collection
Room 27	20th c. painting and artwork
Rooms 28–31, 30, 37, 39, 41, 44 Temporary exhibitions	
Room 33	Californian painting late 19th c.
Room 34	Artwork
Room 35	Early 20th c. painting
Rooms 42, 43, Primitive art from Africa America and the Pacific	

Not all the listed rooms are always open.

Japantown

The Japantown district lies between Geary Boulevard and Post Street and between Filmore Street and Laguna Street. It is the cultural and social centre for the 12,000 or more Japanese ("Nisei") living in San Francisco. Their name for the city is Soko. The first Japanese came to San Francisco 120 years ago, but it was only after the 1906 earthquake that they began to settle in what is now called Japantown. In Japanese the district is called Nihonmachi.

During the Second World War most of the Japanese and Japanese-Americans ("Nisei") were forcibly interned. On being set free most of the former returned to their distant homeland, and it was only slowly that the others moved back to the district in which they had formerly resided.

The opening of the Japan Center in 1968 gave the district a great stimulus. Now there are the 14 storey Miyako Hotel (on the third floor there is

Sights

279

a room with Japanese furnishings and a sunken bath), a theatre, a temple and a shrine, several restaurants and tea-houses, art exhibitions, many shops selling goods imported from Japan, and also the Japanese General Consulate.

Peace Plaza, entered through a gate ("romon") designed by Yoshiro Taniguchi, is noted for its Japanese garden and the five-storey Peace Pagoda. In spring there is a cherry blossom festival (Sakura Matsuri; see also Golden Gate Park, Japanese Tea Garden).

★Lombard Street

A short section of this street on Russian Hill has become one of San Francisco's great tourist attractions. Planted with hydrangeas, it has a 40 per cent gradient and ten Z bends and is known as the "crookedest street". Closed to traffic for a lengthy period when Lombard Street was resurfaced a short while ago, it is now to remain pedestrian-only.

Market Street

Impressive Market Street, one of the few thoroughfares cutting diagonally across the grid-iron street pattern of San Francisco, forms the boundary between the run-down south of the city with its wide roads and the up-and-coming north with narrow streets.
  When there was a danger that the inhabitants of the slums might swamp the northern districts it was thought that the only way to reverse the trend was by a thorough redevelopment of Market Street. Accordingly, between 1964 and 1979, the street was transformed in appearance; trees were planted, the sidewalks repaved with red stone and numerous skyscrapers built.

Market Street leads south-west to Twin Peaks, north-east to Embarcadero Plaza and to the Ferry Building on San Francisco Bay. On the left where Powell Street leads into Market Street is the southern turntable for the cable cars. Behind it rise the 46-storey Hilton Hotel, which was completed in 1971, and the Ramada Renaissance Hotel opened in 1986.

Mexican Museum

The Mexican Museum (open Wed.–Sun. noon–5pm, closed on public holidays) is situated in Fort Mason (Building D). It is the only museum in the United States devoted entirely to Mexican art and folk culture from the Pre-Columbian period to the present day. It is particularly rich in ceramics and paintings by Chicanos, the Mexican farm-hands who come to the United States to help with the harvest.

Every second Saturday in the month at 10am the museum organises a **guided tour** round the many murals in the Mission District quarter of the city where the museum is situated. Many of these murals show the strong influence of Mexican artists such as Rivera and Orozco.

National Maritime Museum

The National Maritime Museum is to be found in the eastern part of the Aquatic Park. Once a prosperous casino, it is now a maritime museum containing models of the different sorts of ships that pass through the Golden Gate – passenger ships, freighters and men-of-war. There is also a library with a collection of historical newspaper cuttings about Californian seafaring, books, pamphlets, log-books, maps and charts. The Photographic Archive possesses about 100,000 pictures of sailing vessels, steamers, harbours and views of the port area of San Francisco, the appearance of which is changing all the time.

Open Wed.–Sun. 10am–5pm (to 6pm in Summer).

In the Maritime State Historic Park (Hyde Street) several **restored ships** are reminders of the time when the harbour was full of sailing ships:

"C. A. Thayer" is a three-master schooner built in 1895. It was first used in the lumber trade, then carried salmon and finally, until 1950, was used for cod-fishing in the Bering Sea.

"Eureka", a ferry steamer in operation from 1890 to 1957, was in its day the largest passenger ferry in the world. Propulsion was by means of paddles.

Also to be seen are the "Wapama", a steam schooner of 1915, the ferry boat "Alma" (1891) and the ocean-going tug "Hercules", which hauled ships into West Coast harbours from 1907 to 1962. The sailing vessel "Balclutha" (1886) is moored at Pier 43 and the submarine "Pampanito" (1943) at Pier 45.

Navy/Marine Corps/Coast Guard Museum

The construction of the Navy/Marine Corps/Coast Guard Museum on Treasure Island was begun at the time of the United States Bi-centennial Celebrations. With displays, documents and pictures the museum illustrates the part played by the US Navy and Marine Corps in the Pacific. A special attraction is the huge mural by Lowell Nesbitt.

Wonderful views of the skyscrapers of San Francisco may be enjoyed during the drive over the San Francisco–Oakland Bridge and especially from Treasure Island. Treasure Island is, it must be added, a man-made island; that is to say, it is a part of Yerba Buena Island which has been reclaimed from the sea. The project was carried out for the 1939 Golden Gate Exhibition.

Nob Hill

Nob Hill, west of Chinatown, rises to more than 100 m (330 ft) and is one of the smartest districts of San Francisco. Before the 1906 earthquake the most prosperous citizens lived here. They began to settle here from the middle of the 19th c. – bankers, industrialists and newspaper owners. They were followed some fifteen to twenty years later by the railroad millionaires who had recently made their fortune, including Charles Crocker, Leland Stanford, Mark Hopkins and Collis Huntingdon.

The name is possibly derived from the word "snob" or – as seems more likely – from "knob", meaning a knoll or rounded hill.

There are still a number of **palatial buildings** on Nob Hill which are worth seeing:

Mark Hopkins Hotel (905 California Street): Hopkins Villa stood here until it was destroyed in the earthquake. It was not until 1925 that the 20-storey hotel was constructed. From its "Top of the Mark" bar there is one of the finest views out over the city.

Fairmont Hotel (950 Mason Street): it was financed by James G. Fair, the "Silver King", totally gutted by fire just before its opening in 1906 and later repaired.

The foyer is considered to be one of the finest public rooms in San Francisco. The exterior lift on the tower, added in 1962, is a special attraction.

Pacific Union Club (1000 California Street): San Francisco's most exclusive club for gentlemen; it occupies the villa built in 1886 for James Flood, another "Silver King" and was renovated 26 years later.

Grace Cathedral

On the west side of Huntington Park (1051 Taylor Street) stands Grace Cathedral, built in 1928 in the Neo-Gothic style and obviously influenced by the architecture of Notre Dame in Paris. It is the seat of the Episcopalian Bishop of California. Florentine works of art were the inspiration of the main portals which take the form of casts from Lorenzo Ghiberti's "Gates of Paradise" at the Baptistery in Florence. The interior houses a number of notable original works of art, including a 13th c. Catalonian crucifix, a Flemish altarpiece of the late 15th c., a silk and gold Brussels Gobelin tapestry dating from the 16th c., a terracotta relief of the Madonna and Child by the Renaissance artist Antonio Rossellino and, on the north wall of the ambulatory, a collection of pages from medieval Bibles.

North Beach

North Beach stretches north of Chinatown as far as Telegraph Hill, where there was an arm of the bay as recently as 1850. It is one of the most enigmatic parts of San Francisco, and inhabited mainly by Italians and their American descendants.

Washington Square

Washington Square is the centre of the Italian quarter. More than 50,000 Italians live here, and a glance at the shops and restaurants is enough to persuade any visitor that the Italian way of life is still practised in this area. In the sixties and seventies it was where the Hippies ("Flower Children") met; this psychedelic movement started here and in other squares in this quarter of the city. The Church of St Peter and St Paul stands in the square.

The south-east part of this area, especially around Broadway and Columbus Avenue which crosses it, is San Francisco's main **entertainment area**, with countless night-clubs, jazz-clubs, bars, cabarets, theatres, restaurants and cafés.

Pacific Stock Exchange

Founded in 1873, the Pacific Stock Exchange now occupies buildings designed by the architects Miller and Pflueger and erected in 1930. The exuberant decoration bears witness to the date of construction. The sculptures are by Ralph Stackpole.

During trading hours it is possible to go into the gallery and watch at close quarters the hectic activity of the stockbrokers. However, intending visitors are required to have a recommendation from a San Francisco stockbroking firm.

Pier 39

Near Fisherman's Wharf (see entry) a complex with 130 shops and 23 restaurants was created on the site of a disused pier. On the ground floor and upper storey of this 300 m (1000 ft)-long pier all has been activity and bustle since its inauguration in 1978. Pier 39 was completely reconstructed by using timbers from old ships and by tearing down other piers in the vicinity, in order to provide moorings for small boats. For several years now, hundreds of sea-lions have taken to congregating in the waters between Piers 39 and 41.

Underwater World

In 1996 an unusual aquarium with an underwater tunnel for viewing the flora and fauna of San Francisco Bay opened on Pier 39. Commentaries are provided on audio cassette, and visitors move through the tunnel on a conveyor-belt. Guided tours every 15 minutes.

Presidio

The name "Presidio" goes back to 1776 when Spanish troops were first quartered on this site. This wooded stretch of land which covers some 600 ha (1500 acres) lies on the northern extremity of the San Francisco peninsula jutting out into the Pacific. It has always been used for military purposes; at present it is the headquarters of the United States 6th Army, but closure is planned. In the park, to most of which the public is allowed free access and from which there are fine views, stands the Officers' Club. Dating from 1776, it is the only relic of Spanish days.

The National Military Cemetery is also part of the Presidio. It has a burial ground where lie more than 15,000 who died in the First World War. Also noteworthy is the gravestone of "Pauline Tyler, Union Spy". She was an actress who served as a Union spy during the course of the American Civil War, winning promotion to the rank of major.

National Military Cemetery

Situated on Lincoln Boulevard (junction with Funston Ave.) is the Presidio Army Museum, housed in an old military hospital dating from 1857. There are exhibitions of relics and documents which illustrate the part played by the military in the development of San Francisco. Open Tue.–Sun. 10am–4pm.

Presidio Army Museum

St Mary's Cathedral

St Mary's Cathedral, the third to bear this name, stands on Cathedral Hill (Gough Street and Geary Street) and was built in 1962. It is by far the most impressive of all the churches in San Francisco. Open daily 8.30am–5pm, Sundays and public holidays afternoons only.

Designed by well-known architects, including Pietro Belluschi and Pier Luigi Nervi, it has a nave without pillars and a dome 60 m (198 ft) high, in which 2 m (7 ft) high stained glass windows like great translucent ribbons come together at the top to form a multi-coloured cross. The four windows in the dome symbolise the elements, fire (west), air (north), water (east) and earth (south).

The altar, at which the celebrant faces the congregation in accord with the recommendations of the Vatican Council of 1962, is surrounded by rows of seats on three sides. Above it hangs a cross and a baldacchino.

San Francisco African-American Historical and Cultural Society

The only museum devoted to the culture and history of the African-Americans west of the Mississippi is to be found in San Francisco (Marina Boulevard, Fort Mason, Building C. Open Tue.–Sat. 10am–5pm

Permanent exhibits include documents and pictures relative to their history in California and the part played by them in the American Civil War of 1861–65

Temporary exhibitions of works by artists, especially those working in and around San Francisco, are regularly mounted.

San Francisco Fire Department Pioneer Memorial Museum

On Presidio Avenue No. 655, behind the massive doors of this museum, is kept a remarkable collection of photographs, equipment and documents that come from the various fire brigades of San Francisco, especially the Volunteer Fire Brigade which was in existence from 1849 to 1866. Much space is given over to documents concerning events during the disastrous blaze following the 1906 earthquake.

There is a special exhibition devoted to Lillie Hitchcock Coit who paid for the erection of Coit Tower on Telegraph Hill as a memorial in honour of the fire brigade, and was herself made an honorary member of a fire brigade company.

★ San Francisco Museum of Modern Art

The new San Francisco Museum of Modern Art in Third Street, next to the Yerba Buena Gardens and the Center for the Arts, opened in January 1995. Prior to this, the museum was housed in the War Memorial Veterans Building on the west side of the Civic Center Plaza. Designed by the acclaimed Swiss architect Mario Botta, a pupil of Le Corbusier and Louis Kahn, the eye-catching new building of red brick has quickly become one of the city's landmarks. Its most distinctive feature is its circular tower, of black and silver grey granite. With an exhibition area twice the size of its predecessor, the San Francisco museum is now the second largest modern art museum in the United States after the Museum of Modern Art in New York.

Unlike the three other major art museums in San Francisco – the Asian Art Museum and M. H. de Young Memorial Museum (both in Golden Gate Park) and the California Palace of the Legion of Honour (see entries) – the Museum of Modern Art is a private institution. Though its origins go back to the 1890s, it was set on a firm footing only in 1916, thanks to the efforts of the San Francisco Art Association.

Unique Until a museum of modern art opened in Los Angeles in 1986, the San Francisco Museum of Modern Art was the only one of its kind on the West Coast. However the architecture of the building was out of keeping with its function, namely to display 20th c. art. As part of a modernising process, works by the American sculptors Tony Smith and Peter Voulkos were positioned in front of the Art Deco façade, and in the entrance hall the statue of George Washington was replaced by a geometric design in steel by the Californian sculptor Bruce Nauman.

Permanent collections Not surprisingly, Californian artists receive special attention, closely followed by American painters and sculptors who have made the West Coast their cultural home, such as Mark Rothko, Jackson Pollock, Clyfford Still, Robert Motherwell and Philip Guston. The museum's collections now also contain works by nearly every important modern European and American artist, including French (in particular Henri Matisse and Georges Braques, but also Paul Cézanne, Fernand L‚ger, Camille Pissarro, Jean Dubuffet, Pierre Bonnard and Georges Rouault), German (Max Ernst, Max Pechstein, Hans Purrmann, Kurt Schwitters, Hans Hartung, Karl Hofer, George Grosz, Ernst Ludwig Kirchner, Franz Marc and Fritz Winter), Russian (Alexej Jawlensky and Wassily Kandinsky) and Spanish (Joan Miró and Pablo Picasso).

The museum possesses sculptures by Hans Arp, Constantin Brancusi, Henry Moore, Alexander Archipenko. Jacob Epstein, Henri Laurens, Jacques Lipchitz and Marino Marini.

Modern day artists As well as the American artists already mentioned, the museum exhibits works by others who have made names for themselves in recent years. Among them are Stuart Davis, William de Kooning, Frank Stella, Jim Dine, Helen Frankenthaler, Arshile Gorky, Adolph Gottlieb, Robert Indiana, Elsworth Kelly, Kenneth Noland, Georgia O'Keeffe, Claes Oldenburg, Ad Reinhardt and Mark Tobey. The museum also has a large collection of photographs, including original prints by Ansel Adams, who died in 1984.

Open Tue.–Sun. 11am–6pm, Thu. until 7pm; admission free on the first Thursday in the month.

San Francisco–Oakland Bay Bridge

This bridge links the city with Oakland and the towns on the east side of the bay. It was opened in 1936, six months before the Golden Gate Bridge (see entry). The bridge is some 13.3 km (8 mi.) long, which makes it one of the longest steel bridges in the world. It consists of two inter-connected suspension bridges on the San Francisco side, a tunnel through the island of Yerba Buena and a lattice-work bridge on the Oakland side.

In the **earthquake** of October 1989 a 15 m (50 ft) length of the bridge collapsed and numerous cars were buried in the debris. The 50 year-old bridge was shown not to be earthquake-proof, as the massive concrete construction served merely to intensify the shock waves. A thorough renovation has since been successfully completed.

San Francisco Zoological Gardens

San Francisco did not begin to lay out its zoo until quite late (1929), but now it is one of the six most important in the United States (Open daily 10am–5pm). Its designers took the Carl Hagenbeck Zoo in Hamburg, Germany as their model. The chief attractions are the snow leopards, polar bears, elephants, pigmy hippos, white rhinos and the monkeys which inhabit an island of their own. The enclosure for primates was added in 1985.

There is also a **children's zoo** here which is open every day from 11am until 4.30pm Children are able to play with young animals and feed them. They can also have rides on giant tortoises and on roundabouts.

Spreckels' Mansion

This mansion is in the Pacific Heights quarter of the city, two blocks away from Van Ness Street. It is worthy of attention on account of the man who had it built, Adolph B. Spreckels, son of Claus Spreckels, an immigrant from Hanover who became the "Sugar King" of California, and also because of its architecture. It was designed by the architect George Applegarth on the lines of a French Baroque palace, and con-structed in white stone. Applegarth was also commissioned by Spreckels to build the California Palace of the Legion of Honor in Lincoln Park (see entry).

Telegraph Hill

Telegraph Hill rises 90 m (295 ft) on the north side of the inner city. It is one of San Francisco's 43 hills. Rather like Montmartre in Paris, it has many artists' studios on its slopes as well as villas for the well-to-do middle classes.

There is at present no telegraph installation on Telegraph Hill, but the name goes back to the semaphore station erected on what was then a barren hilltop at the time of the Gold Rush.

Coit Tower stands 150 m (500 ft) above sea-level on the top of Telegraph   ★Coit Tower

Hill. The inside of the tower is decorated with 16 monumental murals, the work of 25 painters and their 19 assistants. They were undertaken as part of the work creation scheme designed to alleviate the Great Depression. It is also one of the best vantage points from which to view San Francisco, though it is not quite as high as the Twin Peaks (see entry).

The **name** "Coit Tower" recalls Lillie Coit (1843–1929), an honorary member of a fire fighting company. She had it built in honour of the fire brigade. The architect Arthur Brown jnr., who was also responsible for the City Hall (see Civic Center) and other public buildings constructed it in 1934. It takes the form of a free-standing column in which many claim they can recognise the valve of a fire hose.

Apart from the murals at ground-level, those inside the tower can be viewed only on Saturday mornings from 11am.

Pioneer Park
Coit Tower is surrounded by Pioneer Park. This was a stony barren hillside until it was laid out as a park when the Centennial Celebrations of the United States took place on Telegraph Hill. The bronze statue of Christopher Columbus is especially noteworthy.

★Transamerica Pyramid

Since its completion in 1972 the Transamerica Pyramid, which can be seen from virtually everywhere in San Francisco, has become the new symbol of the city. It is situated at 600 Montgomery Street, north of the Wells Fargo Bank Building, in the middle of the financial quarter. Designed by the architect William Pereira of Los Angeles, it has 48 storeys and reaches up 260 m (853 ft) into the sky. It belongs to an insurance and finance company bearing the same name.

Construction Unlike conventional buildings, the pyramidal tower with its lattice-like cladding, is said to be particularly resistant to earthquake. The main building, square in section, is 150 ft (45 m) wide at the bottom and 14 m (46 ft) wide at the topmost floor, This section is surmounted by a 45 m (150 ft) high hollow spire illuminated from within. The sides of the pyramidal spire are clad in aluminium sheeting.

The lines of the tall **spire** are broken by the external lift-shafts (18 lifts) which run up the east and west sides of the building as far as the base of the spire.

Twin Peaks

These two unique and uninhabited hills, almost 300 m (1000 ft) high, are not in fact the highest of San Francisco's 43 hills, a distinction belonging to Mount Davidson which is some 10 m (33 ft) higher. However, they are easier to get to (No. 37 bus) and offer what is perhaps the finest views out over the city and the bay (there are frequent mists from the Pacific).

View Twin Peaks are the only hills in San Francisco not to have been built over and remaining in their original state. From them you can look down over San Francisco and the bay; there is nowhere better than this from which to appreciate the vastness of this impressive city. The Spaniards called the twin peaks "Los pechos de la Chola" (i.e. the Breasts of the Indian Maiden).

Even on warm days strong cool breezes blow in from the Pacific, especially in the late afternoon. Warm clothing is therefore recommended.

The Transatlantic Pyramid contrasts with the old Columbus Tower ▶

Union Square

San Francisco really has no central point, but Union Square comes nearest to fulfilling this function. It is here, or in the immediate vicinity, that numerous lines of communication come together, and here are to be found important shops (Macy's, Magnin, Neiman-Marcus, Saks Fifth Avenue) and hotels (Hyatt Union Square, Westin St Francis, Sir Francis Drake); the most important theatres are just a short step away in Geary Street. The south-west corner of the square, where Geary Street and Powell Street meet, is reckoned to be the liveliest spot in all San Francisco.

History The site of Union Square was presented to the city by its first American Mayor, John W. Geary. Its ornamental palm trees are unique in central San Francisco. Since 1942 there has been a vast underground car park beneath the square.

Union Square received its name during the American Civil War (1861–65) when mass demonstrations took place here in favour of the troops of the Northern Union and against the secessionist Southern States. In 1902 a **Corinthian column** of granite with a bronze goddess of victory was erected here in commemoration of Admiral George Dewey's triumph in the Bay of Manila during the short Spanish-American War of 1898.

Political demonstrations still take place in Union Square, where in warm weather most of the benches are occupied throughout the day by strollers and poor people from the slums south of Market Street (see entry).

Be sure to look into the foyer of the **Westin St Francis** (see Practical Information, Hotels), a famous hotel in Union Square. From the top floor of the hotel there is a magnificent view over the city's financial quarter and beyond to the harbour area and Alcatraz Island, the former penitentiary.

★Wells Fargo History Room

At 420 Montgomery Street, the main street in the Financial District, stands the 43-storey, 564 ft (171 m) high Wells Fargo Bank Building. Its History Room is a rich source of information for all who wish to learn about the early history of California from the time of the Gold Rush (1848) to the 1906 earthquake.

There is a particularly fine example of a Concord coach, in which the Wells Fargo Express Co., founded in 1852, transported passengers and freight, especially gold. A special display is devoted to Black Bart who between 1877 and 1885 ambushed 28 coaches on his own. He often left comic verses at the scene, claiming to be a "Robin Hood" figure.

World of Oil

This museum in the Standard Oil Company of California building (555 Market Street; open Mon.-Fri. 9am-4pm) will fascinate anybody interested in the story of oil from its discovery to the development of its countless by-products.

The history of oil is depicted to visitors by means of models of the equipment used in the oil-fields and by three dioramas. There is also an 18 minute multi-media show called "Magic of a Refinery" which is put on several times a day. It requires no fewer than 26 projectors.

★San José   l 1

Santa Clara County
Altitude: 27 m (90 ft).
Population: 822,000

This rapidly progressing town, situated 60 km (37 mi.) from San
Francisco, is also one of the oldest in the country. Its population has
increased ten-fold since the end of the Second World War, and will probably exceed that of San Francisco when the next census is taken. In spite
of all its efforts, however, it still does not have a proper town centre;
even more so than Los Angeles, it is simply a collection of suburbs
strung together.

History San José was founded in 1777, under the name of Pueblo de San
José de Guadalupe. The Mission established 20 years later is now situated outside the town in Fremont, while the Santa Clara Mission built in
the pueblo now forms part of the town of Santa Clara (see entry),
founded during the Gold Rush period.
    By 1848 there were still only 700 people living in San José; when it
gained the status of a town two years later, however, it boasted 3000
inhabitants.

Economy San José lies in the extremely fertile Santa Clara Valley, where
a great variety of fruit, grapes and vegetables are cultivated. The agricultural products have always been despatched from San José, where
the first canning factory was built in 1871. Nevertheless the town could
muster only 21,500 inhabitants at the beginning of the 20th c., but 40
years later there were 57,000. Then the real upswing began, giving San
José its reputation of being the town with the greatest population
growth in the world.
    The chief branch of industry continues to be the processing of agri-
cultural products. This is followed by the computer, chemical and
engineering industries (especially atomic engineering) which have contributed greatly to San José's economic growth.

The town's **cultural** life has not kept pace with its unbridled demographic
and economic development, in spite of having a big Performing Arts
Center, a Symphony Orchestra and a large Congress Building surrounded
by nine hotels which was opened in 1989. The expansion of the nearby airport, which at present deals with six million passengers and is expected
to be able to take two or three times as many by the end of the century,
will not be able to compensate for the town's cultural shortcomings.

Sights

This Victorian gentleman's residence (525 South Winchester Boulevard)
with 160 rooms must be the strangest ever. When it was built in 1884 by
Mrs Sarah Pardee Winchester, who inherited the Winchester rifle-
making firm, it was a farmhouse with eight rooms. For some 38 years
carpenters and other craftsmen worked day after day on this house
which by the time Mrs Winchester died had been extended considerably
but was still unfinished. Mrs Winchester, taken by the building craze,
insisted on drawing up all the plans herself, although she was far from
being a trained architect. Numerous curiosities were the result: staircases leading nowhere – one even ended at the ceiling – doors opening
on to blank walls and windows which are nothing of the sort because
they do not look out on to anything. The entrance hall was big enough
for her coach to drive into. She bought so much furniture that most of it
lay unused in the cellars.

★Winchester
Mystery House

Winchester Mystery House – a peculiar house with highly imaginative but impractical architecture.

Superstition The number 13 occurs conspicuously often in the construction of this house. There are 13 bathrooms, many of the rooms have 13 windows, several windows of Tiffany glass exhibit 13 jewels; there are rooms with 13 wooden panels, many of the staircases have 13 steps and 13 coat hooks can be counted in the bedrooms. Superstition? A fortune-teller is supposed to have advised her, following the death of her husband, to build a house to protect herself from the ghosts of all those who had been killed by a Winchester rifle.

From June to September there are **tours** from 9am to 5.30pm. Opening times vary during the rest of the year.

Rosicrucian Park, Egyptian Museum

In Rosicrucian Park is the headquarters of the Union of Rosicrucians of international freemasonry. The movement owes its origin to anonymous 17th century writings, based on the life of the knight Christianus Rosencreitz (14th c.) and his brotherhood of men and which spread the concept of neoplatonic, alchemic and mystic thought.

The Egyptian Museum in the park possesses a large collection of Egyptian, Assyrian and Babylonian works of art, a reproduction of an Egyptian rock-tomb and French furniture. An adjoining building houses an art gallery and a planetarium which – like the exhibits – are owned by the Rosicrucians. Open Tue.–Sun. 9am–5pm.

Japanese Garden of Friendship

This 3 ha (7½ acre) garden is a copy of a park in the Japanese twin town of Okayama, and forms an oasis of peace in Kelley Park. There is also a small zoo.

Historical Museum

The San José Historical Museum is also to be found in Kelley Park, near the US 80. Here you can see original buildings and also reproductions of historical buildings, giving you an idea of what San José used to look like. Inside the museum are artefacts relating to San José's Indian, Mexican and early American history. Open Tue.–Fri. 10am–4.30pm, Sat. and Sun. noon–4.30pm.

The new Tech Museum of Innovation at No. 201 South Market Street opened at the end of 1998. State of the art technology is displayed here in a sort of playground for original thought. In the Digital Studio visitors can create their own multi-media experience. In the Life Tech section they can take on the role of surgeon and perform a laser operation. The Exploratorium concentrates on the exploration of space and the oceans.

Tech Museum of Innovation

San Juan Capistrano

See Mission Stations

San Luis Obispo   M 1

San Luis Obispo County
Altitude: 71 m (230 ft)
Population: 42,000

This town lies about 300 km (180 mi.) north-west of Los Angeles, at the junction of the US 101 coast road and the CA 1. It is the site of the fifth mission station built by Father Serra (see Mission stations). Serra thought that two volcanic hills nearby resembled a bishop's mitre, and so he gave this otherwise unimportant mission the name of San Luis Obispo de Tolosa (St Louis, Bishop of Toulouse).

Economy Originally the town lived by despatching products from surrounding ranches; gradually tourism and official bodies concerned with the town's development became more important. The California Polytechnic State University, which has about half as many students as San Luis Obispo has inhabitants, boasts important agricultural and scientific engineering faculties.
   The first olive trees in North America are said to have been planted in the mission; two of the 200 year-old trees still exist.

The Ah Louis Store, dating from 1874, is a survival from the time when many Chinese lived in San Luis Obispo. The building originally housed a Chinese bank and post-office, and was where the town's Chinese fraternity used to meet (800 Palm Street; open daily except Sun.; tel. 5434332).
   The San Luis Obispo County Historical Museum contains artefacts of the Chumash Indians, articles from the ranches, and exhibits from the Victorian period, as well as a library specialising in the history of the county (696 Monterey Street; open Wed.–Sun. 10am–4pm; admission free.
   20 km (12 mi.) south of the town stands the Diablo Canyon Atomic Power Station. It is open to visitors twice a day. At 10am and 2pm the 1½ hour tour starts from the Pacific Gas and Electric Energy Information Center.

Sights

San Pedro

See Los Angeles

Hearst Castle: the legendary W. R. Hearst created this grandiose castle as a fitting residence

San Rafael Arcangel

See Mission stations

San Simeon   L 1

San Luis Obispo County
Altitude: 6 m (19 ft)
Population: 100

The village of San Simeon lies on the CA 1, almost exactly halfway between San Francisco and Los Angeles, and about 400 km (240 mi.) from both places. Coming from Los Angeles, take the US 101 as far as San Luis Obispo, and then the CA 1. If you come from San Francisco, take the US 101 south as far as Paso Robles, then the CA 46 west and after that the CA 1.

San Simeon consists of one street with motels on both sides, an average-sized beach and some warehouses.

★★Hearst Castle

Visitors would hardly bother to stop here were it not for a place of great interest which is at first hidden from view – the famous castle. It was built by the newspaper king William Randolph Hearst (see Famous Personalities), and must surely be the most grandiose and magnificent monument ever erected by a private individual (Open daily from 8am until 4pm, 5pm in summer). When Hearst died in 1951 it was still not quite finished, after being in course of construction for 30 years. In spite

Roman swimming bath, with Venetian gold tiles

of having hundreds of rooms there is still not enough space to house all the works of art which Hearst collected during his lifetime.

W. R. Hearst Hearst's father George, himself not exactly a poor man (he left a fortune of 18 million US dollars when he died in 1891), bought a 40,000 acre (16,000 ha) ranch on San Simeon Bay. By buying up more land he enlarged it more than five-fold (230,000 acres (92,000 ha)), until it stretched more than 50 mi. (80 km) along the Pacific. When W. R. Hearst's mother died in 1919 William Randolph was the sole heir and he decided to build himself a new house on the estate. The official reason given for building this showpiece of a castle was that it was a memorial to his mother. The real reason, however, was the desire of his mistress, the moderately gifted film actress Marion Davies, to acquire a residence "in keeping with her standing". He instructed the Californian architect Julia Morgan (see Famous Personalities) to construct for him, on a hill in the Santa Lucia Mountains 500 m (1650 ft) above sea level and almost 10 km (6 mi.) from the coast, a building in which there would be room to house all his art treasures.

Construction A start was made in 1922. The guest-houses were finished first, and later given the names of La Casa del Mar (The House by the Sea), La Casa del Monte (The House on the Hill) and La Casa del Sol (The House of the Sun). Hearst lived in the first and largest of the three houses himself until the main house, La Casa Grande, was built. The three guest-houses had a total of 46 rooms, and at the time of Hearst's death the main house had 100 rooms, including 38 bedrooms, 31 bathrooms, 14 living rooms, two libraries, a huge refectory (dining room), a cinema, a kitchen and a large reception hall. Hearst named the whole place La Cuesta Encantada (The Enchanted Hill). It was surrounded by a garden covering 48 ha (120 acres) with a small zoo. Zebras, mountain goats and Aoudad sheep also grazed on the hill. The last named can still be seen there today.

Hearst Castle: the Spanish-moorish Casa Grande ...

... and Neptune Bath with neo-antique temple façade

Seven years after Hearst's death the family left the castle to the Federal State of California, which erected the **Hearst San Simeon State Historical Monument** here and has managed it ever since. Unlike many other historical buildings, the castle and its contents and fittings have been preserved in their original state, thus giving us an insight into the opulent lifestyle of its erstwhile occupants.

Nobody has ever known for certain how much money it all **cost** Hearst. Estimates have put it at 30 million US dollars (worth about 300–400 million dollars today). What he paid for the works of art, which he began to collect at the turn of the century, cannot even be guessed at. Many of the paintings from his collection can be seen in other Californian museums, such as the Los Angeles County Museum of Art (see Los Angeles).

The **Casa Grande** is obviously copied from the Cathedral of Seville. The 40 m (130 ft)-high tower in the Spanish-Moorish style gives the whole the intended palatial appearance. It is built mainly of reinforced concrete clad with yellow limestone blocks from Utah. Everything had to be transported from the coast to the top of the hill – no light task on roads as they were then (today a made-up road leads to the castle).

The **ground floor** of the house contains the dining room, measuring 30 m (100 ft) long and 7 m (23 ft) high. There are Flemish tapestries on the walls, the hand-carved ceiling imported from Italy portrays saints, and around the room can be seen crests of Sienese families. On this floor also are the reception room, billiard room, cinema, kitchen and pantries.

The **first floor** houses the main library and the monastic bedrooms. The mezzanine below contains the "Doge's Suite", built in the Venetian style, with the balcony of the living room having four-leaved arches like those at the Doge's palace in Venice.

On the **second floor** you will find Hearst's personal suite, also known as the Gothic Suite, with his study and the library where the newspaper publisher liked to relax. The two towers are occupied by the "Celestial Suite", and are connected by a living room from which there is a fantastic view of the Pacific Ocean.

The castle has two **swimming pools**. One, called the Neptune Pool, is in the open; during Hearst's time it was heated all the year round and was popular with his many guests. It is 32 m (105 ft) long and faced with marble. A Greco-Roman temple façade forms the background, while Etruscan columns at each end and statues in white marble complete the antique setting. The other, a Roman bath, is under cover and is so big that Hearst had two tennis courts built on top of it. The concrete building is faced in tiles of brightly coloured Venetian glass and some of gold, a task which took the Italian craftsmen three years to complete. Hearst was said to have derived the inspiration for this from a visit to the 5th c. Galla Placidia Mausoleum in Ravenna.

There is much more to see, of course. For the most part the **guided tours** do not give the visitor sufficient time for more than a fleeting glance at the mainly French and Italian furniture, the Gothic and Renaissance tapestries, and the huge fireplaces. There are also exquisite Persian carpets, numerous Roman mosaics, carved ceilings, a fantastic collection of silver and many wooden, marble and stone sculptures.

There are four different guided tours:

Tour No. 1: one of the three guest houses, a small part of the garden, the ground floor of the Casa Grande (reception room, refectory, billiard room and cinema with a short film presentation).

Tour No. 2: "Doge's Suite", three of the monastic bedrooms, the main library (with more than 5000 books and Greek vases), the Gothic and "Celestial" Suites, kitchen and pantries.

Tour No. 3: Casa del Monte, the new wing with its Spanish ceilings over the cinema, Renaissance painting, many beautiful Persian carpets and a video film of a reception Hearst gave for some VIPs.

Tour No. 4: Casa del Mar, wine cellar, the changing rooms of the Neptune swimming pool and the extensive gardens.

There are one or two tours a day. It is advisable to telephone and book in advance.

Bookings can be taken by Hearst Castle up to eight weeks prior to the visit. In the high season you should book at least a week in advance, and out of season two days before. If you are already in San Simeon you can buy tour tickets at the Holiday Inn. Mastercard and Visa can be used when booking by telephone. It is also advisable to book a motel room in advance.

★★Santa Barbara   O 2

Santa Barbara County
Altitude: 11–259 m (36–855 ft)
Population: 86,000

General

Santa Barbara lies 148 km (92 mi.) north of Los Angeles (about two hours travelling time) and 530 km (330 mi.) south of San Francisco (seven hours travelling). The US 101 passes through the town. Thanks to

Dolphin fountain in Santa Barbara

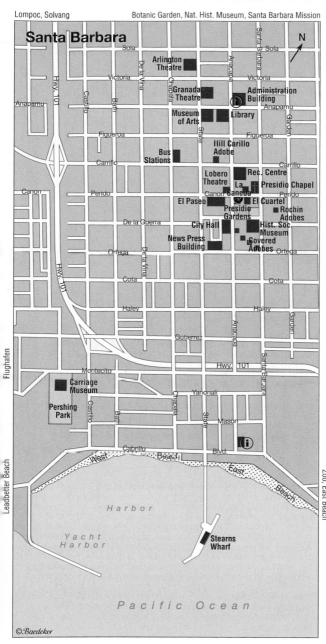

Lompoc, Solvang

Botanic Garden, Nat. Hist. Museum, Santa Barbara Mission

Santa Barbara

N

Sola
Arlington Theatre
Victoria
Granada Theatre
Administration Building
Museum of Arts
Library
Figueroa
Hill Carillo Adobe
Bus Stations
Carrillo
Lobero Theatre
Rec. Centre
Presidio Chapel
La Caneda
El Paseo
El Cuartel
Presidio Gardens
Rochin Adobes
City Hall
Hist. Soc. Museum
News Press Building
Covered Adobes
Ortega
Cota
Haley
Gutierrez
Hwy. 101
Montecito
Carriage Museum
Yanonali
Pershing Park
Mason
Cabrillo Blvd.
West Beach
East Beach
Harbor
Yacht Harbor
Stearns Wharf
Pacific Ocean

Hwy. 101
Anapamu
Canon
Perido
De la Guerra
Ortega
Cota
Haley

Castillo
Bath
De la Vina
Chapala
State
Anacapa
Santa Barbara
Garden

Flughafen
Leadbetter Beach

Montecito, Oxnard, Los Angeles
Zoo, East Beach

©Baedeker

View of Santa Barbara, with the County Courthouse in the foreground

its favourable position and climate – there is some smog and mist especially in August and September, but the sun shines on 84 per cent of all days – Santa Barbara is a favourite holiday resort.

The **ecological movement** is quite strong in Santa Barbara, because an oil slick in 1969 contaminated the whole beach for a long time. That is one of the reasons why there is a prohibition on extracting more oil from the sea. Even though the state government has repeatedly raised the possibility of a renewal of extraction during the last few years, they have been unable to force it through in the face of local opposition.

History

Santa Barbara developed around the tenth of the 21 Mission stations (see entry), built in 1786, and around the excellent harbour. Juan Rodriguez Cabrillo had probably already discovered the channel between the mainland and the offshore island in 1542, but it was not until 60 years later that the Spaniard Sebastiano Vizcaino named the settlement "Santa Barbara", having landed on the coast on that Saint's Day. A further 180 years went by before Governor Gaspar de Portola landed there with his troops in 1782, and Father Junipero Serra celebrated the first Mass in the recently-built Presidio. Serra did not live to witness the completion of the mission, one of the most beautiful in all California.

19th century Like the rest of California, Santa Barbara was slow to develop. The original Mission Church was destroyed by an earthquake in 1812; the second, with a classical façade and two towers, had just been completed when the Mexicans decided to secularise the mission stations in 1833. Santa Barbara's early history is closely linked with the

Spaniards and Mexicans. The town has retained that character to the present day. The first North Americans to come to this area were traders from New England, seeking to buy hides and tallow. On Christmas Day 1846 the town was taken by the Americans without a struggle.

Spanish influence A second earthquake in 1925 reduced a large part of Santa Barbara to rubble. The Mission station was damaged and took two years to repair (its façade was not finished until 1950).

Only a few of the 19th c. Victorian houses are left. Following the earthquake it was decided to rebuild the damaged area in the old Spanish mission style. This gave the town a uniform character unique in California. The most important public buildings in this style are: El Paseo, built round the old "De La Guerra" house, the imposing County Court House and the Santa Barbara Museum of Art.

Many streets also retained their Spanish names. Their Spanish character was further emphasised by fountains, rubbish bins and even letterboxes being decorated with Spanish tiles, especially in State Street, the town's main thoroughfare.

Sights

Today the town is one of the most beautiful in the country and has the great advantage of having most of its places of interest close together, so that they can all be seen quite easily within a short period of time.

The Santa Barbara County Courthouse is a Spanish-Moorish building in the style of a palace, completed after the large earthquake of 1929. The tiles lining the staircase are mainly from Tunisia, while those used on the arches are of Californian origin. The entrance hall on the first floor is a strange mixture of styles; the tiles and a passage way to the loggia are Islamic, the pink window is Romanesque and the archway decorated with angels is Byzantine. The County Supervisor's conference hall is entered through a double door; its murals illustrate the history of the county, beginning with the Indians watching the arrival of the first Europeans led by Cabrillo.

County Courthouse

A lift goes up to the El Mirador bell-tower, from where you may enjoy a fine view over Santa Barbara. In front of the entrance door is a fountain representing the "Spirit of the Ocean". (1110 Ancapa Street, App. 7600.) Open Mon.–Fri. 8am–5pm, Sat. and Sun. 9am–5pm; admission free.

El Mirador bell-tower

The Presidio (fortress), founded by the Spaniards in 1782, was badly damaged in the earthquakes of 1806 and 1812 and became of no importance at all after the American troops entered in 1846. Of the original buildings only El Cuartel, the soldiers' quarters, and the front rooms of the Canedo Adobe remain. The padre's house and the chapel have been restored. (122, 123 and 129 East Canon Perdido Street.) Open daily 10.30am–4.30pm; admission free; telephone: (805) 9669719.

El Presidio de Santa Barbara State Historic Park

This U-shaped adobe house was built between 1819 and 1827 as a political and social centre for the community by the fifth commandant of the Presidio. By adding more houses on the north-west and north-east sides it has been made into the El Paseo Complex, a Spanish street which was used as a copy when Santa Barbara was rebuilt after 1925. (11 to 25 East de la Guerra Street.)

Casa de la Guerra

Until 1941 the Santa Barbara Museum of Art was housed in a former post-office, and during its relatively short existence it has assembled an impressive and diverse collection of exhibits. It covers a wide spectrum, ranging from Egyptian works of art, Roman sculptures and an important Asiatic art department, to works by French Impressionists, 20th c.

Museum of Art

299

Santa Barbara

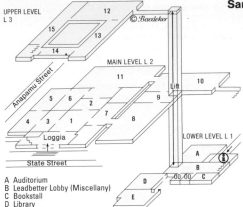

UPPER LEVEL
L 3

© *Baedeker*

MAIN LEVEL L 2

Anapamu Street

Lift

Loggia

State Street

LOWER LEVEL L 1

A Auditorium
B Leadbetter Lobby (Miscellany)
C Bookstall
D Library
E Training Centre

1 Ludington Court (Classical sculpture)
2 Thayer Gallery (Classical ceramics, glass, bronze)
3 Campbell Gallery (Asiatic lacquer work, textiles, prints)
4 Sterling Morton Gallery – West (Near East, Japan, China, India)
5 Sterling Morton Gallery – East (European art)
6 Gould Gallery (European art of 19th & 20th c., Impressionists)
7 Von Romberg Gallery (American 20th c. art)
8 Preston Morton Gallery (American art of 18th & 19th c.)
9 Colefax Gallery (miscellany)
10 Park Wing Gallery (modern art)
11 McCormick Gallery (painting, sculpture)
12 Hammett Gallery (prints, textiles)
13 Wood Gallery (photography)
14 Eichheim Gallery (African art)
15 Ala Story Gallery (International European and American art)

American paintings, photographs, prints, drawings and kinetic art. This little museum is well worth a visit. (1130 State Street.) Open Tue., Wed., Fri. and Sat. 11am–5pm, Thu. until 9pm, Sun. noon–5pm.

Historical Society Museum

This museum is housed in three adobe houses and displays material relating to Santa Barbara's Spanish, Mexican and early American history (including documents and paintings).(136 East de la Guerra Street.) Open Tue.–Sat. 10am–5pm, Sun. noon–5pm; admission free.

Sights outside the main town

Mission Santa Barbara

See Mission Stations

Museum of Natural History

On display are mammals, birds, fish, reptiles, the skeleton of a blue whale, exhibits of plant life and the geology of the Pacific coast and the Channel Islands (see Channel Island National Park), as well as a diorama of prehistoric Indian life. There is also a planetarium with varying displays. (2559 Puesta del Sol, four blocks north of the mission.) Open Mon.–Sat. 9am–5pm, Sun. 10am–5pm.

Botanical Garden

In the Botanical Garden, covering 26 ha (65 acres), native trees, bushes, woodland and field flowers and cacti grow in their natural habitat. There are some 8 km (5 mi.) of easily negotiable paths. A special feature is the dam built in 1806 by Indians under the supervision of the Padre to provide water for the mission and the living quarters. (1212 Mission Canyon Road, about 2½ km (1½ mi.) north of the mission.) Open daily 8am–sunset. Free guided tours Thur. and Sun. 10.30am.

Zoological Gardens

The Zoological Gardens are located in a beautiful setting and include a Children's Zoo as well as elephants, lions, apes, sea-lions and exotic birds. (Ninos Drive, exit to Cabrillo Blvd. east of Milpas Street, near the coast.) Open daily 9am–5pm, in summer until 6pm.

Steam Wharf

The oldest quay still remaining on the West Coast, Steam Wharf is a continuation, three blocks in length, of Santa Barbara's main street (State Street). It extends out over the Pacific, with restaurants, shops and a pier for fishing. Open daily 7am–midnight.

All these interesting places, apart from the Botanical Gardens, lie along Scenic Drive, a road with blue road-signs. You will pass exclusive residential quarters, such as are to be seen in Santa Barbara's suburbs of Goleta, Carpinteria and Montecito. There is a campus of the University of California in Goleta, as well as a railway museum concerned with the railroad history of Southern California. Open daily except Sat. 1–4pm; admission free. Carpinteria, 20 km (12 mi.) south-east on the US 101, has the finest bathing beach in the area.

Santa Catalina Island Q 2/3

Los Angeles County
Altitude: 6 m (20 ft)
Population: 3000

The island of Santa Catalina lies 42 km (26 mi.) south-west of Wilmington, the port of Los Angeles. It is 34 km (21 mi.) long and varies between –½ to 9 mi. (0.8 to 14 km) in width. In the interior there are hills as high as 3135 ft/950 m. The island was discovered by Cabrillo in 1542. He named it "San Salvador" after his ship, but Vizcaino gave it its present name 40 years later, having dropped anchor there on the feast day of Santa Catalina (St Catharine) of Alexandria. The first North American set foot on the island in 1805, and when Governor Pico gave it to an inhabitant of Santa Barbara in 1846 it became first the property of the United States and later was privately owned. Finally it belonged to the chewing-gum manufacturer William Wrigley and his son Philip, who built the main township of Avalon and made the island into a tourist attraction. A casino, deep-sea fishing (tuna, swordfish, sea perch, barracuda and mackerel), diving, swimming, riding and hunting are the main attractions. The interior and most of the coast are uninhabited.

From Long Beach (see entry) and San Pedro (see Los Angeles) there are daily boat and air trips to Avalon.

From June to September **catamarans** sail daily from Huntington Beach to the island (70 minutes), returning after three hours. Information: Huntington Beach Convention & Visitors Bureau, tel. (714) 9693492.

Of the three other neighbouring islands the smallest, Santa Barbara 3.2 km (2 mi.) long and 1.6 km (1 mi.) wide, is included in the Channel Islands National Park (see entry), San Clemente is used for naval exercises and San Nicholas, from where all the Indians were taken to the mainland in 1835, is uninhabited.

See map page 95

Santa Clara I 1

Santa Clara County
Altitude: 27 m (89 ft)
Population: 94,000

Santa Clara, founded in 1852 and the seat of California's oldest university, lies within the urban complex which stretches along both sides of the US 101 south-east of San Francisco. Today this complex is also known as Silicon Valley because of the large number of industries, both large and small, to be found there. Menlo Park, Palo Alto (see entry), Los Altos, Mountain View, Sunnyvale, Santa Clara and San José (see entry) all run into each other without any apparent boundaries. Santa Clara is the very hub of Silicon Valley. It is also known far and wide for its fruit cultivation, started by the priests at the Santa Clara Mission (see Mission

The seaside resort of Santa Cruz is a favourite place of the San Franciscans

white sand and a casino provide necessary entertainment

Stations). Today mainly dried fruits, especially apricots and plums, are exported.

The population of Santa Clara has grown so fast within the last few years and other development has been postponed, so that you will look in vain for a town centre. As a result there are few places of interest to visit.

Santa Clara's University, founded the year after the town became integrated into the State of California, lies on both sides of the Alameda (poplar grove) which links the towns of Santa Clara and San José. On the campus, which is inhabited by some 7500 students, will be found the ruins of the Mission station destroyed in the first half of the 19th c., as well as the 1928 rebuilt mission close by.

Santa Clara University

A few years ago a leisure park on the lines of Disneyland was created in Santa Clara, not far from the US 101. Known as "Great America" it covers an area of 40 ha (100 acres) and is made up of five sections (Hometown Square, Yukon Territory, Yankee Harbor, County Fair and Orleans Place). These depict various aspects of life in America during the 19th and 20th centuries and provide plenty of scope for entertainment of all kinds. (Address: US 101, exit for Great America Park.)

Great America

★Santa Cruz   I 1

Santa Cruz County
Altitude: 6 m (20 ft)
Population: 50,000

Santa Cruz, lying about 115 km (70 mi.) south of San Francisco (on the CA 1), between Monterey Bay and the Santa Cruz Mountains, is very popular because of its 46 km (30 mi.) of beautiful beaches. For the inhabitants of San Francisco it is the first place south of the city where it is possible to bathe, at least in summer and autumn.

History The mission of the same name (see Mission Stations) was founded in 1791 above where the town now lies. In 1797 the Spaniards created the village of Pueblo Branciforte, the inhabitants of which carried out a series of robberies at the mission which led to its gradual downfall. It was the first of the 21 mission stations to be secularised in 1834.

Santa Cruz developed outwards from the Mission Plaza. Its year of founding is given as 1840, but it did not obtain its charter until 26 years later. The township was initially an important harbour from which redwood felled nearby was shipped all over the world. Gradually it became a holiday resort and spa. The long municipal pier is the only one in California with a leisure park. There is plenty of activity here all the year round. "Miss California" is chosen here every year.

About 5 mi. (8 km) north of Santa Cruz, on the CA 9, will be found 1750 acres (700 ha) of forest in which grow some of the most beautiful coastal redwoods (see entry Redwood Highway, also *Baedeker Special* page 308). There are also some 24 km (15 mi.) of trails for walking and riding, as well as camp sites.

Henry Cowell Redwood State Park

Mystery spot About 5 km (3 mi.) north of Santa Cruz on Branciforte Drive there is a most unusual spot, now privately owned, where an optical illusion gives the impression that the laws of gravity are being defied. The phenomenon was apparently first "discovered" in 1939. The eerie effect is heightened by disorientating architecture, conspicuously lacking in right angles.

City Museum

The City Museum contains evidence of the history of northern Monterey Bay, Indian artefacts and an aquarium. (1305 East Cliff Drive.) Open Tue.–Sun.; admission free.

University of California

The Californian Central University's most recent campus lies in the north-west of the town. It was opened in 1965 and already has 9000 students. From the 800 ha (2000 acre) campus there is a splendid view over Monterey Bay. The Joseph M. Long Marine Laboratory is here, with aquaria and a skeleton of a blue whale. Guided tours: Mon.–Fri. 10.30am and 1.30pm; admission free.

Santa Monica   P 3

Los Angeles County
Altitude: 31 m (102 ft)
Population: 87,000

Santa Monica was founded in 1886 at the southern end of the mountain range bearing the same name and of Santa Monica Bay. Although linked to the Los Angeles road network it remains an independent town, highly thought of as a residential area and resort. Its name is derived from that of the god-fearing Monica. She was the mother of St Augustine, one of the four Latin Fathers of the Church. In recent years some industrial firms have become established here, the principal one being the Douglas Aircraft Company. The firm's Douglas Aerospace Museum is near the airport. Open at weekends only; admission free.

Santa Monica Pier

The Santa Monica Pier juts out at the end of Colorado Avenue. It has a shopping arcade, a restaurant and a roundabout. You can also fish from

View of Santa Monica Pier

A fantastic sandy beach at Santa Monica

this pier. Santa Monica's beach is 5 km (3mi.) long and ranks as one of the best in Greater Los Angeles. Palisades Park, with a view over the Pacific, runs along Ocean Avenue between Colorado and San Vincente Boulevards. It is particularly noted for its beautiful gardens.

The towns of Del Rey and Venice, both south of Santa Monica, belong to Los Angeles and have lovely beaches with many facilities for water sports.

Surroundings

Santa Rosa   G 1

Sonoma County
Altitude: 51 m (168 ft). Population: 113,000

The town is situated in the middle of the Sonoma vine-growing area. There are some 100 wine-producers in the immediate vicinity, and the town is one of the main handling centres for the region's products. As it lies only about 85 km (53 mi.) from San Francisco and is easily access-ible by way of the Golden Gate Bridge and the US 101, Santa Rosa has proved to be a favourite place of residence for commuters who do not mind driving this distance.

Luther Burbank, one of America's most important agriculturists (see Famous Personalities), was attracted to Santa Rosa from Massachusetts by the favourable climate and fertile soil. He devoted his life to cultivat-ing new varieties of fruit and vegetables. In the Luther Burbank Memorial Gardens (corner of Sonoma and Santa Rosa Avenues; open daily from 8am until 5pm; admission free) you can learn more about the achievements of this man who is buried there under a cedar tree. You

305

Houseboats in the fishing village of Sausalito north of San Francisco

can also visit the house where he lived and worked. Open Wed.–Sun. 10am–3.30pm.

Peanuts Museum The museum is housed in No. 1 Snoopy Place, the address of the well-known American comic artist Charles M. Schulz. Born in Minneapolis (MN) in 1922 of German descent, Schulz is the spiritual father of the "Peanuts" family, the principal figures of which are Charlie Brown, Snoopy the dog, Lucy and her brother Linus. Since it first appeared in 1950 it has become one of the most successful of all comic-strips.

★Sausalito   H 1

Marin County
Altitude: 4 m (13 ft). Population: 7200

This former fishing village on San Francisco Bay at the northern end of the Golden Gate Bridge is a favourite place for excursions. It is named after the region's first ranch, Rancho Saucelito. This was the spelling of Sausalito in vogue until 1900; the Spanish word "sauce" means willow, and "saucelito" is a small grove of willow trees, for which you will search in vain today. Originally it was a port for whale-hunters and other trading ships.

The numerous **house-boats** which line the harbour today have become the symbol of Sausalito.

Townscape The narrow streets, full of little corners and some linked to others by wooden steps, have added to the appeal of Sausalito. Today it is inhabited mainly by commuters from San Francisco. In the upper parts of the town away from the hustle and bustle, a number of artists have settled by the bay. Their work is displayed in the numerous galleries. Most of the shops are on Bridgeway and in Princess Street.

From Sausalito there is a fine view of San Francisco; an impressive scene is when thick mist envelopes the city early in the morning, while Sausalito is enjoying bright sunshine, and only the tips of the skyscrapers can be seen.

Visitors may be interested to learn that it was in Sausalito that a number of moves towards **healthier living** started, such as holding a national "No Smoking Day". The town council has now decided to make it the first cholesterol-free town in the USA, and in so doing is in competition with Palm Springs (see entry). The latter can in fact boast more restaurants offering fat-free food.

★★Sequoia & Kings Canyon National Parks   K-M 4/5

In the middle south of the Californian Sierra Nevada the Sequoia and Kings Canyon National Parks cover an area of mountainous land with majestic granite peaks, deep gorges, mountain lakes, rivers and superb forests. The two parks are administered as one. They stretch from the foothills in the west on the edge of the San Joaquín Valley – the longest valley in Greater California – to the main ridge of the Sierra Nevada in the east. Here Mount Whitney (4418 m (14,495 ft)) is the highest mountain in the USA (apart from Alaska), and Split Mountain (4285 m (14,140 ft)), Mount Goethe (4047 m (13,350 ft)) and many others are also over 3000 m (10,000 ft). The John Muir Wilderness Area runs along the eastern flank of the National Park area, which adjoins the Inyo National Forest further east.

The two national parks cover the most impressive section of a vegetation belt which is 400 km (250 mi.) long altogether and between 1200 and 2400 m (4000 and 8000 ft) high. In this area can be found groves and whole forests of mighty **redwood trees** (see entry for Redwood Highway, Redwoods) of the species sequoiadendron giganteum (sequoia gigantea) or giant sequoia; saplings of which can be purchased at nurseries. Apart from the yew-needled sequoia (sequoia sempervirens) found on the Pacific coast of California, this species is the only surviving member of the genus sequoia belonging to the family of the marsh-cypress (taxodiaceae), which once grew in profusion in the northern hemisphere.

Flora and fauna As a result of the marked differences in altitude there are three main climatic zones. The dry lowlands and sloping sites below 1500 ft (450 m) above sea level are covered in grass steppes and low scrubland and are free from snow in winter. As well as the extensive native fauna, a large number of animals from the higher regions come here to spend the winter: silver fox, lynx, Californian squirrel, skunk and racoon are often found. The Pacific rattlesnake, which is quite common here, is the only animal in the park which is not a protected species.

The areas at a medium height of between 1500 and 4000 ft (450 and 1200 m) are covered in coniferous forests (red and white fir, Ponderosa and Lodgepole pine, cedar and giant redwood). The damp meadows are lined with aspen. Winter wraps this area in a 6–10 ft (4.5 m) blanket of snow. Red deer and black bear are often seen, and occasionally mountain lions (pumas).

The higher mountainous region consists of sparse woodland, mountain meadows and bare rocky and gravel slopes. Here the animal life is less varied, being limited to the hardier species suited to the weather and feeding conditions. In these lonely hills live mountain sheep, the

Baedeker Special

Living Relic of Times Long Past

Redwoods (*sequoia sempervirens*) grow along the coast from Monterey northwards as far as Oregon. Giant Sequoias (*sequoiadendron giganteum*) on the other hand, are found only in a small part of the Sierra Nevada, specifically the Yosemite, Sequoia and Kings Canyon National Parks. It is not generally known that it was the Austrian botanist Stephan Ladislaus Endlicher (1804–49) who first described these trees in 1847. He chose the name sequoia in honour of Sequoyah, author of the Cherokee alphabet. Elected in 1828 to represent his tribe in Washington D.C., Sequoyah's statue can be seen in the National Hall of Statuary at the Capitol.

With a maximum age of 3200 years, the Sierra or Giant Sequoias live much longer than the far more numerous coastal sequoias, which reach 220 years at most. When it comes to age, neither can match the much less imposing Bristlecone Pine of the Sierra, the oldest specimen of which is said to be 4600 years old. The tallest tree so far measured was a coastal sequoia, which attained 110 m (360 ft).

Generally speaking, the Giant Sequoia, which can grow to a height of 75–90 m (250–300 ft) and a diameter of 12 m (40 ft), co-exists happily with other trees. Its extraordinary life span can be attributed mainly to its resistance to enemies of all kinds and to its astonishing ability to regenerate itself.

Its asbestos-like bark, as much as 60 cm (2 ft) thick in the case of some older specimens, acts as an effective protection against forest fires. In fact forest fires can be rather beneficial to giant redwoods, creating space as other species are destroyed and enabling the sun's rays to penetrate to the mineral-rich forest floor so that saplings thrive. The high tannic acid content of the wood keeps insects and fungal diseases at bay.

The Giant Sequoia's only real enemy is man. However the tree can suffer damage from changes in soil conditions, which may occur during the thousands of years of its life as the result of erosion or washing away of the soil around its comparatively shallow root system (about 1.5 m (5 ft) deep but extending over about half an acre/one hectare). The sequoia trees in the National Parks are safe from technological interference. But storms, particularly lightning strikes, and controlled felling can further reduce numbers.

Propagation of redwoods takes place in a manner somewhat different from

brown wolverine which seeks the lower, milder slopes in winter, and the marmot.

History In pre-Columbian times this region was inhabited by the Potwisha and Kaweah Indians, two friendly tribes who lived by hunting and fishing and did simple basket-work. They spent the winter on the dry, snow-free lowlands, returning in summer to the cool forests of the central mountain regions. Guided by Indians, Hale Tharp was the first white man to penetrate the sequoia regions of the Giant Forest in 1858. He was followed by large numbers of adventurers and gold-seekers who searched in vain for precious metals (relics in Silver City and Mineral King in the south of the park) and in so doing brought to several thou-

that of other conifers. The cones, of which a normal tree has about 600, sometimes containing as many as 1000 seeds, do not fall to the ground of their own accord, but are pulled off by squirrels which nevertheless do not eat the seeds. The authorities have for some time now adopted the practice of deliberately setting fire to sections of the forest, something which previously occurred naturally, so drying out the cones lying on the forest floor. These then open up within a few days. The seeds fall on the ashes, which in the meantime

have cooled, and young trees shoot up within a few months, though admittedly only a small number will survive.

Only a few sequoias thrive outside California and Oregon. The Russians, who settled in Fort Ross early in the 19th c., were the first to plant sequoia seeds and saplings in Europe. Redwoods continue to be of major importance to the timber industry of northern California. Indiscriminate felling threatens more and more of these ancient trees.

"The Senate" an imposing group of trees in this forest of giants

sand Indians living near the Kweah River diseases previously unknown to them, such as scarlet fever, smallpox, measles and fever. Any Indian suffering from these diseases was driven out by white settlers; only ten years after the forest was discovered there were no longer any living in these regions. After the stocks of sequoia had been seriously decimated because of the huge amount of wood obtainable from the trees (one tree was enough to build about 40 houses), the Sequoia National Park was founded in 1890. In the early years the cavalry had to protect the nature reserve from timber thieves.

The species was given the name "sequoia" by the Pressburg botanist Stephan Ladislaus Endlicher (1804–49), who named it after the Cherokee Indian Sequoyah, the creator of an alphabet of symbols representing the

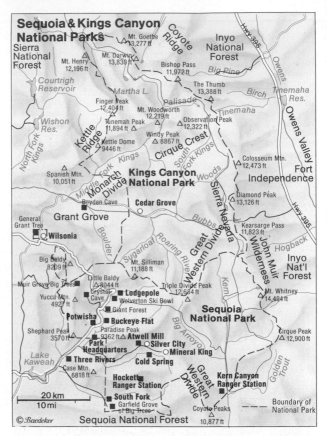

sounds of his tribe's language. In 1828 Sequoyah was elected to represent his people in Washington D.C. His statue stands in the National Hall of Statuary in the Capitol. Kings Canyon derived its name from the river which flows through it, which the Spaniards in 1805 christened Rio de los Santos Reyes, (River of the Holy Kings).

Sights

★Giant Forest

The Giant Forest in the west of the Sequoia National Park is one of the few redwood forests where the trees grow so thickly that no others can survive.

★General
Sherman Tree

In the north-east of the forest stands the General Sherman Tree; 83.8 m (276 ft) tall, with a maximum diameter of 11.12 m (36½ ft) and 31.3 m (103 ft) in circumference at the base, it is one of the mightiest known redwoods. Its age of about 3000 years makes it the oldest living thing on earth.

North-east of Giant Forest is Crystal Cave, a marble cave with rich dripstone scenery. (In the summer months there is a guided tour each day of 0.8 km (½ mi.); warm clothes are advisable.)

Sequoia National Park

To the north of this lies Muir Grove, one of the most beautiful sequoia forests with a lot of old trees. In the extreme north-west of the Giant Forest Area will be found Lost Grove, a 20 ha (50 acre) redwood forest with fifteen specimens measuring more than 3 m (10 ft) in diameter.

★**Muir Grove**

From Giant Forest a road branches off south-eastwards to Moro Rock, a vast monolithic block of granite rock (2050 m (6760 ft) tall; there is a stony path to the top) from where is a fine panoramic view of forest and mountains as far as Crescent Meadow. From here (also the starting-off point of the High Sierra Trail) a footpath leads to Tharp's Log, a hollow tree trunk used by the discoverer of the Giant Forest as a dwelling-hut.

Moro Rock

Immediately north of the Giant Forest lies Round Meadow, surrounded by some beautiful sequoias. Behind it to the north-west stands Sunset Rock (1940 m (6400 ft)) from where there is a good view.

Silicon Valley

The name "Silicon Valley" does not even now appear on any map, being a media invention of the early seventies reflecting the growing importance of the silicon chip in the expansion of the industry of the Santa Clara Valley southwards from San Francisco Bay.

Roughly coinciding with Santa Clara County, this particular area along the US 101 between Palo Alto and San Jose was at one time thoroughly rural, the mild climate and warm dry summers making it ideal for fruit growing and the processing of dried fruit.

Today its concentration of companies manufacturing semi-conductors, computers and space equipment has transformed Santa Clara County into one of the five richest industrial regions in the United States. In 1985 the average income per household was the third highest among metropolitan areas in the USA.

Silicon Valley is the modern symbol of the living American dream, the belief that anything is possible. Many of the electronics companies which are now household names started life in the fifties as tiny enterprises set up in an old garage.

None typifies the Valley's success story more than the now world-famous electronics firm of Hewlett-Packard, set up in 1939 by two engineers, Dave Packard and Bill Hewlett with capital of 538 dollars. This was effectively the date when Silicon Valley was born. From modest beginnings manufacturing measuring instruments in the garage behind Dave Packard's Palo Alto house, once Walt Disney had put in an order for eight of their temperamental but cheap sound generators, the fledgling firm never looked back. By investing heavily in research and pursuing a sound market strategy, the two engineers were able to keep their products abreast of the latest technology and by

the mid-fifties their success was such as to enable them to move into their present prestigious headquarters in the grounds of Stanford University.

Their company philosophy, based on individual responsibility, working together in partnership, and honesty and openness in business dealings, was an example to all. They promoted a team-orientated style of management and nurtured a close relationship with their employees.

From the point of view high-tech industry, the Santa Clara Valley conurbation has also become a model much imitated elsewhere. It is particularly favoured by being situated close to

Silicon chip

several centres of research, development and education such as Stanford University and the Universities of Berkeley, San Jose and Santa Clara, as well as the big research laboratories of major private companies such as Lockheed and IBM. These links are of inestimable value in facilitating the transfer of specialist knowledge and are the principal reason for the frequency and ease with which scientists, technicians and managers interchange jobs.

Even the character of the typical commercial site has been transformed with mainly single-storey buildings located well away from metropolitan

San Francisco replacing the old-style office blocks on the perimeter of the big city. Here there is ample room for parking as well as green and open spaces, some earmarked for future expansion. Business starts are "pump-primed" by various forms of government support – e.g. making land available, much of it for residential development, with good roads and shopping and leisure facilities – and by the award of government contracts for new electronic products.

In the fifties, construction of research and development centres for electronic systems and parts was boosted by federal contracts from NASA and the Pentagon for military, space and atomic research. Investment capital was provided mainly by large banks in the eastern United States, though with a considerable input also from the region itself. Most of those who set up companies were college graduates and employees from research and development laboratories.

In the sixties series production methods and sub-contracting meant that big profits could be made.

Even as early as the seventies, however, over-production and competitive pressures led to many closures and take-overs. With research and development costs spiralling, major organisations began increasingly to pool resources – for example, Stanford University, the Pentagon and a number of private companies jointly set up the Stanford Center for Integrated Systems designed specifically to counter Japanese competition.

The boom in personal computers was followed in the mid-eighties by a further crisis in growth. The short life of many electronic products, which quickly become obsolete, overtaken by new technology, requires investment of massive sums in research and development. It is here that the companies in Silicon Valley benefit most from the continuous flow and interchange of information and ideas.

Hand in hand with short-lived production cycles go constantly changing requirements of work. The insatiable demand for specialist labour which this generates, and the resulting high turnover of staff, can lead – as the experience of Hewlett-Packard has shown – to a lowering of standards among the workforce.

Equally characteristic, on the other hand, is the emergence of a new breed of young, dynamic, technically able and extremely go-ahead staff, ready to sacrifice leisure time in the interests of work and the continual updating of knowledge and skills. Their lifestyle is driven by the myth of unlimited economic growth reflected in such status symbols as expensive cars (an above-average number of Ferrari sports cars), houses and holiday homes.

The reduced level of Pentagon military spending following the end of the Cold War has hit the flourishing electronics industry especially hard. Since the beginning of the 1990s a number of innovative companies have left Silicon Valley, influenced in part also by the recent introduction of onerous local regulations intended to curb further expansion.

Any prognosis for the future of Silicon Valley must be tempered by caution given the emergence of an increasing number of negative considerations: overdevelopment, excessive demand for land due to low-density building, and growing ecological pressures such as pollution of ground water and escalating road traffic. The image of the electronics industry as environmentally "clean" is gradually being eroded.

In response to these symptoms of impending crisis, the so-called County General Plan has been drawn up, prompted largely by calls for action by self-help groups formed mainly among academics and women, demanding zero growth and the right to consultation on such matters as further building on open land. Any major reversal of current trends however, is more likely to come about through radical, permanent changes in attitudes than through centrally-introduced measures.

★Grant Grove and Redwood Mountain Grove

Grant Grove and Redwood Mountain Grove adjoin the Sequoia National Park to the north-west and form a part of the King's Canyon National Park.

★General Grant Tree

In the north of Grant Grove stands a redwood known as the General Grant Tree. It is 81.5 m (268 ft) tall, with a maximum diameter of 12.28 m (40 ft) and a circumference at the base of 32.8 m (108 ft). In the south stands Big Stump, the remains of a giant sequoia felled for the World Exhibition in Philadelphia in 1875, and Stump Basin, a redwood forest which had been completely cleared before it was declared a protected area.

The Redwood Canyon Forest on Redwood Mountain is an example of a sequoia forest which is well worth looking at.

Kings Canyon

Kings Canyon is the valley of the southern arm of Kings River. It is lined with steep walls of rock. The granite peaks of the surrounding mountains dominate the floor of the glacial canyon for more than a mile/1.6 km. Easy paths lead from the Cedar Grove Tourist Center to Zumwalt Meadow with its charming scenery and to the impressive waterfalls known as Roaring River Falls and Mist Fall. The high mountain regions are accessible only on foot or on horseback. Tours to Evolution Basin (north), Bubbs Creek Valley (roughly east) or Kern Canyon (southeast) require a high standard of fitness and some mountaineering experience.

Advice

Roads There are only tracks through the wilderness of the two parks. You can cross them on foot or on horseback. Although both parks are

The Sierra sequoias have a diameter of up to 39 ft (12 m). One of the giants is "The President" in Giant Forest

open throughout the year, the more remote parts are inaccessible in winter. Mountain passes are seldom free of snow before July 1st. The so-called Generals Highway (76 km (47 mi.)) is blocked by deep snow between December and May. It takes the car-driver to the west of the Sequoia National Park. It leads from the Ash Mountain Entrance through Areale Giant Forest, Lodgepole (winter sports, especially in Wolverton) and Dorst, and leaves the park in the north-west, the far side of Lost Grove. From there it crosses the southern tip of the Sequoia National Forest and meets the US 180 (closed in winter) in the Grant Grove Area. This forms the only approach to the Kings Canyon National Park and links the two national parks together. The Generals Highway ends at Cedar Grove, where a 10 km (6 mi.) cul-de-sac continues to Cooper Creek.

Walks There are about 1450 km (900 mi.) of tracks passing through the two parks. The eastern part of both parks, from which motor vehicles are barred, is crossed by the Pacific Crest Trail (here called the "John Muir Trail"), a mountain track which is still being extended. It is 3780 km (1350 mi.) long, passes through various national parks, and follows the line of the ridge of the Sierra Nevada and the Cascade Mountains all the way from the Mexican to the Canadian borders. In the south of the Sequoia National Park the 64 km (40 mi.) High Sierra Trail runs eastwards from the Giant Forest Area, through superb countryside by way of Bearpaw Meadow as far as Wallace Creek, where it meets the John Muir Trail.

Events Campfire programmes: summer evening recitals by the campfire in Giant Forest, Lodgepole, Dorst, Grant Grove and Cedar Grove; guided tours there as well; accompanied riding trips from Wolverton, Grant Grove and Cedar Grove (horses for hire at all of them).

The entrances to the parks are 86 km (83 mi.) south-east of Fresno (see entry) on the CA 190 (Grant Cove Visitor Center) and 56 km (35 mi.) east of Visalia on the CA 198 (Lodgepole Visitor Center). Both **Visitor Centers** are open all the year round; they will advise you on the best way to look round the parks. The three motels inside the park are open only from the end of May to the beginning of September; at other times you will have to look for accommodation in Three Rivers, Visalia or Porterville.

★Solvang   N 1

Santa Barbara County
Altitude: 150 m (495 ft)
Population: 4700

If you take the US 101 coast road south, and turn off at Buellton on to the CA 164, after a few miles you will reach Solvang, the biggest Danish settlement in the United States of America. It was given its name by the Danish-American Corporation in Chicago, who thought the Danish word "solvang" (sunny meadow) was a fitting description of the little town founded in 1911. Several professors involved in founding the town also set up a college, but this no longer exists.

Tourism flourishes in this little town with the **Danish character** on the edge of the Santa Ynez mountains. There are houses in the Danish style and four windmills, and visitors can enjoy cakes and pastries made in the Danish manner and sold in several bakeries and patisseries. In the restaurants you can order karbonader and blomkal and hakkelof med løg (egg). Even a large Sheraton Hotel which opened a few years ago is decorated in the Danish style with Scandinavian furniture. Other hotels in

Danish influence flourishes in Solvang – in its architecture, its food and its customs

the main street Mission Drive, Copenhagen Street or Alisal Road have such names as Kong Fredrik, Dannebrog, Hamlet, Kronborg and Royal København. A stroll through the town makes a "velkommen" change.

Every year a three-day Danish Festival is held in the middle of September. The Santa Ines Mission (see Mission Stations), founded in 1804 in Mission Drive, contrasts with the general ambience of the town.

Sonoma   G 1

Sonoma County
Altitude: 26 m (85 ft). Population: 8200

Sonoma lies some 70 km (43 mi.) north of San Francisco on the beautifully situated US 12, in the valley bearing the same name. Together with Napa Valley this is the most important wine producing region in the United States.

The name "Sonoma" is not, as often assumed, of Spanish origin, but can be traced back to the Wintun Indians who once lived here, and in whose language it meant "nose". However, exactly why this name was chosen when the town was founded in 1835 is uncertain.

History The last of the 21 Californian mission stations (see entry) was built in Sonoma in 1823.

From June 14th to July 9th 1846 Sonoma was the capital of the short-lived Republic of California, the Stars and Stripes of America giving way briefly to a flag with a bear as its emblem. In the morning mist of June 10th 30 cavalrymen from the Sacramento Valley drew up in front of the Casa Grande, the headquarters of the Mexican General Mariano

Vineyards in Sonoma County

Guadalupe, arrested him and his troops and proclaimed the Republic of California without a single shot being fired. William Ide was made President of the Republic.

An American man-of-war arrived in Monterey on July 7th, the day on which California became part of the United States. Two days later an advance guard arrived in Sonoma, thus finally putting an end to the "Grey Bear Revolution". However, the old bear flag lived on and in 1911 became the official flag of California.

Driving up the valley on CA 12 or CA 128, **winery** follows winery. On the eastern edge of Sonoma lies the Buena Vista wine producing concern, founded in 1857 by the Hungarian Count Agoston Haraszthy. He is generally considered to be the father of Californian wine production, even though the Franciscan Fathers had cultivated the first vines for their Communion wine as long ago as 1825. Today the Buena Vista Winery is owned by a German, Hubertus von Wulffen; interesting concerts are held there in the summer months.

The Sebastiani Vineyards & Winery were established much later, in 1904. Nevertheless they remain to this day in the ownership of the founder. There are conducted tours between 10am and 5pm. The Haywood is another winery worth visiting.

The best known **varieties of wine**, all stemming from European rootstock, include Chardonnay, Pinot Noir, Merlot, Johannisberg Reisling and Gewürztraminer, Cabernet Sauvigon and also Zinfandel, a vine developed in America, thrive on the higher slopes.

Also worth seeing is the Sonoma State Historic Park around the plaza. In addition to the San Francisco Solano Mission you will find the former residence of General Vallejos, dating from 1850/1851 (corner of West

State Historic Park

Spain Street and 3rd Street West), the 1834 Mexican barracks (East Spain Street and 1st Street West), the former Toscano Hotel and a row of interesting houses dating from the town's early days.

Sonora   I 3

Tuolumne County
Altitude: 556 m (1825 ft). Population: 4200

The former gold-mining town of Sonora lies near Big Bonanza, the most profitable mine in Mother Lode County (see entry), west of Yosemite National Park (see entry) at the southern end of the CA 49. One year after it was founded in 1848 it had 5000 inhabitants – more than it has today. The gold-rush had just begun and the district soon turned out to be one of the most profitable. The first gold-miners were Mexican and came from the state of Sonora, after which they named their camp. They were followed by Chileans and Americans, who could not get on with the "latinos" and finally drove them out. A similar thing was happening at the same time in San Francisco, where demobilised soldiers stirred up hatred against the "foreigners".

The town, which stretches over seven hills, was the setting for several tales by the American writers **Mark Twain and Bret Harte**, both of whom stayed here from time to time.

Columbia State Historic Park

About 6 km (4 mi.) north of Sonora, on the CA 49, lies the Columbia State Historic Park. Here you can admire the once famous gold-mining town in all its old, restored glory. Thousands of hopeful gold-miners lived here at the time. Although restoration is not yet complete you can already visit most of the houses, including an old school-house, a boarding-house, a fire station and a restaurant. (Tel. (209) 5324301.)

Within a 13 mi. (20 km) radius north of Sonora there are some **caves** well worth a visit. In Moaning Cavern near Vallecito, discovered in 1849, you can see interesting rock-formations from the vantage-point of a 30 m (100 ft) spiral staircase.

Those parts of the caves which have not been built over can be seen in the course of a three and a half-hour guided tour (advance booking advisable; tel. (209) 7362708). The other cave, Mercer Cavern, was discovered in 1885. Here you can see stalagmites, stalactites and aragonites (guided tours lasting three quarters of an hour; to book in advance tel. (209) 7282101).

The Moaning Cavern is open all the year round, but the Mercer Cavern only from June to September; at weekends only during the remaining months of the year.

Stockton   H 2

San Joaquin County
Altitude: 4 m (13 ft). Population: 211,000

Founded in 1849, Stockton is linked to San Francisco Bay by a canal 78 mi. (125 km) long and 30 ft (9 m) deep. Today it is an important distribution centre for grain and other agricultural products grown in the fertile lands around the town.

In its early days it was little more than a place which fortune-seekers passed through on their way to the gold-mines in Mother Lode County (see entry). However, a lot of them returned disappointed and decided to remain in Stockton. It was named after Commodore Robert F. Stockton who had taken possession of California in the name of the United States of America in 1846. Since then the town has developed into one of the two largest inland ports in California (the other being Sacramento). Since the Second World War, in particular, Stockton has experienced a rapid increase in population.

The Magnolia Historic District is well worth a visit. It has some well-preserved mainly Victorian houses, the oldest dating from 1869.

There is also the Haggin Museum, built in Victory Park in 1931. It displays works of art of the 19th and 20th c. Open Tue.–Sun. 1.30pm–5pm.

Sights

In Lodi, some 12 km (7 mi.) north of Stockton on the Joaquin River, can be found the San Joaquin Historical Museum, where a number of historic houses display a variety of items which document the county's agriculture and customs.

Lodi has a dozen vineyards and has become well-known for growing Tokai grapes and producing the famous Tokai wine.

Surroundings

★Tijuana S 4

Baja California – State of Mexico
Altitude: 5 m (16 ft). Population: 750,000

The best way to get to Tijuana from San Diego is by tram. They leave every 15 minutes from behind the Amtrak Station, Broadway and Kettner Boulevard. There are usually parking spaces available at the railway station. The trams take you as far as the American border town of

Access

Tijuana – Fronton Palacio

San Ysidro, where they turn round. The journey takes about 40 minutes. From there you can walk to Tijuana over numerous ramps. There are no border-crossing problems in either direction.

Tijuana is the most important city on the border between Mexico and the United States, and is more influenced by the latter than any other Mexican town. The city lives mainly by tourism and the refining industry. Every year it attracts many millions of visitors, mainly from the catchment areas of the cities of San Diego (25 km (15 mi.)) and Los Angeles (260 km (160 mi.)).

Therefore it is not surprising that Tijuana claims to be the "most visited city in the world", for in the last few years it has grown so fast that the actual size of its population can only be estimated roughly. Certainly, having completed the 10 to 15 minute walk from the border to the main thoroughfare, Avenida de Revolucíon, the tourist is overwhelmed by the masses of people pushing their way through the streets; the Americans, intent on making cheap purchases free of customs duty, and the locals, many of whom stand around on the sidewalks begging for coins. US dollars bring a good exchange rate.

History Tijuana (in the language of the Chochimi Indians "ticuán" means "near water") has a brief history. The city of today developed from a cattle ranch named Tia Juana (Aunt Anna), built by José Maria Echandi in 1829. It began to grow during the Prohibition Period (1920–33), when the consumption of alcohol was prohibited in the United States and numerous thirsty souls made the short trip across the border.

Border town Its importance lies in the great quantity of duty-free goods on offer together with Mexican folk-art and souvenirs, its various festi-

Tijuana – Mexican traditional art and souvenirs

vals and events and its night-life. The place where it all happens, especially at week-ends, is the main square, the Parque Municipal Guerrero, the shopping area around the Avenida de Revolución and the Bulevar Agua Caliente, with their many hotels, restaurants, shops and varieties of sports.

Tijuana is not just a typical run-down border town with cheap junkshops, it also shows signs of American influence. There is an American shopping-centre, an international airport and a glass-box of a hotel. The further away from the Avenida de Revolución you get the more you find the slum areas being replaced by new houses. More and more people are streaming into Tijuana from the provinces, but complete redevelopment is not financially viable because new slums keep appearing, together with new factories which find cheap labour here (people call these factories "maquiladoras").

However, Tijuana has kept to the old customs. **Bull-fights** (no blood is spilled) are still held here on eighteen Sundays in the year: four in each of the months of July, August and September, the rest spread unevenly over the months of May, June and October. They all start at 4pm. Tickets can be purchased in advance from Ticketron in Los Angeles, in San Diego and at the Amtrak Station, Mexicoach.

In the Hipódromo de Agua Caliente, Agua Caliente Boulevard, there is greyhound racing on Monday, Tuesday, Wednesday and Friday, and horse racing on Saturday and Sunday. Every day except Thursday Jai Alai is played in the Fronton Palacio (Avenida de Revolución, corner of 7th Street). Jai Alai is a most attractive sport in which the players hurl a small ball against a wall from a basket on a long stick. Games are accompanied by tote betting.

Hipódromo de
Agua Caliente

Centro Cultural

One of the first impressions of Mexico is provided by the architecturally interesting culture centre known as Centro, Cultural FONART – which looks rather like a big garage from outside – on the Paseo de los Heroes and Avenida Independicia. Here short films (multi-media shows) about Mexico are shown and there is an exhibition of Mexico's history.

Advice As USA Motor Insurance policies are not valid here it is necessary to take one out with a Mexican insurance company. You can obtain further details from the Baja Tijuana Information Center in San Diego, 7860 Mission Center Court.

Truckee   G 5

Placer County
Altitude: 1774 m (5820 ft)
Population: 2400

Truckee, once a little lumberjack village, has developed only slowly, in spite of its strategically favourable position near Lake Tahoe (see entry) and its superb ski-slopes which are among the best in the United States. As a result the small town still provides a good example of a place which has changed but little since the 19th century.

It owes its name to the river called Truckee after the Paiute Indian, who in 1844 led Elisha Steven's group through the Donner Pass (see entry) which they had discovered. Stevens had in fact made up his mind to be the first to cross the Sierra Nevada to Alta California with a covered-wagon trek.

Hotel Truckee – unchanged since the founding of the town in 1863

History Truckee was founded in 1863 – the same year in which President Abraham Lincoln signed the law which authorised the building of a transcontinental railway. The Central Pacific Railroad Company decided to run the lines right through the middle of Truckee. This led to the development of the timber industry, now long since replaced by tourism as the most important source of income. In 1913 California's first ski-club was formed in Truckee; since then the number has grown to more than twenty.

The following **ski-slopes** are to be found in the immediate vicinity (see also Lake Tahoe):
Boreal, 16 km (10 mi.) west on the US 80, exit to Castle Peak (Nov.–Apr.); Donner Ski Ranch, 16 km (10 mi.) west on the US 80 (Dec.–Apr.); Northstar, 9 km (6 mi.)) on the CA 267 (Nov.–Apr.); Tahoe Donor, 9 km (6 mi.) west on the US 80 (Dec.–Apr.).

One of the most interesting buildings is the 30 room Truckee Hotel which dates from the year the town was founded. The exterior has barely been changed in the 125 years of its existence. Its name has changed, however, for it used to be called The New Whitney.

Truckee Hotel

It is worth making a trip from Truckee (or Lake Tahoe) to Virginia City, 110 km (68 mi.) away in Western Nevada. The city was founded in 1859. The best route is the US 80 east, the NV 395 south and then the NV 341. Virginia City lies immediately above Comstock Lode, rich in gold and silver. Comstock Lode covers an area only 3 km (2 mi.) long and 150 m (500 ft) wide, yet within a period of 20 years gold and silver ore worth more than 400 million dollars (in terms of purchasing power at that time) was mined. A point of interest is that the American Civil War (1861–65) was in part financed by the gold and silver found in this town.

Virginia City

Virginia City is now purely a tourist town which has retained its historical character surprisingly well. Even the "Territorial Enterprise", the newspaper on which Mark Twain began his career as a writer, has now appeared once more in this town of only 800 inhabitants. Ten times as many people lived here between 1860 and 1880; at that time Virginia City was in fact the most important town between San Francisco and Denver.

Ukiah   E 1

Mendocino County
Altitude: 195 m (640 ft)
Population: 15,000

Ukiah, 5 km (3 mi.) from the beautiful Lake Mendocino, lies on the US 101 in a fertile valley which the Indians named Yokaya or Ukiah, meaning roughly south or deep valley. It is the distribution centre for the region's agricultural produce, mainly pears and grapes. The timber industry is also important. In 1898 the International Geodesic Union was founded in Ukiah. It is one of the world's five surveying institutes (all on latitude 39°8′ north).

Universal City

See Los Angeles

University of California

See Davis Irvine, Los Angeles, Riverside, San Diego/La Jolla, Santa Barbara, Santa Cruz.

Vallejo   H 1

Solano County
Altitude: 15 m (50 ft). Population: 109,000

Situated north of San Francisco on the San Pablo Bay, Vallejo was named after the Mexican General Mariano Guatalupe Vallejo, who tried to persuade the Americans to create the capital of California on his ranch. He did succeed – albeit only for one week from January 5th to 12th 1852 – but the location was found to be inadequate, so the parliament was moved to Sacramento. The politicians were not satisfied with that either and returned to Vallejo again between January 3rd and February 4th 1853, before deciding to move again first to Benicia (see entry) and finally, for the second time, to Sacramento.

Naval dockyard In spite of all its vicissitudes the town developed, not least because of the purchase of Mare Island, situated between Mare Island Street and San Pablo Bay just before Vallejo. Today submarines fitted with atomic missiles, and other naval vessels are repaired on this 930 ha (2300 acre) site.

Naval Museum

There is also a Marine Academy in Vallejo. The old City Hall now houses an Historical Naval Museum portraying the history of the town and the naval dockyard (734 Marin Street.) Open daily 9.30am–5pm, Mon. and Tue. to 4.30pm only.

Six Flags Marine World

The main attraction in Vallejo is the Six Flags Marine World leisure park, brought here from Redwood City in 1986 and known until 1999 as Marine World Africa USA. This zoo, aquarium and amusement park rolled into one, has very diverse sections and an instructive programme of events (dolphin and killer whale show, performances by trained Bengal tigers, lions, elephants, birds of prey and other animals) making for considerable variety. Of particular interest are the acrobatic routines on water-skis, and the "Australian Adventure" with kangaroos and koala bears roaming free. Other highlights are the walruses and an acrylic tunnel allowing a really close look at the submarine world of a tropical coral reef complete with sharks. Open daily end of May to beginning of Sep; end of Mar. to end of May and Sep. to end of Oct. Fri.–Sun. only.

Ventura   O 2

Ventura County
Altitude: 15 m (50 ft). Population: 93,000

Ventura lies on the US 101 and is 96 km (60 mi.) north-west of Los Angeles, 48 km (30 mi.) from Santa Barbara, and about 300 km (190 mi.) from San Diego. Ventura is an abbreviation for the San Buenaventura Mission (see Mission Stations). Around this centre the town of Ventura has developed over decades. It lies in the middle of an agricultural region. During the previous century people began to grow citrus fruits, avocados and other produce. Today it is the USA's most important area for the cultivation of citrus fruits.

Boat harbour in Ventura

In the early twenties oil was discovered very near to Ventura. This led to the town's economic upswing, and today there is a large oil refinery here.

Since the end of the Second World War holidaymakers have been enticed to Ventura by the superb beaches, especially the San Buenaventura State Beach, a marina which will accommodate 1500 motor and sailing boats, as well as by the excursion boats plying between here and the Channel Islands (see Channel Islands National Park).

Museums Not far from the Mission stands the Ventura County Historical Museum, with artefacts from the Spanish, Mexican and early American periods (100 East Main Street.) Open Tue.–Sun. 10am–5pm; admission free. The Albinger Archaeological Museum, in the same street, has valuable finds from Indian culture (1500 BC), as well as Chinese and Mexican artefacts. Open Tue.–Sun. 10am–4pm; admission free.

Weaverville   C 3

Trinity County
Altitude: 613 m (2012 ft)
Population: 2800

Weaverville, situated on the CA 299 in North California, is a suitable setting-off point for excursions into the Shasta Trinity National Forest (see Redding). Named after one of the gold miners who established this town outside Mother Lode County (see entry), Weaverville experienced its heyday during the 1850s, when it had more inhabitants than it has now. This was due mainly to the influx of more than 2000 Chinese who

worked in the gold mines. In 1854 a feud, called a Tong War, broke out between the Chinese communities, as a result of which part of the Chinese quarter was burned down and a large number of the people left. Only a few Chinese still live in Weaverville.

California's oldest **Chinese temple** (1874) bears witness to their former presence. It is still used on occasions today. All the objects to be found in this temple, such as valuable carpets and scrolls, were imported from China. The temple stands in the centre of the little town, in Joss House State Historic Park, where an exhibition will tell you all about the life of the Chinese and their contribution to California's development. Open daily 10am–5pm.

The wild gold-mining period, when anything was allowed, has left its mark in the form of the figure of a scantily dressed woman looking down on passers-by from the window of the old **brewery** and pub standing opposite the temple.

The still authentic townscape differs little today from the descriptions given by the American author Bret Harte more than 100 years ago. The items exhibited in the J. J. Jackson Memorial Museum also add to the local colour and history; Indian artefacts, Chinese weapons, fossils and even prison cells brought here from afar can be seen. Open May–Oct. daily 10am–5pm, Apr.–Nov. noon–4pm; admission free.

Jackson Museum

★★Yosemite National Park   I/J 4/5

Yosemite National Park (pronounced "yossémmitty") was founded in 1890, and extends over 1190 sq. mi. (3082 sq. km) in the centre of eastern California. It covers a section of the Sierra Nevada rich in forests and lakes, the scenic highlight of which is the Yosemite Valley, measuring some 13 km (8 mi.) long and some 1–3 km (½–2 mi.) wide. Swollen by melting snows in spring, numerous waterfalls cascade down the almost vertical granite walls of the Merced River Valley (known to the Spanish as El Rio de Nuestra Señora de la Merced). These walls rise to between 900 and 1500 m (3000 and 5000 ft).

Flora and fauna The almost flat valley bottom (at 1200 m (4000 ft) above sea-level) is covered in lush flower-strewn meadows, thick bushes and dense clumps of trees. The vastly different levels to be found in the park (between 400 and 4000 m (130 and 1300 ft)) produce ideal living conditions for a wide range of animals and plants. Thus wild deer, black bear, coyotes, badgers and numerous rodents roam the lower regions, while marmots frequent the inhospitable mountain heights.
    Several clumps of mighty redwoods (sequoia gigantea) are also one of the special sights to be seen in Yosemite National Park.

History The Yosemite Valley was formed over millions of years. Originally there was a wide valley here with a river which in time hollowed out a canyon up to 650 m (2100 ft) deep. During the Ice Age the canyon became filled right to the top with ice and possibly glaciers. The ice widened the canyon at its weakest points and hollowed out the U-shaped Yosemite Valley. The last glacier filled it to a depth of only about one-third, leaving a moraine of ice behind. Behind this moraine the melting ice formed a lake, which slowly filled with deposits, thus forming the plains in the valley on which meadows and forests are found today.

◀ *Yosemite Falls*

Near the entrance to Yosemite Valley stands a colossal monolith known as "EL Capitán"

Development The first men must have come to the Yosemite Valley 8000 to 10,000 years ago, and Miwok Indians (Ahwahnee) lived there for more than 4500 years before the Europeans came. In the middle of the 19th c., when the gold-rush and its accompanying army of adventurers descended upon California and the villages and hunting-grounds of the Indian aborigines, the latter often carried out bloody reprisal attacks on the white man's mining towns and trading posts. Whilst on a punitive expedition against the Indians on March 25th 1851 the Mariposa Battalion became the first white men to enter the valley. They gave it the Indian name of "U-zu-mate", the name of the grisly bear native to these forests.

The reports made by the Mariposa soldiers quickly aroused public interest in this special and beautiful part of the country and the first visitors were attracted there as early as 1851. In 1864, during the Civil War, President Lincoln signed the Yosemite Transfer of Ownership, which ceded the Yosemite Valley and the Mariposa Grove to California, on condition that it was preserved in its state of natural beauty.

The Scottish naturalist John Muir, who came to the Yosemite Valley four years later, became the chief advocate of the National Park concept. Yellowstone National Park was the first to be created in 1872. It was followed by Yosemite in 1890. California then returned the area to the Federal Government, and with the passage of time it grew to its present size.

The first cavalrymen entered the valley along Indian trails; ten years later the first roads were laid and in 1900 the first car came in along the Wawona Road, although cars were not officially allowed until 1913. In 1907 the railway line from San Francisco to El Portal was built along the western boundary of the park, and this remained in use until 1945. The all-weather road from Merced (see entry) was completed in 1926. That was when tourists began to flood into Yosemite National Park; now

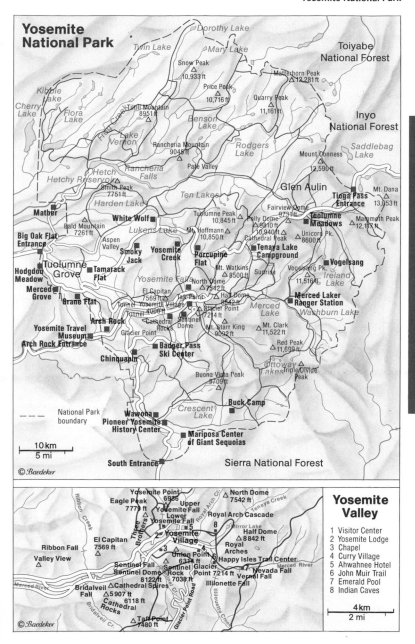

Yosemite National Park

Dorothy Lake
Twin Lake
Mary Lake
Snow Peak
△ 10,933 ft
Price Peak
△ 10,716 ft
Matterhorn Peak
△ 12,281 ft
Quarry Peak
△ 11,161 ft

Toiyabe National Forest

Kibbie Lake
Cherry Lake
Flora Lake
Tiltill Mountain
8951 ft
Benson Lake
Lake Vernon
Rancheria Mountain
9048 ft
Rodgers Lake
Mount Conness
△ 12,590 ft
Inyo National Forest
Saddlebag Lake

Hetch Hetchy Reservoir
Rancheria Falls
Pate Valley
Smith Peak
7751 ft
Ten Lakes
Glen Aulin
Mt. Dana
△ 13,053 ft
Tioga Pass Entrance
Fairview Dome
9731 ft

Mather
Harden Lake
White Wolf
Tuolumne Peak
10,845 ft
Daly Dome
△ 9910 ft
Tuolumne Meadows
Mammoth Peak
△ 12,117 ft
Bald Mountain
7261 ft
Lukens Lake
Mt. Hoffmann
△ 10,850 ft
10,940 ft △
Cathedral Peak
Unicorn Pk.
△ 8600 ft

Big Oak Flat Entrance
Aspen Valley
Smoky Jack
Yosemite Creek
Porcupine Flat
Tenaya Lake Campground
Vogelsang
Hodgdon Meadow
Tamarack Flat
Yosemite Falls
Mt. Watkins
△ 8500 ft
Sunrise
Vogelsang Pk.
△ 11,516 ft
Ireland Lake
Tuolumne Grove
Merced Grove
Crane Flat
El Capitan
7569 ft △
North Dome
△ 7542 ft
Taft Point
Half Dome
8842 ft
Merced Lake Ranger Station
Washburn Lake
Yosemite Village
Tunnel
Glacier Point
7214 ft
Merced Lake
Arch Rock
Tunnel
Cathedral Rocks
Sentinel Dome
Mt. Starr King
9092 ft
Mt. Clark
△ 11,522 ft
Yosemite Travel Museum
Arch Rock Entrance
Glacier Point
Badger Pass Ski Center
Red Peak
△ 11,699 ft
Chinquapin
Buena Vista Peak
9709 ft
Ottoway Lakes
Triple Divide Peak

Crescent Lake
Buck Camp

National Park boundary
Wawona
Pioneer Yosemite History Center
Mariposa Center of Giant Sequoias

10 km
5 mi

© Baedeker

South Entrance

Sierra National Forest

Yosemite Valley

Yosemite Point
6936
Eagle Peak
7779 ft
Upper Yosemite Fall
Lower Yosemite Fall
North Dome
7542 ft
Royal Arch Cascade
Half Dome
△ 8842 ft
Ribbon Creek
Royal Arch Cr.
Tenaya Creek
El Capitan
7569 ft
Ribbon Fall
Valley View △
Three Brothers
Yosemite Village
Mirror Lake
Indian Caves
Royal Arches
Union Point
6314 ft
Happy Isles Trail Center
Merced River
Sentinel Fall
Sentinel Rock
8122 ft
Cathedral Spires
Glacier Point
7214 ft
Sentinel Dome
7038 ft
Nevada Fall
Vernal Fall
Illilouette Fall
Bridalveil Fall
5907 ft
Cathedral Rocks
6118 ft
Bridalveil Cr.
Glacier Point Road
Illilouette Creek
Taft Point
7480 ft

1 Visitor Center
2 Yosemite Lodge
3 Chapel
4 Curry Village
5 Ahwahnee Hotel
6 John Muir Trail
7 Emerald Pool
8 Indian Caves

4 km
2 mi

© Baedeker

some 2–½ million people visit it every year. In 1984 Yosemite National Park received very special recognition from the United Nations who added it to the list of World Heritage Sites, which includes the natural and made-made Wonders of the World.

Yosemite Valley

★El Capitán

Coming from Merced your first impressive view of Yosemite Valley is from Valley View Point at the western entrance to the valley. One of the most magnificent and arresting sights is that of the rock massif known as El Capitán (2307 m (7572 ft)), dominating in bold relief the north-west corner of the valley. The impression made by this mighty monolith comes mainly from its dominant position, its majestic shape and its precipitous walls rising 100 m (300 ft) above the floor of the valley. Its two end walls facing west and south meet almost at right angles; it is an arduous climb to the top.

★Ribbon Fall
★Eagle Peak

Immediately to the west lies the 491 m (1612 ft) high Ribbon Fall in Ribbon Creek. East of El Capitán rise the triple peaks of the Three Brothers, the highest of which, Eagle Peak (2371 m (7780 ft)), provides a superb view of the valley and Yosemite Falls.

★Yosemite Falls

Yosemite Falls are east of Eagle Peak, roughly in the middle of the valley. They are in three parts, with a total overall height of 739 m (2425 ft): the Upper Fall, some 10 m (30 ft) wide, plunges down 136 m (450 ft) almost vertically; the Middle Cascade consists of a number of small cascades (totalling 206 m (680 ft), and the Lower Fall is 98 m (320 ft) high. Yosemite Falls are among the highest in the world and in spring provide the most awe-inspiring sight in the National Park, but they disappear in summer and autumn. In winter a magnificent ice peak, up to 90 m (300 ft) in height, forms on the Upper Fall.

Royal Arches

East of the Upper Fall, on the end face of the Upper Yosemite Fall Cliff, stands a granite needle known as Lost Arrow. Still further east lies Indian Canyon, the soft stone of which shows more marked signs of erosion than that in the Yosemite valley. The rock-wall on the opposite side of the canyon gets its name of Royal Arches from its semi-circular hollows. On the west side will be found the Royal Arches Cascade, a waterfall about 300 m (1000 ft) high, which is normally almost dry but which swells considerably in spring and after heavy rain.

North Dome

East of the Royal Arches, where the valley joins Tenaya Canyon, Washington Column towers above the valley floor. It is a granite tower measuring 585 m (1930 ft), dwarfed however by the barren North Dome (2299 m (7545 ft)).

Mirror Lake

At its east end the Yosemite Valley forks into two narrow valleys, Tenaya Creek (north-east) and Merced River (south-east). Between the square blocks of rock at the foot of the right-hand wall of the Tenaya Creek Canyon can be found the Indian Caves, where Indians once lived. About 2 km (1 mi.) upstream the reflection of the North Dome plays on the clear waters of the beautiful Mirror Lake. The best time to see this is during the still hours of morning and evening when the wind has dropped. Tenaya Creek brings great masses of gravel and mud into the lake, so there is a real threat that it may silt up. It dries up almost completely in late summer and does not fill up again until after the autumn storms. There is a 5 km (3 mi.) path leading round the lake.

★Half Dome

Opposite the North Dome, and forming the east end of the Yosemite Valley, towers the Half Dome (2695 m (8850 ft)) which, as the name suggests, is shaped like a vertically-halved dome. So far it has not been

At the end of the Yosemite Valley can be seen the Half Dome – symbol of the national park

established whether it ever had the other half. It can be climbed from the far side (but only in the warm months of the year) the last stretch to the summit being by cable-car. South of Half Dome is where the Merced River Canyon ends. A little way upstream are Vernal Fall (100 m (330 ft) high) and Nevada Fall (186 m (610 ft)).

At the south-east corner of the Yosemite Valley where it joins the Merced Canyon the rocky peak known as Glacier Point (2199 m (7217 ft)) reaches towards the sky. This is without doubt the loveliest and most popular spot hereabouts from which to look down over the Yosemite Valley into the Merced Canyon with its waterfalls, and across the High Sierra.

Glacier Point

A valley wall runs in an almost straight line from Glacier Point for about 1 mile/2 km. Its lower regions are covered in boulders. It is dominated by Sentinel Dome (2476 m (8126 ft)) and ends in Sentinel Rock (2145 m (7040 ft)), the most prominent rock on the south wall.

★Sentinel Rock

Further west you will come to the two slender Cathedral Spires (1800 m (5900 ft)) and 1865 m (6120 ft) high), side by side with the imposing twinned Cathedral Rocks (2021 m (6630 ft)) opposite the Capitán. Bridal Veil Fall (15–20 m (50–70 ft) wide), cascades down for some 189 m (620 ft) on the lower western slopes of these rocks. It is so called because, when the wind is blowing, the waters take on the appearance of a bridal veil. The Ahwahneechee Indians native to the Yosemite Valley named it Pohono, meaning roughly "spirit that blows the air". The wind blows round the waterfall, sometimes making it move sideways. In the summer months, however, it dries up completely.

★Cathedral Rock
★Bridal Veil Rock

The focus of tourism in the valley is Yosemite Village below the main falls. Here you will find the ranger's office, visitors' centre, museum,

Yosemite Village

331

information centres, accommodation, post-office, shops, riding stables and so forth. In a building west of the Visitor Center is an Indian Cultural Museum with a rich collection depicting Indian cultural history.

Roads and trails

Valley Loop Road runs for 27 km (17 mi.) along both sides of the Merced River through the Yosemite Valley. In the east a road branches off to Mirror Lake.

From Chinquapin (on the Wawona Road) Glacier Point Road leads to Glacier Point by way of Badger Pass (ski-slopes) and close to the southern edge of the Yosemite Valley.

Some of the most beautiful places in the valley and its vicinity can be reached by numerous paths of varying difficulty.

Glacier Point Trail	Glacier Point Trail, leading from Yosemite Village and laid down in 1871 before Glacier Point Road was built, is a difficult route (8 km (5 mi.)) to Glacier Point, with superb views over the valley.
Mirror Lake Loop	A pleasant walk (5 km (3 mi.)) around Mirror Lake, then ascending Tenaya Creek Valley, past the junction with Snow Creek Trail from Tenaya Lake, and then back to Mirror Lake.
Half Dome Trail	A difficult route (27 km (17 mi.)); also suitable for horses) from Happy Isles, going first along the upper edge of the Nevada Fall and then up Little Yosemite Valley to the top of Half Dome.
Inspiration Point Trail	A strenuous way round (4 km (2½ mi.)) from Wawona Tunnel to Old Inspiration Point by the old Wawona Road, which formed the main route to the Yosemite Valley before the Wawona Tunnel was completed.
Vernal Nevada Falls Trail	A mainly difficult road (1–½ mi. (2–½ km)) from Happy Isles in the Merced River Canyon uphill to its two waterfalls.
John Muir Trail	The northern end of the trail starts here and it runs for 340 km (210 mi.) to the Sequoia and Kings Canyon National Parks, through the Californian Highlands as far as Mount Whitney. The trek will take about 20 days, mostly at heights of between 3000 and 4200 m (10,000 and 14,000 ft).
Yosemite Falls Trail	A circular route (12 km (7½ mi.)) from the camp site near Yosemite Lodge to the upper edge of the Yosemite Falls, with beautiful views over the valley from Yosemite Point and Columbia Rock.
Panorama Trail	A difficult route (about 14 km (9 mi.)) from Glacier Point via Illilouette Creek, near its waterfall, then past Panorama Cliffs and through the Merced Canyon to the Nevada Fall.
Pohono Trail	A strenuous route (21 km (14 mi.)) from Glacier Point via the southern edge of the Yosemite Valley to the Wawona Tunnel. There are viewing points at Taft Point, Crocker Point and Dewey Point.
Sierra Point Trail	A steep circular route (2½ km (1½ mi.)) from Happy Isles to Sierra Point, from where you can see five waterfalls all at the same time (Nevada, Vernal, Illilouette and the Upper and Lower Yosemite Falls).

Footpaths also lead to the floor of the valley, e.g., to the foot of the Yosemite Fall and Bridal Veil Fall.

Rest of the park area

From the south entrance the 48 km (30 mi.) long Wawona Road leads to the Yosemite Valley. About 3 km (2 mi.) north-east of the park entrance stands the Mariposa Grove of Big Trees (Spanish "mariposa" means butterfly), the largest of the three groups of giant redwoods in the National Park. There are some 500 fully-grown giant redwood trees (*sequoiadendron giganteum*; see *Baedeker Special page 308*) in this forest area which covers about 1 sq. km (½ sq. mi.) at between 1675 and 2135 m (5500 and 7000 ft) above sea level.

In the lower part of this grove stands Grizzly Giant, 64 m (210 ft) tall and with a basal circumference of 29.4 m (96½ ft), the biggest tree (about 2700 years old) in Yosemite Park.

In its upper part stands the world-famous "Wawona Tree", the top of which broke off under the weight of snow in 1969. A tunnel was made through its trunk in 1881 and the road leads through it.

In the Mariposa Grove Museum there are exhibits on the natural history of the region and its discovery. The road to Mariposa Grove is closed in winter; the giant redwoods can only be reached after a three-mile walk. From Wawona Point (2076 m (6813 ft)) in the north of the grove there is a fine view over the High Sierra and into the San Joaquin Valley.

The **Wawona tourist centre** (hotel) lies about 8 km (5 mi.) north-west of the southern entrance, by the Wawona Road. On both sides of the southern arm of the Merced River will be found the Pioneer Yosemite History Center, an open-air museum with log-cabins, a jail, wagons and a covered bridge dating from the early days of the National Park. Museum staff wear period costume and will answer visitors' questions.

About 43 km (27 mi.) north of the southern entrance, on the far side of Chinquapin, where Glacier Point Road turns off to the north-east and just before the entrance to the Yosemite Valley basin, the Wawona Road passes through the Wawona Tunnel, built in 1933 to preserve the landscape. It is 1.3 km (4200 ft) long. There are then superb views down into the Yosemite Valley. **Wawona Tunnel**

From El Portal the 14 km (9 mi.) long Merced Road leads to Valley View Point at the west end of the Yosemite Valley. The El Portal tourist centre was set up in the south-west corner of the park area as a supply centre for park visitors and placed under the protection of the National Park to prevent over-development. Until 1945 this was the terminus of the 126 km (78 mi.) Yosemite Valley Railroad running from Merced (locomotives and carriages can be seen at the former station, now the El Portal Museum). **El Portal**

The Arch Rock Entrance is about 3 km (2 mi.) north-east of El Portal; 5 km (3 mi.) further on are the 152 m (500 ft)-high Cascade Falls at Cascade Creek and Tanarack Creek. **Cascade Falls**

From Big Oak Flat Entrance in the west of the National Park Big Flat Oak Road (some 32 km (20 mi.) long) leads to Yosemite Valley. About 9 km (6 mi.) south-east of the park entrance is the Merced Grove of Giant Sequoias, the smallest of the three groups of redwoods. To the north-east, on the far side of the Tioga Road (one-way approach road from Crane Flat) stands the Tuolumne Grove of Big Trees, the third of Yosemite Park's groves of sequoias. **Merced Grove**

Tioga Road, 43 mi. (69 km) long (closed in winter), crosses the central area of the National Park in a roughly west-east direction. It branches off from Big Oak Flat Road at Crane Flat and passes through some magnificent mountain scenery, via the High Sierra past White Wolf (just off to the north is a lodge with cabins and tents; to book tel. 3721326) to Tioga **★ Tuolumne Meadows**

Pass (3030 m (10,000 ft)). On its way the road passes the north-west bank of the quiet Lake Tenaya, the rocky banks of which show typical signs of glacial abrasion; it also passes through Tuolumne Meadows (2713 m (8900 ft)); visitors' centre; lodge with tent site, booking necessary), upland meadows surrounded by high rounded hilltops; this is the most extensive sub-alpine meadow in the Sierra Nevada. The Tuolumne River flows through it. This river crosses the National Park some 16 km (10 mi.) north of the Merced River and parallel to it, and on its way it forms a number of waterfalls in the magnificent Grand Canyon of the Tuolumne River. The picturesque May Lake is not far away.

Hetch Hetchy Valley

Further down river is the Hetch Hetchy Valley, somewhat similar to the Yosemite Valley but smaller, with steep rocky walls and high cataracts. Since the completion of the O'Shaughnessy Dam (1923; accessible from Mather) the valley has been filled by the Hetchy Hetchy Reservoir, which supplies drinking water to San Francisco and other towns.

Walks The northern half of the Yosemite National Park has few roads and can be explored only along footpaths and riding tracks. Tuolumne Meadows is the place to set off from for tours into the mountain wilderness (only in summer). Mountaineering experience and climbing equipment are essential.

Notes

Access There are three ways to drive to the park: from the south on the CA 141 (107 km (66 mi.)) from Merced; see entry), in the west on the CA 41 (99 km (61 mi.)) from Fresno; see entry) and in the west on the CA 120 (20 km (12 mi.)) from Lee Vining; the latter route is closed in the winter months because it leads over the 3000 m (9900 ft) high Tioga Pass. From the park entrances it is still a long way to the valley.

On the 120 and 140 roads from San Francisco it is about 320 km (200 mi.) to the park entrance. It would be very tiring to drive there and back in a day and would leave little time for the park itself. One-day coach tours run from San Francisco, and you can also fly but that is rather expensive.

The Yosemite Transportation System offers tours by coach through Yosemite Valley (2 hours), to Mariposa Grove (½ day), to Glacier Point (½ day) or both combined (1 day).

About 7 km (4 mi.)) south of the South Entrance runs the narrow-gauge Yosemite Mountain Sugar Pine Railroad with old-fashioned trains.

Because of the large numbers of visitors to the National Park (some 4 million a year), and the shortage of parking space, motorised access to many points has recently been restricted to the electric **shuttle buses** which ply a regular service. There are plans to expand services in the summer months and bus 1.4 million visitors into the Park.

In **winter** snow-chains must be used! Most side roads from the Yosemite Valley into the surrounding mountains are closed during the winter months, so visits to the National Park are confined to the Yosemite Valley itself.

Because in many years winter conditions in the high mountains persist until June, it is essential to check with a local tourist office whether the Tioga Pass is open to road traffic.

Horse riding Main Stables and Yosemite Lodge Corral in Yosemite Village; facilities also in Wawona, White Wolf and Tuolumne Meadows.

Bicycle hire Yosemite Lodge and Curry Village in Yosemite Valley.

In winter the National Park offers outstanding conditions for **cross country skiing**. The temperature ranges between 14°F (−10°C) and 57°F (14°C).

A wide range of **events** and functions awaits the visitor during the summer months. You should consult the park newspaper "Yosemite Guide" which appears weekly. In addition to the numerous ranger programmes (lectures, etc.) and campfire talks, there are geology walks (guided tours with geological explanations), ecology float trips (accompanied trips floating down the Merced River with ecological commentaries) and mountaineering, riding and cycling tours (cassette recordings of tours available).

For anyone visiting the Yosemite National Park in the high season, in spring and early autumn, and wishing to stay overnight it is essential to book **accommodation** in advance. For the hotels and motels inside the park (see Practical Information, Hotels and Motels, Yosemite National Park) there is a centre which will take advance bookings for the Ahwahnee and Wawona Hotels as well as for Yosemite Lodge and Curry Village. If you have to spend the night outside the park you will have the long journey into the park each day.
You can reach the Yosemite Waterfall in a few minutes if you get off the No. 7 bus at Yosemite Lodge.

Yosemite National Park is open 24 hours a day all the year round. **Information** about walks, together with maps and any permits necessary, can be obtained from the Visitor Center.

**Practical
Information
from A–Z**

Practical Information from A to Z

Accommodation

See Camping, Hotels and Motels, Youth Hostels

Air Travel

Because of the great distances in the United States in general and in California in particular, air travel is the preferred means of transport. The international airports at Los Angeles (Los Angeles International Airport/LAX) and San Francisco (San Francisco International Airport) are among the most important in the country followed by San Diego International Airport situated north-west of the city centre. In addition to LAX the Los Angeles area is served by Burbank-Glendale-Pasadena Airport near Hollywood and the Long Beach and John Wayne Airports south-east of the city. For further information about individual airports consult the appropriate city entry in the A to Z section.

Bathing

Bathing in the Pacific Ocean in the north of California is seldom possible, because of the cool weather and usually rocky coast. Even in San Francisco, which is entirely surrounded by water, there are no bathing beaches. Only south of Santa Cruz (see entry), the town with a great number of beaches, and where there is an amusement park on the beach promenade, are there many bathing beaches. South of Santa Cruz come:

Pebble Beach (south of Monterey).
Carmel River State Beach, at the south end of Carmel.
San Simeon State Beach, on the coast of San Simeon a few miles from Hearst Castle.
Cayucos State Beach, Morro Strand State Beach and Atascadero State Beach, all north of Morro Bay.
Pismo State Beach in Pismo Beach.
Jalama Beach south of Lompoc.
El Capitan, Refugion and Gaviota State Parks, the three beaches of Santa Barbara.
Point Mugu State Park, south of Oxnard.
San Buenaventura State Beach in Ventura.
Beach with Mediterranean vegetation, near Carmel
Malibu Beach (45 km (27 mi.)) from Ventura County to Santa Monica.
County Line Beach, Leo Carillo State Beach, Zuma Beach, Corral Beach, Surfrider Beach, Las Tunas Beach.

Will Rogers State Beach near Santa Monica.
Santa Monica Beach in Santa Monica.
Venice Beach in Venice.
Sunset Beach south of Long Beach.
Huntington City Beach and Huntington Beach State Park in Huntington Beach.
Newport Beach and Balbao Beach in Newport Beach, Laguna Beach.
Aliso Beach in South Laguna.
Dana Point Beach.
Between Carlsbad and San Diego: Carlsbad Beach, South Carlsbad Beach, Ponto Beach, Leucadia Beach, Encinitas Beach, Moonlight Beach, San Elijo Beach, Cardiff Beach, Solana Beach.
Further south in La Jolla and San Diego: Black's Beach, Shell Beach, Marine State Beach, Windansea Beach, Pacific Beach Park, Mission Beach and Ocean Beach Park.

Bathing is possible in hundreds of lakes in California. The water is generally unpolluted and there is constant supervision. · Lakes

Further information about many of these beaches see the A to Z section.

Banks

See Currency

Boat Excursions

Excursions by boat can be made from many towns (see A to Z) including:
San Francisco: boats of the "Blue and Gold Fleet" operate harbour tours daily from Fisherman's Wharf.
Los Angeles: daily excursions from San Pedro Harbor to Santa Catalina Island (see entry).
Ventura: trips to the Channel Islands.
San Diego: day tours to Ensenada, Baja California and Mexico, and Avalon/Santa Catalina Island; also extensive tours of the harbour and a ferry service to Coronado.
Eureka: excursion in Humboldt Bay.
Morro Bay: tours of the bay.
Inland waters: there are boat trips on Lakes Tahoe (see entry) and Shasta, and on the Sacramento River.

Bookshops

As in other parts of the USA there are numerous bookshops in California. In the larger towns there are also specialist antiquarian bookshops, the addresses of which can be found in "Yellow Pages". See also below, Newspapers and Periodicals.

Business Hours

See entry · Chemists

See entry · Banks

Shops and offices

There are no official business hours in the USA. Every shop or restaurant can remain open as long as the proprietor wishes.

Shopping malls and marketplaces (shopping precincts, arcades): Mon.–Fri. 9 or 10am–8 or 9pm, Sat. 10am–7pm, Sun. 11am–6pm; other town centre shops: Mon.–Sat. 10am–5.30pm.

Some department stores stay open later in the evening on one or more days a week and on Sundays. Some supermarkets are open throughout the week and for 24 hours a day.

In smaller places shops, etc. generally close at 7pm.

Museums

The times of opening of museums and similar establishments are given in the A to Z section under their individual names.

Restaurants

In smaller places restaurants are normally open until 9.30 or 10pm and in large cities until midnight or 1am – at weekends often until some hours later. Most bars and discothèques do not close until 4am.

Camping

There are excellent facilities in California for this popular activity. The National Parks, monuments and forests which are looked after by the Ministry of the Interior, the numerous State Parks for which the California Government is responsible, and the steadily increasing number of private trailer camps (trailer parks) provide more space every year.

Booking

For a stay in a State Park camp site (max. eight weeks) advance booking is necessary with MISTIX (tel. (800) 4467275). In addition to the advance booking charge there will also be a nightly site fee. A comprehensive list of these camp sites (California State Camping Guide), can be obtained for a small charge in almost all the State Parks, or by post for a small charge from the Department of Parks and Recreation, (P.O. Box 942896, Sacramento CA 94296).

Information about camp sites in the National Parks can be obtained from the Western Region Information Office, National Park Service, Fort Mason, Bldg. 201, San Francisco, CA 94123, tel. (415) 5560560.

MISTIX (tel. 1–800–283–CAMP) will reserve places for those wishing to camp in the National Forests. Information about camping in the Forests is available from the USDA Forest Service, 630 Sansome Street, San Francisco CA 94111, tel. (707) 5628737.

Private campsites

Private campsites offer greater comfort. These are represented by the chain KOA: Campgrounds of America (KOA), Executive Offices, Billings, MT 59114–0558, tel. (406) 2487444

Information

Information on camping is also available from the American Automobile Association (see Motoring Assistance).

Car Rental

Visitors to San Francisco only will not normally need to rent a car; distances are small and public transport good. If travelling about the state or staying in Los Angeles or San Diego on the other hand, a hire car is virtually essential.

Documents

A valid national driving licence is generally sufficient, however a credit card (Visa, Mastercard, Eurocard) is an absolute must, or a very high deposit will be charged.

Normally the minimum age for hiring a car is 25 years, but in California drivers as young as 21 can hire a car in return for a "risk surcharge" payable by credit card. Age

Many firms offer attractive budget deals (e.g. for weekly hire) as well as discounts in shops and restaurants and certain hotels and places of interest. While basic hire charges are often quite low it is most important to obtain adequate insurance cover (third party liability, comprehensive accident and excess); this can work out quite expensive. Charges

Payment is best made by internationally recognised credit card; cash customers may be asked for a substantial deposit. Deposit

Most car rental firms have desks at airports as well as city centre offices in the major cities such as Los Angeles, Sacramento, San Diego and San Francisco. To avoid disappointment, especially in peak season, bookings should be made by telephone in advance. All car rental firms, including the major companies listed below, have freephone numbers (prefix 800): Rental firms

Alamo Rent-A-Car; tel. 1–800–327–9633
Avis Rent-A-Car; tel. 1–800 331–1212
Budget Rent-A-Car; tel. 1–800–601–5385
Dollar Rent-A-Car; tel. 1–800–800–4000
Hertz Rent-A-Car; tel. 1–800–654–3131

Several specialist operators – e.g. Campertours Worldwide – offer package tours to California. These include return charter flights and hire of a caravan. Caravans

Chemists

American Drug Stores, occasionally called pharmacies, are quite different from European chemists; for most of them dispensing prescriptions is only a very small part of their business.

You can find most drug stores in the "Yellow Pages" of the telephone directories which are available in almost every hotel and motel room. Information

Normally from 9 or 9.30am until 6.30 or 7pm; some are open until 9pm or even later. There is no special night service outside these times. In an emergency it is best to go to the nearest hospital, which will be open 24 hours and have its own dispensary. Business hours

Clothing

According to the season and region you should take appropriate clothing (see Facts and Figures, Climate). As well as light summer wear a warm pullover for cool evenings and air conditioned buildings is advisable. From May to October no rainwear is necessary except for tours into the mountains where sudden summer storms often occur. For trips into the desert headgear of some kind and sunglasses are absolutely necessary. When using good class restaurants a jacket and/or tie is often demanded; otherwise casual leisure wear is sufficient. Swimsuits should, of course, be taken.

Consulates

The United Kingdom has Consulates General in Los Angeles and San Francisco.
11766 Wiltshire Blvd., Los Angeles, CA 90025; tel (310) 4773322.
Suite 850, 1 Sansome Street, San Francisco, CA 94104; tel (415) 9813030.

Crime

Crime, particularly in the cities of Los Angeles and San Francisco is a problem and there it is mainly carried out by gangs. Whenever possible cars should be parked in an underground garage, for thefts from vehicles (especially in San Diego) are a frequent occurrence. If you have to leave a car during the daytime on the street in a quiet district, it is sensible to put all movable possessions in the boot. After dark you should stay away from parks and beaches. It is also advisable to avoid rundown districts such as Watts in Los Angeles and Western Addition in San Francisco. In the cities it is rare to see police on foot. Police patrolling in vehicles warn tourists in San Francisco not to photograph the Victorian houses with the Transamerica Pyramid in the background from Alamo Square.

Except for valuables which you have to carry about with you, such as a purse, a passport or a wallet, other items should be handed to hotel reception for safe keeping and a receipt for them obtained.

Currency

The unit of currency in the USA is the US dollar (US $). There are notes with values of 1, 5, 10, 20, 50 and 100 US dollars (in internal banking business there are also larger notes), and coins of 1 (penny), 5 (nickel), 10 (dime) and 25 (quarter) cents; occasionally 50 c (half-dollar) and 1 dollar coins can be found.

Exchange rates

The exchange rate of the dollar fluctuates against most foreign currencies. Exchanging in America entails accepting a poor exchange rate and greater commission than in Europe, therefore visitors are recommended to change their money into US dollars before they leave Britain, and above all to make sure they have sufficient change (notes of $1 to $10 and coins) available. Shops and restaurants generally do not accept foreign currency; the larger hotels will do so but charge higher commission.

Notes

You should note that all American currency notes are of the same size and colour, and can only be distinguished by the value printed on them and by the picture on the black front and the green back of the note. There are no restrictions on the import and export of foreign and US currency, but if bringing in more than 10,000 US dollars you must fill in a customs declaration in the aircraft.

Banks

Banks are generally open for normal business Mon.–Thu. 8.30am–3pm., Fri. 8.30am–6pm. At weekends and on public holidays only the bank counters at the international airports are open.

In the major cities foreign currencies can be changed into dollars in the large bank headquarters, such as the Bank of America (in San Francisco: 345 Montgomery Street, in Los Angeles: Downtown, 525 S. Flower Street).

It is advisable to buy travellers' cheques from American Express or Barclays before flying to California (a commission of 1 per cent is charged), as these can readily be changed in banks and are accepted in hotels and restaurants as cash, on production of a passport. If stolen or lost, telephone the emergency number and they will be replaced free of charge – usually within 24 hours, if necessary by courier. Eurocheques are not accepted.

You are recommended to take credit cards – American Express, Mastercard or Visa, particularly as these credit card companires in the USA operate a discount system in conjunction with other businesses. They are useful for paying bills of all kinds – for airline tickets, in hotels and motels, petrol stations and most shops. When you rent a car credit cards are accepted as a security deposit, whereas cash is not liked.

Many credit cards enable the user to obtain money, using his PIN number, from machines in banks and often in supermarkets. Card holders can also take advantage of the various discount schemes negotiated by credit card companies in the US, involving a wide range of goods and services.

Customs Regulations

Articles for personal use (clothing, toilet articles, jewellery, photographic and film apparatus, binoculars, portable typewriters, portable radios, video and television apparatus, sports equipment and even a car for 1 year) can be imported without payment of tax. In addition adults can bring in 1 quart (about 1 litre) of alcoholic drink, 300 cigarettes or 50 cigars or 3 pounds of tobacco. In addition every person can import presents up to a value of 100 US dollars including, for adults, up to 1 gallon (3.78 litres) of alcoholic drink and 100 cigars. There are special regulations for the import of live animals, meat, fruit and plants (information can be obtained from customs offices).

Distances

See large map at end of book

Electricity

The standard voltage in the US is 110–115 volts AC. Unless of dual-voltage type, appliances brought from Europe can only be used with a transformer.

European plugs do not fit US sockets. Adapters (and transformers) are best obtained before setting out for the United States, though if necessary they can be purchased in the US at a drug or department store.

Emergencies

Emergency Calls: Police, Fire Brigade, Ambulance everywhere 911.

Events

Throughout the country help can be obtained by ringing 1–800–336–HELP.

Motoring
assistance

See Motoring Assistance; Information – Motoring Clubs.

Events

January 2nd

Tournament of Roses Parade, Pasadena

January

Palm Springs International Film Festival, Palm Springs
Southwest Arts Festival, Indio
The Cushion Memorial Sled Dog Race, Mammoth Lakes
Chinese New Year Festival & Parade (end of January to beginning of February), Chinatown in Los Angeles and San Francisco
Whale Watching (migration of whales from the north to Baja California), Newport Beach
Colorado River Country Music Festival, Blythe

February

Chinese New Year Festival & Parade (see January)
Whale Watching Trips (festival celebrating the arrival of the whales on their migration south), Dana Point, Newport Beach
Napa Valley Mustard Celebration (sampling mustard from all over the world), Calistoga
Mardi Gras (Shrove Tuesday carnival with parades, street bazaars, masked balls etc.) in San Luis Obispo, Pismo Beach, Los Angeles and elsewhere
Italian Festival (Festival of dancing and gourmet food), Palm Springs
Pollyanna Doll Show and Sale (dolls, teddy bears and toys), Petaluma
Bob Hope Chrysler Classic (celebrity golf tournament with Bob Hope), Coachella Valley
National Date Festival and Riverside County Fair, Indio
Pacific Orchid Exposition, San Francis
Winterfest (winter sports and dancing), Chester, (jazz and arts and crafts), Laguna Beach

March

International Asian American Film Festival, San Francisco
Dixieland Monterey (Dixieland Jazz Festival), Monterey
Santa Barbara International Film Festival, Santa Barbara
Irish Faire (Irish festival), Laguna Beach
Snowfest (winter carnival with winter sports events), Truckee
City of Los Angeles Marathon, Los Angeles
Newsweek Champions Cup (tennis tournament), Indian Wells
Hot Air Affair (hot air balloon race), Monterey
Whale Festival (whale-watching), Mendocino, Fort Bragg, Newport Beach
Wine Festival (sampling of Californian wines), Monterey
Santa Barbara International Orchid Show, Santa Barbara

March/April

Shasta Dixieland Jazz Festival, Redding
Easter Sunrise Services (held in many places on Easter Sunday; those in Hollywood and Furnace Creek, Death Valley, are particularly festive)

April

Wine Country Celebration (vintners' festival with gourmet chefs and wine tasting), Yountville
Good Old Days Celebration (folk festival with historical pageants, arts and crafts), Pacific Grove
Santa Fe Market (festival of Indian art and culture), San Diego
Toyota Grand Prix of Long Beach (car rally through the town centre), Long Beach

Pasadena Spring Art Festival (art exhibition and street festival), Pasadena
Red Bluff Round-Up/Rodeo (one of California's biggest rodeos); other Wild West shows are held in Auburn, Needles, Clovis and Springville
Stockton Asparagus Festival, Stockton
Japanese Cherry Blossom Festival, San Francisco
Festival de la Familia (Latin American festival), Sacramento
Temecula Valley Balloon and Wine Festival, Temecula
Scottish Games and Gathering, Roseville

San Francisco International Film Festival (USA's oldest film festival), San Francisco — April/May

Cinco de Mayo Festival (Mexican Independence Day celebration among Latin communities, especially in Los Angeles, San Diego, San Jose, Delano, San Francisco and Santa Barbara) — May
Traditional costume festival (Oktoberfest in May), Hayward
Sacramento Jazz Jubilee (the world's biggest Dixieland jazz festival), Sacramento
Carnival (Caribbean festival), San Francisco and Long Beach
Mother Lode Round-Up Parade (rodeo shows), Sonora
Rodeos in Redding, Ramona, Lake Elsinore
Living History Day (historical crafts demonstrations), Petaluma
West Coast Antique Fly-In & Air Show (vintage and home-built aircraft), Watsonville
Classic Car Parade, San Rafael

Shakespeare Festival (open air performances), Sonoma (until July) and Garberville — June
Hollywood Bowl Arts Fair, Hollywood
Rodeo, Garberville Folsom, Crescent City, Red Bluff, Guerneville
California Police Summer Games, Modesto
Lesbian Gay Freedom Day Parade and Celebration, San Francisco
Monterey Bay Blues Festival, Monterey
Living History Days (festival with historical costumes), San Jose
Juneteenth Festival (folk), San Jose, Berkeley
Father's Day Ferraris on Rodeo Drive, Beverly Hills
Summer Solstice Parade, Santa Barbara
Ojai Wine Festival, Ojai
Redwood Run (annual meet of Harley Davidson motorbike enthusiasts), Piercy
Pioneer Wagon Train, Mariposa
Ox Roast (picnic with ox roast, wine tasting and music), Sonomo
Festival at the Lake, Oakland

World's Largest Salmon Barbecue, Fort Bragg — July
Annual Jazz Jubilee, Mammoth Lakes
Rodeos at Lakeport, Fortuna, Salinas
Lotus Festival (festival of Asian art and culture), Los Angeles
Sonoma Valley Wine Festival & Liberty Ride (wine tasting and races), Sonoma
Celtic Festival and Highland Games, Mammoth Lakes
Gilroy Garlic Festival, Gilroy
U.S. Sandcastle Contest, Imperial Beach
Feast of Lanterns, Pacific Grove
Lake Tahoe Summer Music Festival (opera, orchestral, jazz, open-air performances), Tahoe City
Op Pro and US Open of Surfing Competitions, Huntington Beach
Santa Barbara Greek Festival, Santa Barbara

Hollywood Bowl Summer Festival (music festival), Hollywood — July to September
Sonoma Valley Shakespeare Festival (open-air performances), Sonoma

Events

August	Old Spanish Days (Santa Barbara's biggest festival, with parades, rodeos, dancing and Spanish markets), Santa Barbara
	Toshiba Tennis Classic (women's tennis tournament), Carlsbad
	Sawdust Festival, Art-a-Fair, Festival of Arts and Pageant of the Masters (three-day event), Laguna Beach
	Latin American Festival, San Diego
	International Sea Festival (including water skiing), Long Beach
	Reggae on the River (biggest reggae festival in the western USA), Piercy
	Antique Flea Market, San Juan Baptista
	Nisei Week Japanese Festival (including Japanese folk dancing and parades), Los Angeles
	Jazz Festival in San Jose and Long Beach
	Monterey Historic Automobile Races, Monterey
August/September	California State Fair (one of the USA's largest agricultural fairs), Sacramento
September	Greek Festival (Greek music, dancing and food), Sacramento, Monterey
	Sausalito Art Festival, Sausalito
	Jazz Festivals, Guerneville, Catalina Island, Santa Barbara, Los Angeles (Simon Rodia Watts Towers), Vallejo
	San Diego Street Scene (biggest music festival in California), San Diego
	Danish Days (parades, music, dancing, arts and crafts), Solvang
	Valley of the Moon Vintage Festival (oldest wine festival in California), Sonoma
	California International Air Show, Salinas
	Simon Rodia Watts Towers Jazz Festival, Los Angeles
September/October	Harvest Festival, celebrated in many places including Napa, San Jose, Monterey, Bakersfield

The Danish folk festival in Solvang is celebrated as in Denmark with national costumes, folk dancing and brass bands

Oktoberfest, many places including Big Bear Lake, Huntington Beach,
Santa Barbara, Lakeport, Carlsbad
Sonoma County Harvest Fair (wine festival), Santa Rosa
Italian American Cultural Festival, San Jose
Los Angeles County Fair (largest market in southern California), Pomona

Cabrillo Festival (multicultural folk festival), San Diego
Wine, Art and Jazz Festival, Mariposa
Halloween Festival, many places including Death Valley, West
Hollywood (Los Angeles), Anaheim and San Francisco
Pioneer Days Celebration (folk festival with parade, contests and displays), Twenty-Nine Palms
Harbor Festival, Morro Bay
Fleet Week, San Francisco

October

San Francisco Jazz Festival, San Francisco

October/
November

Asian Pacific American Festival of Performance and Visual Art, Santa
Monica
Fall Art Festival, Pasadena
Christmas Crafts Fairs, many places including Milpitas, Nevada City,
Santa Cruz
Hollywood Christmas Parade, Hollywood
Death Valley 49ers Encampment (folk festival celebrating the first crossing of the desert by pioneers of the West; camp fire atmosphere, fiddle
playing competitions, dancing etc.)

November

Christmas Parade (celebrating the start of Christmas), many places
including Hollywood and Coronado
Christmas Tree Lighting (traditional ceremony of lighting the Christmas
candles), many places including Riverside, Ferndale and Fortuna
Winterfest, Solvang, Sacramento

November/
December

Santa Claus Parade, San Francisco
Old Town Christmas Parade, San Diego
California International Marathon, Sacramento
Las Posadas (candlelit procession), Los Angeles
Newport Harbor Christmas Boat Parade (parade of boats decorated for
Christmas), Newport Beach, Marina del Rey, etc.
Festival of Lights/Mammoth Mountain Winter Carnival (light and laser
show, ice castles, entertainment, food), Mammoth Lakes

December

Food and Drink

If you do not wish to eat in restaurants (see entry) because of lack of time
or money, you will not go hungry. Typical American snacks – hamburgers, hot dogs and pizzas – can be obtained almost everywhere.

Snacks

Most English people are today familiar with hamburgers, a ring of
minced meat, usually beef, perhaps flavoured with onion or cheese and
sandwiched within a roll.

Hamburgers

A hot dog consists of a sausage with mustard, sandwiched between the
two halves of a long roll.

Hot dogs

Pizza consists of a base of thin pastry which is garnished with tomato
sauce, slices of sausage, herbs and cheese and is often eaten hot.

Pizzas

In coffee shops, drug stores and lunch counters a favourite quick snack

Sandwiches

is a sandwich with corned beef, roast beef or pastrami served on rye bread with a gerkin, together with a cup of coffee.

Drinks
At breakfast and even at other meals the Americans drink lightly roasted and thin coffee or "postum" (caffeine free coffee). A second cup of coffee, or tea (made with teabags) is often provided without further charge. Drinking chocolate and soft drinks, such as cola, tonic or fruit juice, sodas, club sodas (plain carbonated water) or milk and milk shakes, can be obtained everywhere. These are often served "iced" unless otherwise ordered. Root beer, which was originally made of the root and bark of trees and manufactured after fermentation into a slightly alcoholic drink, can often be obtained in drug stores and from automatic machines. It is now produced from water, sugar, dark dye and various spices, is no longer alcoholic and at first taste not very attractive. Beer is always served cold and is rather lighter than the beers found in Great Britain; it is served by the glass, stein, seidel, schooner or pitcher. Brands often encountered are Budweiser, Schlitz, Falstaff, Pabst, Busch, Lone Star, Coors, La Crosse and Miller as well as the popular and expensive imported beers. Before a meal it is usual to drink a cocktail, a mixed drink based on gin, vodka, vermouth or rum which is often given a fanciful name. Spirits (liquors) favoured by the Americans are: whiskey (Bourbon, Scotch, Canadian, Rye, Irish or blended), vodka, gin, rum, brandy. In restaurants water, generally ice cold, is provided free with meals.

Wine
See entry

Getting to California

Most visitors to California come by air either on direct flights from London and other airports or go first to New York and fly on from there. There are services from New York and other American towns to San Diego, Sacramento, Oakland, and to Palm Springs. Many Californian towns have air services to other places in America (see A to Z Los Angeles, San Diego and San Fransisco, and Practical Information, Air Travel). Most US air companies offer discounts of one sort or another on flights.

Change
Before you begin your journey you should make provision for small payments (see Tipping, Post, Telephone and Telegraph, Taxis) by having sufficient change with you, especially notes of one and five dollars, as proffering large denomination bank notes can cause difficulty and incurs the risk of fraud.

Hotels and Motels

The major cities – Los Angeles, San Francisco and San Diego – are well supplied with hotels; prices however tend to be high compared with accommodation charges in smaller places.

Prices
The prices given are for a double room per night and are illustrative only:
Luxury hotels: over $200; $$$$
High amenity hotels and motels: $150–$200; $$$
Good quality hotels: $100–$150; $$
Reasonably priced hotels: $60–$100; $

No charge is made for children occupying the same room as their parents; however, additional adults do incur an extra charge.

There is a state-wide Sales Tax and an Occupancy Tax which varies from place to place; together they add 15–20 per cent to the bill.

Only in exceptional circumstances is the cost of breakfast included in the price of the room.

Many of California's hotels and motels belong to one of the major American chains, and it is possible to obtain vouchers for these at favourable prices from their agents in Europe. Hotel vouchers can also be obtained, or rooms booked in advance at travel agents.

Chains

Overnight bookings can often be made quoting a credit card number. Many hotels and motels, particularly those belonging to one or other of the hotel chains, have freephone reservation facilities. Where a listed hotel has such a facility, the freephone number (prefix 800) is given. When calling from within the United States but outside the state of California, dial 1 before dialling 800.

Reservations

Best Western; tel. (800) 5281234
Comfort Inns; tel. 800–4–CHOICE
Days Inn; tel. (800) 3252525
Hilton; tel. (800) 4458667 or 800–HILTONS
Holiday Inn; tel. 800–HOLIDAY
Howard Johnson; tel. (800) 6542000
Hyatt; tel. (800) 2331234
La Quinta Inns; tel. (800) 5315900
Marriott; tel. (800) 2289290
Quality Inn; tel. (800) 2285151
Radisson; tel. (800) 3333333
Ramada Inn; tel. 800–2–RAMADA or (800) 2282828
Red Lion Hotels & Inns; tel. (800) 5478010
Sheraton; tel. (800) 3253535
The Ritz-Carlton; tel. (800) 2413333
Travelodge; tel. (800) 2553050
Vagabond Inn; tel. (800) 5221555
Westin Hotels & Resorts; tel. (800) 2283000

Hotel and motel chains with freephone reservation facilities

Hotel reservations at special tariffs (all categories) for Los Angeles, San Diego and San Francisco can be made by telephoning 1–800–964–6835.

Special tariffs

In the US as also elsewhere, "Bed and Breakfast" accommodation (B&B) is becoming an increasingly popular alternative to spending the night in a hotel. For accommodation with character and personal service, privately-run houses are recommended. Whilst Bed and Breakfast accommodation may be no less expensive than a hotel, it has clear compensations, ranging from romantic historical buildings with antique furnishings where the owner's living room doubles as hotel lobby, to charming country houses in idyllic settings, simple cottages and Bed & Breakfast Hotels. A list of such accommodation is available from:

Bed and Breakfast

California Association of Bed & Breakfast Inns,
2715 Porter Street, Soquel CA 95073
A brochure can be obtained from the California Office of Tourism, Dept. B & B, 801 K Street, Suite 1600, Sacramento, CA 95814; tel. (916) 3222881.

A selection of accommodation

Holiday Inn Select, 801 Truxton Avenue, $, tel. (661) 3231900, Fax –2844. Next to the Bakersfield Convention Center, this elegant new hotel has a generous 259 rooms. It is an ideal place to spend a night or two if you are travelling from south to north.

Bakersfield

Hotels and Motels

Calistoga

The Mount View Hotel, 1457 Lincoln Ave., $-$$, tel. (800) 8166877. It is well worth stopping over in this simple, but comfortable hotel (22 rooms and 8 suites) on the main street of Calistoga, a town famous for its wine. Annexed to the hotel is a mineral bath, also offering fango packs and mud baths.

Carmel

Mission Ranch, 26270 Dolores St., $-$$$$, tel. (800) 5388221. Noisy feasts and weddings had been held in these old buildings for over 130 years, until they started to become dilapidated in the 1980s. The ranch was then bought by Clint Eastwood, who restored it to create a homely inn with 31 rooms.

Catalina Island

The Zane Grey Hotel, 199 Chimes Tower Rd, $$, tel. (562) 5100966. Former home of the writer Zane Grey; 17 rooms and a magnificent sea view.

Dana Point

★The Ritz Carlton Laguna Niguel, 33533 Ritz-Carlton Drive (off Pacific Highway), $$$$, tel. (949) 2402000. Very expensive luxury hotel complex in a magnificent setting looking down over the Pacific, with all imaginable sport and leisure facilities. Throughout the day, a piano player conjures up an atmosphere to suit these distinctive buildings.

Eureka

The Carter House, 301 L St, $-$$$, tel. (707) 4451390. Thirty-four generous rooms, furnished with antiques in three Victorian houses, some with their own whirlpool and fireplace. Good restaurant and wine cellar with a wide selection. Magnificent view of the Marina.

The Eureka Inn, 518 Seventh St., $$, tel. (800) 8624906. In the centre of the old town of Eureka, this Tudor-style building has 105 rooms. The lobby is impressive, with massive wooden beams, leather sofas and a large fireplace. In the evenings a blues or jazz band plays in the Rathskeller Pub.

Mammoth Lakes

Sierra Lodge, 3540 Main Street, $-$$, tel. (760) 9348881. This comfortable, relatively reasonably priced mountain hotel is situated in the immediate vicinity of several restaurants in Mammoth Lakes. The rooms, which are all large, have kitchen facilities and a balcony with a view of the mountains. Guests can relax in the open-air whirlpool.

Long Beach

Travelodge Hotel, Resort & Marina, 700 Queensway Drive (corner of Panorama Drive), $$, tel. (562) 4357676. Moderately priced, renovated hotel situated on the bay; swimming pool and tennis courts.

Los Angeles
Downtown

★Los Angeles Athletic Club, 431 W. Seventh Street, $$$, tel. (213) 6252211, (800) 7529232. This sports club with its long tradition and 72 tastefully furnished hotel rooms (some of them luxury) on the upper floors not only provides a good base for those staying in Downtown Los Angeles on business, but also for tourists passing through. Facilities include a well-equipped fitness center, various sports equipment, two swimming pools and restaurants.

The Westin Bonaventura Hotel, 404 S Figueroa St (corner of 4th St), $$$, tel. (213) 6241000. This hotel, with its five mirror-glass silos, is an architectural feature of the town centre. Although chiefly used by travellers on business, it is worth seeing.

The Biltmore Hotel, 506 S Grand Ave (corner 5th St) $$$, tel. (213) 6241011. Also regarded as one of the sights, this Beaux-Arts style hotel, built in 1923, has 700 rooms. The old entrance on Pershing Square is particularly impressive.

Hollywood

Radisson Hollywood Roosevelt Hotel, 7000 Hollywood Blvd. (between Highland and La Brea Aves), $$, tel. (800) 4238262. Celebrities from the world of films, art and literature used to meet here, among them Errol Flynn, Ernest Hemingway and Salvador Dali. Its lobby, two storeys high and built in Spanish colonial style with wall paintings, is well worth seeing, as is its large swimming pool.

Château Marmont Hotel, 8221, Sunset Blvd. (corner of Crescent Heights Boulevard), $$$, tel. (323) 6561010. This building, dating from 1927, resembles a fortress, which may explain its appeal for Greta Garbo. It has been carefully restored, preserving the patina of past times, and its 64 rooms and suites still attract celebrities.

★The Beverly Hills Hotel, 9641 Sunset Blvd, $$$$, tel. (310) 2762251. This luxurious "rose-pink palace" has attained symbolic value for the hedonistic lifestyle of the residents of the exclusive area of Beverly Hills. Surrounded by tropical vegetation, it has a rich tradition and offers every service imaginable for a (very expensive) luxury hotel. However, it is well worth having a look, which costs nothing (!). — Beverly Hills

Hotel Bel Air, 701 Stone Canyon Rd, $$$$, tel. (310) 4721211. This extremely exclusive hotel offers complete seclusion in the centre of Los Angeles, at great expense. The 92 rooms have open fireplaces and in the extensive grounds there is a lake with swans and a waterfall. — Bel Air

Barnabey's, 3501 Sepulveda Blvd. (corner of Rosecrans Ave), Manhattan Beach, $$–$$$$, tel. (310) 5458466. Elegant Victorian-style hotel (124 rooms) with marble statues, antiques and a swimming pool in the garden. Near the airport. — Manhattan Beach

The Stanford Inn by the Sea, Coast Highway 1 (not far from the Comptche-Ukiah Road), $$$, tel. (800) 3118884. On a hill overlooking Mendocino Bay, this luxurious hotel with its 23 rooms and 1 suite is surrounded by garden terraces bright with flowers. Llamas and swans and a pool surrounded by tropical plants conjure up an idyllic atmosphere and the service is excellent. — Mendocino

Martine Inn, 255 Oceanview Blvd., $$–$$$, tel. (831) 3733388. This small hotel is situated high above the Pacific Grove cliffs. The rooms have sea views or, if facing away from the sea, an open fireplace. — Monterey Peninsula

Beazley House, 1910 First St., Napa, $$–$$$, tel. (800) 5591649. Eleven luxurious rooms in a former turn-of-the-century vine-growing estate; a bed and breakfast inn built in colonial style with plenty of atmosphere and personal service. — Napa

Hyatt Newporter, 1107 Jamboreea Rd (off Pacific Highway), $$$, tel. (949) 6441700. Large hotel complex with golf course, tennis courts, pool and sauna. Concerts are held in the open-air auditorium every Friday in summer. — Newport Beach

The Ritz Carlton, 68–900 Frank Sinatra Drive, Rancho Mirage (near Palm Springs), in summer $, in winter $$$$, tel. (760) 3218282. This luxury hotel has elegantly furnished rooms with beautiful views, being built on a hillside amongst well-kept gardens. The cooled pool is particularly soothing in the desert heat of summer. — Rancho Mirage

★Hartley House, 700 Twenty Second St., Sacramento, $$, tel. (800) 8315806. Turn-of-the-century house, lovingly cared for, with comfortable, stylish living rooms, and five romantic rooms. In the evening, guests are made welcome with classical music, freshly baked cookies and, at times, open fires. Breakfast is served by the owner in person. — Sacramento

Fountain Suites Hotel, 321 Bercut Drive, $$, tel. (800) 7671777. This modern hotel in the centre of Sacramento (300 rooms) is ideal for business people, having several conference rooms, and also offers good service for passing tourists.

The Delta King, 1000 Front Street, Old Sacramento, $$, tel. (800) 825-5464. Very special overnight accommodation can be experienced on this restored 1920s paddle steamer, which has been restored into a floating hotel with 44 luxury rooms. It is docked in Old Sacramento harbour.

San Diego
Downtown

Heritage Park Inn, 2470 Heritage Park, $–$$$, tel. (760) 2996832. Not far from San Diego old town, this Victorian house, built in 1889 is furnished with antiques, and has nine rooms, offering bed and breakfast.

Coronado

★Hotel del Coronado, 1500 Orange Avenue, $$$–$$$$, tel. (760) 5228000. This luxury hotel, built in 1888, was made famous by the film "Some Like it Hot" with Marilyn Monroe, Jack Lemmon and Tony Curtis. Numerous state presidents and other famous people have stayed in this hotel (690 rooms) directly by the sea. The white building with its red-roofed towers looks like a castle (see A to Z: San Diego).

La Jolla

The Bed and Breakfast Inn at La Jolla, 7753 Draper Ave., La Jolla, $–$$$$, tel. (760) 4562066. Romantic hotel with fascinating architecture and 16 rooms, all furnished differently. This luxury establishment offers beautiful views of the Pacific and the formal gardens and terrace.

San Luis Obispo

★Madonna Inn, 100 Madonna Road, $–$$, tel. (800) 5439666. This world-famous hotel complex is worth a detour. Each of its 109 rooms is fancifully decorated, with a different theme, so there is something for every taste: romantic honeymooners, spoilt European guests, and those just passing through.

San Francisco
Union Square

★The Westin St. Francis, Union Square, 335 Powell Street, $$$$, tel. (415) 3977000, 1192 rooms, 83 suites. Traditional grand hotel in the heart of the city with old-world charm. The splendid hotel lobby with its black marble statues and crystal chandeliers is most impressive. The rooms are furnished with genuine antiques and provide magnificent views of the financial district skyline. When it opened in 1904, the St. Francis was the largest and most elegant hotel in the USA west of the Mississipi. The latest in a series of extensions, the new hotel tower was built in 1972. From the 32nd floor you can see the whole city centre, as far as Fisherman's Wharf. A special feature of the hotel is its "money wash" (coin-cleaning service) which was introduced in 1938, to save the ladies' white gloves from getting dirty.

Plenty of crowned heads have stayed in the Hotel St. Francis, in addition to US presidents and showbusiness personalities.

Sir Francis Drake, 450 Powell St., $$$, tel. (415) 3927755. A somewhat more attractively priced alternative, just around the corner. European-style elegance with new baroque elements, gothic windows, marble walls and murals in the lobby depicting the life of the eponymous discoverer. The 417 rooms have furniture made from mahogony and cherry wood.

Marriott Hotel, 55 Forth St., $$$$, tel. (800) 2289290. When it opened in

1989 critics of this architecturally individualistic colossus south of Union Square dubbed it the "Jukebox". Facilities include a swimming pool, fitness center, ballroom, Japanese restaurant and several bars.

Park Hyatt San Francisco, 333 Battery St., $$$–$$$$, tel. (800) 2231234. This elegant hotel at the Embarcadero Center has 323 rooms, most of which have a magnificent view of the city and bay, and offers the kind of service to be expected of a luxury hotel. The lobby has an impressive bronze sculpture, reaching up three storeys.

Financial District/Chinatown

Holiday Inn at Chinatown, 750 Kearny St., $$$, tel. (800) 4248292. This 27-storey hotel towers up between Financial District and Chinatown, and has an open-air swimming pool at the top. Its 566 rooms have impressive views of the city. The hotel owes its special charm to its blend of oriental features and western standards.

Inn at the Opera, 333 Fulton Street, $$–$$$, tel. (415) 8638400. Famous opera singers such as Luciano Pavarotti have stayed in this small (46 rooms) but elegant luxury hotel not far from the Opera House. The rooms are decorated in pastel colours and have large baths.

Civic Center

★The Ritz-Carlton San Francisco, 600 Stockton at California Street, $$$$, tel. (415) 2967465. It is worth going to see this monumental luxury hotel, built at the turn of the century in neo-classical style, and recently restored. Genuine antiques, valuable carpets on the marble floors, piano music at afternoon tea. One of Nob Hill's grand hotels.

Nob Hill

The Bayberry Inn, 111 West Valerio St., $–$$, tel. (805) 68231099. Playfully romantic inn with eight rooms, named after different kinds of berry.

Santa Barbara

The Inn at Pasatiempo, 555 Highway 17, Pasatiempo Drive, $$, tel. (831) 4235000, (800) 8342546, Fax 4261737. This rustic, relatively large hotel is reached on Highway 17, direction San Jose/Oakland. Guests can eat well in Peachwood's Grill and Bar, entertainment is provided at weekends, and there is a small swimming pool and a golf course nearby.

Santa Cruz

Shangri-La Hotel, 1301 Ocean Ave (corner of Arizona Ave), $$$, tel. (562) 3942791. Idyllic hotel in the centre of Santa Monica, with 55 rooms, most overlooking Palisades Park and the ocean.

Santa Monica

Miramar Sheraton Hotel, 101 Wilshire Blv (corner of Ocean Ave), $$, tel. (319) 3943731. This affordable hotel with 310 rooms is very popular with European tourists.

Original architecture in San Francisco: "The Jukebox" (Marriott Hotel)

The Lodge at Pebble Beach, 17 Mile Drive, on Monterey Peninsula

The Sovereign Hotel, 205 Washington Ave (between Ocean Ave and 4th St), $$, tel. (562) 3959921. This small hotel, designed by Julia Morgan, the architect of Hearst Castle, pleasantly combines traditional and modern features.

Santa Rosa

Hotel La Rose, 308 Wilson St., $–$$, tel. (800) 5276738. This historic house, dating from 1906, has 49 cosy rooms (breakfast included) with European turn-of-the-century charm, at acceptable prices. This is an ideal base for visiting the Sonoma Valley vineyards. The hotel restaurant "Josef's" with its French cuisine is recommended.

Solvang

The Chimney Sweep Inn, 1554 Copenhagen Drive, $–$$, tel. (800) 8246444. Quiet, romantic guesthouse with 22 rooms in the main building and six cottages with bathroom and kitchen ($$–$$$), an idyllic garden with waterfalls and a mineral bath.

Yosemite National Park

The Ahwahnee, in Yosemite Valley by the Merced River, $$$$, tel. (559) 2524848. Like an impregnable fortress, blending harmoniously with the spectacular landscape, this popular and expensive mountain hotel, which has 123 rooms, has to be booked well in advance. Magnificent views of the Yosemite waterfalls and Glacier Point.

Wawona Hotel, at Mariposa Grove of Giant Sequoias, $, tel. see above. This traditional hotel, built in Victorian style and classified as a historical monument, has been in business for over a hundred years. The 50 rooms with bath and 54 with shower are relatively good value. There is an adjacent golf course and swimming pool.

Yountville

★Vintage Inn, 6541 Washington Street, Yountville, $$$, tel. (707) 9441112, 80 rooms. Ideal for honeymoons, this romantic hotel, built in country house style, is situated in a vine-growing estate, and each guest is welcomed with a bottle of white wine. The large rooms all have fire-places and the facilities include a swimming pool and tennis courts.

Information

California Trade and Commerce Agency, Division of Tourism
801 K Street, Suite 1600, Sacramento, CA 95814
Tel. (916) 3222881, Fax –3402
Internet address: http://www.gocalif.ca.gov.
(detailed information on all regions)

Central
Information Office
in California

Visitor Information Centers in California

CofC = Chamber of Commerce; VB = Visitors Bureau
C & VB = Convention & Visitors Bureau
VB & C = Visitors Bureau & Convention

Abbreviations

Anaheim/Orange County V & CB, 800 W. Katella Ave.
Anaheim, CA 92803, tel. (714) 7658888, Fax 9918963

Anaheim

Greater Bakersfield C & VB, 13–25 East St.
Bakersfield, CA 93302, tel. (661) 3255051, Fax –7074

Bakersfield

Barstow Area CofC, 409 East Frederick St.
Barstow, CA 92311, tel. (760) 2568617, Fax 2567675

Barstow

Berkeley CofC, 1834 University Avenue, 1st Floor
Berkeley, CA 94703, tel. (510) 5497000, Fax 6442052

Berkeley

Beverly Hills VB, 239 S.Beverly Drive
Beverly Hills, CA 90212, tel. (310) 2481015, Fax –20

Beverly Hills

Big Bear Lake Association, PO Box 1936
Big Bear Lake, CA 92315, tel. (760) 4346093, Fax 4346056

Big Bear Lake

Bishop CofC, 690 North Main Street
Bishop CA 93513, tel. (760) 8738405, Fax –6999

Bishop

Buena Park C & VB, 6280 Manchester Blvd., Suite 102
Buena Park, CA 90621, tel. (714) 5210261, Fax –851

Buena Park

Carlsbad C & VB, PO Box 1246
Carlsbad, CA 92008, tel. (760) 4346093, Fax 9319153

Carlsbad

Catalina Island Cof C and VB, PO Box 217
Avalon, CA 90704, tel. (562) 5101520, Fax –7606

Catalina

Crescent City – Del Norte County CofC, 1001 Front St.
Crescent City, CA 9531, tel. (707) 4643174, Fax –9676

Crescent City

Dana Point CofC, P.O. Box 12
Dana Point, tel. (949) 4961555, Fax –5321

Dana Point

Death Valley National Monument Information Office
Death Valley, CA 92328, tel. (760) 7862331, Fax –3283

Death Valley

Eureka/Humboldt County CofC, 1034 Second Sreet
Eureka, CA 95501, tel. (707) 4435097, Fax –5115

Eureka

Information

Fresno	Fresno City and County C & VB, 808 M St. Fresno, CA 93721, tel. (559) 2330836, Fax 4450122
Grass Valley	Nevada County CofC, 248 Mill St. Grass Valley, CA 95945, tel. (530) 2734667 and (800) 6554667
Laguna Beach	Laguna Beach Hospitality Association and CofC, 357 Glenneyre Laguna Beach, CA 92651, tel. (949) 4997229, Fax 4970105
Lake Tahoe	Lake Tahoe Visitors Authority, PO Box 7300 Incline Village, NV 89452, tel. (775) 8313993, Fax –9172
Lassen County	Lassen County CofC, PO Box 338 Susanville, CA 96130, tel. (530) 2574323
Lompoc	Lompoc Valley CofC, 1115 "I" Street. Lompoc, CA 93438, tel. (805) 7364567
Lone Pine	Lone Pine CofC, PO Box 749, CA 93545, tel. (760) 8764444
Long Beach	Long Beach Area C & VB, One World Trade Center, Suite 300 Long Beach, CA 90831, tel. (562) 4363645, Fax 4355653
Los Angeles	Los Angeles C & VB, 633 West 5th Street, Suite 6000 Los Angeles, CA 90071, tel. (323) 6247300, Fax 624–9746 685 S. Figueroa St. (Corner of Wilshire Blv.), tel. (213) 6898822
Mammoth Lakes	Mammoth Lakes VB, PO Box 48, Mammoth Lakes, CA 83546, tel. (760) 9342712, Fax –7066
Modesto	Modesto C & VB, PO Box 844 Modesto, CA 95353, tel. (209) 5775757, Fax –16486
Mono Lake	Mono Lake Committee Information Center PO Box 29 Lee Vining, CA 93541, tel. (760) 6476595
Monterey	Monterey Peninsula CofC and V & CB, 380 Alvarado St. Monterey, CA 93940, tel. (831) 6485360, Fax 6493502
Mount Shasta	Mount Shasta VB, 300 Pine Street Mount Shasta, CA 96067, tel. (530) 9264865, Fax –0976
Napa Valley	Napa Valley C & VB, 1310 Napa Town Center Napa CA 94559, tel. (707) 2267459, Fax 2552066
Oakland	Oakland C & VB, 1000 Broadway, Suite 200 Oakland CA 946074020, tel. (510) 8399000, Fax –5924
Oxnard	Oxnard Visitors Bureau 400 Esplanade Drive, Suite 100 Oxnard, CA 93030, tel. (805) 4858833
Palm Springs	Palm Springs Tourism, 401 S. Pavilion Palm Springs, CA 92262, tel. (760) 7788415, Fax 3238279
Palo Alto	Palo Alto CofC, 325 Forest Ave. Palo Alto, CA 94301, tel. (650) 3243121
Pasadena	Pasadena C & VB, 171 S. Los Robles Ave. Pasadena, CA 91101, tel. (626) 7959311, Fax –9656
Redding	Redding C & VB, 777 Auditorium Drive, Redding, CA 96001, tel. (530) 2254100, Fax –4354

Riverside C & VB, 3443 Orange St.
Riverside CA 92501, tel. (909) 7877950, Fax –4949

Riverside

Sacramento C & VB, 1303 J St., Suite 1600
Sacramento, CA 95814, tel. (916) 2647777, Fax –7788

Sacramento

Salinas Area CofC, PO Box 1170
Salinas, CA 93902, tel. (831) 4247611

Salinas

San Bernadino C & VB,
201 North E Street, Suite 103, San Bernardino, CA 92401, tel. (909)
8893980, Fax 8885998

San Bernadino

San Diego C & VB, 401 B Street,
San Diego, CA 92101, tel. (760) 2323101, Fax 6969371

San Diego

International Visitor Center, 11 Horton Plaza,
San Diego, CA 92101, tel. (619) 2361212

San Francisco, C & VB, 201 3rd St., Suite 900
San Francisco, CA 94103, tel. (45) 9746900, Fax 2272602

San Francisco

San Jose C & VB, 333 W. San Carlos St., Suite 1000
San Jose, CA 95110, tel. (408) 2959600, Fax 2953937

San Jose

San Luis Obispo Visitor and Conference Bureau,
1041 Chorro St., Suite E,
San Luis Obispo, CA 93401, tel. (805) 5418000, Fax 5439498

San Luis Obispo

Santa Barbara Visitor and Conference Bureau,
510 State St., Suite A, Santa Barbara, CA 93101, tel. (805) 9669222,
Fax –1728

Santa Barbara

Santa Clara C & VB, 1850 Warburton Ave.
Santa Clara, CA 95050, tel. (408) 2449660, Fax 2447830

Santa Clara

Santa Cruz County Conference & Visitors Council, 701 Front St.
Santa Cruz, CA 95060, tel. (831) 4251234, Fax 1260

Santa Cruz

Santa Monica C & VB, 520 Broadway
Santa Monica, CA 90401, tel. (562) 3937593, Fax 3196273

Santa Monica

Solvang VB, 1511–A Mission Drive
Solvang, CA 93464, tel. (805) 6886144, Fax –8620

Solvang

Sonoma County C & VB, 5000 Roberts Lake Road, Suite A
Rohnert Park, CA 94928, tel. (707) 5247589, Fax 5247231

Sonoma

Sonoma Valley VB, 453 First St. East
Sonoma, CA 95476, tel. (707) 9961090, Fax –9212

Lake Tahoe Visitors Authority, P.O. Box 16299
South Lake Tahoe, CA 96151, tel. (530) 5445050

South Lake Tahoe

Stockton San Joaquin CofC, 445 W. Weber Ave., Suite 220
Stockton, CA 95203, tel. (209) 5472770, Fax 4665271

Stockton

North Lake Tahoe CofC, PO Box 5578
Tahoe City, CA 96730, tel. (530) 5833494, Fax 5814081

Tahoe City

Ukiah CofC, 495 East Perkins St.
Ukiah, CA 95482, tel. (707) 4624705, Fax 2088

Ukiah

Vallejo   Vallejo C & VB, 301 Georgia St., Suite 270
Vallejo, CA 94590, tel. (707) 6423653, Fax 6442206

Ventura   Ventura V & CB, 89–C S. California St.
Ventura, CA 93001, tel. (805) 6482075, Fax –2150

Insurance

It is essential to take out short-term health and accident insurance when visiting the USA, since the costs of medical treatment are high. It is advisable to have baggage insurance and (particularly if you have booked a package holiday) cancellation insurance. Legal protection and third party liability insurance are also to be recommended. Arrangements can be made through your travel agent or insurance company; many companies organising package holidays now include insurance as part of the deal.

Within the United States foreign visitors can effect insurance through the following companies:

American International Underwriters,
777 South Figueroa,
Los Angeles, CA 90017.

Address in the UK:
120 Fenchurch Street,
London WC3M 5BP.

Language

Differences abound between British and American usage. Some of the more commonly encountered are listed below:

British	American
appointment	date
attractive, dainty	cute
autumn	fall
bill	check
biscuit	cookie, cracker
bonnet (of car)	hood
boot (of car)	trunk
boot polish	shoeshine
braces	suspenders
buffer	bumper
caravan	trailer
chemist (shop)	drugstore
Christian name	first name
cinema	movies (movie theater)
cloakroom	checkroom
cupboard	closet
eiderdown	comforter
first floor	second floor
flat	apartment
fortnight	two weeks
gangway	aisle
glasses (spectacles)	eyeglasses
graduation (university, etc.)	commencement
ground floor	first floor
holiday	vacation
label	sticker

British	American
lift	elevator
lorry	truck
luggage	baggage
maize	corn
nappy	diaper
past	after
pavement	sidewalk
petrol	gas, gasoline
platform	track
policeman	cop
post	mail
post code	zip code
railway	railroad/railway
refrigerator	icebox
repair	fix
return ticket	round trip ticket
ring up, telephone	call
rubber	eraser
second floor	third floor
shop	store
single ticket	one-way ticket
subway	underpass
summer time	daylight saving time
surname	last name
tap	faucet
tin	can
toilet	ladies/men's room
	powder/rest room
torch	flashlight
tram	streetcar
trousers	pants
trunk call	long-distance call
undercut	tenderloin
underground	subway
viewpoint, viewing platform	observatory
Whitsun	Pentecost

Spanish names

Spanish is the second language of the State of California. In the southern part there are more than 3 million Spanish speakers, especially Mexicans. Spanish is also of geographical importance and is met in many variations, for instance in city and street names.

The five largest Californian cities, Los Angeles, San Diego, San Francisco, San José and Sacramento bear Spanish names. In the following list a few of the most important Spanish words are given:

Spanish	English	Spanish	English
água	water	caliente	hot
alameda	poplar hedge	camino real	royal road
álamo	poplar	cañada	valley
alta	high	casa	house
arroyo	workhorse	cerrito	little hill
borego	lamb	cerro	hill
brea	pitch	cienega	marsh, bog
buena vista	fine view	colorado	red
calabasa	pumpkin	costa	coast
diablo	devil	nevada	covered with snow
dos rios	two rivers		
el dorado	the golden land	oro	gold

Spanish	English	Spanish	English
encina	oak	oso	bear
encinita	little oak	palo alto	high tree
escondido	hidden	pescadero	fishing ground
flora (flores)	flower (flowers)	pinos	firs
fresno	ash	playa	beach
gorda	wide	potrero	meadow
hermoso	beautiful	punta	point
hondo	deep	rio	river
laguna	lagoon, lake	salinas	saltmarshes
loma	low hill	san, santa	saint
lobo	wolf	seco	dry
los gatos	the cats	sierra	mountain chain
madera	wood	soledad	loneliness
mariposa	butterfly	sur	south
merced	pretty	tiburón	shark
mesa	table mountain	toro	bull
molino	mill	trinidad	trinity
monte	hedge or thicket	viña	vineyard
morro	round stone block	vista	view, sight

Leisure Parks

California is the birthplace of the large, commercially operated leisure and amusement park. This is where the legendary cartoonist Walt Disney set up Disneyland, now imitated all over the world, as long ago as 1955.

The main leisure parks are described in the A to Z section, Disneyland under Anaheim, Knott's Berry Farm under Buena Park, Sea World under San Diego, Six Flags Marine World under Vallejo and Legoland, opened in 1999, under Carlsbad.

Six Flags California

The film company Time Warner established the Six Flags California theme park in the mountains north of Los Angeles in Valencia (Santa Clarita), 26101 Magic Mountain Pkwy, tel. (805) 2554815. The Park's attractions include the Batman Stunt Show and the Laser and Special Effects Show. Recently the USA's largest white-knuckle ride was opened here. Known as "Superman: The Escape", it reaches a breathtaking 160 km (100 mi.) per hour. The new water park, Six Flags Hurricane Harbor is another recent addition. Open daily from 10am, April to 1st October, and at weekends and on public holidays during the winter months.

Medical Assistance

Information can be obtained from hotel or motel reception desks or from local hospitals (see Emergencies).

Motoring

AAA

Americal Automobile Association (AAA), Headquarters, 1000 AAA Drive, Heathrow, FL 327465063, tel. (407) 4447000.

The AAA is the largest of America's automobile clubs with offices throughout the country, giving out brochures, lists of accommodation

and other information, although they do not send such information abroad.
If you need help, telephone 1–800–AAA–HELP.

Regional AAA Offices in California:
California State Automobile Association, 150 Van Ness Ave., PO Box 1860 San Francisco, CA 94102, tel (415) 5652012.
Automobile Club of Southern California, 2601 Figueroa St., T.A.B. 30432 Los Angeles (Downtown), CA 90007, tel. (213) 7413686.

Breakdowns

If you have a breakdown in a rented car (see Car Rental) you should immediately inform the rental firm and await further instructions. Towing away a car often is a very costly proceeding unless you are a member of the American Automobile Association (AAA) or a similar organisation which offers free repair and towing services. You will find in "Yellow Pages", under "Automobile Repairing Services", addresses and telephone numbers of firms which can repair the vehicle if it can be driven to their premises.

Rented car

Visitors bringing vehicles not made to US standards into the United States should ensure they are in good working order. While most big cities are likely to have a garage capable of carrying out repairs to foreign vehicles (see "Automobile Repair Services" in "Yellow Pages"), spare parts may not be readily available.
    See also Information, Automobile Clubs.

Vehicles from abroad

Accidents

Remain calm and polite. Keep a clear head and do the following things in order:

1 Secure the scene of the accident, i.e. switch on hazard lights, set up warning signs (flashing torch, red triangle, etc.) at a suitable distance.

2 Look after any injured person. Send for an ambulance if necessary.

3 Notify the police.

4 Note the names and addresses of others involved, and the registration number and make of other vehicles involved, together with names and numbers of insurance policies.
    The place and time of the accident and the address of the police station involved are important.

5 Make sure that you obtain evidence. Write down the names and addresses of any witnesses not involved. Make sketches of the scene of the accident or, better still, take a few photographs from different angles.

6 Do not admit any blame for the accident or sign any written admission of responsibility.

Museums

For all the following museums see under the relevant place name in the A to Z section.

Museums

Berkeley	Judah L. L. Magnus Museum
	Phoebe Apperson Hearst Museum of Anthropology
	University of California Art Museum
Long Beach	Long Beach Museum of Art
Los Angeles	California State Museum of Science and Industry
	George C. Page Museum of La Brea Discoveries
	Los Angeles County Museum of Art
	Los Angeles County Museum of Natural History
	Museum of Afro-American History and Culture
	Museum of Contemporary Art and Temporary Contemporary
	Southwest Museum
Malibu	J. Paul Getty Museum
Oakland	Oakland Museum
Palm Springs	Palm Springs Desert Museum
Pasadena	Norton Simon Museum of Art
	Huntington Library, Huntington Gallery and Botanical Gardens
Palo Alto	Stanford Museum of Art
Sacramento	California State Historic Railroad Museum
	Crocker Art Museum
	Sutter's Fort State Indian Museum
San Diego	Museum of Contemporary Art
	Natural History Museum

Stylish ambience in the Crocker Art Gallery in Sacramento

Indian art in the M.H. de Young Museum in San Francisco

San Diego Museum of Art
La Jolla Museum of Contemporary Art
Scripps Aquarium Museum

Asian Art Museum	San Francisco
California Academy of Sciences	
California Palace of the Legion of Honor	
M. H. de Young Memorial Museum	
San Francisco Museum of Modern Art	
Egyptian Museum	San Jose
San Jose Historical Museum	
Santa Barbara Historical Society Museum	Santa Barbara
Santa Barbara Museum of Art	

Newspapers and Periodicals

Quality newspapers and magazines can be obtained only in the towns of Los Angeles, Sacramento, San Diego, San Francisco and San Jose. There are also numerous local newspapers where details of local events can be found. It is customary in the USA to purchase newspapers almost exclusively from automatic newspaper machines which can be found everywhere.

The most important daily newspapers in California are: Los Angeles: "Los Angeles Times", one of the leading dailies in the USA
San Francisco: "San Francisco Chronicle" and "San Francisco Examiner"

Daily newspapers

San Diego: "San Diego Union" and "San Diego Tribune"
San Jose: "San Jose Mercury News" (of which there is an electronic version known as the "Mercury Center")

Magazines
The monthly "Los Angeles Magazine" and the "California Magazine" (also published in Los Angeles) are very readable, as is the "San Francisco Magazine".

Opening Times

See Business Hours

Post and Telephone Services

As in Great Britain the postal and telephone services are run by separate undertakings. The US Post Office is responsible only for postal services (US Mail) including money transfer inland or abroad. Telephone and telegraph services are operated by private companies.

Post

Tariffs
Letters within the United States: 32 cents for the first ounce (28g) and 23 cents for each additional ounce; postcards: 20 cents.
Airmail letters to Europe: 60 cents for each half ounce (14g), 95 cents for the first ounce and 39 cents for each additional half ounce; postcards 50 cents; aerograms 45 cents.

Stamps
Visitors are advised to buy stamps at a post office, because in many hotels stamps from automatic machines cost more. It is advisable to purchase stamps in small places where the post offices tend to be in the centre; in cities it is often a long way to the nearest post office.

Post offices
City centre post offices in major cities are open 24 hours a day; elsewhere Mon.–Fri. 9am–5pm or 6pm, Sat. till noon.

Poste Restante
Within the United States the letters must be marked "general delivery" and can be collected at main post offices.

Postal codes
The postal code (zip code) is put after the name of the place and the shortened name of the state (for California CA). Each code consists of five digits.

Post boxes
Post boxes are blue with "US Mail" in white lettering.

Telephone

Because telephone and telegraph services in the US are privately operated, calls cannot be made from post offices.

Making a call
Local calls from a coin-operated box (in streets, hotels, drugstores, tobacconists, etc): wait for the dialling tone then insert 30 cents (for a three minute call) and dial the subscriber number. A further 25 cents must be inserted for each subsequent period of three minutes. (N.B. Hotels and motels often charge double or even three times the rate.)

Calls within the USA from a coin-operated box: dial 1 followed by the area code and subscriber number. The operator will come on the line and tell you how much to insert.

Reverse charge calls: no coins are needed, simply dial 0 and ask the operator for a "collect call". Assuming the recipient of the call agrees, it will be charged to their account.

International calls from a private phone: dial 011 for international calls followed by the country and local codes (omitting the 0 in the case of UK codes) and the subscriber number.

From a coin-operated box: dial 0 and follow the operator's instructions.

Some US telephones and subscriber numbers now incorporate letters of the alphabet as well as numeric digits.

From the UK to the USA	001	Dialling codes
From the USA to the UK	011 44	

At the beginning of 1999 many area codes in California were changed. Access codes
The codes for the main towns and areas are as follows: Sacramento 530 or 916, San Francisco 415 or 650, Los Angeles and area 323, 213, 310 or 562, San Diego 760 or 619.

For other Californian area codes see Hotels and Restaurants.

Slightly reduced rates apply between 5pm and 11pm, and considerably reduced rates between 11pm and 8am and at weekends. Off-peak tariffs

Phonecards have several advantages, particularly when making long distance and international calls (avoiding the often high cost of calling from a hotel while obviating the need for large quantities of small change). Cards of various sorts are available from a number of companies including: Phonecards

Chargecard from BT
AT & T Calling Card from AT & T
MCI Calling Card from MCI
Sprint Foncard from Sprint
T.N.C. Travel Card from T.N.C.

Most telegrams are nowadays sent by phone, there being very few Telegraph Offices. Companies specialising in overseas telegrams include Western Union which has offices in many hotels, railway stations and department stores. Others can be found listed in local telephone directories. Hotel reception desks will also handle telegrams. Telegrams

Public Holidays

As everywhere else in the United States of America, California has relatively few official public holidays, and even on these, with the exception of Easter Sunday, Christmas Day and New Year's Day, many businesses remain open. However, banks, exchange offices, government and municipal offices and schools remain closed. No extra day is added to the Christian holidays (Easter Sunday, Whit Sunday and Christmas Day).

Religious festivals excepted, the dates of most public holidays apart from Independence Day are fixed year by year. Usually the Monday immediately before or after the official date is chosen, thus creating a long weekend.

New Year's Day (January 1st); Martin Luther King Day (January 18th); Official holidays
Lincoln's Birthday (February 12th); Washington's Birthday (February

365

15th); Good Friday; Easter Sunday; Memorial Day/Decoration Day (Last Monday in May); Independence Day (July 4th); Labor Day (first Monday in September); Columbus Day (2nd Monday in October); Veterans Day (November); Thanksgiving (4th Thursday in November); Christmas Day (December 25th).

Radio and Television

Radio

Radio and television sets are provided in almost every hotel or motel room. Apart from news, live radio programmes are rarely transmitted. Most stations make use of records and tapes; some broadcast classical music but the great majority specialise in jazz and rock.

Some stations transmit programmes intended for one of the many ethnic groups in California, others broadcast news or music all day. Daily programmes can be found in the daily newspapers.

Television

The daily programme of the following television stations can also be found in the daily papers – the weekend programme in the weekend editions – (see Newspapers and Periodicals) which are often provided in hotel and motel rooms. The numerous transmitting stations in the United States are essentially run by three television companies: the National Broadcasting Company (NBC), the Columbia Broadcasting Company (CBS), and the American Broadcasting Company (ABC) which obtain most of their revenue from advertising. In addition almost every large town has a local station which generally transmits repeats of old material. If you wish to avoid the advertising slots (in peak hours every 15–20 minutes) you should switch to the state-run television station Public Broadcasting System (PBS) which normally transmits programmes without advertisements; in Los Angeles this is Channel 28 and in San Francisco Channel 9.

Railways

In view of the constantly dwindling rail traffic in the United States, tourists will seldom have the opportunity of using trains. In California, in addition to local trains from the stations of the large cities (except San Francisco which has no station and so it is necessary to use Oakland), there are still a number of useful connections. You can go from Oakland to the capital Sacramento, to Santa Barbara, Los Angeles and San Diego by rail. In addition there is a rail connection from Oakland/San Francisco or from Los Angeles to Chicago (journey time about 50 hours), and you can continue from there to New York. In 1993 Amtrak introduced "Sunset Limited", a transcontinental service between Los Angeles on the Pacific coast and Miama, Florida on the Atlantic coast, crossing, in all, eight US states with stops at Phoenix, El Paso, San Antonio, Houston, New Orleans, Mobile, Pensacola and Jacksonville. The journey takes 58 hours (information from local travel agents and Amtrak agents in the US and Europe).

Restaurants

There are an enormous number of restaurants in California, ranging from the most expensive high-class establishments with Americanised international cuisine, to the restaurants of country inns. Typically of America are "diners", which are reminiscent of railway dining cars, and drive-in restaurants where you can be served in your car by a "carhop" (generally a girl). No town lacks a snack bar in which hamburgers, frankfurters, pizzas and other typical American dishes are served. Seafood restaurants, most of which are situated on the coast, are especially to be recommended.

See entry; also A to Z section Sonoma, Napa and other places well known for their wines.

Wines

See entry.

Tips

It is advisable to book a table at the more expensive establishments, especially over long weekends and during the main holiday season. In most good restaurants, you will be asked whether you want to be in the "smoking" or "non-smoking" area before being shown to your seat.

Booking

Selected restaurants

JW's, 700 W Convention Way, tel. (714) 7508000. Imaginative international cuisine in a restaurant that calls to mind a library (booking advisable).

Anaheim

Yen Ching, 574 S Glassell St (corner of La Veta Ave), tel. (714) 9973300. Good Chinese dishes in contemporary surroundings.

The Hacienda, 1725 N College Ave (corner of 17th St.), Santa Ana, tel. (714) 5581304. Popular for weddings, with reasonably priced Mexican dishes.

Guild House, 1905 Eighteenth St., tel. (661) 3255478. For anyone staying in Bakersfield between June and September, lunch (good and cheap) at the Victorian Guild House should be tried (Mon.–Fri.) The honorary cooks (all profits are donated to a children's clinic) know just how to create a homely atmosphere.

Bakersfield

Basque restaurants: French/Basque cattle breeders settled in Bakersfield in the 19th c. and Basque food became a local speciality. The following two Basque restaurants are good value for money: Wool Growers (620 E 19th St., tel. (805) 3279584); Maitia's Basque Restaurant (tel. (661) 3244711).

★Pacific's Edge, Highway 1, tel. (831) 6243801. Situated high above the Pacific between Carmel and Big Sur, this restaurant is a popular meeting place for gourmets from all over the world and is very expensive. Konrad Adenauer, The Beatles, Madonna and the Emperor of Japan have all been here to sample the finest Californian cuisine made with fresh local produce.

Carmel

The Hog's Breath Inn, San Carlos Street (between 5th and 6th Avenue, tel. (831) 6251044. Very popular, comfortable restaurant with excellent food. Owned by the town's ex-mayor, Clint Eastwood.

Tuck Box English Room, Dolores Street/corner of 7th Street, tel. (831) 6246365. Good breakfast café, in a cosy cottage.

555 East, 555 East Ocean Blvd. (corner of Linden Ave), tel. (562) 4370626. Good traditional American cooking in an old-fashioned, darkened dining room.

Long Beach

L'Opera, 101 Pine Ave, tel. (562) 4910066. A turn-of-the-century bank building with green marble columns and modern lighting, where both classical and modern Italian dishes are served.

Restaurants

Los Angeles Downtown

★Checker's Restaurant, 535 S. Grand Ave (between 5th and 6th St. in Checker's Hotel, tel. (213) 6240000. Very elegant, expensive restaurant with excellent service and Californian cooking.

★Rex-II Ristorante, Olive/6th Sts., tel. (213) 6272300. One of California's most exclusive restaurants, in the elegant Oviatt building. Nouvelle Cuisine and Italian gourmet dishes for the most discerning tastes.

West of Downtown

Campanile, 624 S La Brea Ave. (between 6th St. and Wiltshire Blvd.), tel. (323) 9381447. This Spanish-style building with its glass roof once belonged to Charlie Chaplin and offers a romantic setting with good Californian cooking.

City Restaurant, 180 S La Brea Ave. (corner of 2nd St.), tel. (323) 9382155. Wide variety of international dishes served in a former warehouse.

Jackson's Farm, 439 N Beverly Drive, Beverly Hills, tel. (310) 2735578. Rustic American cooking in a farmhouse style restaurant.

Hollywood

Le Dôme, 8720 Sunset Blvd., tel. (310) 6596919. Lunchtime meeting place for film celebrities, with expensive French cuisine.

★Spago, 1114 Horn Ave. (side street off Sunset Blvd.). Famous chef Wolfgang Puck attracts not only famous actors, but also other gourmets who can afford an expensive culinary treat.

Cafe La Bohème, 8400 Santa Monica Blvd., tel. (323) 8482360. This guesthouse on two levels, with imaginative lighting and décor serves reasonably priced international dishes.

★The Belvedere, 9882 Little Santa Monica Blvd (in the Hotel Peninsula Beverly Hills), tel. (310) 7882306. Classic gourmet cuisine.

Toscana, 11633 San Vicente Blvd. (Brentwood), tel. (310) 8202448. Relatively reasonably priced, modern restaurant with good Italian cuisine.

Coco Plazzo, 8440 Sunset Blvd., W Hollywood, tel. (213) 8486000. Italian food cooked to perfection in the stylish and fashionable setting of the Mondrian Hotel.

Malibu

Granita, Malibu Colony Pllaza, 23725 W Malibu Rd (side street off Pacific Coast Highway). Mediterranean cuisine of the famous owner Wolfgang Puck (see Los Angeles, Spago), served in an artistically decorated inner room of neoclassical design.

Mammoth Lakes

Chart House, Old Mammoth Road, tel. (760) 9344526. Architecturally delightful restaurant with grills and a salad bar.

The Lakefront Restaurant, Twin Lakes Road, tel. (760) 9342442. Intimate ambience, ideal for special occasions. Good Californian cooking.

Matsu, Main St & Joaquin, tel. (760) 9348277. A taste of the Orient.

Ocean Harvest, Old Mammoth Road, tel. (760) 9348539. Fresh fish dishes served in this restaurant, with a glorious view over the mountains.

Monterey

Gilbert's Red Snapper, Fisherman's Wharf, tel. (831) 3753131. Very good fish restaurant.

Captain's Gig, Fisherman's Wharf, tel. (831) 3735559. Good value fish restaurant.

Whaling Station Inn, 763 Wave Street (near Cannery Row), tel. (831) 3733778. Rustic d,cor, good grilled fish.

Showley's Restaurant at Miramonte, 1327 Railroad Avenue, St. Helena, tel. (707) 9631200. Enjoy the culinary wealth of the Napa Valley in the homely atmosphere of this old country house, built in 1907. Proof of this restaurant's excellent value for money (main courses 13–20 $) is provided by the fact that many local people are regular customers. It serves Californian food with French, Italian, and even Mexican influences.

St. Helena

Vintners Court, 1600 Atlas Peak Road, Napa, tel. (707) 2575428. Award-winning restaurant with Californian cooking. Open Wed., Thu., Sat., 6pm–10.30pm. Seafood buffet on Fridays from 6pm onwards; brunch on Sundays.

Napa

Zapata, 3958 Bel Aire Plaza, Napa, CA 94558, tel. (707) 2548888. Restaurant with Mexican décor and cuisine; grill dishes.

Kitayama, 202 Bayview Pl (corner of Bristo St.), tel. (949) 7250777. Relatively good value, excellent Japanese meals, consisting of several courses.

Newport Beach

Five Feet, 328 Glenneyre St. (corner of Forest Ave), tel (715) 4974955. Modern Chinese establishment with open kitchen (very good; booking advisable).

Silver Dragon, 835 Webster St., tel. (510) 8933748. Excellent, reasonably priced Chinese restaurant. The giant prawns with almond-caramel sauce are unforgettable.

Oakland

Shangri La, 3363 Grand Avenue, tel. (510) 8399383. Situated by Lake Merrit, this restaurant offers a Mongolian buffet, on the "all you can eat" principle.

★Blue Coyote Grill, 445 N. Palm Canyon, tel. (760) 3271196. Mexican dishes, large portions, moderate prices – served in a cool garden restaurant. Colour scheme deep royal blue.

Palm Springs

Mexi Alfredo's, 292 E Palm Canyon Drive, tel. (760) 3201020. Very good Italian restaurant.

Billy Reed's 1800 N. Palm Canyon Drive, tel. (760) 3251946. Good home cooking in old-fashioned surroundings.

★Mi Place, 25 E Colorado Blvd., tel. (626) 7953131. Old Pasadena's most popular restaurant, with a large percentage of regular customers, offers excellent Italian cuisine at low prices (booking advisable) in a modern setting. The imaginative desserts are among the best and would satisfy any gourmet.

Pasadena

★Auberge Du Soleil, 180 Rutherford Hill Road, Rutherford, tel. (707) 9631211. From the terrace restaurant of this romantic hotel, built in Mediterranean style, there is a magnificent view of the vineyards and the Mayacama Mountains. Meals offered range from simple bar snacks to refined French-style gourmet dishes (main course 25–30 dollars) or complete meals for around $ 60.

Rutherford

Rio City Cafe, 1110 Front St, Old Sacramento, tel. (916) 4428226. This restaurant with its terrace occupies a picturesque position on the Sacramento River.

Sacramento

The Firehouse, 1112 Second St., Old Sacramento, tel. (916) 4424772. Complete meals are served in the elegant interior of this restored, former fire station, whilst more simple dishes can be enjoyed in the romantic courtyard.

Fuji, 2422 13th Street, tel. (916) 4464135. For 30 years, the "Fuji" has been a byword for fine Japanese cuisine, served by waitresses in kimonos.

Ristorante Piatti, 571 Pavilions Lane, tel. (916) 6498885. The best Italian restaurant in the town.

Garbeau's Dinner Theatre, 12401 Folsom Blvd. (by Highway 50), Rancho Cordova, tel. (916) 9856361. While you eat, be entertained by theatrical performances or songs from the musicals.

San Diego
Downtown

★Dobson's Bar & Restaurant, 956 Broadway Circle (Downtown), tel. (619) 2316771. Not far from the Horton Plaza, this popular gourmet restaurant is located in an elegant turn-of-the-century building. Meeting place for business people and local politicians (expensive).

★Rainwater's Kettner, 1202 Kettner Blvd., tel. (619) 2335757. Award-winning, expensive American cooking (e.g. steaks and "prime ribs") on the second floor of an historical building.

Bella Luna, 748 Fifth Avenue, tel. (760) 2393222. Small, inconspicuous Italian restaurant in the Gaslamp Quarter, with hearty Italian home cooking.

Alizé, 777 Front St., tel. (619) 2340411. Good Creole cuisine prepared by the chef, who spent some years on the French Caribbean islands of Martinique and Guadeloupe (expensive).

★The Fish Market & Top of the Market, 750 North Harbor Drive, tel. (619) 2323474. Two highly recommended fish restaurants: one simple, friendly establishment, and on the floor above the refined alternative, with a magnificent view towards Point Loma and the Coronado Bridge.

Trattoria La Strade, 702 Fifth Avenue, tel. (619) 2393400. Top Italian restaurant in the Gaslamp Quarter.

La Jolla

Marine Room, 2000 Spindrift Drive, tel. (619) 4597222. Recently renovated fish restaurant with sea view (expensive).

Trattoria Acqua, 1298 Prospect St., tel. (619) 4540709. Friendly, rustic establishment at La Jolla beach, serving good, relatively reasonably priced north Italian cuisine.

San Francisco
Fisherman's
Wharf

Alioto's, 8 Fisherman's Wharf, tel. (650) 6730183. Popular meeting place on the harbour with a view of the Golden Gate Bridge (booking necessary). Authentic Sicilian dishes have been cooked here since 1933.

Downtown

Harbor Village Restaurant, 4 Embarcadero Center, tel. (415) 7818833. Chinese restaurant with elegant décor and crystal chandeliers.

★La Folie, 2316 Polk St. (between Green and Union St.), tel. (415) 7765577. French cuisine for gourmets (expensive) in relaxed, informal surroundings.

★Postrio, 545 Post St. (in the Prescott Hotel, not far from Union Square), tel. (415) 7767825. Tables must be booked well in advance in this popular restaurant serving good Californian cooking.

The Dining Room, The Ritz-Carlton, Stockton St., tel. (415) 2967465. Elegant, stylish and expensive, this restaurant offers excellent French cuisine, an impressive wine cellar and accomodating service in a fine setting.

LuLu, 816 Folsom St. (between 4th and 5th St.), tel. (415) 4955775. One of the best, and comparatively reasonably priced restaurants in San Francisco. This artistically converted warehouse serves excellent fish dishes. Under the same roof is the LuLu Bis (four-course meals) and a small café.

Manora's Thai Cuisine, 1600 Folsom St. (corner of 12th St.) and 3226 Mission St. (South of Market; near Valencia St.), tel. (415) 8616224. Both these establishments are among the city's best Thai restaurants.

Imperial Palace, 919 Grant Avenue, tel. (415) 9828889. This 30-year-old establishment in the heart of Chinatown offers the best Cantonese cuisine in San Francisco: almost 100 good-value dishes or a seven-course meal for 17 $. | Chinatown

Osome, 1923 Fillmore St., tel. (415) 3462311. Good Japanese restaurant in Japantown. | Japantown

Rue de Paris, 19 North Market St., tel. (408) 2980704. Best, romantic French restaurant in Santa Clara Valley; moderate prices. | San José

77 Saint Peter, 71 N San Pedro St., tel. (408) 9718523. Stylish Italian restaurant with Mediterranean atmosphere representing good value for money.

Buona Tavola, 1037 Monterey St., tel. (805) 5458000. Award-winning north Italian cuisine. | San Luis Obispo

Cafe Roma, 1819 Osos St., tel. (805) 5416800. Romantic surroundings and good service with north Italian cuisine.

Imperial China Restaurant, 667 Marsh St., tel. (805) 5441668. Traditional Chinese restaurant.

Izzy Ortega's Mexican Restaurant & Cantina, 1850 Monterey St., tel. (805) 5433333. Family-friendly Mexican establishment.

Aldo's Italian Ristorante, 1031 State St., tel. (805) 9636637. Traditional Italian cuisine. | Santa Barbara

Brophy Bros. Clam Bar & Restaurant, Yacht Basin & Marina, tel. (805) 9664418. Good fish restaurant.

Joe's Cavern, 536 State Street, tel. (805) 9664638. One of Santa Barbara's longest-established (1928) restaurants.

Casablanca Restaurant, 101 Main St., tel. (831) 4269063. Magnificent views of Santa Cruz beach and Monterey Bay can be enjoyed from this romantic establishment. The "Casablanca" is famous for its extensive wine list and fish dishes. | Santa Cruz

Hollins House, 20 Clubhouse Drive (by Pasatiempo Golf Club), tel. (831) 4599177. Very good Californian cooking served in this former clubhouse with view over Monterey Bay.

LA Farm, 3000 W Olympic Blvd., tel. (315) 8290600. Restaurant with international cuisine at moderate prices in an office building. | Santa Monica

Restaurants

★Valentine, 3115 W Pico Blvd. (corner of 31st St.), tel. (310) 8294313. The owner of this restaurant is a native of Sicily and offers exclusive Italian cuisine in elegant, contemporary surroundings (very expensive; booking advisable).

Opus, 2425 W Olympic Blvd. (corner of 26th St.), tel. (310) 8292112. This wood-panelled, luxurious restaurant is reminiscent of a yacht and offers excellent fish dishes and French cuisine.

Röckenwagner, 2435 Main St. (between Ocean Park Blvd. and Hollister Ave; in the Edgemar village-like shopping complex), tel. (310) 3996504. Californian cooking and German bread and pastries.

Market Street, 72 Market St. (near Pacific Ave.), tel. (310) 3928720. This meeting point of artists and showbusiness people serves American food and was formerly the studio of the famous architect Frank Gehry.

Santa Rosa

Mixx, an American Bistro, 135 4th Street, tel. (707) 5731344. Very comfortable bistro with local cuisine and attentive service.

Josef's Restaurant & Bar, in the Hotel La Rose (see Hotels), 308 Wilson Street, tel. 5718664. Swiss chef Josef Keller knows his stuff: good European, especially French, cuisine.

Kenwood

Kenwood Restaurant & Bar, 9900 Sonoma Highway, tel. (707) 8336326. At weekends people from San Francisco flock to this small garden restaurant in Sonoma Valley, which offers excellent dishes, e.g. roast duck with orange sauce and wild rice, or rack of lamb with wild mushrooms.

Yosemite National Park

The Ahwahnee Dining Room, in the Yosemite Valley by the Merced River, tel. (559) 3721489. Large dining room with high ceilings and large

The Rio City Café facing the Sacramento River in the old town

picture windows set in a wildly romantic landscape (dress code must be observed).

Wawona Hotel Dining Room, not far from Mariposa Grove of Giant Sequoias, tel. (559) 3756556. Good home cooking in a comfortable establishment reminiscent of the Victorian era.

Shopping

See entry

Opening hours

Shopping streets such as those found in Europe exist only in a few large towns and tourist centres. Otherwise there are only very limited possibilities for shopping "downtown". However every self-respecting town can offer at least one "mall" (a very large, car-friendly shopping centre usually situated on the periphery), a market place, a "galleria", a flea market and a factory outlet.

While supermarkets are the principal retail outlets in smaller towns, the larger cities have a wide range of speciality shops. Addresses are listed in "Yellow Pages", copies of which are found in most hotel rooms.

Speciality shops

San Francisco in particular is a shoppers' paradise. The following is just a selection of the city's many shopping areas: The Anchorage, 2800 Leavenworth Street at Jefferson; The Cannery, 2801 Leavenworth Street, between Fisherman's Wharf and Aquatic Park; The Crocker Galleria, entrances on Post and Sutter Streets, between Montgomery and Kearny; Embarcadero Center, between Sacramento and Clay Streets, Battery Street and Justin Herman Plaza; Ghirardelli Square, 900 North Point at Larkin, near Fisherman's Wharf; Pier 39 (Embarcadero), two blocks east of Fisherman's Wharf; Rincon Center, 121 Spear Street; San Francisco Shopping Center, Market & Fifth Streets; south of Market Street (south of Market, SoMa).

San Francisco

Los Angeles' most famous shopping mile is the exclusive Rodeo Drive in Beverly Hills. You can also go on a shopping tour of Melrose Avenue between La Brea and Crescent Heights, Olvera Street in Los Angeles' El Pueblo, the Garment District south of downtown or Santa Monica Promenade

Los Angeles

Shopping malls and marketplaces include: Baldwin Hills Crenshaw Plaza (Westside), 3650 Martin Luther King Blvd.; Beverly Center (Westside), 8500 Beverly Blvd.; Broadway Plaza (Downtown), Seventh & Flower Streets; Century City Shopping Center and Marketplace (Westside), 10250 Santa Monica Blvd.; Glendale Galleria (The Valleys), 2148 Glendale Galleria; The Oaks, 22 W. Hillcrest Drive, Thousand Oaks; Westside Pavilion (Westside), 10800 W. Pico Blvd.

Department stores: Neiman Marcus, Friars Road & Highway 163; Nordstrom, Horton Plaza, 1st Street and Broadway. In the Gaslamp Quarter there are art galleries and antique shops, in La Jolla/Golden Triangle fashionable boutiques, in the old town the Bazaar del Mundo, La Esplanade and Old Town Mercado.

San Diego

Clothing and shoe sizes in the US differ from those in, for example, Europe; often clothes are simply marked small ("S"), medium ("M"), large ("L") or extra large ("XL"). To avoid disappointment items should be tried on before purchase.

Clothes sizes

Spanish Names

See Language

Sport

Baseball

In no other state is the American national sport of baseball so well represented as in California, where there are five first-class teams: the Giants (San Francisco) and the Dodgers (Los Angeles) play in the National League; the Padres (San Diego), the Angels (Anaheim) and the Athletics (Oakland) play in the America League. The season lasts from the end of April to the beginning of October.

Football

First-class football teams in California are: the 49'ers (San Francisco), the Invaders (Oakland) and the Chargers (San Diego). The season lasts from September to December.

Basketball

Basketball is also widespread in California. The Los Angeles Lakers are perhaps the best known team.

Horseracing

Horseracing with totalisator and bookmaker betting can be found in San Mateo near San Francisco, in Del Mar north of San Diego, in Santa Anita Park in Arcadia and in Long Beach not far from Los Angeles.

Surfing and sailing

On almost all the 75 beaches between Los Angeles and Cambria surfing is one of the most popular sports and very typical of California; originally it came from Hawaii. Surfers – even beginners – practise this sport throughout the year in Ventura. The mighty waves on the cooler

Riding the waves: surfing is a popular sport

northern coast, however, are only suitable for experts. Surfers can find out about wind strength on Californian beaches by telephoning (800) 94632255. Information is updated by computer every ten minutes. There is good sailing also in the bleak north (including the Bay of San Francisco). Beginners, however, should either sail close to the coast or in the quieter south, perhaps in Mission Bay near San Diego. Sailing craft can be rented from most marinas. Inland waters such as Lake Shasta, Lake Tahoe and the Sacramento River Delta Lands offer equally good opportunities for sailing.

For snorkelling enthusiasts the Pacific provides waters full of fish and marine flora (Lovers Cove near Santa Catalina Island). For divers the south coast (sunken ships, starfish in La Jolla Cove near San Diego), and the north coast (Abalone molluscs) are both equally suitable.

Snorkelling and diving

Tennis and golf are among the most popular activities. The city of San Francisco has more than 100 public tennis courts; San Diego has 70 golf courses and Los Angeles almost as many.

Tennis and golf

Although you would not normally think of winter sports in California there are, in fact, many opportunities for this activity. There are extensive ski areas especially in the Sierra Nevada, Squaw Valley, Mammoth Lakes, Lake Tahoe and Sequoia National Forest. In addition Snow Valley and Green Valley are only about three hours by car from San Diego. There is cross-country skiing in Yosemite National Park.

Winter sports

Swimming

See Bathing

Taxis

There are numerous taxis at airports, stations, hotels and the special taxi stands. To hire a taxi it is only necessary to stop an empty one. In most cities rates are high because of long distances involved. An exception is San Francisco where the distances are much shorter.

The following phone numbers are normally available 24 hours a day:

Metropolitan Express/Skycar: tel. (800) 3383898

Los Angeles

Orange Cab: tel. (619) 2913333
Yellow Cab: tel. (619) 2346161

San Diego

City Cab: tel. 4687200
Luxor Cab: tel. (415) 2824141
Yellow Cab: tel. (415) 6262345

San Francisco

See entry.

Tips

Telephone

See Post and Telephone Services

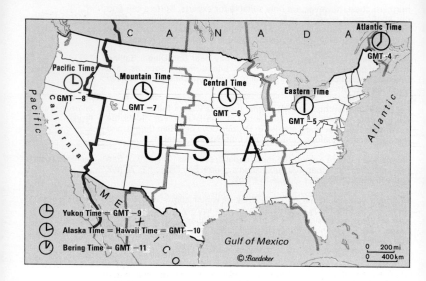

Time

Pacific Time
Like the whole of the west of the United States California is in the Pacific Time Zone, that is three hours behind the east coast of America and eight hours behind Greenwich Mean Time.

Summertime
From the last Sunday in April to the first Sunday in October daylight saving time is in operation and clocks are put on one hour.

Tipping

In the USA, in contrast to European countries, tips are only rarely included in the total bill and have to be given separately. Restaurant and hotel employees are often on very low wages and have to depend on tips.

Hotels
For luggage carried to or from your room a suitable tip is 1 to 2 dollars per item. Room maids should be given 5 to 10 dollars a week, hotel porters 1 to 5 dollars depending on the service, and car park attendents 1 to 2 dollars.

Restaurants
The tip – always left on the table – is normally 15% to 20% of the bill. In the better class restaurants the head waiter (maítre) and wine waiter (sommelier) also expect a tip (5% to 10% and 10% to 15% respectively).

Taxis
The driver should have a tip of 15% to 20% of the amount shown on the taxi meter and more for a short journey.

Hairdressers
Both ladies' and gentlemen's hairdressers expect a tip of 15% to 20%.

Travel groups' coach drivers receive $1.50 from each passenger daily, and tour guides $2.50.

Coach drivers, tour guides

Normally give 50 cents to the shoeshine boy.

Shoeshine

Traffic Regulations

In addition to those applying throughout the USA, every state has its own traffic laws. The regulations as a whole are not too dissimilar from those in Europe.

Drivers who exceed the speed limit can expect severe penalties. In traffic-calmed inner cities and residential areas, limits vary between 32 k.p.h. (20 m.p.h.) and 56 k.p.h. (35 m.p.h.) but may be as low as 24 k.p.h. (15 m.p.h.) in the vicinity of schools, old people's homes or hospitals. On main roads leading out of built-up areas, and on single-carriageway country roads, the maximum speed is generally 72 kmh (45 m.p.h.), reducing to 56 k.m.h. (35 m.p.h.) at night in areas frequented by game. The 32 k.p.h. (55 m.p.h.) speed limit on multi lane out-of-town roads – 104 k.p.h. (65 m.p.h.) on more remote and little-used sections motorway (highways) – was abolished in 1996. Instead states have introduced their own regulations, although most have decided to retain the old limit.

Speed

On single-carriageway roads all vehicles are required to halt when children are boarding or alighting from a yellow-signal school bus. Where the stopping point is a lane marked by a wide green line or protected from oncoming traffic by an impassable barrier, only vehicles travelling in the same direction as the bus need stop.

School buses

Right turns are permissable at traffic lights even when the light is red as long as the vehicle first halts and makes the turn only if the road is clear.

Right turns

Dipped headlights are compulsory during daylight hours (i.e. between sunrise and sunset) whenever visibility falls below 300 m (1000 ft) or on long straight roads with oncoming traffic.

Dipped headlights

Parking is prohibited on out-of-town trunk roads as well as on many roads in built-up areas. If forced to stop, drive up onto the verge.

Clearways

Travel Documents

For a visit to the United States of America you need a passport which must be valid for at least six months after the planned date of departure. From the July 15th 1989 the compulsory visa was abolished, but before arrival in the USA the tourist or businessman must complete form 1–791 which will be provided in the aircraft. A visa is still required in the following cases: people who intend to stay more than 90 days in the USA, students, journalists, exchange visitors, people on official visits, those engaged to American citizens and members of aircraft crews. Visitors who have an unrestricted B1 or B2 visa in their passport do not have to complete form 1–791.

Passport and visa

Before leaving home make sure you have the following with you:

Checklist

Passport (with visa if applicable)
Driving licence (or international driving licence)
Automobile club identification
Travel insurance

Sickness abroad certificate
Tickets, booking confirmations, etc.
Vaccination certificates
Photocopies of important papers (in luggage)
Traveller's cheques, credit cards, cash
Maps, travel guide

Weather Reports

On radio and television (see entry) weather forecasts are regularly given. Weather forecasts can also be obtained by telephone: in San Francisco by calling (650) 9361212 and in Los Angeles (562) 5780478. In other places you will find the appropriate number in the general section of the telephone book.

Weights and Measures

Length		
	1 inch=2.54 cm	1 mm=0.039 in.
	1 foot=30.48 cm	1 cm=0.033 ft
	1 yard=91.44 cm	1 m=1.09 yd
	1 mile=1.61 km	1 km=0.62 miles

Area
1 sq. in=6.45 sq. cm   1 sq. cm=0.155 sq. in.
1 sq. ft=9.288 sq. dm   1 sq. dm=0.108 sq. ft
1 sq. yd=0.836 sq. m   1 sq. m=1.196 sq. yd
1 sq. mile=2.589 km   1 km=0.386 sq. miles
1 acre=0.405 hectare   1 hectare=2.471 acres

Volume
1 cu. in.=16.386 cu. cm   1 cu. cm=0.061 cu. in.
1 cu. ft=28.32 cu. dm   1 cu. dm=0.035 cu. ft
1 cu. yd=0.765 cu. m   1 cu. m=1.308 cu. yd

Liquid measure
The US gallon and other measures of capacity are smaller than the corresponding British (Imperial) measure; one US gallon equals 0.83 British gallons. The following metric equivalences are for the US units.

1 gill=0.118 litres   1 litre=8.474 gills
1 pint=0.473 litres   1 litre=2.114 pints
1 quart=0.946 litres   1 litre=1.057 quarts
1 gallon=3.787 litres   1 litre=0.264 gallons

Weight
1 oz=28.35 g   100 g=3.527 oz
1 lb=453.59 g   1 kg=2.205 lb
1 cwt=45.359 kg   100 kg=2.206 cwt
1 ton=0.907 tonnes   1 tonne=1.103 tons

The US hundredweight is smaller than the British hundredweight (100 lb instead of 112 lb), and the US ton is the short ton of 2000 lb (as opposed to the British long ton of 2240 lb and the metric tonne of 1000 kg or 2204 lb). The metric equivalences given above are for the US units.

In due course the metric system is to be introduced in the USA.

Temperature	Fahrenheit	Centigrade	Conversions
	0°	−18°	
	10°	−12°	$°C = 5(°F − 32) ÷ 9$

Fahrenheit	Centigrade	Conversions
20°	−5°	
32°	0°	°F = (1,8 × °C) + 32
50°	10°	
68°	20°	Ratios
86°	30°	°C : °F = 5 : 9
95°	35°	°F : °C = 9 : 5

When to Go

The best time to go to California is in the spring and early summer (April to June), or late summer and early autumn (September to the beginning of October). In the summer months of July and August it is usually unbearably hot and sultry, especially in southern California, the desert areas, the Central Valley and the northern wine valleys. In spring the landscape is full of flowers and the hills are green. In early summer the grass is already beginning to go brown but even so, the high mountain passes can still be covered in snow into June. In September the temperatures again drop to a more pleasant level, already becoming distinctly colder in October in the high mountain areas and in northern California.

Wine

With a production of 20 million hectalitres the USA takes sixth place in the worldwide production of wine; in the western hemisphere it is second only to Argentina. About 80% of American vineyards are situated in California, where Spanish missionaries brought the grape (Zinfandel) in 1769, but it was not until the middle of the 19th c. that vines were grown here in considerable quantities. Vineyards extended later from California north into the states of Washington and Oregon.

At one time the vintners endeavoured to produce red, rosé and white wines of all kinds at the same time and from the same vineyard; they were not much concerned with the traditional names of the wines and their origins. Gradually they began to produce top-class wines by specialisation and by paying regard to the types of grapes and the most favourable ecological conditions. This development was furthered by the necessity of finding new sites for vineyards because of the exceptional growth of the cities of San Francisco and Los Angeles.

It is astonishing that in the land of coca-cola and pepsi-cola wine has become so popular. Thirty years ago the Americans still drank up to 70 per cent of heavy wines and 30% of light table wine; today this situation has been reversed. Cheap wines which are produced in the Central Valley have followed this trend and have gradually conformed to it. The considerable increase in sales of recent years shows that the Americans are drinking more and more wine, and that Californian wines are forcing their way into the European market.

New developments

Thirty years ago Californian wines were scarcely known in Europe. Since then more and more top-class wines have gradually become appreciated by connoisseurs. The reason for this boom is probably to be found in favourable geographical factors, which, in so far as the varieties of grapes and the areas in which they are grown are together an ideal combination, have made possible a considerable range of high-class wines. Three factors determine the quality of wine (for example in the Napa valley):

Favourable geographical factors

Wine

The type of soil: sunny slopes with porous gravelly loam produce a better quality wine than the heavy clay in the valley bottoms.

Average temperatures: here there are three temperature zones which are suitable for certain types of grape: warm (Zinfandel, Cabernet Sauvignon, Petite Sirah, Barbera, Grenache, Gamay), fairly warm (Merlot, Gamay, Chenin Blanc, Zinfandel, Cabernet Sauvignon), and cool (Chardonnay, Johannisberg Riesling, Gewürtztraminer, Pinot Noir).

Late frost in Spring: this has the worst effect in the valley bottoms.

Modern technology

What the Californian vintner lacks in experience he makes up for with huge investment and intensive research in the field of wine production technology. An important contribution is made by the University of California which carries out investigation into new methods of cultivation, cellar technology, and improved varieties of grape. Although oak casks are still imported from France, nevertheless far reaching modern technology is employed in the preparation of wine: spraying of mist to cool the vines in hot temperatures, combine-harvesting machines, the most modern riddling implements, stainless steel tanks to protect the wine against acid, and the most modern cooling techniques. Thanks to these methods the brothers Julio and Ernst Gallo in Modesto, for example, have been able to operate the largest co-operative wine producing undertaking in the world.

Growing regions

The Californian wine growing regions are, from north to south:

Mendocino and Los Cameros with a cool climate which, however, is favourable for grape varieties which require a cool period for ripening;

Russian River with good table wines which are sold by firms in the Central Valley for blending;

Sonoma Valley with the well-known 19th c. wine cellars of Buena Vista (of Agoston Haraszthy) and Grundlach-Bundschu;

Napa Valley, the centre of Californian high-class wine production with the interesting wine cellars of Robert Mondavi constructed in 1966 in the style of a old mission building. Today this is the most influential wine producing firm in the United States of America;

Rutherford Bench, north of Napa, the "golden area of cultivation" of America which produces the classic Cabernet Sauvignon red wines;

South of the Bay of San Francisco with the small, but very well known, vine growing areas of Livermore Valley and of Paul Macon and Almaden;

South Central Coast with the vineyard areas of Edna Valley (Chardonnay), Santa Maria Valley (Pinot Noir Sanford), Santa Ynez Valley (Firestone) and Paso Robles (Zinfandel of the Martin brothers);

Central Valley with a reliable, often oppressively hot, climate in which grapes with a high sugar content and little acid thrive. Here heavy sweet wines were formally produced, but today thanks to modern technology other wines as well. Almost all the producers of Californian sherry, port and brandy obtain their grapes from the Central Valley.

The Californian wine producing areas can be divided into several climatic zones according to warmth and sunshine. There is first a fairly cool coastal zone, the most important areas of which from north to south are Mendocino, Santa Rosa, Sonoma, Napa, Solano, Alameda, Santa Cruz, Santa Clara, San Benito and Monterey. A warmer inner zone is in the Californian longitudinal valley (Central Valley) with the centres of San Joaquin, Stanislaus, Merced, Madera, Fresno, Tulare and Kern, and the area around Los Angeles including Cucamonga and San Bernadino. In all these areas red, rosé and white wines (and even "champagne") are produced.

Varieties

The most important wines of California are the following, listed according to the extent of the area in which they are produced (in hectares).

380

Zinfandel: a spicy red wine with a raspberry bouquet, also called "Californian Beaujolais"; San Joaquin, Sonoma, Monterey, Napa, San Bernadino (10,750 ha).

Carignane: the most important grape variety of the Mediterranean, used in California principally for cheap blended wines but is in decline (8550 ha).

Cabernet Sauvignon: the finest red wine which develops a fruity bouquet as it ages; Napa, Sonoma, Monterey, Lake (8285 ha).

Barbera: dark red wine of Italian type, needs a warm climate; Fresno, Madera (7025 ha).

Pinot Noir: light red wine generally not particularly good in California; Sonoma, Napa, Monterey, Santa Barbara (3510 ha).

Petite Sirah: heavy red wine which is rich in tannin but which keeps well; Monterey, San Joaquin, Napa, Sonoma (3340 ha).

Merlot: deep red wine often used to fortify Cabernet grapes; Napa, Sonoma, Santa Barbara (830 ha).

Also ruby Cabernet, Grenache, Gamay Beaujolais and Tinto Madeira.

Gamay: genuine French blue grape with white juice which is used here only for rosé wine; Napa, Monterey, Sonoma, Lake (1680 ha).

French Colombard: neutral dry white wine for blending, thrives in cooler regions; Madera, Kern, San Joaquin (15,580 ha.).

Chenin Blanc: produced in upland areas, a wine with good body but with pungency; Madera, Fresno, Merced (11,970 ha.).

Chardonnay: the best dry white wine, light, fruity and full bodied; Sonoma, Napa, Monterey (6324 ha.).

White Riesling: (also Johannisberg Riesling), a dry spirited high-class wine; Monterey, Santa Barbara, Napa, Sonoma (3540 ha.).

Sauvignon Blanc: good to very good earthy wine with a fine bouquet; Napa, Monterey, Sonoma (2645 ha.).

Gewürztraminer: a fine species of grape which produces an exceptionally full-bodied and spicy wine; Monterey, Sonoma, Napa (1340 ha.).

Also Semillon, Pinot Blanc and Grey Riesling.

Palomino.

Well known Californian wine producers and their products

Area	Vintner	Wines
Santa Rosa	Italian Swiss Colony F. Korbel & Bros Martini & Prati Parducci J. Pedroncelli Windsor	Burgundy, Rhineskeller Korbel Brut ("Champagne") Sherry French Colombard Cabernet Sauvignon Chardonnay
Napa, Sonoma, Mendocino	Beaulieu	Burgundy Cabernet Sauvignon Grenache Rosé Pinot Chardonnay Johannisberg Riesling
	Beringer	Pinot Noir
	Buena Vista	Haraszthy Zinfandel Gerwürztraminer Pinot Chardonnay

	Chappellet	Chenin Blanc
	The Christian Brothers	Pinot Noir Pinot St George Gamay Noir Napa Rosé Chateau La Salle Pinot Chardonnay Chablis
	Freemark Abbey	Pinot Noir Pinot Chardonnay Johannisberg Riesling
	Hanzell	Pinot Noir Pinot Chardonnay Chardonnay
	Joseph Heltz	Pinot Noir Pinot Chardonnay
	Ingelnook	Cabernet Sauvignon Charbono Johannisberg Riesling
	Charles Krug	Cabernet Sauvignon Gamay Chenin Blanc Gewürtztraminer
Area	Vintner	Wines
	Louis M. Martini	Cabernet Sauvignon Pinot Noir Mountain Zinfandel Mountain Barbera Gamay Rosé
	Mayacamas	Cabernet Sauvignon
	Robert Mondavi	Cabernet Sauvignon Chenin Blanc Chardonnay Fumé Blanc Johannisberg Riesling
	Oakville	Cabernet Sauvignon
	Sebastiani	Barbera
	Schramsberg	Blanc de Blancs ("Champagne")
	Souverain	Cabernet Sauvignon Johannisberg Riesling
	Stony Hill	Pinot Chardonnay
Livermore, Santa Clara, Monterey, San Benito	Almaden	Pinot Noir, Gewürtztraminer Johannisberg Riesling Blanc de Blancs ("Champagne")

	Chalone	Chardonnay
	Cresta Blanca	Cabernet Sauvignon Premier Semillon
	Concannon	Petite Sirah
	Llords and Elwood	Chardonnay
	Paul Masson	Pinot Noir, Silvaner Emerald Dry
	Mirassou	Santa Clara Zinfandel Cabernet Sauvignon Petite Sirah, Chenin Blanc Monterey Riesling
	Novitiate	Black Muscat
	Martin Ray	Pinot Noir
	San Martin	California ("Champagne")
	Weibel	Pinot Noir
	Wente Brothers	Sauvignon Blanc Pinot Blanc, Chablis Dry Semillon Le Blanc des Blancs ("Champagne")
San Joaquin Valley	Famiglia Cribari	Cribari
	Ficklin	Port
Area	Vintner	Wines
	Franzia Brothers	Zinfandel Light Sweet Muscat
	Royal Host	Conti-Royale Burgundy
	Ernest & Julio Gallo	Hearty Burgundy Pink Chablis, Chablis Blanc
	Joseph Gazarra	Vin Rosé

As an indication of the provenance and quality of US wines the names of the vintner serve well. Imported wines are more expensive, there is not much choice and their quality is dubious. Wine (even red wine) is generally served cool in the USA.   Note

Youth Hostels

Youth hostels (American Youth Hostels; AYH) offer affordable accommodation ($10–15) especially for younger visitors. To stay at a hostel you must be in possession of a valid membership card from either the American Youth Hostels Federation or the International Youth Hostels Federation. There is no restriction on age. Generally speaking youth hostels are less common in the United States than in Europe; in California, however, there are more than two dozen, mostly situated along the coast.

The American Youth Hostels association is affiliated to the International Youth Hostels Federation and the accommodation in its hostels meets the Federations's standards. They are usually open from 7.30am–9.30am and 5pm–10pm, longer in major cities. Address: American Youth Hostels, 733 15th Street NW, Suite 840 Washington, DC 20005, tel (202) 7836161, Fax –6171

Reservations can be made from abroad through the International Booking Network (IBN): IBN Booking Center, San Francisco Golden Gate, 308 Mason St., San Francisco CA 94102, tel 1 (415) 7011320, Fax –2558

Hostels affiliated to the International Youth Hostels Federation are listed below:

Redwood National Peak, 14480 Highway 101, Klamath, CA 95548, tel (707) 4828265

Point Montara Lighthouse, 16th Street (by CA Highway 1), Montara, CA 94037, tel (650) 7287177

Pigeon Point Lighthouse, 210 Pigeon Point Road (by Highway 1), Pescadero, CA 94060, Tel (650) 8790633

Point Reyes, PO Box 247, Point Reyes Station, CA 94956, tel (650) 6638811

Sacramento, 900 H Street Sacramento, CA 95814, tel (916) 4431691

San Clemento Beach, 233 Avenida Granada, San Clemento, CA 926724029, tel (949) 4922848, Fax (949) 3619018

Elliott International (Point Loma), 3790 Udalli Street, San Diego, CA 921072414, tel (760) 2234778, Fax 5217

San Francisco International, Fisherman's Wharf, Bldg 240, Fort Mason, San Francisco, CA 94123, tel (415) 7717277, –3645

San Francisco Downtown, 312 Mason Street, Union Square, San Francisco, CA 94102, tel (415) 7885604; 175 beds

Sio Coast Hostel, 16, 17 Santa Rosa San Luis Obispo, CA 93401, tel. (805) 5444678, Fax –3142

Santa Crux, 321 Main Street. Santa Crux, CA 95061. tel (831) 4238304, Fax (831) 4298541

Los Angeles Santa Monica, 1436 Second Street, Santa Monica, CA 90401, tel (310) 3939913. Fax 1769

Sanborn Park Hostel, 15808 Sanborn Road, Saratoga, CA 95070, tel (408) 7419555

Index

Index

Principal Sights of Tourist Interest

★★

Death Valley	98
Disneyland (Anaheim)	68
Hearst Castle (San Simeon)	292
Getty Center (Los Angeles)	146
Monterey	189
Pasadena	209

★★

Redwood Highway	222
San Diego	232
San Francisco	249
Santa Barbara	296
Sequoia & Kings Canyon National Park	307
Yosemite National Park	327

★

Anza-Borrego Desert State Park	74
Berkeley	83
Carmel	93
Channel Islands National Park	95
Eureka	106
Fort Ross State Historic Park	109
Joshua Tree National Monument	114
Lake Tahoe	117
Lassen Volcanic National Park	119
Lava Beds National Monument	121
Long Beach	122
Mammoth Lakes	171

★

Mission Stations	174
Mono Lake State Reserve	186
Oakland	198
Palm Springs	204
Palo Alto	206
Point Lobos State Reserve	217
Point Reyes National Seashore	220
Sacramento	224
San José	289
Santa Cruz	303
Sausalito	306
Solvang	315
Tijuana	319

The places listed above are merely a selection of the principal sights, of interest in themselves or for attractions in the surrounding area. There are many other sights in California to which attention is drawn by either one or two stars.

Imprint

170 colour photographs
47 maps and plans, 1 large map at end of book

German text: Astrid Feltes-Peter, Henry Marx, Prof. Dr Wolfgang
Hassenpflug (Climate)

Editorial work: Baedeker Redaktion (Astrid Feltes-Peter)

Cartography: Franz Huber, Munich; Christoph Gallus, Hohberg-
Niederschopfheim; Hallwag A.G. Bern (large map)

General direction: Rainer Eisenschmid, Baedeker Stuttgart

English translation: David Cocking, Alec Court, Julie Waller

Revising and additional translation: Wendy Bell, Rosmary Quinton

Source of illustrations: Archiv für Kunst und Geschichte (13), Dieterich
(5), Walt Disney Company (1), Drechsler-Marx (42), Feltes-Peter (75),
Fine Arts Museums San Francisco (1, Frick (5), HB-Bildatlas (2), IMB (1),
IFA (1), Kelpischewski (1), Lade (5), Messerschmidt (1), Möhle (2),
Reincke (1), Schapowalow (3), Scherm (1), ZEFA (3)

Front cover: Tony Stone Images. Back cover: AA Photo Library (K. Paterson)

3rd English edition 2000

© Baedeker Stuttgart
Original German edition 2000

© 2000 The Automobile Association
English language edition worldwide

Published by AA Publishing (a trading name of Automobile Association
Developments Limited, whose registered office is Norfolk House, Priestley
Road, Basingstoke, Hampshire RG24 9NY. Registered number 1878835).

Distributed in the United States and Canada by:
Fodor's Travel Publications, Inc.
201 East 50th Street
New York, NY 10022

The name *Baedeker* is a registered trade mark.

A CIP catalogue record of this book is available from the British Library.

Licensed user:
Mairs Geographischer Verlag GmbH & Co.
Ostfildern-Kemnat bei Stuttgart

Printed in Italy by G. Canale & C. S.p.A., Turin

ISBN 0 7495 2258 5

Notes

Notes

Notes

Notes